The Constitution of Socialism

Historical Materialism Book Series

The Historical Materialism Book Series is a major publishing initiative of the radical left. The capitalist crisis of the twenty-first century has been met by a resurgence of interest in critical Marxist theory. At the same time, the publishing institutions committed to Marxism have contracted markedly since the high point of the 1970s. The Historical Materialism Book Series is dedicated to addressing this situation by making available important works of Marxist theory. The aim of the series is to publish important theoretical contributions as the basis for vigorous intellectual debate and exchange on the left.

The peer-reviewed series publishes original monographs, translated texts, and reprints of classics across the bounds of academic disciplinary agendas and across the divisions of the left. The series is particularly concerned to encourage the internationalization of Marxist debate and aims to translate significant studies from beyond the English-speaking world.

For a full list of titles in the Historical Materialism Book Series available in paperback from Haymarket Books, visit: www.haymarketbooks.org/ series_collections/1-historical-materialism.

The Constitution of Socialism

A World Without Capital

Tim Platenkamp

Haymarket Books
Chicago, IL

First published in 2025 by Brill Academic Publishers, The Netherlands
© 2025 Koninklijke Brill NV, Leiden, The Netherlands

Published in paperback in 2026 by
Haymarket Books
P.O. Box 180165
Chicago, IL 60618
773-583-7884
www.haymarketbooks.org

ISBN: 979-8-88890-804-4

Distributed to the trade in the US through Consortium Book Sales and
Distribution (www.cbsd.com) and internationally through Ingram
Publisher Services International (www.ingramcontent.com).

This book was published with the generous support of Lannan
Foundation, Wallace Action Fund, and the Marguerite Casey Foundation.

Special discounts are available for bulk purchases by organizations and
institutions. Please call 773-583-7884 or email info@haymarketbooks.org
for more information.

Cover art and design by David Mabb. Cover art developed from *Rhythm
69 no. 9*, based on designs from the William Morris block printed
pattern book and Hans Richter's storyboard for *Rhythmus 25*, as well as
Kazimir Malevich's film script *Artistic and Scientific Film—Painting and
Architectural Concerns—Approaching the New Plastic Architectural System*.
Oil and wallpaper on canvas (2007).

Printed in the United States.

Library of Congress Cataloging-in-Publication data is available.

Contents

Preface

This book is an outgrowth of my commitment to socialism and a long-standing interest in the question of what might replace capitalism. At age fourteen, I joined the youth wing of the Socialist Party in my country in order to channel my interest in the promotion of social justice. This was the start of a long process of intellectual development and ideological exploration, which exposed me to various bodies of political thought. Along this journey, I grew increasingly disillusioned by the simplistic solutions to complex problems furthered by the various factions of socialists. While more sophisticated arguments are stripped down into simpler ones for the purpose of public consumption, I noticed a more general theoretical poverty in relation to the question of what might replace capitalism. Something of a siege mentality had beset the socialist movement, in my opinion, causing our active cadre to become inward-looking, rarely wading outside the safe confines of recycled arguments. Critical challenges contesting the feasibility of socialism were met with suspicion and promptly rejected as the partisan efforts of biased functionaries doing the bidding of the bourgeoisie. Consequently, socialists are barely being exposed to a number of exceedingly important questions that require serious input of thought.

As it turns out, the literature devoted to figuring what could replace capitalism is several orders of magnitude smaller compared to the volume of literature devoted to picking apart capitalism. Not appeased by equivocation, I was unswayed by the 'sloganistic' approaches to socialism ('democratise', 'socialise', 'communise') which spurred me on to investigate these matters more deeply. What I hoped to find out was whether my commitment to socialism was sound, which hinges on whether it can realistically materialise by the hands and actions of 'actually existing people'. Doubts and questions playing on my mind had acted as a brake on my political involvement, particularly inhibiting my activism on behalf of the Socialist Party of the Netherlands and their youth wing, which I had joined as a member in two consecutive periods in 2007–2009 and 2016–2021; as well as my activity on behalf of Communist Platform, which I had joined shortly after its founding in 2014 and departed circa 2016, although retaining close, fraternal ties with them. Having linked my fate to socialism, I was apprehensive about the prospect of my personal efforts to the benefit of this political cause ending up a pointless expenditure of energy and time. Familiarising myself with the arguments on both sides of the socialist calculation debate to address my curiosities only raised further questions in my mind. This book, in some sense, is the culmination of a personal project that escalated out of bounds. It was initially intended to assuage my own doubts before I could return to matters of a more immediate urgency, dealing with questions of political action and strategy. Delving more deeply into the literature, however, achieved the opposite, inflaming my appetite instead. As such, this book builds toward my conclusions from the ground up by compiling and synthesising arguments from diverse theoretical backgrounds, which makes this book an appropriate introduction for readers to the topic of modelling socialism. The reader will find the book peppered with references to historical and current sources on socialist economic planning, providing the reader with a useful compendium of literature on the subject to continue their own exploration of the subject.

What is presented here in this monograph amounts to an honest effort to provide a credible alternative to capitalist society, grounded in the political tradition of civic republicanism. In this way, I hope to contribute in a modest way to the revival of socialism. The aim is not to provide a definitive resolution to the crisis of socialism. Instead, I hope to put forth reasonably well-formulated arguments in favour of such a revival by advancing a more or less feasible model of socialism. Contestation, in good faith and by means of measured reasoning, necessarily elevates the quality of discussion. Furthermore, it is my belief that the question of socialist economic planning, which occupies an important place in this book, is the most consequential and at the same time the most neglected question of our movement. Hopefully, my contribution to the debate on socialist planning will be stimulating and thought-provoking, to help draw much-needed attention to this deeply existential question faced by socialism, and in addition, hopefully sheds some light on socialist thought at risk of being overlooked.

The influence of Marxism on the contents of book will be readily apparent. This is in no small part because this theoretical mode of thinking has left its mark on all later developments of socialism in terms of theory and practice, of course. It is my belief, which I will not attempt to prove in this book, that 'dialectical materialism' is a scientific tool by which we can make sense of the causal links that underpin social reality. At the same time, the application of this method of scientific inquiry gradually led me astray from the official canon of Marxism. I found it increasingly difficult to reconcile facts obtained by empirical observation to the theoretical results generated by the conventional application of the Marxist method. Theoretical gaps began forming into a substantial void which, eventually, could no longer be resolved by mere handwaving. Escaping from the intellectual stranglehold of more fossilised forms of Marxism, which constricted my intellectual horizon and stifled ideological development, circa 2018, I began to toy with ideas that were, in relation to orthodoxy, unconventional. The basic suppositions I had previously adopted wholesale as part of the Marxist worldview could no longer be entertained '*a priori*'. In terms of social analysis, I began to accord a greater role to political initiative and ideological articulation, pulling me into the conceptual field of neo-Gramscian Marxism. My intent was to apply this theoretical equipment to close the gulf between theory and practice as I understood it. The nature of socialist society, according to this type of worldview, is no longer pre-given by historically conditioned developments of structural class forces, and therefore a whole range of political thought suddenly became available to appropriate on behalf of socialism. It turned out that the tradition of civic republicanism offered great insights into how to organise the political community on a socialist basis, after making due modifications. I have since attempted to marry republicanism and socialism in a political project of normative republican socialism. My first academic attempt to combine the two traditions into a single union was my master's thesis in Political Science, titled 'The Socialist Community of Citizens', submitted on 5 June 2020 at the University of Amsterdam, of which this book is an expanded revision, thus making chunks of this monograph self-plagiarised.

The book deals primarily with political theory and political economy, and therefore inevitably veers into the terrain of complex theory. Nevertheless, I hope to have written a book that is intelligible – with the necessary effort – to those who are only somewhat trained in reading and processing academic theory. Whilst the reader will be greatly helped by a familiarity with the substance that will be discussed, it is not exceedingly technical and requires no specialist knowledge to penetrate. Certainly, I am no economist by trade or training, and the search for an answer to the fundamental question of what socialist society should look like took me beyond the confines of my own research area. If anything, this fact will spare the reader technical discussions of mathematical models, if only because I lack command of this discipline myself. Lacking a background in mathematics, I have to the best of my abilities gone beyond the equations to grasp the logic behind them in order to make adequate inferences about their potential uses and limitations for socialist society.

Many unpaid hours have been sunk into this book, labouring to complete it during my spare time. There were days I woke up with socialist planning on my mind and went to sleep with socialist planning on my mind. On at least one occasion, the spectre of socialist planning haunted my dreams: I tracked along some lumberjack workers and found them to falsify the labour-hour data of their work collective in order to manipulate plan targets in their favour. Alas, this yielded no new theoretical insights.

I hope my book serves the socialist cause and movement well, providing guidance in exploring these important questions. I further hope to have done justice to the numerous thinkers, authors, and theories that I draw on. I bear full responsibility for the contents of this book; all errors are mine; italics are in original unless otherwise specified.

March 2023
Nieuwegein, The Netherlands

Acknowledgements

This book would not have materialised if not for the help of others. First among those who have supported my efforts is Dr Annette Freyberg-Inan, my Master's thesis supervisor. She first suggested that my thesis could be expanded into a book – it would not have dawned on me to try otherwise – and helped me navigate my first baby steps in academic publishing. Additional academics who have endorsed or encouraged my endeavour in one measure or another are David Laibman, Paul Lucardie, Jean-Philippe Deranty, Jakob Heyer, and Gordon Arlen (which does not imply substantive agreement with the contents of this book).

In terms of moral support and for her patience, my partner Jona Duran is exceedingly deserving of recognition and gratitude.

Further thanks are due to Robin Hahnel for the significant course correction to Chapter 8 afforded to me by his expansive review and incisive criticism, as well as the useful prodding of an anonymous reviewer which helped me make further, final improvements to the manuscript.

I want to thank those who were kind enough to supply me their academic resources, sometimes including unpublished manuscripts: David Schweickart, Paul Lucardie, Bruno Leipold, David Laibman, and Robin Hahnel. Others who have helped me get my hands on difficult to obtain literature were Bram Jumelet, Prateek Vijayavargia, and family members on my mother's side, Arno, Jack, and Esther van Rooijen and their partners, who gifted me a copy of *Selected Essays on Economic Planning* by Kalecki.

Introduction

1   The Crisis of Socialism – Goodbye Lenin!

Over thirty odd years have passed since the demise of the standard bearer of world communism. The red banner of the Soviet Union, its upper hoist distinctly decorated with the hammer and sickle, was permanently lowered from the Kremlin on 25 December 1991. It has been customary ever since – at least, so would it appear – that any publication attempting to rehabilitate socialism is required to introduce the subject by reference to one of two tropes. It either mentions Fukuyama's postulate of the 'end of history' or Thatcher's proclamation that 'there is no alternative' (TINA) – and perhaps both. The latter, so the story goes, expresses the late British stateswoman's belief that the economic decline of socialism had decisively settled the debate between socialism and capitalism in favour of the latter. This 'debate' had been fought out on all fronts, from public discourse to bloody military conflicts; from the ballot box to academic journals. At a certain point, somewhere around the 1970s, communism reached its apogee in terms of spatial expansion. The sense that the odds of winning the debate began tipping in favour of 'international communism' was widely shared. The Soviet Union, in the period immediately following the Second World War, had harnessed tremendous amounts of 'soft power' over their modernisation and development efforts, their heroic triumph over the genocidal forces of fascism, and their support in word and deed for anticolonial struggles. The Soviet Union exemplified the possibilities of escaping material and cultural backwardness by throwing off the fetters of capitalist relations of production. This was proved by the fact that the Soviet peoples had managed to climb out of the periphery of Europe to catapult themselves into the status of an industrial superpower in a matter of a few short decades. By marshalling the enormous reserves of labour and natural resources under the command of political authorities, the Soviet Union proved capable of an enormous industrial and military build-up, constant rates of economic growth, and scientific and cultural advancement. By these means, they secured their place in the hearts and minds of large segments of the world's intelligentsia, the cadres of organised labour, and peasant leaders – especially among those living under the yoke of imperialism. The intellectual and political anticolonial leadership were poised to overcome the indignity and exploitation of colonial subjugation and commonly turned to the official Soviet doctrine of communism to effect the national liberation of their homelands. Having been transformed into the captive means of alien interests, forced to live by the will of foreign, moneyed powers; valiant efforts under the guidance of the doctrine of Marxism-Leninism would enable the well-read and well-trained vanguard cadres in the global periphery to mobilise the popular masses, promising to unshackle colonial subjects from their condition of servitude. In turn, it would permit, by example of the Soviet Union, rapid material development animated by collective zeal and scientific economic planning:

> The Communists who came to power after a long and often heroic struggle looked on the Soviet Union as the paragon of human progress. They were sincerely convinced that the more faithfully they copied the Soviet model, the sooner they would attain the socialism they ardently desired.[1]

In the 1970s, Communist parties had a firm grip on power in a long stretch of neighbouring countries; controlling a continuous landmass beginning where the slopes of the Dinaric Alps descended into the Adriatic sea, where the Bohemian Forest separated the socialist world from the capitalist West, beyond the Urals and into the expansive grasslands and mountainous terrains of Central Asia and Mongolia, reaching the outermost Siberian peaks where taiga turns to tundra; from the Himalayas to the whole of the plains, deserts, and plateaus of China, to the mountain ranges of the Korean peninsula; and ending in the deepest valleys and deltas of Indochina. The geographical diversity of the former communist world was only surpassed by its rich tapestry of languages, cultures, and histories of the diverse peoples that inhabited it.

Throughout the rest of the world were also scattered more geographically isolated revolutionary governments bearing the red banner and ruling in the name of communism – the countries of Cuba, South Yemen, and more than a handful of African countries can be counted among them. By then, about one third of the world's population lived in states modelled after some variant of 'Marxism-Leninism'. Furthermore, many Communist parties were knocking on the doors of power around the globe. In eastern and southern Asia, countries such as India, Malaya and Sarawak, Thailand, Bangladesh, Sri Lanka, and the Philippines had been affected to varying degrees by communist insurgency. The greater Middle East region, too, was afflicted by pockets of armed opposi-

---

1 Kornai 2007, p. 374.

tion prosecuted by communist insurgents. Several liberation fronts of Marxist-Leninist persuasion operated in the Arabian Gulf, in Lebanon, in Palestine, as well as in Kurdistan, employing revolutionary violence against the many Western-backed aristocracies and dictatorships, to further their aim of establishing a people's democracy modelled after the Soviet experience in their respective home countries – mostly without much success, with the exception of South Yemen. Furthermore, throughout the Arab world – in Egypt, Algeria, Libya, Iraq, and Syria – pan-Arabic variations of socialism managed to climb to power. This opened up a rift in the Middle East between the traditionalist powers and the Soviet-backed secular, nationalist governments.[2] Likewise, in Africa, legitimation of anticolonial struggles was commonly couched in the ideology of socialism – if not in the form of Marxism-Leninism, then as African socialism, relying on indigenous communal traditions and heritage as source for inspiration. In the Caribbean and Americas, socialist political forces came to power in Chile, Cuba, Jamaica, Grenada, Nicaragua, and Guyana, either by ballot or by the barrel of a gun. The growing fear of communist influence resulted in the installation of several right-wing military regimes on the American continent – in Chile, Argentina, Brazil, and so on – hoping to reverse the rising tide of socialism. Similarly, in Southern Europe, the responsibility of tempering the gulf of communist opposition was borne by authoritarian corporatist dictatorships that held Spain, Portugal, and Greece in their iron grip. Of course, a number of clandestine and not-so-clandestine operations – e.g. Gladio, Condor – were set up to assist the worldwide 'debate' on behalf of the capitalist world-system and its imperialist, Atlanticist core.

Socialism, in short, began eating away at the colonial empires and spheres of influence of the transatlantic major powers. A dramatic example is Portugal's loss of empire, serving as an illustrative case of the shifting polarities transpiring during this period. The country's imperial overreach saw their military resources stretched thin by overseas campaigns to quell popular rebellions being mounted in four of their five overseas territories in Africa, each

---

2   This by no means signifies that the Soviet-backed camp should be regarded as having represented a unified front. For example, in 1959, Soviet-backed communists, loyal to the Iraqi republic headed by al-Karim Qasim, clashed with Arab nationalists (more specifically, with Nasserites and Ba'athists) in the city of Mosul. Eventually, in 1963, the Ba'athist Party seized political power from al-Karim Qasim. His pro-Soviet sympathies and the growth of communist influence within his administration led the Ba'athists to stage a bloody *coup d'état*. In its aftermath, both known communists and suspected sympathisers were systematically persecuted; the total death toll ranging in the many thousands. As a matter of fact, various conflicts between different factions of the Arab nationalists were far from uncommon (see for instance the volatile nature of Libyan-Egyptian relations during this period).

under the leadership of a political party founded on the principles of Marxism-Leninism. Eventually, the right-wing authoritarian 'Estado Novo' that had ruled Portugal for decades itself fell to socialist revolution in 1974, and all five of Portugal's overseas African territories – Mozambique, Angola, Guinea-Bissau and Cape Verde, and São Tomé and Príncipe – were subsequently converted into sovereign states modelling themselves after the example of the Soviet Union.

In this period of widespread global turmoil, with its shifting frontiers and fluid balance of power, a sense of imminent world revolution descended upon much of the world, including the West, where young people in particular became infected by the spirit of revolution. They revolted against the conservative establishment and became enamoured by the romantic appeals of participating in the world-historical unravelling of capitalism.[3] 'May 1968' has since become the symbolic point of reference for the cultural shift that has transpired in the West since then. It refers to the spring in which a series of protests and strikes by left-wing students and workers brought the French republic to a standstill. Many feared, others hoped, but in any case many felt that this would be the spark to ignite revolution in the West. Even when these expectations did not materialise, the global capitalist centre felt itself rightly under some measure of existential threat, by external and internal adversaries.

Fast forward only a few decades and the 'actually existing socialisms' have left the world stage. The Soviet Union, the flagship of communism, crashed on the rocks of an inert administrative apparatus, alongside the entire socialist bloc. China, Vietnam, and Laos only evaded similar fates by liberalising their economies, inadvertently conceding the superiority of market mechanisms and the profit motive over comprehensive economic planning on the basis of social priorities. Thus, 'Marxism', today, 'as a world-historical force is effectively dead'.[4] As Sheehan despondently reflected:

> The world is 'going our way', the leaders of 'the free world' have declared. The iron curtain has come tumbling down. The Kremlin has been conquered without a single marine opening fire, without a single ICBM being launched. It unravels before me like a nightmare. No more the red flags flying. No more the heads held high and the fists clenched and the voices raised to the strains of The Internationale. No more the larger-than-life murals of workers and soldiers and peasants marching into the future

---

3 See e.g. Verbij 2005.
4 Heywood 2004, p. 83.

shaping the world with the labour of their hands and hearts and minds. Now it is to be Mickey Mouse and Coca Cola and Michael Jackson and Sacchi & Sacchi [*sic!*].[5]

Along with the Soviet Union came crashing down the promise of a potential future beyond capitalism – the supremacy of capital now being a universal fact of life. The withering of Marxism-Leninism worldwide did not result in its displacement by another, perhaps more democratic, form of socialism, as many on the left had gambled it would. For whatever their serious flaws, Marxist-Leninist regimes had embodied the romantic appeals and optimism of a society based on collective meaning and endeavour, a common humanity, and a free and dignified life. Its worldwide abandonment emboldened liberalism, rather than propel forward more attractive interpretations and applications of socialism. The disappearance of the Soviet Union has effectively decreased confidence in all forms of socialism, including in its more moderate incarnations.[6] In the wake of the collapse of the communist bloc, socialists have often embraced the market mechanism as the primary means to generate wealth. The domination of market forces in society is a given. The question that remains is fundamentally pragmatic: How can the forces of private business be harnessed by public authorities to generate socially desirable outcomes? This axiom underpins all public discourse, stifling the formulation of a progressive agenda around which popular forces can rally to challenge the supremacy of capital over nature, labour, government, recreation, and society at large.

'These are the days of our defeat', Sheehan remarked shortly after the fall of the Soviet Union, 'we ought not to pretend otherwise, but defeat is not death'.[7] This, in short, is the crisis of socialism. It is, and remains, cause for contemplative reflection on both the nature and viability of socialism. Socialists, including those opposed to Marxism-Leninism, necessarily had to define themselves in relation to the Soviet Union as it functioned as the movement's natural centre of gravity, due to the enormity of the influence it could exert on world affairs. With the Soviet Union's cataclysmic exit from the world scene, this anchor of socialist orientation has ceased to exist, causing socialists to scatter for new interpretations, insights, and inspiration in order to salvage their political convictions. Socialists logically had to respond in some manner to the Soviet Union's dissolution, and sought to reinvent, realign, reorient, or reaffirm their political beliefs. As Sheehan summarised: 'We stand at a most dramatic

---

5   Sheehan 1989.
6   Heywood 2017, p. 22.
7   Sheehan 1992.

crossroads in the history of the socialist movement. The question we face, let me put it most starkly, is whether or not to go on with it'.[8] Socialist political parties disbanded, reconstructed, reformed, revised, reorganised, or merged in response to the dissolution of the Soviet Union. Many remained faithful to the doctrine of Marxism-Leninism by insisting that 'revisionism', possibly borne out of residual petty bourgeois consciousness, in the Soviet leadership was the cause for its decline, and that it was not due to any innate flaws contained in its ideological apparatus. Marxism-Leninism, in this way, was relieved of all responsibility and the focus was pinned instead on fortifying the doctrine's ideological core against creeping revisionism. Simultaneously, many 'official' Communist Parties and their fellow-travellers conceded that the market mechanism is a necessary instrument on which expansive public services rely. Thus, the programme of the Japanese Communist Party reads: 'In carrying out socialist reforms, it is important to run the economy effectively with flexibility by combining the elements of the planned economy and the market economy'.[9] The Communist Party of Bohemia and Moravia (KSČM) similarly states that '[i]n our view, the socialist economy will be a market economy with strategic planning'.[10] Lastly, the Progressive Party of Working People (AKEL) of Cyprus argues that socialism 'the methods of planned development with the strengthening of the market within the framework of socialism which will secure a balance of the economy and at the same time add to its flexibility'.[11] The Communist Party of Greece (KKE), in contrast, still maintains its belief in centralised planning in conjunction with 'workers' control'.[12] Without attempting to survey all the respective positions of the remaining of 'official' Communist parties, it seems the KKE stands increasingly isolated in their steadfast belief in Marxist-Leninist orthodoxy.

Some 'official' Communist Parties have parted ways with Marxism-Leninism altogether – a handful long before the eventual demise of the socialist bloc. The images and accounts of breadlines, representing underlying economic difficulties faced by socialist countries, combined with the violent repression of protests and open opposition in East Germany in 1953, in Hungary and Poland in 1956, and in Czechoslovakia in 1968, eroded much of the sympathy for the Soviet Union and their doctrine of Marxism-Leninism. Disillusionment crept into several 'official' Communist parties, which gradually began to distance

---

8   Sheehan 1992.

9   JCP 2020.

10   KSČM 2016.

11   AKEL n.d.

12   KKE 2013.

themselves from Soviet-style socialism, instead adopting a more timid 'Euro-communism'. These parties included the Communist parties of France, Spain, Italy, Japan, and Mexico. Other parties only did so after the collapse of the communist bloc. Likewise, the ruling parties of many Marxist-Leninist countries transformed themselves into, or were legally succeeded by, left-of-centre 'democratic socialist' or 'social-democratic' parties in the 1990s. This was the case in countries as varied as Angola, Estonia, Croatia, Guinea-Bissau, Serbia, Slovenia, Albania, Mozambique, Yemen, Congo-Brazzaville, and Poland.

Non-ruling parties underwent transformations of their own. The powerful Italian Communist Party (PCI) reorganised itself into a democratic socialist party following the collapse of the Soviet Union and was quickly thereafter transformed into the centre-left 'Democratic Party'. The Communist Party of the Netherlands (CPN) was similarly liquidated into a centre-left Green party. The Communist Party of Great Britain (CPGB) would not survive the collapse of the Soviet Union either, being disbanded in 1991. Further to the East, in Iran, the concept of 'worker-communism' had been developed by Hekmat, who deserted Lenin in favour of 'going back to Marx'. The Kurdistan Workers' Party (PKK) abandoned Marxism-Leninism and eventually adopted 'democratic confederalism': a vaguely socialist and quasi-anarchist ideology. In the Americas, revolutionary-left parties, such as the FMLN in El Salvador, the Sandinistas in Nicaragua, or the People's Progressive Party (PPP) in Guyana, all initiated their rightward drift away from socialism.

Left-wing critics of Marxism-Leninism – such as democratic socialists, anarchists, and Trotskyists – read into the dissolution of the Soviet Union a vindication of their sustained opposition to Soviet-style socialism, yet failed to capitalise on its bankruptcy. No socialist alternative emerged to fill the vacuum left by Marxism-Leninism. What happened over the course of the 1990s was therefore a spectacular rout of a movement that once promised to be the world-historical movement for the liberation of the whole of humanity. The quintessential ideology of capital found new purchase and was regenerated in the form of 'neoliberalism', and its advocates and policymakers were permitted to mount an offense. With the collaboration of centre-left parties they managed to rollback many social achievements against the ineffectual opposition being mounted by the far-left. The ideological hegemony of liberal capitalism has taken firm roots in the public's consciousness. Even the left has been gripped by it. This, to me, was exemplified by a journalist writing for Britain's most left-wing major newspaper,[13] who denounced a young socialist advocating for the

---

13   M. Smith 2017.

1974 Labour Party election manifesto which called for the transfer of political power to the working class, by commenting disapprovingly, 'let a young man dream'.[14] What was mainstream left-wing electoral politics in the 1970s had become the utopian dream of a naïve young man only a few decades onwards. The socialist movement today is by and large the plaything of political forces beyond our control. The primary cleavage of the twenty-first century, thus far, has been a tug-of-war of centrist cosmopolitans duelling it out with right-wing, conservative nativists – the 'globalist' and 'nationalist' factions, respectively. These political forces set the pace and direction of discourse and determine the political agenda, while the socialist movement remains largely reactive and incapable of taking the helm in public debate, let alone in seats of power.

Today, 'democratic socialism' has suspended its opposition to the fundamental being of capitalism. It may instead be regarded as a 'set of ameliorative values and policies' without pursuing a qualitative break with capitalism.[15] That is, this type of socialism has become an instrument shielding people from the worst excesses of liberal capitalism, but not a means to overcome it. The far-left in Europe retreated from advancing an alternative to capitalism and today commits itself to defending expansive welfare state policies which were abandoned by the centre-left social-democratic parties.[16] When elected to office, European far-left parties hardly challenge neoliberal supremacy – let alone capitalism.[17] The extra-parliamentary 'counter-globalisation' movement, which was kindled in the late 1990s; the Occupy-movement, which emerged in the wake of the so-called 'Great Recession' of 2008; and the broader anti-austerity mobilisations in Europe were ideologically amorphous and the embers of resistance were quickly doused and forgotten without leaving any notable or sustained impact, at least in part due to underdeveloped institutional alternatives advanced by these political poles.[18] Similarly, parliamentary parties of socialist disposition lack a coherent political vision or ideology, and in participating in electoral cycles are consequently forced to fall back on populist or pragmatic reinventions of *postbellum* social-democracy.[19] Even esteemed Marxists have retreated from the core commitment of socialism and ceased to advocate for the overturning of capitalism to instead pro-

---

14   Jeffries 2012.
15   Laibman 2022, pp. 225–47, 226.
16   March 2008, pp. 9–10.
17   March 2008, p. 14.
18   Scholl and Freyberg-Inan 2018; Scholl and Freyberg-Inan 2013; Scholl and Freyberg-Inan 2014; Freyberg-Inan and Birchfield 2005.
19   March 2011.

moting social empowerment, which seeks to expand 'real utopias' within the bounds of capitalism,[20] or advocate an equitable allocation of stock portfolio among citizens,[21] or slightly more ambitiously, advance the concept of 'corpo-syndicalism' based on equal partnerships of employees via shareholding.[22]

This is the sobering state of affairs socialists are forced to confront. The fundamental question that requires addressing is whether the positive programme of socialism can yet be rehabilitated. The dramatic collapse of socialism worldwide should humble and caution socialists, but we should not forego on seeking to move beyond capitalism until our exploration of alternatives has been definitively exhausted. If we are committed to a revival of socialism, we should take seriously the causes of the implosion of socialism at every level. A revival of socialism further hinges on restoring political confidence, which in turn requires the availability of a vibrant and positive political vision that can form the basis of a counter-hegemonic offensive. This vision will need to be ambitious, attractive, coherent, and feasible. The major extant socialist schools of thought that are available for adoption in this respect are anarchism, Marxist communism, and democratic socialism.[23] Democratic socialism barely qualifies as a political vision *per se* owed to its ambiguous character. In its current 'form' (or lack thereof) it cannot serve as the basis for a revival of socialism, since its dubiety will be exploited in such a way that any uncertainties can only be addressed by receding back into the familiar institutional foundations of capitalism. This leaves anarchism and Marxist communism as the remaining eligible candidates. In this book, I will offer a 'third' political vision, that of republican socialism, which is strictly speaking not in direct conflict with Marxism but does challenge certain canonical notions deeply ingrained in the tradition. Republican socialism may further be regarded as a coherent operationalisation of democratic socialism, to the extent that it offers a political vision that is capable of sustaining by democratic procedures a socialist society. The aim here is not to opportunistically render socialism more respectable to our adversaries, but to articulate a course of action for a 'better conceived victory':

> It is only by constructing this new third way on the left that we can open a new third way for history, a third way between the capitalism we have known until now and the socialism we have known until now. (...) The

---

20   Wright 2010.

21   Roemer 1994; Bardhan and Roemer 1994; Bardhan and Roemer 1992.

22   Varoufakis 2020.

23   Busky 2000, p. 2.

idea is to forge a [vigorous] synthesis, drawing from the strengths, the most vital qualities, of [socialist] traditions, testing them constantly in the fire of our own experience, to create something new. The idea is to reconstruct, not something watered down, but something better blended and further developed.[24]

The aim of this book is not to add to the already rather abundant pile of critiques of capitalism but instead to explore positive alternatives to capitalism by the triad of institutional, constitutional, and mechanism design. This may be regarded as putting the cart before the horse, but we have good reasons to investigate the feasibility of socialism before we flesh out normative arguments in favour of it. We cannot afford delegating the task of designing socialism to spontaneous historical processes alone. This would presuppose that a workable – and in relation to capitalism, comparatively superior – socialism must necessarily follow from the concerted efforts of, the traditionally so regarded, working class as revolutionary subject (i.e. the subjective bearer of the objective world-historical development toward communism). The dialectical process of 'Aufhebung' (sublation), in which qualitative improvement cumulates progressively by cycling through a series of 'contradictions', underpins this assumption.[25] If we reject the 'essentialism' implied by this orthodox interpretation of Marxism, and thus reject the notion that the ultimate consummation of historical development is structurally prescribed, we are free to draw greater attention to discussing the organising principles of socialist society. We should carefully test the assumption that socialism will be a higher form of human social organisation in theory before we might consider doing so in practice. To do otherwise is to take a leap of faith, to put trust in untested and unsubstantiated assumptions, which runs afoul of claims to 'scientific socialism'.

It makes little sense to embark on a highly risky venture involving an enormous expenditure of energy to implement socialism only to in the end having to find out that some of the difficulties in putting socialist ideas to work in actual practice will inevitably cause it to collapse back into capitalism. All criticisms that can be rightly or wrongly levied against capitalism are more or less null and void if there is no viable means to make socialism into a living reality. Especially in light of the disappearance of 'actually existing socialisms' we should first of all ask the question what a feasible socialism could look like. This is a

---

24   Sheehan 1992.
25   See for example: Wheat 2012.

deeply existential question for socialism and merits a much higher consideration than the afterthought it is usually reduced to. Furthermore, enormous creative energy and thought has already been poured into socialist practice. This body of practical knowledge involved in socialist construction has yielded invaluable insights that can potentially allow us to enrich and reformulate the theory of socialism in reference to this body of empirical data. Some of the most innovative and insightful contributions to the theoretical canon of socialism in the previous century have come from the minds of those with hands-on experience in the construction of socialism – important contributions that are now at risk of being overlooked and phased out of memory. The quantity and quality of collective knowledge that has been accumulated over the past centuries and that has now become available for activists, strategists, and theorists to draw on enables a much closer examination of the nature and functioning of socialism without sliding into 'pie-in-the-sky' utopianism.

This book will specifically attempt to revitalise socialism by marrying it to the republican political tradition. In recent years there has been a growing body of literature devoted to exploring a converging relationship between republicanism and socialism. Mostly, this literature has been devoted to exegeses which seek to discover hidden or forgotten republican themes in the writings of historical figures or in social movements.[26] This can be seen as a project of 'socialist republicanism', a less voluminous branch of what has been termed the 'neorepublican research program'.[27] The normative aspect of this project is severely underdeveloped (which is understandable given that it is only now escaping its embryonic phase), although some basic normative theory is being introduced.[28] In order to move this project forward, normative arguments and proposals need to be developed and fleshed out. Toward this purpose, I will draw from the conceptual repository of republicanism in order to define the parameters by which we will subsequently review diverse socialist proposals and attempt to piece together a normative institutional framework of 'socialist republicanism' or, if one prefers, 'republican socialism'.[29] This vision should give socialist political actors the sense of direction and confidence that

---

26   Gourevitch 2015; Leipold 2017; Roberts 2017; Lewis 2019; Muldoon 2019; Thompson 2019; Leipold, Nabulsi, and White 2020.

27   Lovett and Pettit 2009, p. 13.

28   Muldoon 2019; O'Shea 2019; Muldoon 2021.

29   Overall, I prefer 'republican socialism' to 'socialist republicanism' especially where it concerns normative political theory, since it fits, in terms of its 'epistrophe', when we discuss different forms of socialism – democratic socialism, republican socialism, libertarian socialism, etc.

is needed to restore offensive initiative and to reconfigure dominated classes and social groups around a counter-hegemonic pole.

The republican conceptual repository lends itself to various interpretations and has been employed in service of widely diverging political positions, from radical labourism to laissez-faire liberalism.[30] Republicanism, then, is not intrinsically wedded to any particular ideological disposition. The justification for investigating the possibility of a union between republicanism and socialism – as far as this inquiry is concerned – lies in the attempt to rehabilitate socialism. It is not the purpose of this exploration to pass judgement on whether or not socialism is the conclusion that should follow logically from republican premises. I proceed from the assumption that republicanism can potentially positively influence the attractiveness and viability of socialism, which I will seek to test in this book by designing an institutional arrangement that reflects both republican and socialist values. Herein I will not discriminate between neo-Roman and neo-Athenian concerns, but focus broadly on republican values, particularly a mixed constitution, civic virtue, republican liberty, and self-government.

---

30   Gourevitch 2015; Irving 2020.

PART 1

Diagnosis

∴

Socialism in Theory – Promise and Possibilities

If we are interested in staging a revival of socialism then it stands to reason that we ought to have a clear and credible account of its failure hitherto – a diagnosis, in a word. To provide such an account, we will need to focus in particular on the question of the economic feasibility of socialism. Socialism is, after all, fundamentally an arrangement of economic relations, a way of distributing collectively owned goods, resources, and materials. It is relevant for our inquiry, therefore, to provide an overview of both the socialist theory of economic planning and its practice. The purpose in doing so lies in isolating the factors that have been shown historically to be major caveats in the construction of socialism. This will enable us to work out the implications for a workable and durable socialism in Part 2 of this book. In this chapter follows what amounts to an exposition of the main developments of the ideas concerning the economic organising principles of a socialist commonwealth. We will concern ourselves in particular with how communist society was conceived of by its main historical exponents (specifically, by Marx and Engels and their followers) in the first section. The second section of this chapter deals with an exposition of the main arguments involved in the socialist calculation debate. Very briefly by accounting for the historical origins of the sociopolitical movement of socialism, we then proceed to the theoretical framework of socialist planning which it birthed, and the economic calculation debate which was ultimately sparked by it.

1   The Communist Mode of Production and Distribution

The lineage of 'modern socialism' can be traced back to both utopian 'proto-socialism' and radical republicanism.[1] So-called 'Babouvism' may be regarded as the first bud of modern socialist thought. This political tendency found its origins in Babeuf, a radical republican active during the French Revolution, and who is widely considered to have been 'first revolutionary communist' in history.[2] Radical republicanism and socialism, which sprang from the out-

---

1   Moss 1976; Moss 1993.
2   Higonnet 1979.

ermost left wing of the French revolutionists, took shape in response to the concrete material conditions that they confronted. Their ideas were expressions of the will and interests of, in particular, the urban poor – the 'sans-culottes'. The radical impulses and sentiments of the urban working classes, beginning in Europe, were shaped into a self-asserting labour movement by political agitators and organisers, and were supplied philosophical and theoretical underpinnings by such thinkers as Saint-Simon, Fourier, Proudhon, Lassalle, and Marx and Engels. The latter two worked out an ambitious, systematic, and scientific theoretical foundation for the labour movement,[3] by combining French socialism with British political economy and German philosophy, as Lenin simplified.[4] Marx's political theory and strategy borrowed from the republican tradition in a number of ways as well. Particularly its critique of wage-labour expressed in a vocabulary familiar to republicanism, as well as its advocacy of self-government.[5] Marx's ideas (or more accurately, the analytical tools he helped to develop, which can be summarised as 'dialectical materialism'), encapsulated in the term 'Marxism', gradually eclipsed rival radical political movements, such as the Owenites, Proudhonists, Bakuninists, Babouvists, and Lasalleans. It remains the most popular coherent socialist body of thought in the world till this day. Logically then, Marxism will take centre stage in this book, by taking its theoretical and political principles as the point of departure for most of the discussions which contrast republican socialism with the views of existing schools of socialist thought on the nature of socialist society. Given the impact of Marxist theory on the practice of economic planning in the twentieth century, we will need to briefly summarise its key tenets in relation to the communist modes of production and consumption. While it is true that Marx and Engels had published few thoughts on what communist society would look like, we can work out the implications from various clues scattered throughout their works. It further follows from the premises of the dialectical method that the Marxist account of capitalism cannot be separated from its theory of communism – in other words, to understand the Marxist conception of communism we need to understand its account of capitalism.

Unlike many socialists before him, Marx believed that communism would spring from political struggle, rooted in the antagonistic relationships within production that underpin the material reproduction of capitalist society. He theorised that communism would emerge from the concrete material 'contra-

---

3   Chattopadhyay 2005.
4   Lenin 1913.
5   Roberts 2017; Leipold 2020b.

dictions'[6] of capitalist society – rather than from moral principles abstracted from objective conditions, as many of his 'utopian' predecessors and contemporaries believed. In the words of Bordiga:

> communism presents itself as the transcendence of the systems of utopian socialism which seek to eliminate the faults of social organisation by instituting complete plans for a new organisation of society whose possibility of realisation was not put in relationship to the real development of history.[7]

The 'utopian socialists' conjured up their blueprints for a socialist community without regard for the prevailing material circumstances that constrain human action and condition social consciousness. Instead, they tended to regard socialism as the realisation of a universal, timeless morality, which would require a mere force of conviction and moral fortitude to bring about. Communism, according to the Marxist account, would be the culmination of a world-historical dialectical process rooted in the unfolding possibilities of material circumstances. More concretely, it would require political struggle waged by the class of wage-workers against the class that owed their material existence to private ownership of means of production. The industrial expansion of manufacturing methods socialised the labour process, by drawing more individual labours into the process of mass production. At the same time, social production maintained its essentially individualised pattern of ownership over factories and workshops, resulting in the benefits of large-scale mechanised manufacturing flowing into the hands of the non-labouring class of idle owners. Since the material reproduction of labourers depends on their ability to sell their labour-power to the class whose material reproduction depends on squeezing surplus product from labourers by means of their private control over production, the two classes are locked into social conflict. The material interests of workers are connected to the social character of production and are therefore ultimately disposed to collective action on the basis of their common position in relation to their class adversaries and fated to effect the socialisation of the means of production. The capitalist class, on the other end, has a vested and shared interest in maintaining the existing system of capitalist property relations since their continued welfare and dominant position depends on their ability to appropriate surplus product in the form of profit.

---

6   That is to say, the 'opposition of structural principles', in Giddens 1990, p. 145.
7   Bordiga 1920.

History, according to Marx, developed according to an intelligible pattern,[8] which could be understood dialectically, by reference to the transforming material constitutions of societies.[9] The material reproduction of a given society, which depends upon the specific historically constituted mode of production, was assumed to be the principal source of human social organisation and development. Marx, applying the dialectical method of discerning between the outward appearance and inner essence of a phenomenon, summarised it thus:

> The specific economic form, in which unpaid surplus labour is pumped out of direct producers, determines the relationship of rulers and ruled, as it grows directly out of production itself and, in turn, reacts upon it as a determining element. Upon this, however, is founded the entire formation of the economic community which grows up out of the production relations themselves, thereby simultaneously its specific political form. It is always the direct relationship of the owners of the conditions of production to the direct producers – a relation always naturally corresponding to a definite stage in the development of the methods of labour and thereby its social productivity – which reveals the innermost secret, the hidden basis of the entire social structure, and with it the political form of the relation of sovereignty and dependence, in short, the corresponding specific form of the state.[10]

More concretely, in relation to capitalism, large-scale industrial manufacturing in nineteenth century Europe dispossessed the immediate producers, who had until then employed their individually owned and controlled means of production at their leisure. Individual labour was replaced by expansive, socialised mass production. Despite the labour process attaining a social and collaborative character, the structure of ownership did not fundamentally alter, it remained 'individualised' or 'private'.[11] The workers, as a result of this process of proletarianisation were thus subjugated to the will of capitalists.[12] This structural feature of socialised labour and private or capitalist appropriation is, per Marxist theory, the primary contradiction of capitalist society, and the source of social antagonisms the proletariat and capitalist class.[13] While the

---

8   In Sheehan 1993.
9   Wheat 2012; Wood 1995.
10   MECW 37: 777–8.
11   MECW 24: 310.
12   Leipold 2017, p. 3.
13   MECW 24: 310–11.

force of law is not the only instrument in securing the continued reproduction of these fundamentally asymmetrical relations of production, the enforcement of contracts by means of legally sanctioned physical coercion carried out by the repressive arm of the state is nonetheless crucial. Consequently, the state in Marxist theory is considered the arbiter of the class structure on behalf of the dominant class.

In capitalism, different units of production – individual capitals – exist that execute their functions in mutual independence. The production of commodities often requires the productive contributions of several different, autonomous firms through which commodities pass before being available for final use. 'Autonomous', in this process, is the operative word.[14] The co-ordination of production between different units is achieved through bargaining, bidding, and exchange of commodities on the market, rather than directly through social direction via interpersonal relations, whether vertically or horizontally structured. As Chattopadhyay explained: '[I]n a society of generalised commodity production, where products result from private labours executed in reciprocal independence, the social character of these labours – hence the reciprocal relations of the creators of these products – are not established directly'. Therefore, '[t]heir social character is mediated by exchange of products taking commodity form'.[15] It is only where social labour is indirect, or fragmented according to separate capitals, that products need to assume the form of a commodity in market exchange. According to Marxist theory, this gives rise to the so-called 'law of value', emerging out of the competition of capitals, which acts as impersonal disciplinary mechanism, driving down the quantity of abstract labour-time used in production to the social average.[16] Consequently, '[w]ith the inauguration of [socialism] there begins the process of collective appropriation of the conditions of production by society', which means that 'with the end of private appropriation of the conditions of production there also ends the need for the products of individual labour to go through exchange taking the commodity form. In the new society individual labour is directly social from the beginning'.[17] In other words, when the co-ordination of social production occurs through social relations directly, products would not need to become subject to exchange to realise their social character and would therefore not be transformed into commodities at all. Producers and consumers would simply

---

14   Chattopadhyay 1994.
15   Chattopadhyay 2005, pp. 5, 630.
16   Tsushima 1956.
17   Chattopadhyay 2005, pp. 5, 630.

divide the various tasks required in social production amongst each other to service the various social wants of the community.

The entire mode of capitalist production therefore depends on the continued reproduction of social, co-operative labour, which is distributed among individual capitals, each with their own particular motives and strategies for accumulation, and co-ordinated indirectly, through the exchange of commodities. Capitalism is therefore regarded by Marxism as an inherently unstable system, depending on the adjustments of social production through competitive private exchange – the 'anarchy of the market' – and the capitalist appropriation of social wealth. The antagonistic opposition of the social classes that follows from these contradictions would produce class conflict, which, according to Marxism, will assume a political struggle for supremacy, and ultimately permit the proletariat, aided by their numerical superiority and their collective creative, productive powers, to seize state power. Since the source of conflict rests on the objective separation of the producers from the means of production – a condition which would be universalised through the outward, expansionary processes associated with the regime of capital accumulation – the struggle for political power would, in theory, also assume a universal scope. Consequently, labour conflicts isolated to each individual capital, in which the modern state acts as arbiter intervening on behalf of the capitalist class, would eventually escalate into the struggle for political supremacy involving the working class as a whole. All means of production would be wrestled out of the hands of the capitalist class and be transformed into public property. Through this process of expropriation and socialisation, socialised production would be brought into harmony with the property relations.[18]

This 'harmonisation' entails that the scope of the direct social character of production would no longer be limited to within units of production but instead encompass the entirety of society. Where market forces discipline capitalists in a roundabout way, indirectly, the disciplinary mechanism within workplaces is direct, exercised by means of the authority of the owners (or the employees they hired to act on their behalf). The managers employ a particular repertoire of rewards and penalties in order to extract as much relative and/or absolute surplus product from the workforce. As such, the class of producers stand in direct opposition to the class of owners. Robertson had observed that firms were 'islands of conscious power in this ocean of unconscious co-operation'.[19] Co-operation in the sphere of social production in capitalism is

---

18   MECW 24: 323.
19   Cited in Coase 1937, p. 388.

achieved by two primary means. Within firms, interpersonal (usually hierarch-ical) relations, and therefore conscious command directs the combined efforts of the workforce; while the individual efforts of separate units of capital are co-ordinated unconsciously, in the sphere of market exchange. As Coase noted:

> Outside the firm, price movements direct production, which is co-ordin-ated through a series of exchange transactions on the market [indirectly social]. Within a firm, these market transactions are eliminated and in place of the complicated market structure with exchange transactions is substituted the entrepreneur-co-ordinator, who directs production [dir-ectly social].[20]

Within enterprises workers take directions and execute the orders issued by their superiors collectively. In other words, the abolition of private property makes possible the social integration of enterprises into a single association, upon which the social character of production is given the 'freedom to work itself out'.[21] Thereby, the 'anarchy' of market forces would be replaced by the collaborative and planned organisation that is already practised within the set-ting of individual firms[22] – albeit presently orchestrated at the behest of the capitalist, instead of by the producers themselves.

Thus, if the social organisation internal to firms is expanded to encompass all of society – forming into a union of communal property – logically, products cannot become commodities since no transactions will need to occur to divide them amongst the members of the community. Under directly social relations wherever they may form or exist, material resources used in production are simply distributed according to the will of whoever directs production, in order to generate certain results. In communism, the means of production belong to society – i.e. they are the common possession of humanity – and are managed by a vast, co-operative association of producers. Individual units of production will become integrated into a co-operative whole.[23]

Consequently, '[p]roduction is now geared for use, not for augmenting value. Indirect social labor, based on the value-form of mediation, is replaced by direct social labor, based on "transparent" interpersonal relations between the produ-cers'.[24] As Engels explained:

---

20   Coase 1937, p. 388.

21   MECW 24: 325.

22   MECW 24: 323, 325.

23   For example: Bukharin and Preobrazhensky 1920.

24   Hudis 2005.

From the moment when society enters into possession of the means of production and uses them in direct association for production, the labour of each individual, however varied its specifically useful character may be, becomes at the start and directly social labour. The quantity of social labour contained in a product need not then be established in a round-about way; daily experience shows in a direct way how much of it is required on the average. Society can simply calculate how many hours of labour are contained in a steam-engine, a bushel of wheat of the last harvest, or a hundred square yards of cloth of a certain quality. It could therefore never occur to it still to express the quantities of labour put into the products, quantities which it will then know directly and in their absolute amounts, in a third product, in a measure which, besides, is only relative, fluctuating, inadequate, though formerly unavoidable for lack of a better one, rather than express them in their natural, adequate and abso-lute measure, *time*.[25]

Under such conditions, accumulation will no longer be a means to despoil and deprive the working class, which results in the accelerated concentration of wealth into the privileged upper stratum of society, the capitalist class. Instead, accumulation will be turned into an instrument – under the conscious dir-ection of the producers themselves – to raise the quality of life for all.[26] The experience of the Paris Commune in 1871 appeared to bear out these theor-etical propositions. The working classes in Paris, in response to their imme-diate economic and political circumstances, especially as they related to the Franco-Prussian War of 1870, radicalised in the process of open mutiny and began asserting themselves as independent class force against the government of landlords and capitalists in Versailles. They organised their own defence, elected their own representatives to the municipal council of the Commune, and planned to reorganise the Parisian industrial base. The Commune of Paris was guided politically by the Blanquist faction and economically by the Proud-honist faction, promoting the association of workers in each factory and the incorporation of these producers' associations into a single union; 'in short, an organisation which, as Marx quite rightly says (...) must necessarily have led in the end to communism'.[27]

Given these contours of communist society, derived from materialist ana-lysis, we can make reasonable inferences about the inner workings of the com-

---

25   MECW 25: 294.
26   Chattopadhyay 2016, p. 60.
27   MECW 27: 188.

munist mode of production. Theoretical experimentation of this nature has only the faintest resemblance to the ideological output historically produced by some of the utopian socialists, who departed from ideal circumstances and worked their way backward. Instead, describing the mechanisms operating in a communist society might be done by first taking into account certain historical developments, and that these unfolding processes will necessarily socialise the levers of production and, owed to the material contradictions contained within capitalist property relations, eventually also cause the means of production to assume their socialised character. What remains is for the implications of a system of socialised ownership to be worked out.

The co-ordination of social production in a socialist community would be organised on the basis of direct social relations between producers – so much is clear. We can thus speculate that different production units would communicate and deliberate amongst each other directly, presumably via a sort of all-encompassing production and distribution co-operative with functional and geographic divisions. The co-operative network of production associations and industrial syndicates would not only need to measure the social costs of the various products (the amount of material and labour contained in them) but also compare this expenditure of effort to the social usefulness of the results of productive activity to be able to make measured decisions between various choices among techniques and output mixes. On the basis of such evaluations, the associations of producers would need to decide on the best use of resources by combining factors of production in a way that minimises expenditure compared to a given level of social demand. There has been a tendency in Marxism, especially in the early stages of its development, to assume that all this would be rather uncomplicated.

Each individual association of producers in communist society would be the conditional and temporal custodian of a particular amount of commonly owned productive resources. They possess, we can speculate, knowledge of the composition of input and equipment needed to obtain the maximum output required to satisfy a particular level of demand. On the basis of the available productive capacity and materials (data for which can be aggregated immediately as they are transmitted by the lower levels to higher administrative levels), the various associations of producers would be able to determine what they each need to contribute to the total output, consistent with the estimated or communicated level of consumer demand.[28] The principal accounting tool to aid this process would be labour time, the 'natural' unit of account, as per

---

28   See for example: Ticktin 1997, pp. 145–67; and GIC 1930.

Engels, freed from the distorting effects exerted by market forces on price levels. As products pass through the chain of production, their time of procurement would be tracked; thus, the costs of different products would be expressed in terms of the average social labour time incurred in their production. The magnitudes of labour-power required to produce a given article of consumption would become immediately clear, since it is established directly by means of mutual adjustment within the vast co-operative association that would cover all sites of production in society, and is therefore transparent to all links in the supply chain. The social labour time embodied in products would not have to be gauged indirectly, from the exchange ratios of commodities observed in the market; rather, this information emerges from the unified system of bookkeeping of the associations of producers and the interpersonal relations of production between them.[29] On the basis of that information the social costs of goods can be compared to their relative usefulness in satisfying different consumer preferences. Using these computations, society will try to allocate resources in such a way that producers can manufacture as much useful output whilst minimising the amount of resources required.

The entire sphere of social production and consumption would be treated as if part of a single co-operative workplace, without internal or external market relations. According to Marx then, communism is based on 'production by freely associated men, [which] is consciously regulated by them in accordance with a settled plan'. In such a society, the 'labour power of all the different individuals is consciously applied as the combined labour power of the community'.[30] Thus:

> The total product of our community is a social product. One portion serves as fresh means of production and remains social. But another portion is consumed by the members as means of subsistence. A distribution of this portion amongst them is consequently necessary. The mode of this distribution will vary with the productive organisation of the community, and the degree of historical development attained by the producers.[31]

Put differently, part of the total product of society is earmarked for addressing the wear and tear of equipment and to expand the productive base of society – its expanded reproduction. What remains of the stock of fixed assets after this portion has been used to produce more means of production can be used to

---

29   See for example: Lenin 1918; Pannekoek 1950 [1946].
30   MECW 35: 89–90.
31   Ibid.

produce means of consumption. Marx proposed that as the productive forces in communist society develop, the mode of distribution evolves as well. In 'the first phase' of communist society, the level of productivity of the means of production would be insufficient to assure an adequate supply of the means of subsistence which would therefore prohibit their free distribution. That is to say, distribution cannot be based on the principle that the members of the community appropriate from the stock of means of consumption whatever they deem necessary to satisfy their needs and wants. By force of necessity, articles of consumption would instead be distributed proportionately to the individual, productive contributions of producers to social production:

> Labour time would, in that case, play a double part. Its apportionment in accordance with a definite social plan maintains the proper proportion between the different kinds of work to be done and the various wants of the community. On the other hand, it also serves as a measure of the portion of the common labour borne by each individual, and of his share in the part of the total product destined for individual consumption. The social relations of the individual producers, with regard both to their labour and to its products, are in this case perfectly simple and intelligible, and that with regard not only to production but also to distribution.[32]

As such, no private property, no money, and no exchange would exist under communism. Indeed: 'According to nineteenth-century socialist views, socialism would function without capitalist economic categories – such as money, prices, interest, profits and rent – and thus would function according to laws other than those described by current economic science'.[33] Later interpretations would assert to the contrary that the law of value – as corollary of the continued, partial reproduction commodity-money relations – would only disappear in later stages of communist development.[34] According to Marx, in any case, in the first phase of communist development, producers would receive a coupon, note, or certificate, which has stamped on it their contribution measured in hours of labour-time, and with it they can subtract from the stock of consumption goods an equivalent amount of products. Crucially, Marx makes explicit that these certificates are cancelled after use, and are therefore not a medium of exchange.[35]

---

32   MECW 35: 89–90.
33   Bockman 2011.
34   See for example: Laibman 2013; KKE 2013.
35   MECW 35: 104.

According to Ollman 'Marx divides the communist future into halves'.[36] That is to say, two conceptually distinct phases of communist development. Cockshott, Cottrell and Laibman concord with the statement that Marx advanced the idea of 'two stages' of communism – the 'two-stage' legend of communism, if you will – which reflects, I think, a tendency of reification and fossilisation of phrases that have only been used in passing by Marx or Engels.[37] On the contrary, Marx merely illustrated that a communist society which is relatively more advanced would distribute a higher proportion of its products according to the self-determined needs of consumers. Marx's use of 'a' higher phase as opposed to 'the' higher phase corroborates, in my view, that there are not two categorically distinct stages of communist society, only varying degrees of material advancement within communist relations of production. In a more advanced phase of its development, communist society would bear such and such characteristics which separate it from the first or earlier phases of development. The difference between 'the first' and 'a higher phase' of communism was grounded in the notion that the degree to which the means of consumption are distributed either according to individual contributions or self-defined needs, follows from the degree of material abundance enabled by a given level of development of the productive forces. Communist society would thus pass through different stages of material development according to the overall size of the productive forces of its industrial base, in which the ratio of goods distributed freely to goods rationed according to individual contributions would progressively increase in proportion to development of productive capacity. In other words, communism is not cleaved into two categorically separate 'halves', but exists according to a continuum of development proportionate to the quantity and grade of its productive forces.

In direct correspondence to this development, communism would more and more free up the creative and social energy of working people. Liberated from the burden of drudgery, exploitation, and alienation, by virtue of material advances in the development of the forces of production, individuals would become free to develop their faculties at their own discretion. As the development of the productive forces progresses, the necessity for physical toil is decreased, and in proportion to this, leisure, in which the individual can pursue intrinsically motivated creative and productive fulfilment, is increased. It was assumed that people in such social circumstances would volunteer to do stimulating yet productive work due to innate human proclivities for creativity

---

36   Ollman 1977.
37   Laibman 2013, p. 501; Cockshott and Cottrell 1993, p. 21.

and purpose. The division of labour would in this way be overcome gradually, as Marx famously prophesied:

> in communist society, where nobody has one exclusive sphere of activity but each can become accomplished in any branch he wishes, society regulates the general production and thus makes it possible for me to do one thing today and another tomorrow, to hunt in the morning, fish in the afternoon, rear cattle in the evening, criticise after dinner, just as I have a mind, without ever becoming hunter, fisherman, shepherd or critic.[38]

In this way, the sphere of 'work' begins to merge with leisure and this categorical separation in social life will gradually be overcome. Communism therefore prepares the material groundwork for the all-round development of human potential in all members of society.

In addition to abolishing social classes, the social division of labour, money, and wage-labour, communism would also do away with the state. Under a communist regime, the antagonistic opposition between different classes will have given way to the free co-operation by a community of producers and consumers for their overall benefit. The struggles over the distribution of the material product along class lines requires the legal-political mediation by political authority and state power to guarantee the reproduction of class relations to the advantage of the dominant class. Prior to the advent of social stratification and the division of society into classes, that is to say, before the agricultural revolution and the emergence of 'civilisation', human social organisation was constituted purely by egalitarian hunter-gatherer bands without overarching state body. This stage of human development being classified as 'primitive communism' in Marxist historiography. The state, according to the Marxist understanding of historical development, arose as an instrument to insure the dominant position of one class against potential resistance by the exploited classes. Alongside material political force, based on physical coercion, also arises a system of symbolic beliefs – cultural values, social norms, ideological forms – that legitimate the existing order in an attempt to reconcile the working classes with their exploitation. Hence, under conditions of collective appropriation by the community of producers, political authority would phase out of existence, since there are no longer any conflicts proceeding from class antagonisms that require mediation and enforcement to secure the reproduction of class domination.

---

38   MECW 5: 47.

Like primitive communism, industrial communism would have no need for political coercion. Since the association of producers and consumers would decide in what capacity to employ their commonly owned productive resources, and within this scope, would also collectively decide toward what exact collective purposes the resources are to be used (e.g. medical care, infrastructure), the spheres of 'politics' and 'economics' – much like the spheres of work and leisure – merge. What remains is the administration of things, the allocation of material goods between different uses, by the free association of equal producers and consumers. The antagonistic relationships between social classes would dissolve after a period of political and social transformation. In short, communism would be a classless mode of production, distribution, and appropriation, in which there are no competing class interests that give rise to the need for political authority to attend to class conflict on behalf of the dominant class.

To summarise, communism is envisioned by Marxism as a society that emerges out of historical processes that have brought forth the technical forces of mass production under a capitalist regime and the material contradictions contained therein. The private structure of ownership of the tools of production was sublated under the development of the powerful forces of industry, which socialised the process of production but retained the motive of private gain at the level of ownership. The working classes and capitalist classes, themselves birthed by this development, have diametrically opposed material interests engendering social conflict over the appropriation of surplus product. The resolution to this contradiction is the reorganisation of industry on a communal basis. In the words of Marx:

> The capitalist mode of appropriation, the result of the capitalist mode of production, produces capitalist private property. This is the first negation of individual private property, as founded on the labour of the proprietor. But capitalist production begets, with the inexorability of a law of Nature, its own negation. It is the negation of negation. This does not re-establish private property for the producer, but gives him individual property based on the acquisitions of the capitalist era: i.e., on co-operation and the possession in common of the land and of the means of production.[39]

Thus, by combining socialised production with socialised ownership, social production comes to represent a higher form of under communism; being

---

39   MECW 35: 751.

unshackled from the fetters of private property. Likewise, the self-control over production by petty producers, which disappeared on account of mass production, re-emerges in a higher form, by establishing collective, co-operative control by producers over the tools of labour.

Under these conditions, the citizens of communist society would be able to develop themselves in accordance with their human essence, exercising collective control over their social life, free from any and all oppressive and exploitative social structures. These are still the noble aspirations that Marxists today labour to make a reality, against strong odds. If we want to investigate the extent to which these worthy political ambitions are salvageable and applicable to the twenty-first century, in the context of advanced capitalism, we will need to begin by interrogating the main critiques of socialism. For the purpose of this inquiry we will confine ourselves to the question of the practical feasibility of collectivist society itself. In this respect, we should turn to the question of the application of economic calculus under socialism, which Mises and Hayek famously urged was impossible.

2   Economic Calculation under Socialism

The question of economic calculation is straightforward: How can society measure the costs and results of using productive assets in different capacities so as to assign them to their most useful application in order to secure the best possible growth of material wealth? From the 1920s onwards, two central figures of the 'Austrian school' of economic thought, Mises and Hayek, generated the theoretical ammunition to chip away at the credibility of socialism. They proposed that socialism was incapable of performing the calculations necessary to allocate resources efficiently. Since, without the free exchange of goods and their expression of value in monetary terms, socialism would lack the mechanism for determining the least costly ways to do things. The central planning body could never absorb the enormous volume of the technical information, and if it could, they would not be able to digest and convert them into specific production targets for the numerous producers in the economy. Furthermore, the highly decentralised and qualitative nature of knowledge related to economic possibilities and opportunities, makes the aggregation of economic data by the central authorities an impossibility. Socialism was fated to collapse, and the conclusion of actually existing socialisms has served to vindicate their claims.

In order to provide better insight into the problem of economic calculation under socialism we will have to understand the respective Marxist and 'bourgeois' positions in relation to market prices. Marx and Engels saw price levels as outcomes of the anarchy of the market, generating misinformation on which capitalists act. Since the quantities of labour contained in commodities cannot be established directly, the ratio of prices established in the process of market exchange form the basis for investment decisions. Since the responses of firms to market prices are not co-ordinated, any miscommunication contained in the information of market prices compounds the errors of investments and amplifies the effects. This is part of the causes that contribute to disturbances to capitalist reproduction, although it is not in itself considered to be the basic cause of economic crises in Marxist theory.[40] A key element in Marxist doctrine is the notion that prices, which express the ratio at which commodities exchange (their exchange-value), mystify underlying human relations: The relations between people appear as relations between objects (or, 'commodity fetishism'). Marxist theory, borrowing from dialectics, proposes that the essential characteristics of an economy are not found, say, in inflation, interest rates, unemployment figures, or even the growth rate of the national product. These are but surface phenomena, which conceal the essential, underlying production relations which lie beneath and give rise to them, but which become the primary object of investigation in 'bourgeois economics'. The Marxist approach, by contrast, takes the material constitution of society, the mode of production, as the basic object of analysis. A mode of production is a particular configuration of production relations and production methods, which allocates labour-power and extracts surplus product in a certain way.

In the capitalist mode of production, the terrain of social production is fragmented into separate capitals, which each acquire liquid or fixed assets, labour-power, and physical materials in order to sell their commodities at augmented value. Changes in market prices, mediated by market forces, are the primary mechanism by which human labour-power is apportioned. If profit margins increase in a competitive ('healthy') market as a result of a sustained increase in effective demand for a particular product, this indicates that more material resources should be employed producing said commodity. This may assume the form of additional living labour (i.e. workers) or 'embodied labour' (i.e. production goods) – or the intensification of exploitation of workers or resources, or some combination of these options. The reverse may also be true of course, as Marx pointed out:

---

40   Shaikh 1978.

Every individual article, or every definite quantity of a commodity may, indeed, contain no more than the social labour required for its production, and from this point of view the market value of this entire commodity represents only necessary labour, but if this commodity has been produced in excess of the existing social needs, then so much of the social labour time is squandered and the mass of the commodity comes to represent a much smaller quantity of social labour in the market than is actually incorporated in it.[41]

Thus, market demand dictates what is a socially necessary expenditure of labour and what has been a socially needless expenditure. To put it differently, behind the surface phenomena associated with the circulation of commodities lurks a simple truth: all economic conduct is a particular apportioning of human labour-power and appropriation of surplus product obtained from this application of human labour. Prices in the capitalist economy cloak the underlying source of value: quantities of social labour time. Under capitalism, the production process is socialised, but the ownership of productive resources remains private, thus fragmenting the total social capital into individual components which require their indirect re-assembly by establishing exchange relations between them. When productive resources are converted from the private tools of individual owners to the collective property of the community, this hidden truth is laid bare – at least, so says the basic tenet of Marxist theory. It would henceforth become possible for social production to be regulated by interpersonal social relations and consequently, the contributions of individual labours would be immediately transparent and directly part of the social labour. Accounting in labour time would flow naturally from the socialisation of the means of production. Society, if it took possession of the means of production, could simply assess the various needs in society and the availability of resources measured in labour-time, and taking this into consideration, apportion labour to various branches of production corresponding to such needs. Money, as universal mediator of commodity exchange, would lose its purpose and communist society could conduct its affairs in the area of production and distribution much more rationally by means of social planning compared to the chaos of the market economy.

Mises famously turned this argument on its head. Without market prices, and crucially, without a capital market, there would be no way to determine the costs of production goods and the returns on their use in different capacit-

---

41   MECW 37: 186.

ies, rendering it impossible to calculate rationally based on the disparate valuations that collapse relative scarcities, production costs, and consumer preferences into a single scale. While Mises admitted for the possibility of a market for consumption goods under a socialist economic arrangement, and therefore conceded that the use of coupons by consumers to appropriate finished products would yield economic valuations, the socialisation of capital goods would make it impossible to measure and compare the results of economic activity.[42] Consequently, the socialist community could not assign prices to 'higher-order' goods (means of production) that approximately reflect their true value. This effectively means that society would be unable to figure out the best course of action out of all alternative options based on comparisons of costs and returns, thus being condemned to allocate productive resources arbitrarily.

Prices, so the argument goes, absorb innumerable disparate subjective preferences and valuations based on the best local estimates of possibilities and opportunities to turnover a profit. It allows economic agents to act on this information without needing direct knowledge of the large amounts of detailed information contained in (and concealed by) them. This structure of exchange arising out disparate dispositions and valuations cannot enter into the decision-making process of economic agents where none such exchange relations exist, naturally. The market mechanism furnishes consumers and producers with snapshot summaries in the form of market prices that convey the multitude of these qualifications, considerations, and costs that go into decisions, enabling them to make efficient and rational use of these highly diffused pockets of knowledge, which would otherwise be drowned out by the immensity of the volume information. Only when prices can be established freely in the market can this information be absorbed into the circuits of production and exchange, becoming available to everyone participating in the market as buyers and sellers – in relation to economic calculus, market prices serve their purpose. This free operation of market exchange is therefore indispensable to create order out of chaos, to enable participants in the market to navigate the complexity of a modern, expansive industrial economy rationally and efficiently.

It follows that a socialist commonwealth that would seek to allocate resources between different uses without the aid of a price mechanism guided on the basis of market exchange would be 'groping in the dark'.[43] Furthermore,

---

42   Mises 2012, pp. 1–7.
43   Mises 2012, p. 23.

a planned socialist economy which would try to compute costs by assigning by administrative fiat prices to production good would not be any more rational. Such prices would not be the result of bidding on the basis of contextual knowledge of possibilities and opportunities and would therefore not be able to incorporate estimates by producers of the relative usefulness of fixed assets in bringing about particular outcomes. Administrative prices, in other words, are arbitrary and no more useful than the absence of prices in their entirety. As Caplan summarises, 'if the state owns all the capital goods (...) there will be no market for capital goods. With no market for capital goods, no capital-goods prices. And without prices, there will be no numbers to run so as to determine the cheapest way to do things'.[44] In short, there can be no rational economic calculation in a society that abolishes the market in capital goods. Laibman puts the question of economic planning thus:

> How can a central authority absorb and process the mounds of information, about the needs of consumers on one side and production possibilities of producers on the other, and put together a consistent plan to create and distribute goods across the social and geographic territory of a modern economy? This is the 'millions of equations' critique of central planning. It draws on the interdependence of economic actors and the almost unimaginably large number of possible products, techniques of production, routes of delivery, distributions, patterns of consumption, etc., and concludes that creation of a single central plan by a unified human will must be inherently impossible. Moreover, a Central Planning Board that attempts this even assuming that the planners are not subject to temptations of power and misrule would create errors, inconsistencies and chaos, not to speak of massively suboptimal outcomes, that would truly be the 'road to serfdom'. The Central Planner would have to have the 'universal mind' of Laplace; would have to not only solve millions of equations, but do that many times every day, to accommodate changes that are constantly taking place.[45]

The criticisms by Mises had initially been directed at Neurath, a contemporary, in particular. A committed socialist, he had inferred from his study of war economics that calculation *in-natura* alone would be sufficient in socialism.[46]

---

44   Caplan 2004.
45   In Laibman 2020.
46   Cockshott 2008; Neurath 2004.

He observed how, in the face of military expediency, the belligerent govern-ments involved in World War I resorted to mobilising their resources for milit-ary purposes on the basis of the availability of physical input on the one hand, and their value in realising military-strategic objectives on the other. Military-industrial production was planned according to military priorities using cal-culations in physical units to overcome financial constraints. Neurath theor-ised that the same practice of calculation *in-natura* could be extrapolated to the economy as a whole during peacetime. In place of military priorities, social priorities would be identified to guide the allocation of resources. In short, according to Neurath, calculation in-kind in a socialised (at the same time, 'naturalised') economy would transplant monetary calculations and the profit criterium in economic decision-making. He had noted that reducing all economic activity to money-prices concealed (in fact, destroyed) enormous amounts of detailed information. He proposed that the use of elaborate stat-istics regarding the physical quantity of resources and goods could be plugged into tables, which would preserve this information whilst also ensuring that physical inputs match the physical output. However, the complexity of calcu-lation in-kind under real world conditions, and in particular the scale of the required calculations to plan an entire national economy, would be prohibit-ively difficult.[47] The processing of huge sums of material goods expressed only in physical units of measurement would make finding a feasible plan (i.e. one that is internally consistent) impossible. Furthermore, it would be impossible to express costs as a common denominator to compare the different outlays associated with different investment decisions. Even if a feasible plan could be expressed in material quantities alone, there would be no way to subject the distribution of resources to optimisation since the relative costs of alternatives cannot be established to weigh the implications of using different combina-tions of sorts of materials, types of equipment, and categories of labour. That is to say, even if we leave aside the issue of scale for the moment, it would not be possible to compare different feasible (internally consistent) plan variants against rational criteria related to the minimisation of total expenditure and the maximisation of returns accruing to society.

In the first rounds phase of the socialist calculation debate, the most sophist-icated attempt to tackle Mises' arguments came from the camp of neoclassical economics, particularly in the form of the 'Lange'-model (or 'Lange-Lerner' model, or even 'Lange-Lerner-Taylor' model). This marks an important way-

---

47   Cockshott 2008, pp. 13–14.

point in the debate on socialist planning. Lange's basic model, later amended on the basis of input from Lerner and Taylor, proposed that the means of production should be owned publicly whilst a Central Planning Board (CPB) would artificially mimic the market, by acting as the 'Walrasian' auctioneer. This model built on a tradition of sorts whereby neoclassical economists, going back to Barone in 1908, would run theoretical experiments on how a fictitious socialist government wielding a monopoly over capital goods could conduct their economic affairs. Barone had argued that if the collectivist government would depart from a condition where money is absent, all the various financial categories – rent, wages, prices – would re-appear as soon as they should try to allocate assets in a way that would observe the principle of least-cost and max-imum collective welfare. This theoretical exercise allowed him to draw out the conclusion that socialism was more capable of allocating resources rationally compared to the free market, because it could better simulate the conditions resembling those of 'perfect competition' (such as the equalisation of the cost and price levels) which were suitable for the attainment of general equilibrium. Lange built on these insights and proposed that, where ordinarily the market-place secures supply and demand via the buying and selling of producers and consumers facilitated by their private means and motivated by their private ends, the market mechanism could be embodied in the CPB. That is to say, the CPB would auction goods to producers, in place of the sum of isolated choices made in the market; with both costs and results being expressed in monetary units.

The Lange-Lerner procedure proposed that the means of production could be distributed rationally among producers by, as the first step, having the CPB quote an arbitrary set prices for all commodities. These prices are adopted by producers and formulate a supply and demand schedule which is then send back to the CPB, which checks them for consistency. Firms are expected to expand output until the marginal costs equal price, which would maximise hypothetical profits. Since the first iteration is unlikely to generate a fully con-sistent economic plan, new prices will be announced in a process of trial-and-error. This works thus. When there is excess supply of a particular commodity, the price is lowered; when there is excess demand for a particular commodity, the price is increased. The firms are then once again instructed to readjust their output to maximise profit, which involves a process of scaling the quantity of output up or down. Eventually, after a number of successive approximations, prices would convergence on a state of general equilibrium in which supply and demand for all commodities are level. The CPB would assign 'accounting prices' to capital goods on the basis of these calculations in order for to CPB to distribute capital goods in such a pattern that they would maximise overall profits.[48] There are some additional elements contained in Lange's model related to the different time horizons of firms and industrial associations and the rate of accumulation, but the basic mechanism works thus. Central planning of this kind is therefore a *theoretically* viable mechanism for the rational allocation of economic resources, at least within the neoclassical framework of general equilibrium.[49]

In response to this rejoinder favouring socialism, which came out of the very heart of mainstream economics, the Austrian school revised and refined their arguments, spearheaded by Hayek.[50] The Lange-Lerner model based itself on neoclassical axioms, and therefore presupposed access to perfect knowledge and perfectly rational behaviour. These features were projected on the agents involved in the planning 'dialogue'; on both central planners and managers. As such, the model made no effort to define ways in which knowledge would be generated and whether or not the participants would feed each other unbiased data. That is to say, the Lange-Lerner model assumed a 'managerial' view of economic decision-making, which could rely only on explicit cost-benefit calculations, as well as presupposing selfless and rational behaviour on part of both the centre and firms. To neoclassical economics, the question of economic calculation was fundamentally a technical problem that could, in theory, be resolved by the application of the correct technical means. Put differently, by devising and employing the right technical tools the 'hidden' technical variables could be disclosed and put to rational use.

The Austrian scholars had a more sensible understanding of knowledge production compared to their neoclassical peers. Behind the decisions of buying and selling, while generating numerical valuations (i.e. explicit, quantitative information), also lies an 'entrepreneurial' function, Hayek objected, not merely a 'technical-managerial' one. Knowledge does not simply exist externally to the sphere of dispersed economic relations and interactions, but is generated in the process of participating in these activities. Lange's model of central planning using simulated markets was too static, seeking to arrive at a static equilibrium by a clever manipulation of prices. The market, by contrast, actively creates *disequilibria*, moving from one state of disequilibrium to another in a constant flux of change, disrupting any potential stabilisation by introducing new concepts, new applications or new technologies, which is simultaneously the source of sustained growth by muddling through the selection

---

48   Kowalik 1990, p. 147; Lange 1937; Lange 1936.

49   Sherman 1973.

50   Hayek 1940; Hayek 1945; Hayek 2006.

of the best uses of resources among alternatives based on local and tacit knowledge and market competition, which is constantly forging new opportunities
and roadways to explore.

Entrepreneurs generate information as they participate in dynamic processes of market co-ordination. The correct 'variables' are therefore not given,
waiting around to be unveiled by applying the right technical instruments. The
knowledge generated and reconstructed by entrepreneurs is highly contextual,
dispersed, and dynamic, as it takes into account and engages with the constant mutually evolving qualitative local and tacit, fractured pieces of knowledge that cannot be quantified or transmitted to the centre – even if aided by
artificial market mechanisms.[51] The market, according to this view, involves a
learning process that requires active participation:

> for the Austrian school, the essential economic problem is not the max-
> imization of a known, objective function subject to known restrictions
> but, on the contrary, it is strictly economic in nature: it emerges when
> ends and means are numerous and compete, and knowledge of them is
> not given, but instead is dispersed throughout the minds of countless
> human beings who are constantly creating it *ex novo*, and thus one can-
> not know all the existing possibilities and alternatives, nor the relative
> intensity with which each is desired.[52]

Rational economic activity is not an issue of applying known technical variables toward calculable ends, instead revolving around the discovering and
developing of circumstantial economic possibilities and opportunities. Take
as an example an idle tract of land. This vacant lot does not possess innately
or objective economic qualities that can be subjected to optimisation according to purely quantitative metrics at the direction of some central authority –
it does not factor as explicit data into economic calculus. Resources are only
rendered a force for economic purpose when qualitative judgement is passed
on them by entrepreneurial fortitude, envisioning the land as containing boun-
tiful seeds for economic exploitation – whether in the form of an attractive
tourist resort, a productive mining operation, or agrarian cultivation. This lat-
ent potential is contextual, depending purely on the role ascribed to resources
by entrepreneurial intuition or perception, and therefore unavailable to the
surveying eyes of central planners. Knowledge of economic possibilities is only

---

51   Rothbard 1991.
52   Huerta de Soto 2008, p. 9.

discovered due to the crucible of market competition that induces entrepreneurs to continually seek out and discover new opportunities to gain advantage. This type of knowledge, generated and acquired by participating in decentralised market processes, acts as the motor propelling forward the actions and behaviours of economic agents. As such, this economic information cannot be quantified and aggregated into a central databank, to be massaged in such a way that economic functions and resources can be distributed among producers accordingly by means of centralised planning.

Hayek further pointed out that in a Lange-type economy, it would require an army of bureaucrats to take stock of the realities on the shopfloor in order to review the data input submitted by managers to audit their reliability. The planners, after all, are dependent on this data since they themselves are unable to interact with the knowledge dispersed among the many economic agents involved in decentralised processes that continually reconstitute knowledge. Whether or not the production-possibility frontiers that managers of plants and firms submit to the planning authorities as data actually correspond to the true potential of their facilities cannot be gauged from the vantage point of centre. It requires the assumption of altruistic motivation on the end of managers, or alternatively, an expansive bureaucratic system of audits and reviews. In addition, entrepreneurs routinely rely on experience or 'entrepreneurial' intuition to overrule quantitative signals in their decision-making.[53] In order for qualitative knowledge to be absorbed into economic decision-making, the free initiative of producers and consumers should be allowed to play out, the 'Austrians' propose. It would be far too convenient to dismiss this line of attack on socialism out of hand.

Mises drew the conclusion that civilisation may well collapse in on itself if market prices disappeared as a consequence of the nationalisation of capital goods.[54] Rothbard, a philosophical heir to Mises, went as far as to claim that his mentor had shown that socialist society could not function 'above the most primitive level'.[55] These critics, Mises and Rothbard in particular, boasted that they had delivered a deadly theoretical blow to socialism. Socialism, they explained, was not just economically inefficient or morally deplorable, but, far more damning than all of the above, *impossible*. If socialism was economically inferior to capitalism but arguably morally superior, it would leave scope for debate about the comparative merits of one system over the other. Conversely, if socialism proved morally inferior but economically superior to capitalism,

---

53   Grünberg 2023.
54   Caplan 2004, p. 36.
55   Rothbard 2000, p. 201.

it still would permit terrain for perpetual debate on these trade-offs. However, if the very existence of socialism could be demonstrated to be an impossibility, it rules out all debate and socialism can be condemned to the scrapyard of history.

The strength of these particular conclusions is difficult to maintain, we can immediately infer from the empirical record. Far from being 'impossible', 'primitive', or bringing civilisation to collapse in on itself, Soviet socialism endured for almost seventy years and improved the material standard of living considerably, despite deeply unfavourable conditions. Kenny notes that in 1913, the income per capita of the Russian Empire was only about one percent larger than Mexico's. However, by 1989, 'Soviet income per capita was 46 percent larger than Mexican income'. This, '[d]espite suffering through two incredibly damaging world wars, a civil war, the Stalin-induced famines that killed millions in the 1930s, his jail and gulag system that killed millions more, and a range of environmental disasters'.[56] Indeed, in 'a relatively short period of time', Wilczynski summarised, the countries in the communist bloc:

> have been transformed into progressive economies, with a solid and viable industrial base and with practically no help from Capitalist nations. In the two decades 1950–70, the national income of the eight Socialist countries more than quadrupled. During the same period, their industrial output increased seven times and their share in the world's industrial production rose from less than 18 to over 30 per cent.[57]

We can readily dismiss the most damning degree of these conclusions about the feasibility of socialist planning. Moreover, as Caplan correctly points out, Soviet-style socialism was implemented in economies that usually had largely undeveloped market relations to begin with. In other words, the rational conduct of entrepreneurial activity and commercial relations had barely sprouted before being transplanted by the centralised planning of national economies. After an initial burst of accelerated growth of the national product, economic decline in centrally planned economies tended set in only after some while, and stagnation cannot therefore be logically connected to the loss of the ability to perform economic calculations.[58] The claim that socialism is impossible rests on very shaky grounds. In the words of Sen:

---

56   Kenny 2010.
57   Wilczynski 1972.
58   Caplan 2004, p. 41.

The world has moved a great deal since Ludwig von Mises in 1920 foresaw in socialist production 'the senseless output of an absurd apparatus', arguing that 'the wheels will turn, but will run to no effect' (...). The wheels have turned and to some effect all around the globe, and along with the experience of economic planning, the literature on planning theory has also grown enormously.[59]

In response to this type of challenge to the 'Austrian impossibility theorem', the 'Austrians' Boettke and Leeson have attempted to salvage the claim that socialism is impossible by conceding that the central ownership of productive resources could endure in a purely technical sense – i.e. it will not lead to the spontaneous disintegration of the fabric of society, per se – but that socialism cannot attain its objectives due to the aforementioned efficiency problems. Since the Marxist theory of socialism stipulates that it should prepare by industrial means the groundwork for communism, and given its incapacity for rational economic calculus, socialism would be unable to grow the stock of productive assets to the extent necessary to complete the transition to communism and is in this very narrow sense 'impossible'.[60]

This workaround is both theoretically and empirically weak, since it bends the meaning of 'impossible' beyond breaking point and ascribes a historical role to socialism that Marxist theory had typically assigned to capitalism (namely, developing the material preconditions for communism to emerge out of). In any case, not every genre of socialist finds itself in agreement with this 'schematic' model of history and could therefore simply avoid this criticism. Moreover, on the empirical side of the argument, the ability of the Soviet economy to mobilise its resources for the purpose of industrialisation – i.e. to advance the material forces of production to help raise society to a higher form of social development – was arguably its most impressive feat.[61] Caplan, likewise an 'Austrian', therefore concludes that Mises overstated his conclusion, and while he agrees that rational economic calculation is impossible in socialism, it does not follow that socialism itself is impossible, only suboptimal and inefficient.[62] Still, for those committed to socialist renewal this is hardly a comforting conclusion. The 'Austrian' challenges to socialist economic planning, even if overstated, call attention to the problems of using information in a socialist economy: The issue of scale – the 'millions of equations'

---

59   Sen 1975, pp. 447–8; Sen 1975, p. 447.
60   Boettke and Leeson 2005, pp. 155–70, 156–7.
61   Ellman 2014, p. 137.
62   Caplan 2004, pp. 48–9.

problem; the process-specific ways in which information is generated and how economic data can be absorbed by planning agencies; and the importance and use of qualitative knowledge in socialist society necessitate the articulation of a compelling response. To investigate in more detail the degree to which such calculation problems contributed to allocative problems in practice, we will redirect our attention from the theory of planning to its application in practice.

Socialism in Practice – The Soviet Model

Compared to our nineteenth-century predecessors we today enjoy the benefit of the cumulative experience of a series of practical and momentous endeavours to implement socialism. The pioneering role of the Soviet Union in this process makes it a natural point of departure for discussing the practical experience of socialised economic planning. The model of centralised planning was formalised as part of official Soviet doctrine and subsequently adopted or adapted by a great variety of countries, even counting some non-socialist countries among these ranks. While we will make incidental references to the experiences of other socialist countries throughout, the logical focal point of our empirical survey of socialist planning is the Soviet Union. To this effect, we will provide a concise overview of the material reproduction of the Soviet Union and its development over the course of its existence. We will survey the most relevant literature on the history of Soviet-style socialism in general and the Soviet Union in particular. Doing so will allow us to derive inferences about the requirements of a feasible socialism.

Toward this end, it is relevant to provide an outline of the basic features of Soviet-style socialism, to exposit the mechanisms by which it secured its material reproduction, and to try and isolate the main causal factors that can explain the eventual decline of 'actually existing socialism'. The approximately seventy year duration of the Soviet experiment with central planning will be compressed significantly, as we are primarily concerned with the principal features of the planned economy, how they came about, in which ways and why they evolved, and what their main effects were.

Contemporary explorations of socialist planning stand to gain from a comparative analysis to Soviet-style socialism by clarifying where and how they differ, and therefore why new theoretical models would produce a different outcome in reality – particularly, to secure socialism successfully and sustainably. The formulation of a feasible socialism today will have to be rooted in a full appraisal of the collective, historical experience of our political heritage – regardless of where personal political affiliations may be located. A project of socialist renewal will have to enter into a dialogue of past and present, by critically engaging the socialist thought of our antecedents to build on their contributions and findings. This dialogical exchange with our collective past cannot cheat a number of intellectual giants by circumventing the socialist thought that originated from behind the political boundaries that separated the socialist East from the liberal West, leaping back over and past the previous century, to the historical period before the first whispers of the Great October Socialist Revolution could even be detected. Socialist thinkers from within the bloc of socialist countries have grappled with many questions of a practical nature that arose directly out of the requirements of socialist construction, and contemporary socialist thought can benefit from a critical appropriation of these ideas, as we will find.

Of secondary concern in this chapter is the typological classification of Soviet-style socialism. While we are more interested in detailing the factual circumstances of the Soviet economy and its demise, in order to identify what lessons might be learnt from this experience, the chapter will also provide brief commentary on the classification of Soviet-style socialism. Disqualifying historical attempts at building socialism as 'state-capitalism', as we will see, is ill-suited for the purpose of our inquiry, for both conceptual and instrumental reasons. On that account, I am not opposed to using some variant of 'socialism' to describe the Soviet mode of production and distribution – we will alternate between 'actually existing socialism' and 'Soviet-style socialism' and such terms. This commentary is relegated to the addendum to this chapter.

Over the course of this chapter we will describe the Soviet economy *more or less* chronologically, beginning with the early period of revolution and civil war (1917–1921), quickly pass over the period of the 'New Economic Policy', and proceed to the period after the installation of centralised planning in the economy (1929–1965). We will subsequently move on the most relevant and important reform proposals that have been put forward or experimented with during the period from 1966 until 1991. Again, in the addendum is quarantined our brief discussion of 'state-capitalism'.

1   The Experience of War Communism

The immense difficulties associated with the construction of socialism became all too apparent in the immediate aftermath of the protracted Russian Revolution of 1917–1923, in which the Czarist regime was overthrown and eventually replaced by the Soviet government and the founding of the Union of Soviet Socialist Republics. This assumption of power by socialists afforded them the first real opportunity to begin laying the practical foundations for a socialist society. We will deal here in particular with the period of war communism, which lasted from 1918 until 1921. During this brief but critical phase of Soviet history, both theories of and experiments with economic planning proliferated. Some of the ideas that emerged in this period were later modified and adopted as part of the more familiar central planning mechanism of the Soviet Union. In this section we will focus on the material reconstitution of society that followed after the revolution; consequently we will not go over the constellation of conditions that resulted in the overthrow of the Czarist dynasty. Instead, we will focus on the three main institutional factors that drove the social transformation after the revolution.

The first of these factors, before and during the early years of the Soviet government (circa 1917–1918), were a number of novel organisational forms that arose under the influence of socialist and labourist ideas and which played decisive roles in the reconstruction of the Russian economy. Across the vast territory of the (former) Russian Empire, instruments of self-government and self-administration sprang up. Among these were the factory committees and workers' councils, or *soviets*, which would imprint heavily on the course of the revolution. A second factor was the Bolshevik party manoeuvring itself into a leading position among the industrial proletariat and to a lesser extent the much more numerous peasantry – meaning they also outmanoeuvred their political rivals on the left, such as the anarchists, Mensheviks, and Socialist Revolutionaries. Their political objective was the construction of socialism, which according to them entailed, quite correctly, the idea that the narrow and immediate aims of the labour agenda (the focus on the amelioration of work conditions) could not serve as the overall socialist programme. Instead, the construction of socialism would depend on the ability to integrate all sectoral elements under a unified authority which would reflect, not the interests of various separate trades, but the broad interests of the working class as a whole.[1] With the ascendancy of the Bolshevik party to power, for the first time in history socialist ideas were allowed to play out, albeit under circumstances that did not favour them. The third factor which would heavily steer the course of events was social disintegration and anarchy. This disintegration was partly underway under Czarist rule, partly encouraged after the revolution by the Bolsheviks – since revolutionary reconstruction is equally divided between destruction and construction – and partly the result of unforeseen consequences of Soviet policies or forces beyond their control.[2] Let us review the course of events then.

In relation to the first two factors, the principal organs that emerged as the political forms of the working class to advance their agenda were the factory committees, the soviets, and, ultimately, the Bolshevik party. The soviets were

---

1   Carr 1952, pp. 101–3.
2   Carr 1952, p. 72.

representative bodies of workers and soldiers, which came to challenge the authority of the Czar's regime initially, as well as its successor, the Provisional Government (in a relationship qualified by Lenin as 'dual power'[3]). After the October Revolution, in which the provisional government was overthrown and the seat of power was captured on orders of the Bolshevik leadership, a government was formed on the basis of the soviets. The All-Russian Congress of Soviets became the supreme governing body of the emergent Soviet Russia. The soviets were geographically sited political bodies, elected by workers, and largely concentrated in urban areas, reflecting their position as the political weapons of the industrial proletariat. As such, the Bolshevik influence in the soviets was disproportionate compared to general popular support, since the bulk of the peasantry was (initially) disposed toward other socialist parties. By word of Lenin, the Bolshevik vision of socialism declared that the basis of the socialist state would have to emerge from 'a network of producers' and consumers' communes, which conscientiously keep account of their production and consumption, economise on labour, and steadily raise the productivity of labour'. Thus:

> Every factory, every village is a producers' and consumers' commune, whose right and duty it is to apply the general Soviet laws in their own way ('in their own way', not in the sense of violating them, but in the sense that they can apply them in various forms) and in their own way to solve the problem of accounting in the production and distribution of goods.[4]

However, beyond these very amorphous and open-ended sketches, the positive programme of socialist construction of the Bolsheviks is difficult to discern – perhaps understandably so. Given the volatility of events unfolding in rapid procession, they could spare little time and effort for the development of comprehensive plans for the national economy. However, it also reveals a broader undertone, namely that most orthodox Marxists – the Bolsheviks being no exception – had no particular inclination to dedicate much, if any, serious thought to the economic organisation of the association of equal producers, having assumed that direct association of production would release an explosion of the forces of social production more or less automatically.

The factory committees were, in contrast to the soviets, local and industrial in nature. They were organised during the revolutionary gulfs of 1905 and 1917

---

3   Lenin 1917a.
4   Lenin 1917a.

by malcontented workers to represent their interests within a given enterprise, in principle in a supervisory role. However, when factories were deserted by their owners as a result of increasing social disorder, the factory committees tended to assume direct control over productive facilities, and were usually then nationalised by the Soviet authorities.[5] Workers quickly escalated their demands, and with increasing ferocity petitioned or acted to appropriate the factories in order to put them under direct control of the committees.[6] Conditions pushed forward such demands by workers for direct control, and were, even if ambiguously worded, eventually taken up in the political programme of the Bolshevik party.[7] In this way, it appeared that a substantive transformation of the social relations of production, from wage-labour into associated labour, was underway. Yet, at the same time, the aim of socialism was not to liberate the workers as workers of a particular factory, but to liberate the working class as a class.[8] The dissemination of workers' control was not without problems, moreover.

Lenin, like other Bolsheviks, 'assumed that there would be a spontaneous releasing of resources as a result of freeing the population from oppression by capitalists and landowners'.[9] The exodus of the bosses – foremen, owners – did not however offer immediate alleviation of the economic problems that plagued Russia. Further, alongside the owners, factories also saw a flight or removal of specialists – administrative and technical staff – from expropriated factories, which proved imprudent as productivity fell and production costs rose due to the absence of their assistance.[10] The manual labourers were ill-prepared to run the factories without the aid of specialist knowledge, and the acquisition of the requisite skill for the workforce to do so and carry on production would take considerable time.[11] Labour discipline and morale suffered and there were some instances in which the workers decided to sell off the remainder of stocks and pocketing the proceeds.[12] This deplorable fall in morale was characterised by Bazarov, who would later become a chief architect of Soviet planning, as the petty bourgeois, anarchistic sentiment infesting sections of the working population; cynically speculating that 'Today they might

---

5   Pasvolsky 1921, p. 29; Malle 1985, p. 51.
6   Pasvolsky 1921, p. 32.
7   Pasvolsky 1921, p. 57.
8   Carr 1952, p. 72.
9   Read 1996, p. 126.
10   Read 1996, p. 129; Pasvolsky 1921, p. 33.
11   Read 1996, p. 129.
12   Carr 1952, p. 70.

throw an engineer out of their factory in a wheelbarrow, tomorrow they might threaten the trade union leader with the same fate, and the day after – their own factory committee'.[13]

Initially, the factories remained isolated units, which was inconsistent with the aims of socialist construction, at least as understood by Marxism. Some committees would soon discover the need for co-ordination, and attempted to involve the local soviets in their daily economic operations.[14] Organically, in this way, the factory workers attempted to enhance the scale and scope of workers' control by linking their individual factories, and in so doing laid the basis for socialisation under direct association. Attempts to do so were however obstructed by the Bolshevik party, all the while criticising their localism.[15] The substantive transformation of the social relationships of production, in their view, would have to wait until more urgent matters, which required strict discipline, were settled. After all, this proliferation of self-governing organs was met by an undercurrent of social disintegration which the Bolsheviks had initially hoped to co-opt and control, as Bazarov lamented: the Bolsheviks 'did not hesitate to dive in and ride the rapids of this essentially anarchist stream' against better judgement.[16]

The Soviet government, headed by Lenin, for their part realised their error and began moderating the rapid expropriation of factories, by enticing specialist staff and employers to stay, rather than retreat into territory controlled by 'white' counter-revolutionaries.[17] Lenin explained, rather reasonably that 'Without the guidance of experts in the various fields of knowledge, technology and experience, the transition to socialism will be impossible'.[18] Given that the dissemination of 'accounting and control' methods in Russia was weakly developed corresponding to the underdeveloped productive base of society, the requirements of socialist construction demanded a role for 'bourgeois' specialists. Still, it is difficult to escape the conclusion that Lenin believed, rather naively, that the lack of widespread training in the practice of 'accounting and control' was the primary endogenous constraint limiting the consolidation of socialist relations in production. The Bolsheviks initially hoped that the employers, as well as administrative and technical staff, would continue to operate as usual, albeit under the supervision of workers' committees and

---

13   Bazarov 1917.
14   Read 1996.
15   Brinton 1970.
16   Bazarov 1917.
17   Read 1996, p. 126; Malle 1985, p. 50.
18   Lenin 1918.

the Soviet government.[19] This was understood to be 'state-capitalism'. Workers' control (supervision) would prepare the steps for orderly expropriation at a later point.[20] For now, the radical impulses of the working class had to be tempered somewhat, given the level of 'immaturity' of the working class. Indeed, even the outer left-wing of the revolutionaries – the left-wing communists and anarcho-syndicalists – advocated that (at least two-thirds of) factory management be elected by unionised workers, due to their comparatively advanced level of class consciousness. This, Malle points out, 'was a sign that nobody really believed the maturity of the Russian proletariat, as such, to be adequate for self-management'.[21]

Effective administration was further inhibited by the lack of trained and competent cadres.[22] This put the reintegration of Czarist administrative staff into public functions on the political agenda, which was heavily protested by the left-wing communists. Similarly, the Bolshevik party was forced to retreat from some of its other radical policy objectives, such as an egalitarian wage policy.[23] Many owners had in turn hoped that a worsening of the conditions in the workplace would tempt workers to petition the restoration of full authority of the owners, but this proved a miscalculation on their part.[24] Factory owners often frustrated the operation of productive activity and factory committees by various means. In response, nationalisation was pursued punitively against acts of sabotage prosecuted by owners; the nationalisation of factories therefore did not proceed systematically initially.[25]

The disorderly manner in which expropriations and the spread of workers' control progressed inhibited coherent industrial organisation.[26] Numerous variations of workers' control arose during the early stages of the revolution, varying between direct control by factory committees, supervision by factory committees, trade union supervision, as well as *ad hoc* nationalisations at the direction of workers, local soviets, regional soviets, or central authorities. This diluted responsibility in the execution of productive duties on all sides and encouraged disorder, which gave rise to the need to regain central command and re-impose discipline.[27] Reliable rates of industrial out-

---

19   Carr 1952, p. 67.
20   Malle 1985, p. 36.
21   Malle 1985, p. 115.
22   Malle 1985, p. 89.
23   Malle 1985, p. 48.
24   Read 1996, p. 129.
25   Malle 1985, pp. 49–50; Carr 1952, pp. 69, 71–2, 87–8; Pasvolsky 1921, p. 36.
26   Read 1996, p. 126.
27   Pasvolsky 1921, p. 31.

put and supply of inputs were crucial also in relation to equipping the Red Army with the supplies and materiel necessary to prosecute the war against encroaching counter-revolutionaries. In other words, under the force of necessity imposed by armed uprisings against the Soviet government by various counter-revolutionary armies, abetted militarily by a number of Allied nations; general social disintegration; and the need to override the sectional interests of local units by a central authority representative of the working class as a whole, the Bolsheviks would attempt, in one stroke, to assert systematic central control over the fragmented ensemble of localised and highly varied forms of workers' control. Thus, 'when the situation of emergency created by war had become extreme', the Bolsheviks 'announced a maximum unification of all economic activity through a nationwide plan, centralization and concentration of production, and the rational and economic utilization of all material resources'.[28]

'State-capitalism', which promised to be a relatively gradual and peaceful appropriation of productive resources in the hands of Soviet authorities, was replaced by the strategy of 'war communism' in mid-1918, which instead promised to be an accelerated centralisation of resources in the hands of the state to counteract disintegration. Amongst other things, it implemented sweeping nationalisations, banned private trade, introduced one-man management, imposed strict labour discipline, and requisitioned food surpluses from the peasantry to feed the Red Army and industrial proletariat.[29] This centralisation of power was further premised on a rather 'essentialist' understanding of class and class interests as held by the Bolshevik intelligentsia. Since the interests of the proletariat were inscribed in the structural properties of capitalism itself, they could be laid bare by turning the analytical lens of Marxism to the study of capitalist relations of production, and concomitant to this, be grasped by the vanguard of Marxist militants. This idea served to lubricate the sliding suspension of working class self-administration by the Bolsheviks, since power could be temporarily stored in the hands of the most advanced elements among workers until objective and subjective conditions ripened and for a more mature working class to again resume control directly.

Above all, the perils of civil war imposed on the Bolsheviks the need to concentrate resources in their hands so that they could be redirected toward military strategic objectives. Initially, the Soviet government used financial means, backed by administrative pressure, to acquire the resources necessary for the Red Army to continue its military campaigns. Compulsion, however,

28   Malle 1985, p. 304.
29   Nove 1992, p. 40.

quickly displaced financial means.[30] Haphazard and piecemeal nationalisation of factories was replaced by centrally directed, wholesale nationalisation, supplemented with central economic bodies (in particular the Supreme Council for the National Economy, or VSNKh), and, ultimately, one-man management.[31] One-man management was an instrument necessary, the Bolsheviks believed, to restore labour discipline and prevent further fragmentation. Regimentation of labour was required to, on the one hand, impose vitally necessary discipline and restore productivity, and at the same time, to allow directly social relations of communist production to develop embryonically. Appointment of managerial positions by public officials was controversial, and workers often disliked the military-like discipline imposed upon them.[32] The extension of associated labour by organs of workers' power was halted, reversed even. However, by bringing control over the economy under the authority of those workers, organised in the Bolshevik party, who understood the historical mission of the proletariat most clearly and scientifically, workers' management could be halted, at least temporarily while order was restored by addressing the chaos that grew out of poorly executed, spontaneous initiatives of workers. Since productive activity in factories was subordinated to the local and regional soviets (which were controlled, in practice, by their executive committees, which were in turn controlled by the Bolsheviks), Soviet rule still reflected the essential class interests of the proletariat. Over time, however, political participation had declined as a result of workers being tied up in other responsibilities – production or survival – and power was allowed to concentrate in the hands of public officials in the executive committees, who, if members of the Bolsheviks, were subject to the instructions emanating from the party's central committee.[33] In short, political decision-making authority became gradually concentrated in the uppermost layer of the Bolshevik party.

Under war communism, nationalisation would proceed systematically, as the Bolsheviks sought to absorb local economies (and their raw materials) into central economic administration, which was closely connected to military needs. About half of enterprises employing labourers has been transformed into state enterprises by 1920, employing about ninety percent of the total labour force.[34] Nationalisation in the Bolshevik programme reduced the scope

---

30   Davies 1958, p. 26.
31   Carr 1952, pp. 72–4, 83–4.
32   Malle 1985, p. 112.
33   For example: Lucardie 2016, p. 86.
34   Malle 1985, pp. 64–7.

of activities of both factory committees and trade unions.[35] This too reflected the Bolshevik belief that the working class would need to be guided by the most advanced, class conscious segments of the proletariat that were able to transcend 'labourist' tendencies ('trade union consciousness', as Lenin referred to it).[36] Indeed, the proletariat was mostly concerned with a labourist agenda, rather than with the construction and realisation of socialism (often sliding into short-sighted, self-destructive tendencies even).[37]

In the midst of civil war and industrial disorganisation, the unchecked increase of the supply of local notes (money surrogates) and currency coincided with a drop in the circulation of goods as a result of industrial collapse, resulting in hyper-inflation.[38] Runaway inflation and regional price differences made centralised monetary accounting increasingly meaningless, and hence the Bolsheviks turned to planning in physical units: '[t]he strains exerted by war on economic resources and the impossibility of using market signals to direct investments and production compelled VSNKh to make some efforts towards planning'.[39] The Bolshevik party strategic and economic theorists promoted the 'naturalisation' of the 'proletarian economy' by proposing that distribution of assets and goods could be demonetised. Allocation in-kind would help reduce the scope of market distribution and therefore the circulation of money to counter hyperinflation.[40] Much like Neurath, the Bolshevik economists were inspired by the recent experience of war economics. This entailed the concentration of material resources in the hands of the state and the calculation of industrial production in physical units to overcome financial constraints.[41] Under war communism, state enterprises were expected to deliver goods amongst each other on the basis of instructions by authorities. In respect to personal consumption, social services and foodstuffs were rationed at fixed amounts and in turn available gratis.[42] War communism thus entailed emergency policies that were intended to address the civil war and social disintegration, but doing so in a manner that simultaneously laid the groundwork for the consolidation of communism.

The VSNKh was the main central body of economic administration, which had a number of functional and industrial departments, bureaus, and com-

35   Pasvolsky 1921, p. 35.
36   Read 1996, p. 130.
37   Read 1996, p. 131.
38   Davies 1958, p. 29; Malle 1985, p. 179.
39   Malle 1985, p. 215.
40   Malle 1985, p. 166.
41   Malle 1985, pp. 298–9.
42   Nove 1992, pp. 57–8.

mittees under its auspices. The VSNKh, through its main subsidiary (the Committee for Utilisation), would calculate and compare the aggregate demand and supply of goods and services, and direct allocation by issuing orders on the basis of those calculations. The committee then calculated the percentage of fulfilment of said orders as the measure of performance.[43] Regional soviets also operated departments for orders, which assessed which factories were best suited for the production and distribution of goods, determined deadlines, and negotiated and settled upon agreements, which were then listed in their registry and acquired the force of law.[44]

In this way, local initiative and commodity exchange were reduced, and central grip over economic activity increased. It was believed that central control over supply, using denotations in purely physical units, could ensure an effective distribution of goods. The historic era of commodity production and exchange was imagined to end with the introduction of war communism.[45] However, it turned out that the VSNKh did not have 'sufficient information about the existing production units under its control, nor did it have control over enough economic levers'.[46] According to Kritsman, a Bolshevik economist and one of the architects of war communism, the difficulty laid in 'who is going to decide how much iron, for instance, is to be allocated to locomotives, how much to ploughs and how much to knives, spoons and forks'.[47] No attention was paid in practice to the criteria which would allow for the effective and rational regulation of the emerging communist mode of production and distribution. Consequently, 'complementary materials were provided to the factories in arbitrary proportions: in some places they accumulated, whereas in others there was a shortage'.[48] The centralisation of control over supply caused lengthy procedures for indents to be processed, sanctioned, and released, thereby increasing disruption of the supply chain, exacerbating the issue of shortages. Thus, '[u]nused stocks coexisted with acute scarcity'. In short, '[t]he centre was unable to determine the correct proportions among necessary materials and eventually to enforce implementation of the orders for their total quantity'.[49] In the words of Kritsman:

---

43   Malle 1985, p. 215.
44   Malle 1985, p. 232.
45   Malle 1985, p. 194.
46   Malle 1985, p. 303.
47   Cited in Malle 1985, p. 311.
48   Malle 1985, p. 233.
49   Malle 1985, p. 233.

No surpluses can accumulate with the producers, since the product is not superfluous in an absolute sense; as a matter of fact, if such a surplus is formed, it will be immediately allocated when the first demand for it is announced. The multitude of independent allocating organisations, however, unavoidably causes situations in which, for example, an organ demanding paraffin lamps gets all the necessary lamp chimneys (100 per cent) from one economic organisation, but only 60% of the holders from another, 50% of the wicks from a third one, and only 20% of the burners from a fourth. In this case 4/5 of the lamp chimneys, 2/3 of the holders and 3/5 of the wicks will prove to be superfluous and lie wasted. A month later, the burners, so much needed by the first user, will lie unused with another organ needing paraffin lamps. Similar cases are unavoidable with fuels, raw materials, and various complementary materials.[50]

Effective co-ordination by planning authorities was inhibited by the disintegration of the economy, the lack of a set of articulated rational criteria to aid in allocative decision-making, inexperience among administrators, and disorganisation of the administrative apparatus.[51] In respect to the latter issue, there was an immense proliferation of administrative organs, some of 'which never became active or rapidly exhausted their functions', with many such bodies having overlapping responsibilities, sometimes issuing conflicting orders. In short, there was an 'immense gap which had widened (...) between projects and immediate tasks, goals and available means, planning and feasibility'.[52]

There were abortive attempts to develop more sophisticated methods of calculating the material budget, but the need for a common denominator (or unit of account) was widely acknowledged.[53] The replacement of monetary units of account was given serious consideration in theoretical disputes.[54] While at least one theorist proposed a 'salt standard', analogous to the 'gold standard', most attention was afforded to working out some measure of labour time, energy expenditure, or a combination of both; while yet others maintained that planning in physical units alone was sufficient.[55] Calculation *in-natura* was defended mainly by Chayanov, an agrarian economist. His proposal is rel-

---

50   Ellman 2014, pp. 36–7.
51   Nove 1992, pp. 63–5.
52   Malle 1985, p. 215.
53   Davies 1958, p. 44.
54   Malle 1985, p. 185.
55   For a concise critique of combined labour-energy units, see Nove 2011, p. 54.

evant since it shares a considerable resemblance to material balance sheets later used in Soviet central planning. He argued that computing the normal technical coefficient within a given branch of industry should serve as the efficiency criterium, by comparing the observed technical coefficients to the norm of average productivity.[56] Each factor input (labour, capital, etc.) would need to be weighed so as to arrive at a single coefficient, which could then be used to for the purpose of economic calculation. However, this hinges on the relative weights assigned to different factor inputs, which would render comparable the different quantities and quality of inputs, but no theoretical strides in the direction indicating how factors of production should be weighed were made. According to his contemporary, Yurovsky, it would in theory be possible to figure out an internally consistent economic plan by relying on Chayanov's proposals, but there would be no way of determining whether the final plan were more efficient or less efficient (and by how much) compared to some other internally consistent plan. Nor would it have been possible to measure the degree to which the mix of goods in the feasible plan corresponded to the structure of consumer needs and preferences.[57]

Other Soviet economists pondered whether, as Marx and others had argued, social labour-time could be used as the basis for the regulation of production in communist society. The idea of units of labour ('*tredi*'; singular: '*tred*') being used as the unit of account in Soviet society was advanced by Strumilin, Shmelyov, and others.[58] According to Strumilin, the social labour embodied in a particular good should be used as the labour standard by which to compare all other goods.[59] Labour, he reasoned, should be incrementally increased in production until the costs of a particular good, measured in labour units, were equal to the social utility derived from the consumption of that good, as measured by the use of labour notes to appropriate them. This would ensure correspondence between the structure of demand and the structure of investments. Among other things, what remained undeveloped in Strumilin's model was the method for determining how producers would go about acquiring their inputs. In other words, by what criteria could the Soviet government allocate inputs to different production units. If enterprises would re-use labour notes to back indents, then they would simply reconstitute money.[60] Strumilin's proposal lacked a crucial link in its economic mechanism by failing to offer solu-

---

56   Belykh 1989, pp. 426–9.
57   Nove 2011, pp. 54–5; Malle 1985, p. 193.
58   Malle 1985, pp. 190–2; Nove 2011, p. 41; Davies 1958, p. 41.
59   Malle 1985, p. 192.
60   Nove 2011, pp. 47–8.

tions as to how fixed assets, semi-finished products, and raw materials should be allocated in accordance with criteria of efficiency.

Before these and other experimental thoughts could be developed further or come to fruition, the period of war communism came to a grinding close. The Soviet government had wrestled with inexperience, logistical dysfunction, statistical confusion, constant military opposition, open resistance from within all layers of society, and the fallout of ill-advised policies. In respect to the latter, the Bolshevik policy of grain requisitioning particularly contributed to the tearing apart of society at the seams. By intent, the purpose was to secure food supplies to the cities and Red Army, but peasants were in reality left without incentive to produce beyond their own subsistence levels. The policy saw agricultural output fall, causing proletarians to flood back to the countryside. Industrial production, which was also heavily disrupted by makeshift reorganisation and civil war, consequently imploded.[61] Eventually, the policies and civil war culminated in famine, runaway inflation, and industrial collapse. Social dislocation crippled Soviet society, which was still in the process of establishing itself, and decimated the power base of the Bolshevik party. The proletariat had shrunk considerably, and both the urban working class and peasantry had turned away from their initial attraction toward the Bolsheviks and their cause in large numbers. The Bolsheviks had, prior to the October Revolution, gained significant support among the proletariat by supporting initiatives for expansive workers' control;[62] when the Bolsheviks, upon their seizure of power, reversed such initiatives in order to exact labour discipline, popular support declined. The introduction of one-man management, for example, was looked upon unfavourably by the industrial proletariat.[63] It would not be until the late 1980s, under Gorbachev, that a stunted form of workplace democracy ('samoupravlenie'; literally: self-management) were to re-introduced on Soviet territory.

The early Soviet experience includes a range of cautionary tales for future attempts that endeavour to move society beyond the horizon of capitalism. The basis for many mistakes lied in an underestimation of the complexities involved in the implementation of an economic transformation. In general, this should temper both naivety and zeal. While it may be tempting to assume that the primary problem of war communism was a matter of over-centralisation – an absence of horizontal links between production units – the experience also

---

61   Richman 1981, p. 90.
62   Read 1996, p. 130.
63   Pasvolsky 1921, p. 41.

clearly underscores the need for the bring into operation a rational set of criteria to facilitate rational and economical decision-making to render an efficient allocation of resources tractable. While not every kind of socialism calls for a maximum degree of centralisation, nearly all socialists – so it appears – lack a clear idea of what complementary combination of quantitative analyses and incentives would induce producers to make responsible use of resources in place of the profit motive. As such, the example and lessons of Soviet-style socialism extend far beyond the boundaries of Marxism-Leninism and careful scrutiny of this experiment remains highly necessary.

2   General Features of Soviet Planning

Faced with declining popular support and economic collapse, the Bolshevik leadership introduced a period of respite in the form of the 'New Economic Policy', which restored a large degree of private initiative and market exchange before again being transplanted in 1929 by the introduction of the first 'Five Year Plan'. This plan officially covered the period of 1928–1932, although its start was delayed by one year and was officially shortened by one year.[64] After 1929, the Soviet Union reintroduced many of the institutional features of war communism, including wholesale nationalisation, centralised economic planning, and the use of material balances to help guide the allocation of supplies. Here will be provided a brief outline of the general features of the Soviet system as it operated for the duration of the period of the 'classical model', which lasted from 1929 until 1965.

The development and direction of the national economy is determined through a number of fundamental functions. The division of national income between consumption and accumulation, which facilitates the rate of growth on the one end and the apportioning of investment between different branches of production, which determines the direction and pace of development on the other end – as well as the co-ordination of different branches of production.[65] Additionally, we can include the element of local and detailed planning, which involves defining and co-ordinating the exact profile and specifications of the supply and output schedules of different production units. From 1929 up until 1965, all these functions were concentrated in the upper layers of the Soviet state and their planning agencies.[66] The economy of the Soviet

---

64   Ellman 2014, p. 10; Nove 2011, p. 143.
65   Lange 1958, p. 7.
66   Dyker 2013.

Union worked roughly as follows. The political leadership of the Soviet Union would decide upon a number macroeconomic priorities,[67] which the central planning authority, the State Planning Commission (*Gosplan*), translated into output targets and strategic investment goals, based on estimations of the existing productive capacity and resource availability, for a period of (usually) five years, broken down into annual periods (current plans, which were the only somewhat operative plans).[68] Longer planning cycles of ten, fifteen, or twenty years (perspective plans) proved mostly ineffectual.[69] Profit calculations did not factor into the determining of the obligatory output targets. The plan targets were instead expressed as gross output targets related to investment needs. Thus, the preferences of the planning authorities were primarily expressed via their assorted investment plans.[70] The Gosplan would pass down investment plans and aggregate output targets to industrial ministries, which were each tied to a particular sector or branch of the Soviet economy. The ministries then translated the investment goals into patterns of capital formation and specific output targets for the enterprises that operated under their auspices.[71]

The current plans assigned to enterprises defined the operational goals on the basis of ten categories of plan indices for an enterprise with a time horizon of a year. The annual operational plans were formulated on the basis of administrative iterations, with suggestions flowing down and counter-suggestions floating up in a process of 'planning and counter-planning'.[72] Enterprise directors would transmit estimates of productive capacity of their individual enterprises to the planning authorities. The estimated productive capacities were then compiled and aggregated by the centre, which subsequently converted the information into aggregate output targets and investment plans consistent with politically defined objectives. The aggregate output targets were then passed down to the enterprises via the appropriate industrial ministries, each connected to a different branch or branches of industry. The disaggregated output targets were assigned to specific enterprises as part of operational plans for periods of a year.[73] Since labour was considered the only source of value, production goods were rationed (i.e. supplied without charge) to enterprises in

---

67   Kornai 2007, p. 125.
68   Gregory 2004, p. 118.
69   Ellman 2014, p. 10.
70   Gregory 2004, p. 111.
71   Ellman 2014, p. 30; IMF 1991, p. 8.
72   Ellman 1969, p. 70; Ellman 1973, p. 22.
73   Nove 1992, pp. 286–70.

accordance with the current plan targets.[74] A degree of local detailed adjustments was possible within the confines of vertical instructions:

> When the enterprises receive their quotas they specify their requirements in detail (within the limits of the quota) and submit them to the supply organs. On the basis of these specified quotas the supply organs distribute orders between the producer enterprises and organise the attachment of producers to consumers.[75]

In sum, the enterprises were not expected to enter into exchange of their own accord, but were instead instructed to produce a given quantity and assortment, to deliver certain goods to certain places at certain times, to set prices at a given level, and so on, while the producer goods were allocated to enterprises in accordance with such plans.[76] The circulation of commodities – or perhaps pseudo-commodities – among enterprises was determined vertically, from the top down, on the basis of obligatory targets in other words. Exchange between units of production, then, was not regulated by competition of capitals, or according to the rhythms and compulsions set by achievable profit margins. Social production was instead structured by administrative instructions which specified the required gross output.

During the first Five Year Plan, the expectations harboured by the political leadership exceeded what the planning system could deliver manifold.[77] Impressive early results encouraged unwarranted optimism, and upward revisions followed accordingly.[78] This general tendency toward optimism in Soviet planning was in part owed to 'strict pre-publication censorship of all publications', which reinforced the erstwhile illusory beliefs of policymakers.[79] Thus, '[p]lanners and plant managers, who pleaded for some semblance of realism, were labeled as class enemies and wreckers'.[80] The agenda guiding these optimistic plan projections was, of course, rapid industrialisation by mobilising idle resources in order to catch up and eventually overtake the more economically advanced West – not in the least to secure independence from capitalist powers by building up sufficient military strength.[81] As direct corollary, attention for

---

74   Wilczynski 1972, pp. 45–6.
75   Nove 2011, pp. 17–18.
76   Nove 1992, p. 268; Wilczynski 1972a, p. 227.
77   Nove 1992, p. 146.
78   Nove 1992, pp. 189–90.
79   Ellman 1978, p. 253.
80   Gregory 2004, p. 120.
81   Kontorovich 2013; Chandrasekhar 1998, p. 43.

personal consumption remained scant throughout most of the existence of the Soviet Union:[82] 'Socialism (...) has come into existence in underdeveloped economies, surrounded by enemies. Instead of being able to distribute the surplus to the workers, it has been obliged to squeeze out all the more, for industrialisation and for defence'.[83] Priority was thus accorded to the development of heavy industry, including military industry. Toward this aim, the Soviet authorities used wage repression and imposed strict discipline as a means to squeeze high surpluses from labour, which could be reinvested into the expansion of industrial capacity. Collectivisation of agriculture further freed up labour-power to be redirected toward industrial production, and likewise, previously underutilised resources (including unemployed labour-power) would be mobilised to stimulate high rates of accumulation.[84]

This coincided with a period in Soviet life, '[w]hether in literature or in philosophy, in the party's own internal arrangements or in the sphere of economics', in which 'the line became one of stern imposition of conformity, centralized authority, [and] suppression of uncontrolled initiatives'.[85] (The Soviet archives reveal a period of arbitrary and gratuitous political violence typically executed on the whims of General Secretary Stalin or his immediate associates.[86] Indeed, many of the protagonists of the Russian Revolution were executed, imprisoned, or exiled during the 'Great Purge' on fabricated charges, including many economists referred to previously – Chayanov, Bazarov, Yurovsky, Bukharin. The list of victims runs much longer, obviously; the declassified Soviet archives recorded 681,692 executions during the period of the Great Purge.)

In hierarchical administrative organisations, Ellman notes, subordinates tend to project outcomes to superiors that are favourable and reduce transmission of information that reflects poorly on their performance. This would become an endemic problem of Soviet economic planning as we will see, but was further compounded by the monolithic character of the Communist Party and wider society. Information that threatened certain rigid or narrow belief patterns were filtered out of transmission and circulation (sometimes but not always by means of active suppression). This at times resulted in the reliance on heavily distorted information by political authorities in those socialist countries that adopted some form of Marxism-Leninism.[87] Since effect, not intent,

---

82   For example: Wilczynski 1972a, p. 21; Chattopadhyay 1994, pp. 93–4.
83   Robinson 1982, p. xviii.
84   Ellman 1975, p. 860.
85   Nove 1992, p. 142.
86   Gregory 2004, pp. 14–18.
87   Ellman 1978, pp. 250–5.

served as the defining criterion for the qualification of 'sabotage' in practice, the resultant culture created an atmosphere conducive to systemic distortion and the evasion of responsibility. Many excess deaths (although by no means all) under socialist regimes can be attributed to the systemic generation of misinformation by (self-)censorship, rather than malicious conduct. Ellman mentions how in some socialist countries these practices resulted in institutionally and ideologically exaggerated agricultural output data, which in turn contributed to food shortages.[88] The falsified figures inspired more confidence in political leaders than was warranted by the realities on the ground and slowed responses to food crises. The same pattern repeated in military affairs. At later stages in Soviet history (under Brezhnev for example) the censorship of sensitive information and the promotion of servile loyalists and careerists kept the Soviet leadership themselves in ignorance, spurring complacency.[89] The monopoly on political power and the control over the circulation of information by the Communist Party, and the state apparatus wielded to secure the party's leading position in society, thus contributed to economic underperformance.

The vast resources of the Soviet Union could be mobilised in what seemed like a rational and scientific fashion, for the purpose of rapid economic and military development. The economy was marked by macroeconomic stability, full employment, and high rates of growth. Initially, the Soviet Union succeeded in increasing industrial output rapidly by means of the centrally mandated mobilisation of resources,[90] impressively turning it 'from being the most backward country in Europe to the ranks of a global superpower'.[91] The Soviet Union consequently commanded admiration from across the globe over its leaps in modernising economically, socially, scientifically, and culturally and its independent efforts in catching up to the West. This admiration was also shared by a number of Western academics who regarded economic planning as a tendency of global convergence toward rational and scientific policymaking to achieve macroeconomic stability. Whatever the human costs incurred by the Soviet command economy, (the role of forced labour in the process of socialist accumulation in the Soviet Union is well-established)[92] planning appeared as much more rational and scientific than the violent and disorderly fluctuations of market forces and the corresponding boom and bust cycles.[93] This belief of the

88   Ellman 1978, p. 258.
89   Ellman 2014, p. 29.
90   Ellman 2014, p. 12; Nove 1992, pp. 195, 226, 231.
91   Schweickart 2002, pp. 58–9.
92   Nove 1992, p. 193.
93   Ellman 2014, p. 374.

scientific supremacy of planning over the spontaneous, reactive, groping market processes was underscored by the impressive growth rates registered by the Soviet economy (partially falsified)[94] whilst Western economies suffered the malaise of the Great Depression in the 1930s:[95]

> The publication of the First Five Year Plan – a massive work of hundreds of pages full of tables and graphs – followed as it was by the Great Depression, created an image, widely believed throughout of the world, that the Soviet 'centrally planned' economy, unlike the anarchic and inefficient capitalist system, was a rational economic system.[96]

Consequently, under the post-World War II compromise – the 'social-democratic consensus' – European governments began making concerted efforts toward employing macroeconomic management, via a combination of indicative planning, *dirigisme*, industrial policy, and counter-cyclical measures. Similarly, central planning served to illustrate how societies were potentially capable of rapid economic development. The resource mobilisation strategy of the Soviet model demonstrated the potency of this approach. In this way, Marxism-Leninism became the engine behind many 'Third World' liberation movements that sought to escape Western colonial domination.[97] Marxism-Leninism, and regional forms of (quasi-)socialism inspired by it, quickly spread throughout the underdeveloped, exploited peripheries of the world and contested the imperialist core.

In sum, the economic mechanism of centralised planning primarily depended on two techniques, which will be reviewed separately. As Ellman summarised: 'The main technique used to try to achieve efficiency of the plans is the system of norms. The main techniques used to try to achieve consistency of the plans is the system of material balances'.[98] We will try to give due attention to these two key elements of Soviet planning in the two separate sections below.

---

94   Ellman 2008, p. 101.
95   Ellman 2014, pp. 11–12; Nove 1992, p. 225.
96   Ellman 2008, p. 100.
97   Ellman 2014, p. 4.
98   Ellman 1973, p. 27.

3 Material Balances

Under Soviet-style socialism, material tables were the principal method to ensure consistency of input and output, iteratively.[99] Once the output targets had been determined and assigned to various enterprises, it followed that a given amount of material resources were required to meet those targets – depending on the 'technical input coefficient'. It was the responsibility of the planning authorities to ensure that the flow of inputs was consistent with the output targets. Material balances were drawn up for the national level, the territorial level, and the particular [enterprise] level.[100] In sum, 'the allocation of resources was not guided by prices but by material balances expressed in physical terms'.[101]

While the planning process relied heavily on material balances, they never transplanted monetary calculations entirely, as had been attempted under war communism. Such radical ideas did surge, however, in the very early stages of the post-NEP transition to central planning, in which administrative rationing of production and consumption goods played a significant role, but these were never taken up as permanent features of the Soviet system.[102] Accounting prices, expressed in monetary units (roubles), merely supplemented the material balances and did not serve as a criterium for the production of types of outputs and their quantities. Rather, as goods passed through the economy upon instruction of the planning authorities, an accounting price would be stamped on them, which corresponded to the physical throughput on the basis of average costs.[103] Spontaneous price formation was suppressed, since the stability of prices as accounting tool for the planning process had to be maintained. As such, the prices were fixed administratively on the basis of average costs, for periods of up to five or ten years.[104] In relation to allocation of resources 'money is in principle passive', and the transfer of money between enterprises merely served to monitor the implementation of the plan. That is, accounting prices had a circumscribed control function, and did not facilitate the exchange of products as market prices do in a market economy.[105] (Rationing of consumer goods, (re)introduced in 1928, was by and large abandoned in 1935.[106]

---

99   Nove 1992, pp. 268–9.
100   Bor 1979.
101   Wilczynski 1972a, p. 77.
102   Nove 1992, p. 204.
103   Devine 2011, p. 57.
104   Wilczynski 1972a, p. 87; IMF 1991, pp. 9–10.
105   Devine 2011, p. 57; Ellman 2014, p. 31; Brus and Łaski 1989, p. 41.
106   Ellman 2014, p. 310; Nove 1992, p. 222.

The labour-market – meaning the commodification and exchange of labour-power – was likewise heavily circumscribed, insofar as enterprises were only able to bid for labour-power through offering improved working conditions and fringe benefits, until at least the 1950s.[107] Thus, whilst money did play an active role in the labour and consumer markets in the post-Stalin period,[108] we can still not speak of 'generalised commodity production' where all output and input are subject to exchange on the market, to the extent that neither capital goods nor materials were distributed in accordance with the competitive compulsions of market forces.)

This reliance on physical calculations allowed the Soviet economy to overcome financial constraints in the mobilisation of resources – hence, resource constraints became the primary restriction on economic growth. Furthermore, the price mechanism in Soviet socialism was two-tiered:

> In effect, the prices of retail consumer goods were insulated from producers' prices by substantial and highly differentiated turnover taxes or subsidies. Consequently, consumers' preferences had hardly any influence on the size and structure of production until they were acknowledged by central planners prepared to make appropriate adjustments to producers' prices and the allocation of resources.[109]

Wholesale prices therefore bore little relation to consumer demand and did not reflect the relative scarcity of means, in effect.[110] Since prices did not embody such information, their use in Soviet accounting and planning could not serve to promote an efficient pattern of utilisation of productive resources. To the extent that the material balances only recorded the flow of materials, the choice of technique was not subject to economisation. Thus, since production goods were rationed out to producers it was impossible for the material balances to promote an efficient use of these scarce assets. Consequently, there were instances where the quantity of labour-power required for the production of machinery was 'greater than the labour saved by its use'. However, 'it was impossible to calculate whether this was in fact so or not, since the price system was not adapted to such calculations'.[111] Calculation *in-natura* cannot compare costs to results, since physical units of measurement cannot be expressed as a

---

107   IMF 1991, p. 9; Ellman 2014, p. 261.
108   Devine 2011, p. 57; Ironside 2021.
109   Wilczynski 1972a, p. 77.
110   Kornai 2007, p. 224.
111   Nove 2011, p. 34.

single, commensurable coefficient. This prevented central planners from allocating resources according to the criterium that their use in some capacity yields the greatest benefit to society, as the esteemed Soviet economist Kantorovich noted:

> Even if the equipment allocated to enterprises was used effectively from the perspective of a single enterprise, it may be suboptimal from wider considerations. Thus, intricate equipment is used for simple work, with low efficiency, while in other places, where it could be the most effective, the absence of this equipment causes delays or necessitates the use of primitive methods.[112]

The use of material balances, therefore, offered some advantages in overcoming financial constraints to enable the mobilisation of idle resources such as raw material and labour-power, but could not sustain a pattern of efficient utilisation. Resources were put in motion, by coarse and makeshift methods of accumulation to some effect, but many of the potential benefits of their use were squandered in this process.

The ideal-typical procedure of drawing up balances functioned as follows. The Gosplan would announce the preliminary output targets on the basis of investment requirements, and in return receive from managers (via intermediate administrative levels) the estimates of input availability, their reserves, and input requirements. Any imbalances discovered in this process would be resolved by adjusting the material balances accordingly. These updated material balances would then be projected to enterprises, which then again responded with counter-suggestions. Consistency would thus be achieved through an iterative process of planning and counter-planning. However:

> there is normally not time for successive iterations to take account of these secondary effects. The output targets and input allocations on which the revised, approximately consistent, material balances are based become the definitive plan and are passed down through the hierarchy to become binding instructions to the enterprises.[113]

The actual process did not resemble a harmonious dialogue between planners and managers, co-operating to discover an equilibrium of input and out-

---

112   Kantorovich 1965, p. xxiii.
113   Devine 2011, p. 56.

put after a limited number of iterations. Instead, the process relied heavily on haggling over competing interests, the use of arbitrary heuristics to overcome information constraints, the doctoring of information, and the making of messy and makeshift adjustments to accommodate various mutually exclusive demands emerging in the process of planning. This sparked the ire among the participants on both ends of the planning procedure:

> Planners and producers were not fond of each other. Producers felt bombarded with arbitrary instructions that changed from one minute to the next and wondered out loud, 'Why do they need us?' Planners viewed producers as unreliable, distorters of information, and doing their own thing irrespective of the enlightened orders from above. Producers concluded that the less their superiors knew the better.[114]

The process of planning was in practice a 'swirl of negotiation, bullying, petitions, excuses, and pleadings'.[115] Each action elicited counteraction that attempted to cancel out the effects of the initial step. The planners tried to elicit a high performance, while the producers attempted to withhold performance. The planning authorities, knowing the propensity to understate productive capacity of the producers, overstated the initial output targets.[116] Investment decisions taken among higher levels administration were likewise the outcome of an inefficient process of bargaining between self-interested investment hungry departments and subdivisions. Because there were no effective financial constraints to structure investment choices, administrators attempted to expand their department as much as possible. Decisions that resulted from such a process would only afterwards be given 'scientific' and rational justification, by comparing them favourably to alternative projections that were selected for the express purpose of their comparative inferiority. In this way, economic decision-making was manipulated by economic agents whose motivations were deeply irrational considered from the general interest.[117]

A centrally directed administrative economy is not subject to the fluctuations and cyclical movements of the market. Indeed, the growth of national income of the Soviet economy can be observed to have been rather linear. Where negative growth rates could be measured in socialist economies, they usually occurred due to extra-economic shocks. Nevertheless, it should be

---

114   Gregory 2004, p. 151.
115   Gregory 2004, p. 169.
116   Kornai 2007, pp. 121–6.
117   Ellman 2014, p. 168.

stated that in some socialist countries economic causes can also be identified as having contributed to a fluctuation of growth rates.[118] The crucial mediating factor that spurred such fluctuations was the inattention paid to investment criteria related to efficiency.[119] What mattered most of all was to raise investments to the level mandated by the political leadership, quite literally 'whatever the cost'. As a result, the incremental capital-output ratio rose at incredible rates over the course of the 1950s and 1960s, in the USSR as elsewhere in the socialist bloc.[120] Since central planning was based on definite plan periods, there was a predictable pattern of fluctuations (i.e. a cycle): an initial explosion of investment hunger, in which all resources were mobilised to maximise accumulation guided by an excess of optimism, with relatively high growth rates, followed by a period of slowdowns in production and projects, caused by bottlenecks and constraints – or investment tension. In general, '[t]here was a strong tendency for the demand for resources to exceed their supply, with consequent tight balances, rationing, shortages and even frequent bottlenecks'.[121] The Soviet economy has thus been typified as a 'resource-constrained economy'.[122] The explosive rise of investments would come at the cost of consumption or the balance of payments. This disequilibrium then caused planners to halt new projects, to temper investment hunger, and to redirect resources to key investment projects.[123] Growth subsequently slowed down.[124] And so the penchant swung between investment hunger and investment tension. While it does not appear that the overall growth rate of the Soviet national economy was much affected by these tendencies, investment cycles could be observed, at least during the first two Five Year Plan periods, as well as in other countries belonging to the socialist bloc.[125]

In short, the combination of the use of material balances and gross output targets engendered investment hunger and structural misallocation, in place of financial constraints. Then there was in addition the issue of performing the actual calculations of the material balances. When imbalances were discovered (in paper before-the-fact or in practice after-the-fact), alterations of inputs and outputs were required to address them. The balance sheets had to be adjusted and readjusted for hundreds if not thousands of materials for each single

---

118   Ellman 2014, p. 172; Gregory 2004, pp. 107–8.
119   Wilczynski 1972a, p. 180.
120   Wilczynski 1972a, p. 35.
121   Wilczynski 1972a, p. 31.
122   Kornai 1979.
123   Gregory 2004, p. 100.
124   Ellman 2014, pp. 172–3.
125   Nove 1992, p. 226; Gregory 2004, p. 83; Kornai 1979, p. 193.

alteration, which was an exceedingly complicated task.[126] The effects of any alteration of any single output target naturally affects input requirements all the way up the supply chain, necessitating many more alterations. This would have a knock-on effect for many other goods as well, a small change spiralling outward – a bullwhip effect. Each small modification therefore threatened to sink the supply chain into chaos. The notoriously unreliable supply chain caused interruptions of production, which wasted resources by forcing produces located downstream from supply disruptions to sit idle.[127] Furthermore, managers resorted to hoarding assets to immunise their enterprises from supply shortages.[128] Additionally, in an attempt to overcome supply chain issues, enterprises would often wastefully expand their activities in order to produce their own inputs.[129]

It turned out that the Gosplan was incapable of calculating with anything approaching precision, a feasible plan of millions of unique goods given the estimated productive capacity (which, in any case, was distorted by managers) dispersed among tens of thousands of productive establishments.[130] The primary obstacle in this process proved to be human processing power:

> For the compilation of such a plan for the tens of thousands of products for which the USSR state plan sets targets, requires the carrying out of milliards of calculations (mathematically this is a problem of solving a system of linear equations) whereas a man, equipped with a desk calculator can only do 1000–2000 calculations per day.[131]

The planning authorities were overloaded by the innumerable equations they would have to solve: '[I]deally, the aggregate total is made up of the separate requirements of all the users. But there is never time or information available for such perfect planning'.[132] Political command over the economy in practice meant that the Politburo often dealt with one hundred to one thousand points per meeting,[133] and high-ranking politicians, including the General Secretary, dealt with many intricate details of production, from the volume of vodka to

---

126 Nove 1992, p. 199.
127 Ellman 2014, p. 249.
128 Ellman 2014, pp. 12–13; Wilczynski 1972a, p. 34.
129 Kornai 1979, p. 249; Gregory 2004, p. 179.
130 Nove 1991, pp. 33–5; West 2020, p. 40.
131 Ellman 1973, p. 24.
132 Nove 1992, p. 365.
133 Gregory 2004, pp. 127–8.

be produced to the quotas for agricultural output in a given region.[134] Yet, even though 'the number of Politburo decisions appears large, it represented a miniscule portion of all the decisions required to run an economy composed of thousands of enterprises, spread out over the world's largest country'.[135] Thus, '[w]hereas the market makes the millions of resource-allocation decisions in a market economy, they must be made by harried, overworked, and under-informed officials' in a centrally planned economy.[136] Consequently, only a very small number of high-priority goods (variously estimated to have been between 2,000 and 200,000 in the 1980s) were fully covered by the material plan, out of the 24 million or so of unique goods that were produced in the 1980s annually.[137]

Given the labour intensity of performing the required calculations, annual production plans were frequently announced to the enterprise halfway through the year, retroactively, or at times, not at all.[138] Likewise, control figures were set haphazardly and arbitrarily.[139] Some enterprises in the 1930s had not received annual plans for several years. Many factories were therefore compelled to plan their own activities, and plans were only drawn up afterwards as a matter of record. This 'non-planning' blinded the central planning authorities from certain economic realities and allowed intermediate administrative bodies to syphon off resources.[140] Moreover, as political preferences altered during the course of a planning period, abrupt changes to the output targets had to be announced to redirect resources to the new strategic priorities.[141] The inevitability of inconsistencies contained in the material balances and the unreliability of supply, as well as the rationing of materials and equipment, reinforced tendencies by managers to understate their productive capacity in reports to superiors.

We can therefore distinguish two primary information problems in the practice of socialist planning: (i) the volume of information that the central planners were expected to digest exceeded their computational abilities; and (ii) the material balances could not incorporate information about the relative scarcity of productive assets and materials, and therefore could not serve to allocate resources to their most productive uses. Hence, if even if consistency

---

134   Gregory 2004, p. 115.
135   Gregory 2004, p. 128.
136   Gregory 2004, p. 72.
137   Cockshott and Cottrell 1999.
138   Ellman 2014, p. 39.
139   Gregory 2004, pp. 117–18, 124.
140   Gregory 2004, pp. 122, 144, 160.
141   Kornai 2007, pp. 125–6.

between input and output across the economy could be obtained by adjusting the material balance sheets, there was no way to ensure an optimal structure of outlays. As consequence of these issues, a pronounced demand for make-shift and *ad hoc* decisions emerged to keep the system afloat. The planners, for example, complemented gross output planning with the use of impromptu information derived from complaints, petitions, or emergency telephone calls, to rectify mistakes and address the most acute shortages.[142] The functioning of the planned economy further depended on unplanned activity and unofficial exchange between enterprises.[143] Attempts to resolve such problems 'by administrative measures resulted in the proliferation of centralized government agencies and the expansion of bureaucracy, further complicating the situation'.[144]

The Communist Party also played an important in patching up the gaps in central planning. Party committees at all levels of administration acted as enforcers of the national priorities as promulgated by the Politburo and Gosplan, with party officials exercising tutelage over workplaces. They could circumvent the complicated maze of bureaucratic agencies. Party committees and officials would direct the activities of enterprises and intermediate bodies through political control over managers and in this way helped realign productive activity with the centrally determined strategic priorities.[145] Local party officials would also lobby on behalf of local enterprises for additional inputs when required.[146] Political entrepreneurship, which often took place via backroom dealings, was a key part of the Soviet economy. This made the system susceptible to political favouritism and corruption, since politically well-connected enterprise managers were able to leverage their personal connections to acquire scarce goods.

Behind the veneer of rational planning thus lied considerable administrative chaos. Economic policymakers were compelled to rely on their intuition, more so than on any dispassionate analysis on the basis of robust information that accurately captured the real conditions of industries. A number of key assumptions that underpinned planning practices in the Soviet Union turned out to be more convention than scientific. For example, the priority accorded to heavy industry over light industry was little more than a supposition; while the increase in planned output in an industry was based on some arbitrary per-

---

142   Gregory 2004, p. 6.
143   Gregory 2004, p. 177; Ellman 2014, pp. 40, 45.
144   Gerovitch 2008, p. 336.
145   Nove 1992, pp. 270–1.
146   Ellman 2014, p. 82.

centage increase rather than statistical analysis of potential growth. Because 'of their ignorance of many aspects of the past and present situation and uncertainty about the future, and also because of the complexity of economic life, decision-makers in the USSR made extensive use of rules of thumb'.[147] Still, the complexity of Soviet central planning during the earlier periods was mitigated because it dealt particularly with large strategic priorities (large-scale investment, raw material, production goods, heavy industry). Furthermore, the crudeness of the resource mobilisation strategy was partially offset by large reserves of idle resources. For the purposes of extensive growth and shock industrialisation, therefore, the material balances proved fairly useful, in spite of the disproportions spawned into existence by their use.

4   The System of Norms

Having so far discussed the method of material balance sheets of physical quantities and their limitations, we will now turn to the second, interconnected key element of Soviet planning, the system of norms. As noted previously, material balances were the primary method to achieve consistency and the norms the primary means to achieve efficiency. The short-lived period of war communism lacked rational criteria related to the allocation of resources. Even in theoretical debates, the status of workable criteria remained severely underdeveloped. In the absence of the main tools available to producers in a typical market economy – private property, factor markets, commodity exchange, and the profit motive – alternative norms had to be drawn up that could stimulate the most efficient use of resources under socialism. In the Soviet Union, from 1929 onwards, a great number of plan indices and production norms were deployed to serve as the criteria to measure, evaluate, and incentivise performance.

Since the allocational mechanism of the Soviet system was based around material balances, which denoted the physical quantities of input and output, the reproduction the system relied on enterprises producing the specified production quotas of gross output. Plan (over-)fulfilment was therefore the primary performance indicator of enterprises in the Soviet economy. Since neither ideological zeal nor concern for the general interest proved sufficient to encourage producers, the system of production norms was coupled to a system of material incentives. This roughly meant that bonus payments were allocated

---

147   Ellman 2008, p. 102.

to enterprises when they fulfilled or exceeded their production quotas. As previously mentioned, in administrative hierarchies, due to asymmetrical knowledge, subordinates tend to manipulate the data they transmit in their favour. Indeed, in Soviet practice, managers tended to deliberately under-report productive capacity and stocks, while also overstating cost projections, to then overproduce at lower than estimated costs in order to maximise bonuses and to secure more supplies.[148] This had two dimensions, a static and dynamic one. Managers would convince planning authorities of low production possibilities in order to easily exceed their obligatory production targets. The margin by which they subsequently exceed their output quotas would, however, likewise be small since otherwise planners might revise the quotas upward by significant amounts for subsequent plan periods – the so-called 'ratchet effect'. The first, static issue 'biases enterprise representations of production possibilities downward to induce a lower quota' while 'the dynamic incentive problem biases enterprise performance toward lower fulfillment levels'.[149] In this way, the data that the Gosplan used to determine the gross output targets were chronically distorted.[150] The extent of this distortion is revealed by the fact that output targets were frequently fulfilled with a mere fifty percent of the supposedly 'required' input.[151]

The gross output targets were defined by the planning authorities in a number of different ways, each of which produced their distinct and well-recorded defects:

> [P]lan targets set in physical output terms result in distortion: since enterprises are rewarded in proportion to plan-fulfillment, they have perverse incentives to bias the assortment of output toward either heavier components (when targets are set in terms of weight), or lighter ones (when targets are set in terms of number). Similarly, targets set in money terms lead to equally perverse incentives to increase cost.[152]

Similarly, because production targets were determined by vertical instructions, and performance was measured as compliance with said instructions, there was no necessary correspondence between output and consumer demand (which could otherwise have been determined via horizontal links). Output

---

148 Wilczynski 1972a, p. 33.
149 Weitzman 1976, p. 252.
150 Gregory 2004, p. 140.
151 Gregory 2004, p. 180.
152 Laibman 1992, p. 64.

was therefore frequently mismatched in relation to consumer requirements. There was no particular incentive to take into account consumer needs, since the plan targets reflected the preferences of planners based on partial information at best: 'it was not uncommon for the piling-up of stocks of useless goods to exist side by side with prevalent shortages of both consumer goods'.[153] Ellman characterises this as 'production for plan rather than for use'.[154] Crucially, not much attention was accorded to the efficient allocation and use of production goods, which were rationed without charge. Producers would petition for the highest amount of capital goods as they could possibly obtain, regardless of whether they could use them productively or not. Similarly, since '[e]nterprise success was judged not by efficiency but by total [gross] output' it 'was easier to reach targets by expanding employment than by increasing labour productivity'.[155]

Little attention was also paid to the quality of output – especially toward the end of a given plan period, in which production was accelerated to meet output quotas, a phenomenon known as 'storming'.[156] By evaluating enterprises according to quantitative metrics of the degree of output target fulfilment, regardless of the grade of output, there was no incentive to deliver quality materials and goods. As such, enormous amounts of output, volumes of materials, ranging from tires to steel rails and wood and coal, had to be discarded as waste annually.[157] Since there was no inbuilt mechanism to encourage quality of output, the delivery of substandard quality was made a criminal offence in the 1930s.[158] Punitive measures could hardly be expected to improve matters since underlying, systemic causes were not remedied. In other words, the difficulty in setting effective standards to assess the quality of work and products resulted in perverse effects, both in terms of productivity and the grade of output.

In relation to the volume of means of consumption, consumption norms were drawn up to determine output levels, i.e. 'the quantity of a particular good or service required per head of the population'.[159] Planners would determine the number of articles – shoes, shirts, and so on – per capita that were supposedly needed, which ran into the obvious problem of deciding what the

---

153   Wilczynski 1972a, p. 99.
154   Ellman 2014, p. 34.
155   Wilczynski 1972a, p. 28.
156   Ellman 1973, p. 45; Nove 1958, p. 6.
157   Beissinger 1998, p. 121.
158   Nove 1992, p. 271.
159   Ellman 2014, p. 293.

appropriate norm should be for each category of commodity. This let to continual revisions of the norms and the use of advertisements to try and dispose of any excess stock that resulted from mistaken estimations. The norms, throughout the existence of the Soviet Union, remained largely arbitrary and an unreliable instrument for setting output targets for means of consumption.[160]

The system of norms had further drawbacks beyond the manipulation of data and the tendency to produce substandard output. A key factor which explains the economic decline of the Soviet Union was the inability to propagate novel technology as a result of poor incentives. Managers were systemically encouraged to behave in a risk-adverse manner.[161] They consistently obstructed the implementation of technological innovations since this would disrupt the production process, thereby threatening the fulfilling of output targets, without pay-off in the longer term.[162] Moreover, central command over economic activity could not account for the emergence of new technologies:

> It is hard to get any new invention applied or new product introduced if it did not feature in the original plan. The plan directs its implementers, but it also ties their hands, making it one of the sources of economic rigidity and lack of flexible adaptation.[163]

In addition to the structurally reinforced innovation aversion exhibited by managers, more contingent brakes on economic growth were the restrictions placed on scientific and trade interaction with the capitalist world, as well as over-centralisation, which is tied to monopolistic complacency.[164]

The only recourse for growth available to Soviet authorities, in the absence of a continual improvement in technical productivity, was the mobilisation of physical resources, which inevitably ran into the more or less natural limitations of this strategy. Beyond a certain point, most idle natural resources and labour-power will have been incorporated into the national economy. Furthermore, the process of excavating raw material in the Soviet economy became increasingly costly, since those resources that had been most accessible had been extracted first, thus increasing operational costs at later stages of extraction.[165] Demographic developments slowed down the growth of the working

---

160 Ellman 2014, p. 295.
161 Ellman 2014, p. 38.
162 Devine 2011, p. 64.
163 Kornai 2007, p. 128.
164 Ellman 2014, pp. 38–9; Kornai 2012, p. 28.
165 Allen 1958, p. 197; IMF 1991, p. 12.

aged population – the supply of new labour-power to the national economy – and therefore also the growth of production.[166] The mobilisation strategy, consequently, could not indefinitely bear the brunt of responsibility in terms of accumulation. It became crucial that, instead of relying on a quantitative growth of factor inputs, Soviet authorities should urge a qualitative growth in the productivity of these inputs. Thus, such developments necessitated a shift in strategy from quantitative, extensive growth to increasing the productivity of resource usage (i.e. intensive growth). Without the ability to improve technical productivity, the socialist economies were deprived of any feasible means to grow their national incomes.

Finally, we will consider briefly the issue of labour incentives. The Soviet model of economic development – based on shock industrialisation via resource mobilisation – required the tightening of labour discipline, since worker morale remained low. There were those exceptions, especially in the early period of centralised planning, where workers showed genuine ideological zeal to help build communism with the instruments of their own hands and minds.[167] Overall however, '[t]hose who bore the main brunt of the burden of rapid growth had little chance of influencing the priorities laid down by the Party'.[168] Labour productivity would perpetually lag behind the Western world, even after an initial promising boost in the first few or so plan periods, which was mainly due to a combination of expanded wage differentials and efforts to bring up the technical skills of the Soviet workforce, as well as the moral incentives associated with the Stakhanovite movement.[169] In the period of the first Five Year Plan, due to the high ratio of accumulation relative to consumption, inflated wages could buy very little, which contributed adversely to morale and productivity; by contrast, the end of rationing and the introduction of penalties for labour-related offences productivity recovered and reduced absenteeism somewhat.[170] Furthermore, workers enjoyed little control over their activities and were under threat of arbitrary authority of managers, which contributed to low morale, low productivity, absenteeism, and slacking.[171] There was little positive motivation available for workers participate conscientiously in production, in short:

---

166 Ellman 1986, pp. 530–42.
167 Nove 1992, p. 193.
168 Wilczynski 1972a, p. 21.
169 Nove 1992, pp. 233–5.
170 Nove 1992, p. 211.
171 Ellman 2014, pp. 248–9.

One can scarcely expect an enthusiastic attitude to production in a factory where the workers are producing something other than that which is really required in order to fulfil the plan, find it impossible because of shortages to obtain numerous desired commodities, and have no more control over their working lives than workers in a capitalist factory.[172]

The workers enjoyed even less control over the returns of their enterprise, and 'prolonged overfulfilment of piecework norms was likely to lead, not to prolonged high earnings, but to an upward revision of the norms'.[173] Understandably, this did not help to raise labour productivity either.

5   Reforming the System – From Optimism to Cynicism

Soviet planning had reached its zenith by the 1950s.[174] Around this time, it was commonly considered a matter of time before the USSR would catch up with the West.[175] Thus, 'Although Soviet plans have normally been inconsistent, this has not prevented the economy flourishing'.[176] When the transition to an intensive growth regime (one driven by technical progress) had to be made, however, the shortcomings of Soviet-style central planning came to a head.[177] The Soviet system – in the wake of the Second World War and Stalin's collectivisation and industrialisation drive – was marked by a deeply disharmonious structure. This fact was partially concealed by macroeconomic indicators that showed the Soviet economy to experience constant rates of growth. Despite strides in these areas, the economy 'suffered from severe disproportions, shortages, and arbitrary pricing. The central planning system was struggling with the task of assigning production quotas to each and every economic unit and distributing the output according to the continuously revised national plan'.[178] While calls for economic reform had been made from the 1930s onwards, often in confidential memos,[179] the need for a change of course asserted itself when macroeconomic indicators began their slow decline. Growth rates gradually slowed down and eventually began to stagnate in the 1970s when the benefits

---

172   Ellman 1973, pp. 530–42.
173   Ellman 2014, p. 264.
174   Ellman 2014, p. 12; Wilczynski 1972a, p. 20.
175   Ofer 1988, p. 2.
176   Ellman 1969, p. 71.
177   Nove 1992, pp. 322, 366, 390; Wilczynski 1972a.
178   Gerovitch 2008, p. 336.
179   Ellman 2014, p. 52.

of the resource mobilisation strategy (i.e. extensive growth) had worn off.[180] During the Stalin era, household consumption had been a of concern second to the strategic development of heavy and military industries. As such:

> The planners have not been much troubled by the consistency problem, as they were primarily concerned with strategic problems, for example the relationship of industry to agriculture, and the allocation of investment between industries, and the development of specific products (e.g. tanks), specific plants (e.g. the Dneiper and Bratsk hydro stations and the Magnitogorsk iron and steel complex), of specific programmes (e.g. the space programme), and of specific industries (e.g. oil). In all these their successes were striking. (It was the non-priority sectors that suffered from inconsistencies.) Compared to these crucial questions the calculations necessary to ensure consistency were regarded as a mere 'game with figures'.[181]

However, as fewer benefits were being reaped by the quantitative growth strategy of national income, the pressure to introduce reforms bubbled up (in spite of ideological and institutional opposition) in varying degrees in all socialist countries, with the exception of Albania which retained strict ideological adherence to 'Stalinist' orthodoxy.[182]

According to Soviet doctrine, the direct allocation of goods secured the social character of labour directly, bringing the units of production under the control of a single directing centre. This allowed for conscious and rational control over the direction and pace of economic development, eliminating market competition, economic crises, the 'exploitation of man by man'. Socialism was thus free of contradictions and conflicts being organised on the principles of democratic centralism, and all Soviet citizens would share equally in the common interest to promote the development of the material forces of production and labour-power could be put to rational use as the object of social production and planning. The individual and collective interests aligned utterly – therefore, if practice indicated conflict between the two it was regarded a matter of wrecking and sabotage by subversive elements rather than an issue of incentive design. No fundamental, practical or technical problems were acknowledged in the scientific orchestration of comprehensive planning.[183]

---

180   Chattopadhyay 1994, p. 88; Nove 1992, p. 389; Itoh 1995.
181   Ellman 1969, p. 71.
182   Wilczynski 1972a; Ellman 2014, pp. 52–3; Sturmthal 1961, pp. 379–96.
183   Wagener 1998, p. 11.

These ideas reflected the optimistic rationalism of Marxist orthodoxy (of which the conception of the whole economy as a 'single great factory' is a more or less immediate outgrowth), which contained thought based around the notion that society moved along the rhythms laid down by objective laws and further that these laws could be understood and subsequently controlled by conscious efforts under the right conditions. These ideas were carried over into Marxism-Leninism and put into action by the Soviet authorities where workers were put into service of the construction of socialism from above. According to Soviet doctrine, 'the plan was a law that had to be obeyed without question', since the conception of the plan 'was an "economic law" of socialism' and further 'there could be no true interests of economic agents different from those of the national economy as a whole'.[184] Labouring under these assumptions it was the belief that 'the system in itself is viable, potentially optimal'. Therefore, if 'something went wrong, the suspects were individuals who did not understand the paradigm fully, who worked for their private interests or, who failed'. As such, diagnosing systemic failure 'was taboo' since 'there must be a possibility to improve, to make the system perfect'.[185] Hence the tendency to hold fast to the ideological reins and to remain vigilant and suspicious of 'deviationist' ideas cropping up.

Despite this tendency to preserve the ideological core of Marxism-Leninism, the economic maladies – which of course ran counter to principles related to the absence of contradictions under the socialist organisation of society – gave rise to voices petitioning for improvements to the planning mechanism. The increasing pressures on authorities to reform the system and to accommodate intensive methods of accumulation more effectively was obviously felt strongest in those socialist economies with the highest degree of industrial development, where the potential for extensive growth was stretched thin and the opportunities for the mobilisation of idle resources depleted most quickly and where, as a direct consequence, the growth rates of national income obtained by these economies were the lowest recorded among all members of the socialist bloc – in particular, Czechoslovakia and Hungary. The achievement of the primary objective of developing a solid productive base implied that the reliable supply of finished products to households could no longer be relegated to a matter of secondary importance. A shift in strategic focus became inevitable to accommodate the increasing expectations of consumers. Thus:

---

184   Sutela and Mau 1998, p. 58.
185   Wagener 1998, p. 12.

By the 1960s this traditional attitude had begun to alter. The economy had become so complex that the gains from the administrative allocation of resources to the key sectors began to be rivalled by the losses from the misallocation of resources throughout the economy.[186]

Economists, planners, policymakers, and administrators in the Soviet Union and across the communist bloc were forced to reckon with the economic realities of slow technical progress and chronic imbalances in the supplies of input compared to output targets. Gradually then, attention shifted from achieving the key strategic developmental objectives to addressing matters of over-centralisation associated with directive planning. Economists began cautiously circulating ideas about how to relieve the centre of certain responsibilities and to allow a greater scope for local initiative – this movement to reform, which was of loose affiliation, was dubbed 'reform socialism' by Kornai.[187]

This growing awareness of the need to address the degenerative currents within the economy resulted in number of (abortive) attempts to reform the economy. We will subsequently go over the most important and relevant proposals and attempts.

Prior to any experimentation with major structural reforms, a series of modest modifications to the system of centralised planning had been introduced. To bring Soviet reality in closer alignment with the 'single great factory' paradigm, attempts were made in the area of 'personnel changes and purges, by organizational changes, by the implementation of shifts in investment allocation as well as by the reformulation of centralized pricing rules and also incentive schemes'.[188] Under Stalin's successor, Khrushchev, modifications included the increased involvement and consultation of managers and local and regional officials in the drawing up of the draft plan in 1955.[189] Another attempt of Khrushchev's to overcome over-centralisation of industries, which resulted in deficient co-ordination among them, was to the sever direct lines of subordination to the centre for units that were of local significance. This had perverse effects, firstly, since '[s]upply chains were severely disrupted, because different enterprises within a single supply chain often ended up under the control of different regional councils' and, secondly, authorities attempted to correct these disruptions by introducing a plethora of agencies to mend broken supply

---

186   Ellman 1969, p. 71.
187   Kornai 2007.
188   Sutela and Mau 1998, p. 40.
189   Nove 1992, pp. 350, 353.

chains, thus contributing to bureaucratic hypertrophy.[190] Thus, 'Khrushchev's infamous experiment with *sovnarkhozes* provided a cure that was probably worse than the disease'.[191] This category of reform did not address the underlying structural causes that, for example, led managers to distort information and made them avoidant in implementing technical improvements.

Thus, the reform movement was born out of the impotence of these minor adjustments. This movement in the Soviet Union and the socialist bloc countries more generally grew on the back of wider sociopolitical undercurrents that began making themselves felt. Since political rule by the Communist Party was not reinforced by popular vote, the political leadership had to maintain stability by offering rising standards of living in exchange for civil compliance, a more or less tacit 'social contract'.[192] However, no unified interest can be discerned among the socialist working classes, with different layers and categories of workers bearing different aspirations and interests. The internal contradictions of socialism began pulling the political leaderships of socialist countries into particular, and at times incoherent, directions. At certain conjunctures, popular grievances boiled over into open struggles by workers for an increase in pay or the retention of rationing of foodstuffs, as well as the introduction of workers' councils, to which authorities responded with a combination of physical repression against uncontrolled initiatives and concessions to bring workers back into the fold of the Communist Party. At the same time, social pressure also emerged in the form of the new generation of educated, professional workers to be afforded a higher status compared to 'blue-collar' workers and a corresponding income differentiation. Intellectuals, meanwhile, called for the ability to exercise open criticism, and economists advocated for an expansion of either commodity-money relations or cybernetic optimal planning, or both. There was no clear overriding goal among these tendencies, and this constellation of social forces had to be balanced to secure the position of the Communist Party. At this point, sincere belief in some alternative, more democratic form of socialism widely circulated among the intelligentsia (although cases of strategic lip service can also be recognised); and demands from below for workers' councils seemed to reinforce this tendency. A compromise of sorts among these various tendencies led to reform proposals and experimentation with a market mechanism embedded in the framework of centralised planning in various socialist countries – chiefly Hungary's 'New Economic Mechanism', the GDR's

---

190   Gerovitch 2008, p. 336.
191   Sutela and Mau 1998, p. 42.
192   Cook 1992.

'New Economic System', and Czechoslovakia's 'New Economic Model' – sometimes alloyed with workers' councils. The socialist optimism that marked the progressive reform elements among these varied impulses was carried forward to the greatest extent in Czechoslovakia, where the Communist leadership under Dubček began to promote 'socialism with a human face', which ended dramatically at the hands of the Warsaw Pact invasion in 1968.[193]

The objective requirement for structural adjustment is of course not a unique feature of socialist economies and could scarcely be considered an indictment as such. Under the capitalist system, the requirement for restructuring imposes itself regularly when the circuit of capital breaks down whenever the acute limits of accumulation are approached. The political leadership will tend to respond to crises of over-accumulation by adopting a particular strategic approach that shifts the balances of forces between labour and capital or different fractions of capital, to form a new power bloc or reforging the existing power bloc on the basis of a new social compromise, in order to reanimate the circuit of capital. Arguably, the operational autonomy of public officials in most capitalist societies helps them to overcome the narrow interests of different capital fractions to help synthesise a social compromise.[194] This makes capitalism particularly suited to structural adaptation. On the other hand, no such operational autonomy exists in administrative-command economies, where the exercise of political functions and economic functions is fused, further cemented by the basic tenets of the ideological framework, entrenching interests and biasing public officials to the current way of operating the system, making Soviet-style economies less adaptable to challenges that might arise.

The inability to address the pronounced excesses of the system prompted renewed interest in theoretical debate centred on the functioning of the socialist system. In the words of Kantorovich:

> in our country the necessity of further improvements of the control mechanism, some defects in the use of resources, incomplete realization of the potential advantages of the planned economy were pointed out repeatedly. It was obvious that such improvements should be based on new ideas and new means. This led to the natural idea to introduce and use quantitative mathematical methods.[195]

---

193   For a deep dive into Czechoslovak reform socialism, see Yörümez 2021.
194   Jessop and Overbeek 2019.
195   Kantorovich 1975.

Until 1928, there had been ample leeway for discussion within the confines of questions concerning strategies of socialist construction, but this space for the relatively free circulation of ideas was closed at the introduction of the first Five Year Plan.[196] As Nove put it, at that point 'real argument ceased, to give way to abuse'.[197] The post-Stalin 'thaw' lifted some of these restrictions and re-opened limited space for discussion regarding planning methods.[198] This allowed for the emergence of various reform proposals to address the growing problems associated with manual control over the national economy, falling into three (overlapping) categories: (i) the expansion and strengthening of market ('commodity-money') relations; (ii) the application of mathematical methods; and (iii) economic cybernetics. These proposals were advanced by a faction of mathematical economists known as the 'optimal planners'. According to this faction of economists, the Soviet economy should move toward a form of 'indirect centralisation' based on local solutions to centrally transmitted optimisation problems:

> Direct, traditional centralization was based on hierarchically determined compulsory enterprise-specific targets. In an optimal plan, however, shadow prices can be used to decentralize the planning task in the sense that once they have been derived with the constrained optimum, shadow prices can be used as parameters. (...) In a perfect setting, plants have no reason to act against the wishes of the centre. Given the economic environment formed by the parameters, factories under these conditions are free to find out all by themselves what the centre wants them to do. That is also in the plants' own best interests. Incentive problems have been solved. This idea was the main inspiration of Soviet reform economics from early 1960s all the way until *perestroika*. It was formulated by Kantorovich, specified by Novozhilov and widely disseminated by Nemchinov. In various forms, it was propagated by a generation of Soviet reform economists (...).[199]

The basic rationale behind reform proposals was framed as follows. The material balances that formed the basis for central planning were crude, yet proved to be a fairly effective instrument for the purpose of rapid industrialisation.

---

196 Kontorovich 2013, pp. 15–16.
197 Nove 1992, p. 219.
198 Nove 1992, pp. 367–8. Brus and Łaski 1989, p. 51; Gerovitch 2008, p. 337.
199 Sutela and Mau 1998, p. 45.

Since the strategic objective of industrialisation and military parity with the West had since been realised – that is to say, the usefulness of crude material balances had been exhausted and outlived their usefulness – other methods had to be devised to improve ('further perfect') economic planning.[200] This was obviously a form of rationalisation, since 'the practice of taking the index of gross output as the basic success indicator of an enterprise' and other such core features of the administrative-command system, 'are the cause of waste which cannot be justified at any stage of development'.[201] Some Soviet academics turned to mathematical and cybernetic approaches that find a successor for the crude material balances. The reform socialists were optimistic that regeneration was feasible:

> Input-output [methods were] supposed to create consistency in plans; growth economics would substantiate longer-range planning than had been actually possible before; enterprise models would assist in developing incentives; regional models would provide the basis for spatial planning; and efficient computers would overcome the informational overburden of traditional data.[202]

For example, according to the optimal planners, the price mechanism would need to be reformed thus:

> (a) Prices must be either determined in free competitive markets where consumer's sovereignty prevails, or derived computationally from the optimal plan. (b) The contribution of all resources (i.e. in addition to labour) to production must be accepted as cost and reflected accordingly in prices. (c) Prices must be based on the costs of marginal enterprises in the industry producing a particular article. (d) There ought to be a closer correspondence between retail and producers' prices. If they must differ (over and above wholesale and retail margins), the rates of turnover taxes should be reasonably uniform, at least for broad classes of products. (e) Prices must be fairly flexible to indicate the conditions of supply and demand as reflected in conventional markets or in computationally simulated 'shadow markets'.[203]

---

200   Ellman 1973, p. 59.
201   Brus 1972.
202   Sutela and Mau 1998, p. 43.
203   Wilczynski 1972a, p. 78.

From the 1950s onwards, there was an explosion of both literature and agencies working on the subject of cybernetics. This impulse gave birth to initiatives that promised to deliver a computerised information network – a predecessor to the internet.[204] Since central planners would in theory have to carry out fifteen milliard calculations to produce a consistent plan, electronic computers would be able to reduce the time to compute an optimal plan to a matter of minutes, it was believed.[205] A nation-wide network of computers would be able to solve the millions of equations required to compute such a plan, argued mathematical economists.[206] The application of cybernetics would involve the automatic regulation of production by central control. The main innovation advanced by Soviet cybernetics was that data-processing would be connected to dynamic control functions. Thus, data would not just be compiled and prepared in order to subject it to analysis and draw conclusions; data would be coded and applied in such a way that they form the parameters that regulate the processes of production and distribution as part of a system of automatic management.[207] Cybernetic approaches to communism would enable a reduction of the maze of administrative controls and agencies, improve transparency, and empower local units at the expense of public officials. Steps taken in the direction of a cybernetic information network were a cause for alarm for US authorities, fearing it could help realise the USSR's ambition of overtaking the West.[208] One of the pioneers of Soviet cybernetics, Glushkov, 'argued that his proposal would not centralize all decision-making, but only top-level strategic planning'. According to his vision, 'it would be possible to design a system that would provide quasi-market incentives for individual enterprises through computer modelling. He argued that this would work even more efficiently than actual market[s]'.[209] In short, many in the Soviet Union pinned their hopes on cybernetics to renovate Soviet planning.

In the 1960s, cybernetics won official support from the Communist Party, being adopted in their political programme, declaring that 'Cybernetics, electronic computer and control systems will be widely applied in production processes',[210] for reasons that the party leadership believed this to be a promising scientific avenue that could improve the flow and processing of information

204   West 2020; Gerovitch 2008, p. 335.
205   Wilczynski 1972b, p. 31; Kantorovich 1965, p. 149; Lange 1971, p. 111.
206   West 2020, p. 39.
207   Maiminas 1979.
208   Gerovitch 2008, pp. 335–6.
209   Gerovitch 2008, p. 342.
210   CPSU 1961, p. 66.

without upsetting entrenched interests tied up with the Soviet system as a whole.[211] Thus, the Soviet authorities hoped that cybernetics could be integrated into central planning without a major overhaul of the existing institutional framework while the central role of the Communist Party in society could be preserved. However, the notion of a central supercomputer, linked up to a network of electronic computers, absorbing the manual computations of the Gosplan, was factually abandoned by the early 1970s, since the processing power of supercomputers proved to be wholly inadequate. Hodgson estimated that – taking the approximate number of unique goods produced in the Soviet Union, some twelve million he estimates – it would take eighteen years or so to produce a fully integrated optimal plan using the computer technology available in the 1980s.[212] Consequently, if cybernetics were to be in any way technically viable, it would need to be coupled with decentralisation and local initiative. The basic conception of cybernetic planning that emerged in the Soviet literature – in place of the electronically enhanced central planning that the political authorities hoped to realise – was one that allowed for self-governance of lower units, within general parameters that were centrally determined.[213] Since this implied dislodging established institutions and reducing their sway over the Soviet republics, the diffusion of cybernetic organisation was constrained by powerful political interests, which limited its practical application to 'a patchwork of ministry-subordinated data banks'.[214] With that, the revolutionary potential of cybernetics was squandered. As Kantorovich remarked, attitudes in relation to new methods and innovations cycled through a series of steps, 'from scepticism and resistance through enthusiasm and exaggerated hopes to some disappointment and dissatisfaction'.[215]

As a matter of practical difficulty, it also proved challenging to apply optimising algorithms. In 1939, Kantorovich introduced a method – known as 'linear programming' or 'linear optimisation' – to solve constrained optimisation problems. This is an algorithmic technique (when the problem involves more than three unknowns) that performs dual calculations that can determine how to maximise an objective function given a set of constraints. It can thus compute the optimal means to achieve given output targets by discovering and assigning relative weights to various inputs in relation to this objective func-

211   Gerovitch 2008, p. 340.
212   Hodgson 1998, p. 422; Hodgson 1984, p. 170.
213   West 2020, p. 40.
214   Gerovitch 2008, p. 347.
215   Kantorovich 1975.

tion.[216] Initially, his methods were rejected by planning authorities since the system of central planning, they retorted, worked perfectly. However, the post-Stalin thaw allowed mathematical models to come into the limelight. When implemented in practice, optimisation programmes were mostly confined to regional application, applied to specific branches with comparatively stable technical coefficients. The quantity and quality of both computers and data was such that optimisation programmes could not be run for solving problems of greater scales.[217] Thus, 'Many applications are episodical, they don't became regular and are not united into a system'.[218] According to Kantorovich, 'planning deficiencies exist as a direct result of economic science lagging behind the requirements needed in the building up of a communist state'.[219] This apparently applied with equal force to the level of electronic computing power.

The problems in the application of optimisation programming extended beyond issues of political and computing constraints, as the system of norms was also biased against their use. If a feasible solution to a constrained optimisation problem would demonstrate the optimal use of resources, one which would minimise expenditure, say, it would likely conflict with one of the many plan indices that promoted a maximisation of *gross* output.[220] For example, in the transportation branch, gross output targets were given as magnitudes of ton-kilometres. Naturally, this created the perverse stimulus for unnecessarily lengthy hauls to maximise said ton-kilometres. By optimising their shipping routes, in accordance with the solutions found by the application of mathematical methods, transporters would be doing themselves no favours by reducing the amount ton-kilometres since, in accordance with the system of norms and material incentives tied to it, they should maximise them.

As long as the plan fulfilment remained the primary operational criterium, the central planning system would continue to suffer from its various defects.[221] Given these problems, which affected all branches of industry, one of the aims of the reform proposals was therefore to modify the performance indicators to reduce the disincentives they triggered into existence. If the application of mathematical and cybernetic methods to the problems of the planned was blocked by practical and political obstacles, the final remaining solution was curbing over-centralisation by means of an expansion of horizontal

216   Kantorovich 1965; Lange 1971, p. 86; Cockshott 2008.
217   Kornai 2007, p. 405; Wilczynski 1972a, pp. 74–5.
218   Kantorovich 1975.
219   Kantorovich 1965, p. xxii.
220   Ellman 2014, p. 46; Ellman 1973, p. 10.
221   Nove 1992, p. 368.

linkages facilitated through market exchange. This pragmatic logic dominated among the neo-Marxist school of 'reform socialism':

> The reformist Marxists were profoundly affected by the inefficiencies of the command system, but they (...) ascribed failures not to central planning as such, but to excessive centralization, which clearly exceeded the capacity of the planners to collect and to process the flow of information. This seemed to be the result of the attempt to cover, by detailed obligatory target planning and physical allocation of resources, all aspects of current operations of state enterprises: size of output and its composition, labour and material inputs, sources of supply and directions of sales, prices, financial outcome, and so on. Decisions of this kind could and should therefore be left to the enterprises themselves, the horizontal relations of which could be co-ordinated by a regulated market.[222]

While we can unequivocally say, especially in hindsight, that it is true that 'reform socialism' planted the seeds for the eventual restoration of capitalism, attempts to improve centralised planning were motivated by a sincere commitment to the regeneration of socialism, and their diagnostics and innovations can cautiously inspire theoretical renewal today – if we admit frankly their limitations for socialist construction. But if we are tempted to lay blame solely at their feet for the disappearance of socialism, a few things might be kept in mind: (i) the imbalances and waste were real conditions experienced by Soviet-style economies, and opportunities for extensive growth were fast depleting; (ii) political interests, in addition to technical obstacles, blocked alternative strategies for socialist renewal; (iii) the 'marketeer' faction of reform economists seized on pre-reform or 'Stalinist' period claims of the 'law of value under socialism' to advance their proposals.

The dead-end of cybernetics and the restricted utility of mathematical tools left reformists with only one option; to advance proposals for the harnessing – i.e. expanding and strengthening – of market relations by according a greater role to horizontal contracting and increasing the role of profitability in accounting and control – ideas of which the economist Liberman was the principal advocate. Profitability, after all, provided a synthetic value index that simultaneously promotes a minimisation of expenditure and a maximisation of returns. By substituting plan fulfilment (and a host of contradictory norms) for the rate of profit many disincentives would vanish, and the

---

222   Brus and Łaski 1989, p. 75.

need for a great number of supplementary and convoluted plan indices would be greatly reduced. Furthermore, by expanding the role of markets, intensive growth was to be promoted by creating favourable conditions, which included: 'decentralization, flexibility and adaptability of the structure of production to demand, strengthened incentives based on efficiency, competition and, in general, the operation of the market mechanism where it is considered to be desirable'.[223]

The Kosygin-Liberman reforms of 1966–1969 were the first major reforms that were implemented in practice which attempted to remedy the structural problems affecting the Soviet economy. The reforms were the result of a tug of war between the two rivalling factions, the 'optimal planners', whose chief concern was efficiency, efficacy, and optimisation; and the orthodox 'political economists', who primarily feared that this would risk restoring the operation of capitalist categories in the Soviet economy.[224] Since cybernetic modelling proved to be a *cul-de-sac*, the only recourse for reformers lay in the expanding of 'commodity-money' relations. The aim of the reforms was to reduce the responsibility of the central planning authorities in resource allocation, which would instead need to 'concentrate on the long-run macroeconomic effectiveness of investment, i.e. on the major proportions between different branches and regions of the economy, and particularly on those developmental needs which are strategic to technological progress'. Meanwhile, 'the microeconomic details of planning and construction of investment projects are left to enterprises, branch associations and banks'.[225] At the ousting of Khrushchev in 1964, and the ascendancy of premier Kosygin and General Secretary Brezhnev, the debate was 'settled' by political fiat and critics were subsequently silenced,[226] thus clearing the path for the reforms to be implemented. However:

> The situation was paradoxical. The fundamental ideas for change were developed by one group of economists. Normative documents were prepared by another group, generally of much more moderate persuasion. The practical implementation was carried out by yet a third group, a number of whom were out-and-out opponents of the central ideas of the reform.[227]

---

223 Wilczynski 1972a, p. 48.
224 Boldyrev and Düppe 2020.
225 Wilczynski 1972a, p. 180.
226 Tubis 1973, pp. 91–2.
227 Sutela and Mau 1998, p. 61.

The reforms were ratified in 1965, and implemented over the following years, from 1966 until 1969.[228] As per the official data of the national accounts of the various socialist bloc countries, the highest growth rates in national income were obtained by the industrially least developed national economies, with growth rates recorded of upwards of ten percent; while the economies with comparatively low rates of growth were among the economically most advanced economy – the empirical record bearing out that the principal cause of the decline of socialism being the difficulty in promoting intensive methods of accumulation.[229] The fact that reforms appear, at a superficial glance, to precede economic decline has given rise claims that the reforms *caused* economic decline rather than being a *response* to decline, by reducing the political command over the economy in favour of market relations, thereby restoring harmful capitalist elements.[230] As we have seen, however, falling macroeconomic indicators can be traced back to underlying causes that preceded the period of economic liberalisation, and were present from the very beginnings of central planning based on material balances. The levels of growth to which supporters of unreformed Soviet-style socialism direct our attention as proof of the harmful effects of loosening the reins by central planners, observe the tail end of unsustainable extensive growth.

The argument that creeping 'revisionism' should be assigned blame is deeply implausible. This can scarcely account for the structural emergence of reformist thought from within every socialist country, often from within the Communist Party itself, by people deeply reared by and socialised into the doctrine of Marxism-Leninism, and in spite of concerted efforts to curb counterrevolutionary views, by means of recurrent political purges, control over media and the dissemination of official doctrine, all to prevent the emergence of revisionists that eventually crept up everywhere and ended up victorious across all these countries. If there are structural outcomes we have to disclose structural causes. If no socialist country has been spared 'revisionism', being affected by it according to varying rates and degrees, then clearly its emergence is not merely due to some accidental contingencies that have to be ironed out, and there must have been compelling and structural pressures that explain why diverse minds, from diverse class origins, ethnic backgrounds, and a range of countries were drawn in the direction of very similar conclusions. This convergent evolution of reform thought took shape in response a climate of economic decline that can be traced to systemic flaws, primarily of over-centralisation

---

228   Ellman 2014, p. 36.
229   Wilczynski 1972b.
230   Ball 2010; KKE 2009; Keeran and Kenny 2010.

associated with planning by detailed directives and economic waste caused by relying on obligatory gross output plan targets. It is with the socialist optimism of the reform Marxists – which spread throughout the ranks academia, public authorities, and the Communist Party before being displaced, not by a faithful recommitment to orthodox Marxism-Leninism, but by bitter cynicism – that today's socialists should critically engage in order to identify the structural causes that allowed market relations in socialist countries to envelop planning mechanisms, eventually leading to the complete liberalisation and collapse of their economies and societies.

The Soviet reform package attempted to tackle the issue perverse incentives by subjecting the system of norms to significant modification. The set of indicators of economic performance were reduced. Under the administrative-command system, the meeting of output targets as stipulated by the plan was the primary indicator of performance, since the reproduction of the system depended on the required input being available to manufacture the outputs necessary to meet the various investment and consumption needs of society. The system of norms, hitherto, took no particular notice of the rate of return of individual productive establishments. The overriding aim was the realisation of politically determined plan priorities, regardless of the costs and profits involved.[231] Enterprises operated under soft budget constraints, therefore, since funds were reallocated between enterprises if so demanded by the expediencies of the plan.[232] Profit-and-loss accounting for individual enterprises had, in fact, already been official practice since the 1920s. Its function in the planned economy, however, was to encourage economisation of resources in relation to planned quantities of output, which were not set in relation to profit considerations. The profit *motive* in production then, did not operate, even if profit-and-loss accounting was practised.[233] The Kosygin-Liberman reforms accordingly made profitability and sales performance priorities in an attempt to rectify the perverse behaviour (particularly the adoption of cost-inducing production methods; and neglecting consumer needs in terms of the grade and type of output) promoted by existing performance indicators, although they did not displace plan (over-)fulfilment as overriding aim.[234]

In addition, the reforms also attempted to tackle the issue of underutilisation of productive capacity. Production goods under the 'classical' system were allocated at zero costs to enterprises in accordance with plan objectives. Man-

231   Nove 1992, p. 296.
232   IMF 1991, p. 9; Ball 2010.
233   Nove 1992, p. 296; Smirnov, Radaeva, Esin, and Rusakov 1979.
234   Ellman 1977, pp. 22–42.

agers therefore tended to lobby for additional free allocations of means of production rather than use existing capacity more productively. To reduce hoarding and to promote the most efficient uses of the limited supply of production
goods, capital charges were introduced in combination with the expansion of
the role for profit.[235] The use of production goods would thereafter require the
payment of a fee, a certain fraction of the costs of production, to be paid to the
authorities as a sort of 'rent', thus factoring means of production into the total
operational costs of enterprises. The idea being that if production goods could
not be used productively, the capital charge imposed on enterprises would
encourage managers to choose the amount of equipment carefully so that overall, the means of production could be used in the capacity where they might
prove most expeditious.

The reintroduction of profit, Soviet theorists proposed, would not resemble
the role of profit in capitalist markets. The profitability of productive activity
would be used only as a control tool, to realise planned output levels while
encouraging a reduction of costs by incorporating the rate of profit into the
success index of the enterprise. Profits obtained by producers would, moreover,
not be pocketed by private individuals, but serve social ends.[236] Since the overall measure of performance of an enterprise became more closely connected
to its rate of profit, enterprises faced somewhat hardened budget constraints,
which successfully reduced the rate of loss-making enterprises in the Soviet
economy.[237] The main defect it sought to address, however, was the persist-
ence of managers to understate productive capacity to allow their enterprises
to overproduce relative to their obligatory plan targets.[238] However, given the
frequency of supply shortages (related mainly to the unreliability of material
balances in achieving consistency), enterprise directors still aimed at slack targets – which could absorb disruptions of supply, and also allowing output in
excess of quotas to be produced with relative ease – and therefore continued
the practice of biasing data. The structure of material incentives still primarily rewarded plan fulfilment and over-fulfilment despite all modifications, and
could scarcely be expected to yield different results.[239] Since the initial reforms
failed to force a breakthrough, a constant series of minor adjustments followed
in relatively close succession. Each modification to the system of compulsory
targets generated only limited overall impact:

---

235   Ellman 1977, p. 25; Wilczynski 1972a, pp. 41–2.
236   Wilczynski 1972b, p. 49.
237   Ellman 1977, p. 77.
238   Ellman 2014, p. 36.
239   Ellman 1977, pp. 31–2; Nove 1992, pp. 383–4; Kornai 2007, pp. 145–7.

They issued instructions that user demand should be met. They modified the bonus systems so that the achievement of purely quantitative
targets should not be sufficient, that the assortment plan had also to be
fulfilled, that costs had to be reduced, the wages plan not exceeded, and
so on. They experimented with a kind of value added indicator known
as 'normed value of processing'. Each of these 'success indicators' had its
own defect, induced its own distortions. Thus, insistence on cost reduction often stood in the way of the making of a better-quality product (...)
The greater the number of indicators, the more likely it was that they
would be inconsistent. Similarly, the greater the number of items and
subitems planned and allocated by the centre, the greater the burden on
the planners and the likelihood of error or delay.[240]

Suppose that manufacturers were instructed to reduce materials consumption in an effort to reduce waste in the economy this might instead compel
producers to reduce the quality of output, conflicting with customer requirements, rather than economise resources more carefully. After all, the response
by producers to such instructions depends on a series of other norms whose
combined effect might be some altogether unintended outcome. For example,
if producers intended to increase their profit but were incapable of horizontal
contracting, being instructed to deliver a certain amount of output at a certain moment in time, they could very well reduce expenditures to lower the
quality of output while being secured of customers that have been instructed
by planners to absorb their output. Furthermore, the increased scope of profit
could not serve as a rational indicator of success insofar as accounting prices
remained largely arbitrary values assigned for the purpose of supervising plan
fulfilment, rather than express relative costs and scarcities – to the extent that
the monetary expressions of costs did not correspond to an actual amount
of material or effort used up in production, profitability was a poor measure
of performance.[241] Strained planning authorities, unable to compute rational
prices corresponding to the costs of production, sometimes relied on the heur-
istic of market prices observed in capitalist economies to come up with valuations for domestic products. Khrushchev reportedly once quipped that 'when
all the world is socialist, Switzerland will have to remain capitalist, so that it
can tell us the price of everything'.

The relaxation of repression in the post-Stalin period had resulted in a cres-
cendoing of complaints by consumers calling for the increased availability and

---

240   Nove 1992, p. 367.
241   Nove 1992, p. 384.

quality of goods.[242] By introducing 'sales' as a performance indicator, it was hoped that output would more closely align with the requirements and preferences for goods. The enterprises were not, however, free to determine the assortment of output based on consumer demand. Instead, each enterprise would receive an aggregated plan. The enterprise was then expected to enter into contractual agreements with customers, after which the plan was referred to higher levels of administrations for approval. This increased the scope of customer input in determining output, and by the same token therefore, reduced the role of higher administrative bodies thereby strengthening the scope of commodity-money relations.[243]

However, public officials balked at any suggestion of incorporating 'subjective preferences' (the structure of consumer demand) in the formation of the value index under socialism since this violated the Marxist theory of value and was thus promptly rejected as.[244] The reform proposals of the 'marketeer' faction bore a likeness to market socialism, in the eyes of the political leadership of the Communist Party.[245] Many of the more substantive reforms were therefore blocked by political interests and the implementation of Kosygin-Liberman reforms were ultimately partially aborted by institutional logic. The breadth, and concomitant to this, the potential for the successful accommodating of a new impulse in the process of socialist construction, was ultimately constrained. Direct allocation, or rationing, of production goods remained the main method for the distribution of productive assets among enterprises, for example. The alternative of horizontal contracting for the acquirement of means of production, semi-manufactured goods, and physical materials; the introduction of wholesale trade in other words, within the confines of administrative central control, did not make it much further than a fairly successful but brief and local experimental phase. Hence, the focus of the reforms again retreated into the familiar territory of improving the existing institutional mechanism of centralised planning, rather than the strengthening of horizontal links and improving local initiative. In this respect, attention was directed to enhancing both the information availability to planners and the techniques to process data.[246] As such:

> [T]he system actually implemented was a compromise, in which institutional changes designed to encourage enterprise management to use

---

242   Wilczynski 1972a, pp. 20–1.
243   Ellman 1977, p. 28.
244   Nove 2011, p. 42; Cockshott and Cottrell 1993, p. 79; Dobb 1967, p. 157.
245   Ellman 1973, p. 133.
246   Ellman 1977, pp. 28–9.

its initiative were effected (e.g. the material incentive fund was created, and formed on a new basis) but they were prevented from having their desired effect by the retention of aspects of the former system of economic administration (the view that inferiors should carry out orders and the formula for determining current managerial bonuses which gives effect to this view).[247]

Soviet growth figures from the 1960s onwards, during the period of Brezhnev's rule, showed decline and stagnation (later dubbed the 'era of stagnation' by Gorbachev). Macroeconomic indicators confirm that the half-hearted reforms were unable to stimulate intensive accumulation. But no substantive efforts were initiated to reverse the negative trends, and the window of opportunity to flesh out reforms and pursue more sustainable and effective solutions had closed as the Brezhnev administration settled into complacency: 'Political attacks soon followed. Censorship was tightened, the possibility of publicly discussing economic problems diminished. Economically, the country deteriorated. The technological gap between the USSR and industrial Western countries widened'.[248]

Indeed, by 1973 only three percent of production goods were bought and sold on the wholesale market, with the rest being allocated directly by political authorities.[249] Other minor reforms sparingly passed by the Politburo were usually stillborn or impotent. 'The authorities were (...) aware of the shortcomings in trade', but addressed these symptoms 'by resorting to administrative methods' such as '[s]tate inspection, the intervention by trade unions or local consumer protection societies, complaints in the press – usually without much lasting improvement – rather than going to the basic causes of these deficiencies'.[250] For example, in the 1980s it was decreed that new performance indicators should be formulated for the transport industry, although no indication was supplied by authorities on how to render transportation more efficient. As such, the transportation branch continued to rely on targets set in ton-kilometres to everyone's deep discontentment.[251] The primary problems of the Soviet economy therefore remained, in summary, 'stagnant technologies', 'resource hoarding, poor information, and poor incentives' which 'resulted in increasing allocative inefficiency'.[252] Or as Devine sums up:

---

247 Ellman 1977, p. 33.
248 Sutela and Mau 1998, p. 62.
249 Nove 2011, p. 29; Ellman 1977, p. 29.
250 Wilczynski 1972a, p. 213.
251 Hanson 1983, p. 1.
252 Escoe 1996, p. 79.

The manifestations of the underlying systemic problems are evident enough: falling rates of economic growth; continuing difficulties in agriculture; poor innovative performance; rising capital-output ratios and evidence of unemployed fixed capital; low labour discipline and morale; low quality output; generalized inefficiency; and low levels of consumer satisfaction.[253]

At this stage, politically complacent conservatism under Brezhnev had been consolidated and the urgency for reform was not sufficiently heeded. The abolition of the 'party maximum' under Stalin had opened the ranks of the Communist Party up to corruption, since privileged benefits – from lodgings and leisure, to provisions – could be obtained by climbing the party's ranks. This pivoted the composition of party membership toward careerists, and entrenched their interests in preserving manual and arbitrary control over the levers of the economy.[254] Thus, the 'selection mechanism for higher personnel was biased in favour of political conformity and against professional qualification' to stabilise party rule.[255] Political corruption, administrative inertia, an atmosphere of public frustration, and economic stagnation marked the Brezhnev period out as an era of general social decline. Under his leadership, social necrosis crept through the social and institutional fibre of Soviet society and chipped away at the belief in a future for socialism.

Over a number of decades, the bombastic veneration of communist ideals via official channels rung progressively hollower and was met with increased public cynicism, even affecting the layers within government and party.[256] Khrushchev's proclamation that communism would be built within a definite time frame was officially abandoned in the final decade of the Soviet Union's lifespan. A testament to the fact that the official communist ideology of the Soviet Union had become a more or less empty husk. Official propaganda was cancelled out by the combination of sobering daily experience under socialism – which, to say the least, did not live up to its ideal – and the uncontrollable penetration of Western popular culture into Soviet civil life, which projected an idealised version of Western life.[257] Popular discontent was, at least in part, fuelled by the purchasing power of ordinary workers falling behind money-

---

253 Devine 2011, p. 60.
254 Veduta 2022.
255 Wagener 1998, p. 14.
256 Nove 1992, pp. 396–7; Wilczynski 1972a, p. 112; Ellman 1973, pp. 144–5; Nove 2011, p. 43; Kornai 2007, pp. 384–5.
257 Nye 2004.

wages, as direct corollary of repressed inflation; while officials (the *'nomen-klatura'* and *'apparatchiks'*) were able to use their personal connections and exclusive shops to acquire scarce means of consumption.[258]

As the Soviet Union lingered, a much more cynical generation of Soviet leaders and policymakers rose through the ranks of the Communist Party disillusioned by the failing promises of communism. Likewise, the optimistic reform socialists were gradually replaced by a pessimistic generation of economists:

> It is impossible in this change to overestimate the generation gap in Russian economists. The socialist reformers were among those Soviet intellectuals to whom the formative experience had been the anti-Stalinism of the 20th Party Congress in 1956. A surprising number of them were actually born in 1936–7, at the height of the terror. Their thinking was that of socialist renewal. The economists of the Gaidar [the architect of shock liberalisation and privatisation] generation were typically born in the mid-1950s. Their years of formative experience were the years of Brezhnevite stagnation. They had little trust in the socialist perspective.[259]

Sometimes candidly, sometimes secretly, sometimes sincerely, sometimes deceptively, they professed support for a restoration of capitalism, usually under the guise of reinventing socialism as a social-democratic mixed economy. Yeltsin – formerly a member of the Politburo, who, in his capacity as its first president would oversee the passage of Russia into capitalist waters by means of destructive shock therapy – in 1989 expressed a sentiment which had increasingly found traction, even amongst party officials, when he professed himself a social-democrat and stated that '[t]hose who still believe in communism are moving in the sphere of fantasy'.[260] This degeneration of ideological rigidity and party discipline was in no small part the result of would-be careerists pursuing party membership, which was a precondition for social climbing.[261]

After the halted structural adjustments of the Kosygin-Liberman period, no substantial reforms would be undertaken until 1985–1987. Instead, attempts to reverse negative trends involved the familiar recipe of refining existing institutional features, i.e. dealing with symptoms rather than underlying causes. For instance, when labour morale dipped, it was addressed by tightening discipline;

---

258 For example: Ironside 2021.
259 Sutela and Mau 1998, pp. 54–5.
260 In Breslauer 2002.
261 Devine 2011, p. 119.

the response to poor grade output was increased surveillance and quality control; and instructions to increase investments in new technologies were issued to address slow technical progress. Predictably, the policies, like those before them, were mostly ineffectual.[262] As such, the reforms in the late 1980s were a last-ditch effort to address the chronic inefficiencies that debilitated the Soviet economy. In the late 1980s, increased military spending and the fall in prices of primary commodities such as oil on the world market – on which the Soviet Union depended heavily[263] – put additional strain on the buckling economy.

Starting in 1985, a process of major restructuring of the Soviet economy began. If successful, the reforms would transition the Soviet Union into market socialism, with somewhat expanded political rights, at the cost of expansive social rights.[264] Effectively two reform tracks were developed: 'market socialism based upon self-management and market socialism based upon such quasi-state capital managers as banks or funds',[265] which would ultimately be combined incoherently.

Like the Kosygin-Liberman reforms before it, the restructuring ('*perestroika*') reforms attempted to devolve responsibilities in an effort to stimulate productivity and overcome bureaucracy-induced atrophy of morale and initiative. The restructuring of the economy would need to remedy 'inefficiency, poor quality, and lagging technological development'.[266] Gorbachev re-attempted to expand the latitude of enterprises in setting prices, negotiating contracts, and investment decision-making. Additionally, budget constraints were hardened in order to motivate managers to improve productivity and efficiency, rather than seek refuge in subsidies or financial assistance.[267] This ran into more or less the same difficulties of both internal opposition from officials and institutional incoherence which had inhibited the full implementation of earlier reforms of the 1960s.[268] As Ellman had cautioned:

> The elements of the economic system are closely linked together, and this must be borne in mind when introducing reforms. The price system, the supply system, the incentive system, the criteria used, and the degree of centralisation are inseparably interconnected. For example, to give the

262   IMF 1991, p. 19.
263   IMF 1991, pp. 14, 23–4.
264   IMF 1991, p. 25; Cook 1992, p. 37.
265   Sutela and Mau 1998, p. 52.
266   IMF 1991, p. 19.
267   Ellman 2014, p. 253.
268   Nove 1992, pp. 394–5.

enterprise more autonomy in determining its assortment pattern, given the existing price system, is scarcely likely to increase efficiency.[269]

Due to the years of neglect under Brezhnev, reforms had to be expedited. However, an overhaul of the entire institutional arrangement would risk certain collapse of the whole edifice. Careful navigation, evading erring too much into one direction or the other, was required to preserve the Soviet Union on the foundations of some genre of socialism.

In 1987 followed an additional reform, the 'Law on State Enterprises', which promised to be a substantial revision of the fundamental nature of the Soviet economy. Rather than receive centrally mandated gross output targets, enterprises would, starting in 1988, be free to enter into contractual agreements with suppliers and customers, horizontally, and would be permitted a greater degree of independence in investment and reinvestment decision-making. Thus, detailed planning and the co-ordination of activities would be delegated downwards, to the enterprise level. Meanwhile, strategic planning as well as control of macroeconomic proportions would remain in the hands of central authorities. Further, the planning authorities would prescribe a number of mandated state orders, to ensure that enterprise activity could be directed toward what was considered politically expedient – political command, then, remained an instrument, albeit circumscribed, in theory. In practice, state orders would account for ninety percent of the output:

> This was partly a result of planners and branch ministries wanting to ensure supplies of low-profit or lossmaking items. But it also reflected pressure from enterprises themselves who, in an economy prone to chronic shortages and distribution failures, wanted the assurance of a guaranteed source of inputs to meet their own state orders.[270]

Further, independent economic accounting ('*khozraschet*') was increased as enterprises were expected to self-finance, i.e. rely on their own revenue for investment. Enterprise directors were, however, unaccustomed to negotiating via horizontal links along the supply chain. There was a lack of knowledge, experience, and information flows that could facilitate this effectively.[271] Horizontal links, therefore, remained underdeveloped, and consequently, in face of uncertainty, enterprises scaled up their hoarding, exacerbating disruptions of

---

269   Ellman 1973, p. 55.
270   IMF 1991, p. 26.
271   Nove 1992, p. 398.

supply.[272] This was further compounded by the fact that enterprises were now at liberty to change the assortment of output:[273]

> Given the freedom to decide on the distribution of their production funds (the income of enterprises), they focussed strongly on the wage base. In addition they tended to alter their production focus towards more expensive goods, which resulted in increasing incomes for enterprises, hidden inflation and a shortage of consumer goods.[274]

Thus, perverse incentives combined with greater freedom to act on them logically exacerbated many economic problems. The traditional supply links, which were in the process of disintegrating, conflicted with the horizontally established supply links, which were only in an embryonic stage of development. The overall result was economic chaos:

> The only practical outcome of [reform] inclinations was the 1987 [Law on State Enterprises] which decreed elected managers and enterprise self-finance. The intention was to have 'more democracy, more socialism' and to undermine the powers of the ministries. Among the outcomes were high inflation and the beginnings of spontaneous privatization.[275]

Previously, in the experimental phase of the Kosygin-Liberman reforms, vested interests in society – within the Communist Party and various other political institutions – handicapped the implementation of the reforms. Intermediate bodies would sometimes refuse to acknowledge the special status of some factories that were mandated to experiment with horizontal contracting.[276] The result was a partial retreat from the Kosygin-Liberman reforms in practice, a compromise of half-measures which was overall little effective and allowed the problems to fester until they threatened the Soviet system with acute collapse. Similarly, the application of cybernetics, as we saw, was deliberately circumscribed owing to political interests, in addition to technological constraints. In the 1980s, local authorities again 'proved generally uncooperative', and thwarted the issuing of new licences for private businesses and co-

---

272   IMF 1991, p. 27.
273   Ellman and Kontorovich 2013, pp. 23–4.
274   Kalyuzhnova 1998, p. 22.
275   Sutela and Mau 1998, p. 53.
276   Tubis 1973, p. 95.

operatives.[277] To curtail bureaucratic sabotage of the reforms, Gorbachev promoted the notion of open public discussion, scrutiny, and criticism – in a word, 'openness' ('*glasnost*'). This included, but was not limited to, the introduction of worker participation at the workplace-level through the election of committees.[278] Glasnost resulted in an open outpouring of unabated criticism of the Soviet system by economists and others. Where previously human error and scapegoats were the means to deflect criticism from the Soviet system itself, the underlying causes could now be subjected to scrutiny.[279] The economists used their new-found freedom to call attention to egregious misallocation, waste, distortions, falsified data, and the systemic causes that underpinned such problems.

The role of the Communist Party in society was also reduced. The dislodging of the Communist Party from its economic role proved ill-advised, however, at least in the short-run. As noted previously, the Communist Party played an integrative role in the Soviet economy, by aligning the conduct of all layers of the administrative hierarchy, from the enterprise upwards, with central directives. The withdrawal of the Communist Party increased the anarchy of production by rendering central command ineffective, without an appropriate alternative being in place.[280] Of course, the reforms:

> were bound to conflict initially if the reform were truly radical, as it would involve at least short-run disruption of traditional links between suppliers and customers and modernization based on an evolving restructured base rather than the traditional industrial structure.[281]

In some sense, the reforms were hastened with disastrous effects, yet haste was appropriate given the moribund state of the economy as a result of the decades of neglect under Brezhnev. The reforms were too little in some sense, but too much in another. They challenged vested power in a way that would drag the entire system along with it. The dissolution of the Soviet Union, then, cannot be attributed to the loss of political command, as is typically claimed by contemporary advocates of Marxism-Leninism.[282] (In addition, it is difficult to draw out the political implications of such an analysis. If political purges, strict

277   IMF 1991, p. 22.
278   Devine 2011, p. 77.
279   Nove 2011, p. 43.
280   Ellman 2014, p. 82.
281   IMF 1991, p. 25.
282   Ball 2010; KKE 2009; Keeran and Kenny 2010.

ideological instruction and a monopoly on power by the Communist Party has repeatedly shown itself inadequate in addressing revisionism, it is unclear how future endeavours might result in a different conclusion.) There were, as we have hoped to summarise succinctly, very real innate material causes – internal contradictions, if you will – to the decline of Soviet socialism. Ultimately, the inability of socialism to reform itself on a democratic basis, to reconcile the contradictions of central direction with the need to strengthen horizontal link-ages and to issue correct incentives, ultimately shifted reform thought further in the direction of liberalisation. The failure to reform along the lines of the proposals of the reform socialists during the peak of their momentum has foreclosed an enormous opportunity for socialist renewal. By the time some half-attempt in this direction was made, the popular belief in socialism had already largely evaporated. As Sheehan remarked in her personal reflections:

> After Gorbachev came to power and all through the upheavals of 1989, I still found it possible to hope that the promises of glasnost and peres-troika would be fulfilled, to believe that the time had come for socialism with a human face, socialism with a fresh and truthful voice, socialism with democracy, socialism with economic efficiency, socialism with a flourishing civil society. But by 1990, it became clear that this was not on, not for this period of history. It became painfully clear that what we were witnessing was the restoration of capitalism and not the renewal of social-ism.[283]

We now face an uphill struggle in breathing new life into the idea of socialism.

Addendum: Sharing in the Illusion – On the Question of State-Capitalism

The aim of this chapter has not been to give undue weight to the defects of the Soviet system, at the expense of sketching a more balanced narrative. The intention is not to prove what is now conventional wisdom: that Soviet social-ism was horridly inefficient economically, and barbarously oppressive polit-ically. This is hardly worth the trouble rehashing. As a matter of fact, today it is impossible to suggest otherwise. An incontestable consensus has taken shape passing final judgement that socialism was an irredeemable and cata-

---

283   Sheehan 1989.

strophic economic failure, a contemporary prism through which we now per-
ceive and judge the entire history of socialism. While this consensus is not
entirely without its merits – the problems of socialism were real and deeply
rooted – we should 'be wary of a historical amnesia that blinds us to the actual
accomplishments of these first experiments in socialism':[284]

> What are we to make of it now? Was it a false dawn of a new day that has
> not yet come? Or will it disappear without trace? How many times have
> we heard in recent times voices from Eastern Europe speaking of scrap-
> ping 74, 51, 46 years of history and starting again at zero? There will be no
> starting again at zero. This vast experiment in human history has cut too
> deeply into the psyche, too deeply into the rhythms of history, to disap-
> pear without trace.[285]

In reconnecting our current study into socialism to the historical literature, we
find a somewhat different treatment of socialism; one that does not fully correspond to the current one-dimensional reputation borne by socialism. For all
their faults, many of these countries managed to grow their economies at rapid
rates, allowing workers to enjoy growing incomes with small pay differentials,
combined with free access to many social services, all this in spite of – I am
tempted to stress – the enormous amounts of waste co-produced by the system of centralised planning. Many socialist countries achieved growth rates
that rivalled the economic 'miracles' of the likes of South Korea or Singapore.
This earned socialism a certain level of prestige that few are today willing to
afford it.

The list of estimable feats accomplished by the Soviet Union that we can
counter-pose to the long list of structural deficiencies is exhaustive indeed. It
includes a wide range of social benefits: from a high level of cultural and social
development of the Soviet citizenry (in spite of political censorship); widely
available social and healthcare services at zero or low costs; far-reaching gender
equality in the natural sciences; a high average caloric intake (contrary to conventional wisdom); affordable living space (average housing costs amounted to
2–3 percent of household budgets); and more[286] – not to mention the unima-
ginable hardships and sacrifices endured by the peoples of the Soviet Union
in their resolve to halt the extermination campaign of Nazi Germany and their
allies, stopping the physical annihilation of entire ethnicities in its tracks, at

---

284   Schweickart 2002, p. 58.
285   Sheehan 1989.
286   Keeran and Kenny 2010, pp. 2–3.

an inconceivable loss of civilian and military life of up to 26 million Soviet citizens. As socialism collapsed, social security dissipated, average caloric intake plummeted, corruption surged, material deprivation exploded, the popular dissatisfaction with capitalism grew when the spoils of shock privatisation were pocketed by an ascendant oligarchy. It is hardly surprising considering such developments that nostalgia for the communist past is fairly widespread in many formerly socialist countries (nor, for that matter, should it be surprising that the general population in these countries are vulnerable to the poisonous influences of chauvinism).

At the same time, there can be no doubt that unconscionable atrocities of significant scale were committed in the name of communism generally, and Marxism-Leninism specifically. There is no need to distort and diminish such facts in an attempt to stave off criticism from socialism. If we proceed to identify ourselves with the socialist tradition we inadvertently reconcile ourselves to this legacy and should therefore assume responsibility.

Marxism-Leninism is not an aberration of some truer version of Marxism, falsely camouflaging itself under the colours of Marxism or Leninism. Many of the basic principles of Marxism-Leninism can be traced rather directly to the origins of Marxism. Particularly the belief in the rational and conscious direction of regimentally socialised production and the notion that individuated particular interests do not exist or can be perfectly reconciled to the social interest under socialism. Such notions are not alien imports, but outgrowths of kernels present at the inception of 'classical' Marxism, nurtured to fruition under the duress of the particular conditions in which the Russian Revolution took place (including the strategic and ideological orientation of the Bolsheviks themselves). In this respect, 'anti-Leninist' Marxism is an aberration. We necessarily inherited and build upon the chequered legacy of Marxism-Leninism, and moving forward requires full cognizance of this knowledge. Thus our current objective of socialist regeneration will have to move straight through the Soviet experience which occupies a central place in our movement's history, rather than by circumventing it – in effect, our socialism can only be one of post-Marxism-Leninism.

While we obviously do not bear personal or criminal responsibility for the criminal actions of communist governments, we do bear responsibility for our self-identification and ideological affiliation that links us to the history of these egregious acts and therefore, in our capacity as advocates for socialism, owe some accountability. This would entail: (i) an acknowledgement and recognition of the facts themselves and of the fact they were perpetrated by socialist regimes and in the name of socialism; and (ii) a clarification as to how socialism, going forward, should stray from flagrant, violent, arbitrary excesses by unveiling the structural causes that sustained such behaviour, rather than dismissing them as personal errors, historical contingencies, or ideological drift. In other words, to rehabilitate socialism we need to exhibit a serious commitment to improvement in this area. The position that we should learn from the past cannot stand as an excuse to refrain from criticising some of the historical choices and actions made by socialists, sweeping these matters under the rug. There is no mechanically carrying out the *telos* of history alleviating anyone of their moral responsibility for the choices made within historical circumstances not of their own making – actions that produce material effects are always mediated by reflective thought and calculations.

On that account, the purpose of detailing, albeit concisely, the flaws of the Soviet economic mechanism is to recover lessons that could help future socialist initiatives. Logically then, this chapter has focussed on the deep-seated weaknesses of the Soviet model, since these will have to be remedied by any prospective socialist endeavour. Given the clear failings of Marxism-Leninism in this respect, it may be tempting to disassociate from this bastard child of communism, denying kinship altogether. Indeed, many theorists have done so by disqualifying the Soviet experience as 'state-capitalism'.[287] A few words will be reserved here to address this typological matter. While it is of secondary importance, insofar as lessons might be recovered for socialism from a variety of non-socialist practices, it does direct our attention to the question of what socialism is and is not, which evidently conditions our approach to socialism.

The basic argument of the theory of state-capitalism, for all its variety and particularities, is that the *fundamental characteristics* of capitalism were operational and dominant in the Soviet Union, albeit concentrated in the state – hence, *state*-capitalism (with the notable exception of Bordiga, who rejected that a meaningful distinction could be drawn between liberal-capitalism and state-capitalism). The argument is briefly as follows. Instead of a judicially fractured class of individual capitalists, each owning an individual share of the total capital, all capital in Soviet society was legally concentrated and considered state property, controlled by the hands of the officials at the apex of the party hierarchy. This caste of party officials exercised effective control over the means of production, choosing how to combine them with labour and physical materials to ensure a cycle of expanded reproduction of capital. By directing this process of capital accumulation through exclusive domain over the levers of state power, these public officials carved out a portion of the surplus product for themselves, in the form of privileged access to material benefits inaccess-

287   For an overview of theories see Van der Linden 2007.

ible to ordinary workers, reinforcing the idea of a class of proletarians exploited by a layer of bureaucrats, which was, in functional terms, capitalist.

Since workers were separated in every meaningful way (legally and actually) from the means of production, they confronted the objective tools of their labour as alien condition. Without any other recourse to acquire means of subsistence but to surrender their labour-power to the collective owner of the total capital of society, the party-state, in exchange for wages, the Soviet worker was effectively reduced to the status of proletarian. In other words, their propertyless circumstances compelled workers to enter into a relationship of wage-labour with the state to secure their material reproduction. By means of this relationship, surplus product was squeezed from the producer in order to fund the industrialisation drive (or the accumulation of capital) and helped finance privileged access to comforts and amenities for those that made up the ranks of the bureaucracy. Having no control over the conditions of production, the means of production, and surplus product, the working class was no more free from exploitation than their proletarian counterparts in the West. Aside from the formal appearance of universal state ownership, all the elements of the capitalist mode of production seem to have operated in the socialist bloc countries.

One would be tempted to draw the conclusion that the socialist outer appearance of the Soviet Union was part of an ideological façade inadvertently concealing the underlying, capitalist essence contained in the mode of production. The structural imperatives of capitalist relations were absorbed and internalised by the political leadership, all the while earnestly professing themselves Marxists. The socialism of the Soviet leadership was the subjective form assumed by the objective requirements by history for the development of capitalist relations of production. By taking these outward professions and ideological forms to be the motive force behind the social transformation, we fall into the trap of idealism that Marx had described: 'the "conception" of the people in question about their real practice is transformed into the sole determining and effective force, which dominates and determines their practice' and we therefore come to 'share in the illusion of the epoch'.[288] By a perverse twist of history, a unique constellation of objective and subjective forces had aligned to cause this ideological 'illusion', which cloaked the bourgeois revolution taking place in Russia in the form of Marxism. It is by piercing this outward appearance that we grasp the inner logic and expose the rapid industrialisation as a strategy for commodification and proletarianisation orchestrated by the Soviet regime for the harnessing of the forces of capitalist development. Soviet socialism was,

288 MECW 5: 55.

in effect, markedly more capitalist in nature than the regime it replaced. The party-state, then, was functionally bourgeois in overthrowing absolutist fetters and promoting capitalist relations of production.

Chattopadhyay further argued that the law of value asserted itself in an essentially indistinguishable way from its operation under the liberal capitalism of the West.[289] Namely via the competition of capitals. The law of value is the disciplinary mechanism guiding the choices of capitalists. It does so through the confrontation of individual capitals on the market. It is here that the *social* character of production is established by comparing the results of 'private labours' of individual capitals, their commodities, by means of exchange relations in the market. The market subsequently disciplines the various firms according to the extent that they have used up more or less social labour time in the production of their output, relative to the current level of social demand. It is this competition of capitals (which by no means implies an ideal-typical, textbook version of the free market) that underpins the logic of the capitalist mode of production. Should we discover any other disciplinary mechanism as the instrument structuring the allocation of resources in a particular mode of production, it cannot be qualified as capitalist – this serves as our basic criterium for the classification of capitalism, therefore.

Chattopadhyay's argument, which is arguably the most sophisticated variant of the theory of state-capitalism (at least as far as my knowledge extends), posits that the exchange of commodities between state enterprises can be understood as the confrontation between distinct units of capital, and hence as 'competition of capitals'. The circulation of commodities was assured via exchange on the market, facilitated by money (the universal equivalent of commodities). While in a formal-judicial sense, each enterprise belonged to a single owner (i.e. the party-state), the fact that commodities changed hands upon payment necessarily implies that they were engaged in external exchange relations between separate units. The content behind the formal-judicial, 'phenomenological' appearance reveal the existence of relations of reciprocal independence between firms. Each enterprise acting to augment the value of commodities as they passed through, exchanging them to realise a profit to appropriate surplus product on behalf of the party-state. If, by contrast, all labour in the Soviet Union was immediately part of the total labour of society, as in societies of a pre-industrial and communal character for example, the objectified results of labour would not have to assume the form of commodities to realise their social character. In their mutual interrelations, each Soviet 'enterprise'

---

289   Chattopadhyay 1994.

traded their objects of labour amongst each other to co-ordinate the social labour executed independently and 'privately' (meaning, without being structured by means of direct social direction). By virtue of the relations established in exchange, the social character of these objects was established indirectly thus transforming them into commodities. Furthermore, the trade of commodities was subjected to profit-and-loss accounting to discipline the manufacturers and suppliers in reducing costs and increasing returns. Under capitalism, this compulsion to improve value is not imposed from without by some authority, but emerged from endogenously, by the emergent forces generated in the processes of market competition.

   If this reasoning is correct, it follows that the accumulation of capital into the hands of the functional bourgeoisie was the motive force behind production and distribution under Soviet rule. Moreover, this imperative should exist independently of conscious will, emerging instead in the process of the competition of capital on pain of bankruptcy, or at any rate, inferior performance in the area of profit. The enterprise managers, where it concerns the execution of their economic tasks, merely embodied the function of capital, the logic of capital accumulation acting through them. The proof submitted by Chattopadhyay to substantiate his theory of state-capitalism is that this was more or less freely admitted by the political leadership of the Soviet Union. They explicitly proclaimed, he points out, that the Soviet Union should grow their national income to surpass the West, and thereby prove the superiority of socialist methods of accumulation. This process of capital accumulation was cloaked in a veneer of socialist ideology, a sort of 'red-washing' at the surface-level of the USSR. At best, as per the state-capitalist theorem, we can admit that this was a different, alternative strategy to accumulate capital, but not that the rudimentary laws of motion capitalism were suspended in the Soviet Union. Hence, submitted Chattopadhyay, the Soviet economy can be described, explained, and understood by reference to the same categories developed by Marx to analyse capitalism.

   The crude 'structuralist functionalism' of this sort of reasoning aside, the reasoning may seem attractive at first glance. It appropriates the dialectical language of Marxism to seemingly penetrate the outward appearance, the formal socialist façade, of Soviet society to reveal the hidden, capitalist essence underneath – the dirty little secret of Soviet 'socialism'. In so doing, it absolves socialism of responsibility for the terrorism and economic dysfunction of the Soviet Union (and emulations elsewhere). Socialists do not have to grapple with difficult questions, or to deal with the fallout of the Soviet Union, or to subject their views to introspection. The slate of socialism has been wiped clean by a theoretical sleight. However, the theorem of 'state-capitalism' quickly falls apart under closer examination of the inner working of Soviet-style economies. Especially in the early pre-reform period of Soviet planning (roughly from 1929 until 1965), production was organised on the basis of administrative-political control. Firms did not set output targets on the basis of profit-and-loss considerations. As a matter of fact, they did not set output targets at all. Instructions of this kind were passed down the hierarchy of planning offices. While enterprises made counter-suggestions, they had no real discretion concerning their operations. Enterprises could not exchange goods freely, in the interests of accumulating capital or maximising their profit, but were subject to orders passed down by political fiat. That is to say, the allocation of resources, and the regulation and co-ordination of social production was determined via a vertical chain of command. In other words, through instructions within *directly social relations* – even if the transparency and labour time calculations, which were supposed to underpin the communist mode of production, could not be established directly as a result of substantial information constraints involved in direct co-ordination.

For the law of value to manifest it is required that individual units of capital confront each other and establish exchange relations, which gives rise to competitive compulsions (acting back on producers as an alien, external force) outside of conscious control. In the Soviet economy, on the contrary, the volume of production in aggregate and disaggregate terms were determined by the central planning authorities, based primarily on political criteria. Output targets were not set on the basis of profit calculations at either the central level or at the level of individual enterprises. The overriding aim was to grow the stock of means of production – this much is true. But this accumulation imperative did not grew out of competitive pressures involved in the war for profits. The goal of economic activity under Soviet-style socialism was consciously defined and subsequently imposed by political means. According to Kornai, Soviet-style socialism was 'a semimonetized system':

> In terms of formal features, the classical socialist system is a monetized economy. But if one analyzes the actual processes behind the formal facade (...) it turns out there is merely an apparent monetization in many respects, since the role played by money in some of the relations is only weak or secondary. The desire to abolish money (...) has been granted in part after all.[290]

---

290   Kornai 2007, p. 131.

Thus, the reverse of the state-capitalist theorem appears to be true. The outward appearance did not consist in a 'socialist façade' concealing generalised commodity relations; instead the extant money-commodity relations camouflaged the extent to which centralised planning had in actual fact been demonetised and decommodified.

Since, in the Soviet Union, the allocation of goods was organised on the basis of instructions issued by planning authorities – prices, sales, and even labour-power (under Stalin) were fixed administratively, rather than determined by the market – money played a mere passive role.[291] It logically follows that the law of value could not have been operational in the Soviet Union then. Stalin's comments in chapter 3 of *Economic Problems of Socialism in the USSR* that indicate the contrary seem misguided. Such admissions are frequently invoked as a shorthand proof of the Soviet regime's degeneration, but they are a poor substitute for substantive inquiry into the actual material reproduction of Soviet society. (Lenin's comments about 'admitting' to building state-capitalism in Soviet Russia have suffered similar abuse.) Planning, for example, was done in physical units using material balances as money-values were largely arbitrary. This in itself is a damning piece of evidence that knocks down the foundation of the theorem of state-capitalism: if prices are arbitrary and fixed administratively (i.e. they do not correspond to actual costs) they cannot, axiomatically, refract the socially necessary labour time embodied in products and therefore social production cannot be regulated by the law of value. Thus, even if commodities in the Soviet Union were exchanged freely on the basis of said arbitrary prices, the law of value could not be operational because prices would not bear any correspondence to actual labour values.

While it is certainly true that money was transferred alongside physical throughput as it passed from one enterprise to another, this does not mean we can infer from this the existence of 'commodity exchange', the 'law of value', nor the 'competition of capitals'. The circulation of commodities was, after all, achieved by the issuing of binding instructions by planning authorities based on material balance sheets, and expressed these orders in gross output targets, usually measured in physical units. When allocation under the Soviet economic system is analysed in its dynamic, *active* interaction, one is quickly forced to concede that money in Soviet planning played a subordinate, secondary role. In the sphere of production and allocation, it acted as a supervisory tool to audit producers and check their compliance in fulfilling their obligatory output targets. Material goods were transferred, of course, but not upon the initiative of

---

291   Kornai 2007, p. 133.

the enterprises, and certainly not according to their financial bidding or commercial interests – except in the sphere of illicit exchange.

The existence of prices, exchange, and the commodity-form under Soviet-style socialism were surface phenomena that did not correspond to an underlying organising principle of market competition. The existence of commodity exchange – an economic phenomenon predating capitalism, incidentally – in itself does not automatically call into existence the competitive market pressures that make the continual expansion of productive powers of capital a force of economic necessity. Only when the development of the productive forces engender a cycle of expanded reproduction outside immediate, conscious control, in other words when the sum of market exchanges becomes an unconscious, externalised force that acts back on producers, can we speak of social production being regulated by the competition of capitals. In this capacity, the behaviour of firms and choices by capitalists are subject to law-like forces of the market – the 'law of value', in Marxist thought. The logic contained in the circuit of capital is not the conscious will of any one in particular. On the contrary, in the Soviet Union, the imperative to grow the stock of production goods did not emerge spontaneously from market pressures independent of an overarching consciously defined purpose, but was instead an expression of explicit political will, imposed by administrative command. Accumulation, it should be remembered, is not at all synonymous with the accumulation of *capital*. Communism would be oriented toward an accumulation of use-values to usher in an age of abundance, for example. The cycle of expanded reproduction in the Soviet Union was not propelled forward by market compulsions, but instead reflected conscious political command which structured production and distribution by administrative means in an attempt to secure politically formulated strategic objectives – the Soviet mode of production abided an entirely different logic than one that grows out of the competition of capitals.

Chattopadhyay's preoccupation with the forms of appearances of Soviet society – despite his best efforts to go beyond them – lead him astray, since money and commodity exchange were but forms of appearance behind which lied the essence to the material reproduction of Soviet society: political-administrative command.

If the argument becomes instead that the central planners acted singularly as the collective capitalist over the entire economy, then the argument about the law of value falls flat on its face insofar as the 'law of value' does not operate internal to enterprises, and therefore, by analogy, would not have operated within the Soviet Union. Where Chattopadhyay offered arguably the most coherent and sophisticated theory of state-capitalism, the theory of Cliff, an unorthodox Trotskyist, is arguably the most widely held. Unlike Chattopadhyay,

Cliff admits that administrative-political command over the Soviet economy necessarily implies that the law of value could not operate within the domestic economy. According to him, however, the law of value was imprinted on the Soviet economy through its interactions on the world market.[292] This argument too seems untenable. First, in relation to the Soviet economy's own internal reproduction, to the extent that the law of value does not regulate social production, which Cliff conceded it could not, the Soviet economy cannot be classified as capitalist in nature. Second, the interaction of the Soviet Union on the world market after World War II was largely confined to trade with other socialist countries, and, moreover, trade policy insulated economic units from the external effects of trade through variable taxes and subsidies, to align the price levels to the administratively fixed accounting prices – a 'price equalization mechanism'.[293] Furthermore, the commission of trade between socialist countries (and frequently capitalist countries as well) was done through barter. Thus, it 'was not customary to measure foreign trade in terms of money and profit'.[294] The retort, that the USSR was forced to compete indirectly, namely politically and militarily, with the Western imperialist core, is unconvincing since the logic of military and political competition is conceptually distinct from the competition of capitals. If, as noted previously, the accumulation regime is not driven by a logic of competitive pressures that emerge from market relations, we can disqualify any claim of capitalism.

Van der Walt argues somewhat similarly that anarchists may disregard the argument that the law of value did not operate within the Soviet Union.[295] First, the tradition of anarchism is not beholden to the theory of the law of value, he points out; anarchists do not typically regard this as the defining characteristic of capitalism. Second, he argues, the Soviet Union could be regarded as a gigantic indivisible capitalist firm, which was forced to compete internationally. Of course, the latter argument – theoretically less polished than Cliff's – holds no real weight, since the Soviet Union barely took part in international trade. If we abstract all the particularities and strip capital down to its essential functions, then we arrive at a conception of capital that would roughly encompass the following. A 'unit of capital' participates in the exchange of commodities, to acquire their input (labour-power, materials, equipment), augmenting them in order to produce output which is then sold on the market to obtain returns, to recoup their investments, to carve out their share in the

292   Cliff 1974, Chapter 7.
293   Brus and Łaski 1989, p. 41; IMF 1991, p. 10; Kornai 2007, p. 358.
294   Kornai 2007, p. 359.
295   In Van der Walt and Schmidt 2009, p. 105.

market, and thus to turnover profit. Capitalist firms set investment targets in relation to the imperative to grow, in other words, to actively involve themselves in commodity exchange to conquer some part of the market to secure their profits. By contrast, the Soviet government set investment goals in relation to domestic priorities, while attempting to isolate itself the market as much as possible, by minimising the inputs acquired on the market and consuming their products domestically as much as possible, not seeking to obtain profits by exporting it back to the world market. It would be difficult to qualify this pattern of behaviour as, at its most charitable, anomalous for capital to withdraw from markets and to forego profit maximisation in favour of domestic consumption of resources.

Upon examination, we inevitably arrive at the conclusion that we cannot prod, probe, twist, or massage the facts to fit the Soviet Union into the classification of capitalism. It begs the question as to how it should be categorised instead. Ticktin has argued that it was a social deformation, a historical aberration. He maintains that the Soviet mode of production was socially non-viable and therefore does not warrant the predicate 'mode of production' at all.[296] Due to its inherent dysfunctionality, it was a temporary abnormality destined to disappear. Indeed, with its many deformations, it is difficult to not describe the Soviet Union as an aberration of sorts. Detractors of socialism will of course contend that any attempt to do away with capitalism will inevitably lead to such distortions, proving socialism's impossibility. According to this logic, it would be fallacious to dismiss the claim that the Soviet Union was socialistic on account of the malformations, since these inevitably arise when society attempts to transform itself in a socialist direction. Likewise, it would also be fallacious to argue that the existence of deformations in Soviet-style socialism disprove its socialist credentials even under the assumption that an alternative, feasible socialism is viable. It does not follow from the premise that since the Soviet system was fundamentally dysfunctional (or 'socially non-viable') that it cannot also be described as socialist – we must surely admit the theoretical possibility of socialism, in one form or another (perhaps all of them), being socially non-viable. Finally, while opportunities for a renewal of socialism from within were exceedingly slim, it is a stretch to say that reform was categorically out of the question and collapse inevitable. Currents to reform socialism on a new basis emerged from within and, in the case of Czechoslovakia, had to be stopped by military force from without – a contingent factor, to be certain.

---

296   Ticktin 1992.

> What was done was done in the name of socialism and it encompassed the efforts of honest men and women who believed in it and worked for it and who did achieve much that deserves to be called socialism. (...) We need to defend the socialism of the past, in these days of unprecedented slander of it, even as we take a severely critical view of it. It was a radical shift in productive relations, a radical social transformation. It was imperfect, glaringly, screamingly, tragically so. It came to embrace elements utterly alien to its original impulses.[297]

It is far easier for those to the left of Marxism-Leninism to selectively romanticise and appropriate untainted communist heroes and martyrs, as well as popular songs and communist symbols as icons for their own ends – perhaps Hannie Schaft, Amílcar Cabral, Margarita Tutulani, Rosa Luxemburg, Stjepan Filipović, or Fred Hampton – who are beyond controversy insofar as they never exercised power, than it is to account for the full scope of communist history, including its darker episodes. We cannot lay claim to the social advancements and heroic sacrifices of socialism, without also admitting complicity in criminal errors.

Thus, for now I am satisfied with settling, tentatively, on the postulation that the Soviet Union was some form of socialism – and by extension, that 'actually existing socialism' or 'Soviet-style socialism' are appropriate labels to designate this type of mode of production. This leaves open the possibility that it could be characterised as a *socialism with aberrations*, a *socialism with malfunctions*, a *socialism maladapted to the purpose of socialism* or whatever else. Further commentary on this question lies beyond the scope of this inquiry. What is relevant here is that the Soviet leadership sought, for better or for worse, to move beyond the relations and categories of capitalism, and succeeded in displacing market competition and the profit motive from an industrial regime for the first time in history, guiding production and distribution instead by direct allocation, calculated mostly in physical quantities, and directed production by setting gross output targets. This momentous development in the history of socialism warrants due consideration and substantive scrutiny, rather than withdrawing into disowning and repudiating the experience as 'state-capitalism', scrubbing the record clean, precluding having to face difficult questions of socialist construction. To afford socialism a fighting chance going forward, we have to resolutely confront the uncomfortable and the inconvenient instead of sanitising our history.

---

297   Sheehan 1989.

Socialism in Practice – The Yugoslav Model

The attempt in the late 1980s to carry the Soviet Union into a new era on the back of market socialism, if this experiment had been allowed to be played out, would not necessarily have been some final revelation, turning socialism back from the brink of collapse. So much is proved by Yugoslavia. There is no need to shy away from the ultimate conclusion of this experiment, since the tragic disintegration of the country's socialist project at the hands of irredentism, separatism, and chauvinism, in the wake of protracted economic crisis, is well-known. What justifies our revisitation of the Yugoslav model of socialism is its unique experimentation with a form of market socialism that combined competitive market exchange with labour-managed firms, which took place from 1952 until 1989. This set Yugoslavia's socialism apart from Soviet-style socialism. It was 'the most comprehensive longer-term attempt to establish popular selfgovernment in history'. As such, analysing it 'is a very useful starting point for the future'.[1]

The roots of this unique experiment lie in World War II. After the liberation of Yugoslavia at the hands of the communist-led partisan front from occupation by the Axis powers, the Yugoslav communist leadership did not simply follow obediently in the tracks of Soviet-style socialism. The Yugoslav communists defied dictates issued by the Kremlin and charted a distinctive path in the construction of socialism in their homeland. Instead of using state-centric methods of accumulation, the Yugoslav regime promoted various organs of self-government in an attempt to involve the working population directly in the running of the economy and wider society. Formal decision-making power was devolved downwards, to workers' councils. The decentralisation of decision-making power meant that the principal mechanism for the co-ordination of economic activity became market exchange between labour-managed firms. This socialist experiment was, and remains, unique. In the eyes of many commentators, it marked Yugoslavia out as a living alternative to the self-serving bureaucracy that characterised Soviet-style socialism. In spite of its distinct trajectory, institutional makeup, and motives, the collapse of Yugoslav-style market socialism coincided with the collapse of Soviet-style administrative-command socialism, curiously enough. It is worthwhile therefore to disclose

---

1 Jakopovich 2015, p. 62.

the causes behind the decline of Yugoslav socialist self-management since, on the surface, it embodied many of the core principles of socialism.

We find that there are two dimensions to Yugoslavia's collapse: ethnically structured political divisions and economic decline. Between these, we will be mostly occupied with the latter factor. The economic history of socialist self-government in Yugoslavia can be divided into four periods. The period immediately preceding the construction of self-management can be classified as the adoption of a Soviet-style command economy; followed by the first phase of socialist self-government, which can be characterised as market socialism with administrative controls; a second phase of competitive market socialism, which enhanced the scope for market exchange; and a final phase of bottom-up planning. Or to use Mencinger's terms: a period of 'mixed administrative and self-managed market economy', 1953–62; 'labour-managed market economy', 1963–1973; and the 'contractual economy' after 1974.[2] We will again, as in the previous chapter, provide an account of the events more or less chronologically.

1   Laying the Groundwork

The independent course of socialist construction that took place in Yugoslavia can be traced to the partisan struggles during World War II. During the war, Yugoslavia saw itself occupied by the fascist forces of the Axis powers. Partisan formations, headed by marshal Tito of the National Liberation Army – which was connected to the Communist Party of Yugoslavia – waged armed resistance against the occupation forces and their domestic collaborators. These valiant efforts eventually culminated in triumph over their adversaries, while having relied little on direct aid supplied by the Allied forces – including the Soviet Red Army – in securing the independence of Yugoslavia. During their national war of liberation, the USSR had urged the Yugoslav communists to join forces with the reactionary resistance, the Četniks. The leadership of the Yugoslav communists did not, however, heed these instructions to co-operate with the royalist Serbians, who frequently crossed divisions and engaged in tactical and strategic collaboration with the Axis forces. By their own sacrifice and resolve, the antifascist partisans liberated the territories of Yugoslavia, and used their independence from foreign powers to chart a course of their own design. They elected to establish a socialist government, against the express

---

2   In Brus and Łaski 1989, p. 91.

wishes of the Soviet leadership, who were not keen to upset the fragile geopolitical balance of power between themselves and their transatlantic allies. The
relatively autonomous direction of the Yugoslav communists was in part the
result of the conditions of war, which saw a huge upsurge in party membership. This transformed the party from a small band of hardened 'Stalinists' into
a mass party with a relatively open character.[3] Unlike the 'satellites' installed
by Soviet authorities in the countries of Central and Eastern Europe that they
had liberated from Nazi occupation, Yugoslavia's liberation was effected by the
Communist-led People's Front itself, and garnered a large degree of popular
legitimacy as a result.[4] Its political programme of social transformation, which
promised to uproot premodern vestiges and the social uplifting of the population, likewise earned it widespread popular favour.[5]

After the consolidation of their victory in the national war of liberation,
and the conclusion of Second World War, and in spite of their differences
with the Soviet government, the Yugoslav administration formed themselves
on the basis of the central tenets of Marxism-Leninism. For the duration of
the very first few years of their existence, they began to construct socialism
in the style of the Soviet Union. The USSR in turn pledged assistance in the
form of loans and experts to aid in recovery efforts and the construction of
socialism in Yugoslavia.[6] The results of the administrative command economy
in this period are familiar: increased volumes of investment to expand productive capacity, a corresponding increase in industrial output, declining real wages
and decreased household consumption.[7] This period was also marked by a
great number of imbalances and irrationalities,[8] some of which could no doubt
have been straightened out to an extent, had the system continued to operate.
For instance, no incentive model had been in place, leaving supervision and
sanctions as the only means to motivate workers, officials, and managers alike,
which resulted in an overgrown bureaucracy, even compared to the standards
of the Soviet Union.[9]

The Soviet Union used their leverage to force the Yugoslav leadership to
realign themselves with Soviet geopolitical goals, as the Kremlin threatened
to withhold aid. Meanwhile, the Yugoslav government too sought to return to

---

3   Kirn 2019, p. 73.
4   Kukić 2018, p. 3.
5   Kirn 2019, p. 73.
6   Kirn 2019, p. 115.
7   Ellman 2014, p. 54.
8   Sirc 1979, pp. 4–9.
9   Sirc 1979, p. 8.

the good graces of Stalin.[10] In 1948, however, the chasm had proved too wide, and the Yugoslav and Soviet leaderships split definitively over irreconcilable differences, and Soviet support for Yugoslav efforts in building up socialism was withdrawn. Yugoslavia, which had incurred tremendous costs as a result of the war and occupation, threatened to fall into economic and political isolation. However, at the same time, the self-reliance of the Yugoslav communists mobilised domestic support for the communists in general and leadership of Tito in particular.[11] The Yugoslav communists now had to rely on their own capacities to retain popular legitimacy, and the poor performance of the administrative command period – at least in relation to the material standard of living for the working classes – formed a poor basis to mobilise domestic support.[12] This imposed on the communist leadership the imperative to design a different, independent route to the construction of socialism, which could unite the popular masses behind the leadership of the Communists.

The main architects and proponents of the independent Yugoslav road to socialism were to become Đilas, Kardelj, and Kidrič.[13] In their analysis – which aligns closely with that of 'Western Marxism' – the Soviet Union displayed irredeemable deformities. They pointed to the stifling effects of bureaucratisation and the lack of worker participation in both workplace and government as bastardised features of Soviet socialism, in addition to the human costs of millions of fatalities due to famine, political repression, and inhospitable internment conditions.[14] State-socialism, they believed, would breed a parasitic bureaucracy, deforming into state-capitalism, and thus arose the need to

---

10   Kukić 2018, p. 3.
11   Kirn 2019, p. 79.
12   Ellman 2014, p. 54.
13   Kirn 2019, p. 97.
14   During the Cold War there was undoubtedly political cause to exaggerate the number of victims of these various Soviet campaigns (or at least highlight those estimates which tended toward the higher ends of the scales) – which in turn permitted Marxist-Leninists to dismiss these half-truths as untruths. Frequently, twenty or so million excess deaths are attributed to them, on the basis of Cold War era estimates (see Conquest 2008, p. 486). After the collapse of the USSR, the Soviet archives became declassified and open to independent investigation. They revealed that the mass deportations and executions that took place in the Soviet Union had been explicitly documented in numerical detail (Gregory 2004, p. 8). Scrutiny of these documents has allowed researchers to draw more definitive conclusions about both the nature and scope of political repression in the Soviet Union. It has resulted in a substantial downward revision of the estimated, cumulative death toll of political violence. The archives, however, also disclosed the purges as 'centrally planned quasi-military series of attacks on the population', orchestrated by Stalin (see Ellman 2008, pp. 115–16), dispelling theories that the terror had slid into excess by more or less uncontrolled actions of overzealous officers, undertaken independently of central direction.

realise the socialist promise of popular participation, they reasoned. Kidrič further warned against the use of administrative controls would cause distortions to the extent that these conflicted with 'objective economic laws'. This foreshadowed the increasingly loose leash market forces would be afforded in Yugoslavia.[15] Toward these ends, a system of socialist self-management was fashioned and rolled out by the government. Labour-managed firms operating in the context of a heavily regulated market, would become the trademark feature of the distinctive Yugoslav socialism.[16]

Political leaders, and crucially Tito – now president – after some reservations, had come around to the idea of socialist self-government as it had been proposed by the original three architects. For their part, they remained committed to the Marxist-Leninist model of the vanguard one-party state.[17] Yugoslavia, whilst being comparatively freer than the Soviet Union,[18] would still maintain a considerable authoritarian slant, particularly through pre-publication censorship. Although more violent forms of political repression were also employed, including politically motivated executions ranging in the many hundreds and a notorious re-education internment camp (especially geared toward the 're-socialisation' of adherents of Stalin) as well as a reliance on violent police action to break up strikes.[19]

The divergence from the 'official' model of centralised planning was rationalised in such a way as to justify a new approach without writing off Marxism-Leninism altogether. An administrative mobilisation of resources had been necessary to kickstart high rates of accumulation to prepare for higher forms of socialism, but this crude method could now be surpassed, political leaders declared. The Yugoslav model of self-governing socialism, then, was:

> interpreted within a national framework – as an application of Marxist ideas to the given stage of development and specific conditions of Yugoslavia, not as a universal alternative to Stalinism or as a continuation of the initiatives of worker democracy seen in the previous decades.[20]

This new direction of the country, then, did not constitute a break from Marxism-Leninism, merely a distinct application of this doctrine, shaped in part by the unique domestic and geopolitical requirements of Yugoslavia.

---

15 Sirc 1979, p. 3.
16 Sirc 1979, pp. 42–3; Kirn 2019, pp. 100, 122–3.
17 Kirn 2019, p. 103.
18 Uvalić 2018, p. 32.
19 Kirn 2019, p. 96; Sirc 1979, p. 55.
20 Musić 2011, p. 174.

2   Toward Self-Governing Socialism

Unlike the Russian Revolution, in which organs of workers' power emerged spontaneously from within labour movement and on initiative of the working classes, Yugoslavia's experiment with workers' self-management would be introduced from above, legislatively[21] – and moreover, it was formulated by the party's inner circle without input from the working population, or even the leading cadres of organised labour.[22] The policy of self-management was promulgated in 1950. It was hoped that it would lay the groundwork for the withering away of the state, by distancing the state bureaucracy from direct control over the means of production.[23] The theoretical design of workers' self-management tracked closely the writings of Marx and Lenin.[24] Đilas, who was both the principal initiator of the self-management proposals and eventually the main critic of the Yugoslav government, relied on a close reading of *Das Kapital* to conclude that Yugoslavia should faithfully follow Marx's ideas and implement a system based on the free association of equal producers.[25]

In practice, workers' self-management was rolled out over a number of years, starting in 1952, and would be subjected to substantial revisions in 1965 and again in 1974–76, before being abolished in 1989. The system of socialist self-management converted virtually all productive property to the legal status of 'social property', bringing them under the direct management of the workers' council and the board it elected.[26] Unlike centrally planned economies, market socialism was characterised by horizontal contracting between suppliers and customers that could be freely explored and developed within the confines of the framework of administrative controls and regulations. Under the regime of market socialism, output and investment decisions were shaped by enterprises in relation to typical market signals: The prices commodities would exchange for on the market, the rate of return, the rates of interest, and so on. The motive structuring the choices of producers in relation to these market signals was the material incentive to generate as much residual income above the costs of production, per worker. Meanwhile, the government attempted to curb the worst excesses of unfettered commerce by interfering in the market activities of enterprises, by levying taxes, distributing subsidies, or imposing price controls.

---

21   Kirn 2019, p. 97.
22   Musić 2011, p. 175.
23   Musić 2011, p. 174.
24   Kirn 2019, p. 98; Musić 2011, p. 173.
25   Sirc 1979, p. 1.
26   Sirc 1979, p. 45.

The internal organisation of the labour-managed firm was structured as follows. The law stipulated that the workers' collective of the enterprise was to be the source of supreme authority and would act through an elected workers' council. The workers' council would meet monthly, and install a board of directors for daily decision-making. One-third of the seats in the workers' councils were to be reserved for manual or shopfloor workers. In addition, there was an enterprise director, who was appointed by the local committee (in effect, the party), but this decision had to be ratified by the workers' council.[27] The labour-managed firm had appreciable discretionary authority in relation to investment decisions and in their internal affairs. This was the way in which workplace democracy was provisioned. In terms of labour productivity and effort, the Yugoslav model outperformed Soviet-style socialism; workers' incomes being tied to performance, giving them a vested interest in participating in management.[28] The efficacy of worker participation varied, with lesser and higher degrees of active participation attained across enterprises, industries, and republics.[29] Especially for the duration of the early period, before 1965, that there was a fairly widespread willingness to participate in workplace decision-making.[30]

The labour-managed firms would buy input and equipment, combine them with their labour to transform it into output, and dispose of the output on the market, in accordance with their consideration for the highest possible profit (or more specifically, residual income maximisation per head of the workforce), which naturally depended on the price levels of both input and output. The price policy in the period of 1952–1964 combined administrative controls with market forces. Prices were administratively fixed through negotiations between planning authorities and enterprises:

> Prices would be used to assess the 'social' value of output, and, hence, could not be determined in a typical free-market setting, but rather through 'agreements' reached between enterprises and higher-level planning bureaux. This typically meant that the Federal Office for Prices and similar planning agencies would either freeze prices at levels consistent with overall macroeconomic goals, or prices would float within a strict range determined by the planning authorities.[31]

---

27 Sirc 1979, p. 39; Musić 2011, p. 175.
28 Ellman 2014, p. 264; Estrin 1991, pp. 187–94.
29 Kirn 2019, p. 117.
30 Devine 2011, p. 95.
31 Prychitko 2002, p. 46.

On the basis of these prices – which thus came into operation under the influence of market forces and administrative corrections – enterprises were free to
negotiate contracts with suppliers and customers, and decide upon the rate of
reinvestment (after taxes) of enterprise profits (or 'income', as it was officially
termed). Administrative restrictions were placed on many other enterprise
decisions. For example, the decision to divide enterprise profits between reinvestment and wages had to be approved or ratified by local political committees. Another aspect of administrative control was government-directed investment.[32] As an example, interest charges generated income for various public
investment funds, which funnelled finance back into the economy on the basis
of politically determined social plans.[33] Command planning was thus largely
replaced by market relations, but policies in the form of administrative controls and some form of indirect planning remained in place to steer the activity
of the labour-managed firms into producing socially desirable outcomes (as
interpreted by the ruling League of Communists, which possessed the monopoly power on doing so). In this way, the free operation of market forces would
be restricted to help bring about the social ambitions of Yugoslavia's political
leadership.

The results were as mixed as the system itself. Macroeconomic indicators
showed impressive results, but internal contradictions of the system below the
surface level were noticeable. The initial reforms, in the period from 1951 until
1964, allowed the standard of living to climb, with growth rates that exceeded
both those of Western and Eastern Europe.[34] The restructuring also improved
work conditions, and labour productivity managed to recover from its poor
record under the initial phase of centralised planning. Meanwhile, expansive
welfare services freed a first generation of adolescents of lower class backgrounds from various social fetters. They could raise themselves up on the
social ladder by the generous provision of publicly funded higher education.
Yet trouble lurked as the interference by public institutions in the operation of
the market reproduced some of the irrationalities of the administrative command system, such as poor linking of output with consumer demand and an
imbalanced structure of investments. The Yugoslav economy simultaneously
suffered from a number of economic ailments that were more familiar to liberal
market economies than they were to socialist ones, such as inflation, unemployment, rising levels of inequality, and vulnerability to economic shocks and

---

32   Prychitko 2002, p. 46; Sirc 1979, p. 20.
33   Sirc 1979, p. 28.
34   Kirn 2019, p. 117.

business cycles.[35] In addition, there was the issue of the low volume of investment, which was a uniquely Yugoslav economic ailment; and short investment horizons, which, in appearance and effect, more closely corresponded to the risk-adverse behaviour of managers observed under a system of centralised planning, but had distinct system-specific causes in Yugoslavia's case. These problematic undercurrents of the Yugoslav economy undermined its long-term stability. Here we will attempt to summarise and expound their causal relations.

The administrative command period had initiated a period of imbalanced growth. The rate of accumulation in the industrial sector exceeded the rate of growth of available raw materials. This resulted in bottlenecks and underutilised industrial capacity. The prejudice toward favouring heavy industry, imported from Soviet practice, continued to exercise influence on policymakers even after the Yugoslav-Soviet split. Political authorities saw to it that loss-making enterprises in heavy industry were not permitted to go under. Generous subsidies were made available toward this end. The logic of socialist self-management demanded evermore financial assistance being funnelled to firms, owing to a number of reasons.

First, administrative interference actively shaped the commercial activities of labour-managed firms, but the public officials responsible for shaping investment decisions did not also share in the responsibility for their outcomes. Since officials were not part of the work collective, their income was unaffected by the market performance of these enterprises; and conversely, the amount of profit per worker obtained by enterprises was not the result of activity freely undertaken by them without outside, administrative intervention. For instance, losses recorded by enterprises might be blamed on price controls imposed on producers by a planning bureau; although theoretically it might still have been possible for them to turnover a profit in spite of such controls, and the actual cause of their loss-making might in actual fact have been poor direction of the enterprise by the workers' council. It would amount to counter-factual speculation about the extent to which low revenue could be accounted for by the choices of producers themselves, compared to the effects of choices imposed by public officials, or perhaps some other extraneous circumstance. It would require close audits of the causes to come to some reasonable conclusion, since contextual knowledge might be concealed by labour-managed enterprises in a bid to acquire subsidies to compensate their losses.

---

35   Ellman 2014, p. 54.

Second, since the workers' councils are not the owners of the assets they manage, they can hardly be expected to be responsible for the value of the capital of their enterprise. Workers that join an existing enterprise would be made partially responsible for the current value of the enterprise, insofar as their income is influenced by it, without having had the opportunity to influence this value. By good fortune alone, workers might join an enterprise with a positive value, and would be able to obtain a higher than average income, while less fortunate workers might be compelled to join enterprises with major liabilities. Since workers were not technically speaking 'entrepreneurs' it was unfair to expect them to assume all the risks of investment decisions, especially where they had to take-on the risk of choices made by previous members. Further, workers under a socialist market economy were exposed to greater degree of income instability than those in liberal market economies, which is obviously undesirable from a socialist standpoint.

The payment of subsidies to compensate income losses due to the fluctuating fortunes of market forces was motivated by an honest concern for the welfare of workers, but produced the unintended consequence of removing the incentive to work efficiently and effectively. The extra income generated by profitable enterprises were taxed away and reallocated to loss-making firms. Without the need, imposed by the discipline of the market, to efficiently produce output for which consumers expressed demand, stocks of unsold goods accumulated. Thus, '[l]ow utilisation of capacity was due much less to insufficient effective demand than to the inconsistencies of the production structure', which manifested as a mismatch of supply and demand.[36] The material interest of producers to correct the structure of investment to align with consumer requirements gradually eroded. Any losses incurred because output could not be sold would be covered by the cross-subsidisation between enterprises or payments out of public funds. The key component of the system of socialist self-management, the labour managed firms, generates these irrational economic policies:

> The asymmetry of membership rights, the fact that one cannot force members to stay in their LMF against their will, means that it is the lender, or society, that has to bear the costs of failed investment projects. This can come in either of two ways. Members can leave a failing LMF, or, even worse, may be able to press the public into subsidizing it so as not to increase the rolls of the unemployed.[37]

---

36   Sirc 1979, p. 86.
37   Keren and Levhari 1992, p. 668.

By and large, workers remained committed to their own narrow self-interest, and opportunities to work and plan less diligently were readily seized. As a matter of fact, it was not unheard of that worker-members of loss-making enterprises enjoyed higher incomes than those of profitable firms, which, as one can imagine, scarcely induced workers to consume fewer resources in production or plan their investments more meticulously. The interference of local political authorities in the affairs of the enterprise further reinforced the idea that workers should not feel responsible for the outcome of their decisions.[38]

The difficult to navigate maze of complicated administrative rules, controls, and regulations suppressed in large part the free initiative of enterprises.[39] This was of course how they were intended to function. The Yugoslav leadership, being upright socialists, knew market forces to be the adversary. By placing administrative limitations on the free conduct of exchange, they hoped to curb unconscious pressures exerted by the forces of the market. However, administrative regulations and policies were also a source of social tension and conflict between the labour-managed firms and socialist government. By imposing terms, conditions, and *ad hoc* policies, the free operation of markets was stifled, sowing confusion and ire among producers.

Furthermore, consistent with the applied principles of Marxism-Leninism, it was assumed that workers shared in sovereignty, exercising power directly, therefore no institutional mechanisms had been in place to deal with grievances and labour conflicts. Thus, '[e]ven if the workers council represented the majority, various minorities could still feel badly treated'.[40] Strikes ('work stoppages', in official terms) exploded as a consequence. Logically:

In a purely competitive and 'free' self-management system, workers would have no reason to *strike against themselves*. In practice, nonetheless, the high degree of government intervention in enterprise affairs provoked adverse reaction in workers. Workers were striking not against enterprise, but against government policy.[41]

Worker-members opted for strike action since the official channels for self-management were subordinated to the political power of the League of Communists, and thus workers had 'no *real* influence – despite the claims of the

---

38   Sirc 1979, p. 92.
39   Sirc 1979, pp. 20–1.
40   Sirc 1979, p. 194.
41   Liotta 2001, p. 6.

(one-party Marxist) state – on decision-making, production process, or social policy'.[42] So, decisions related to the rate of taxation to raise a certain amount of funds for investment were made in an unaccountable manner by non-democratic procedures, at the central level far removed from both the control and daily perceptions of the public. Since political participation at this administrative level was limited to a clique – the upper layers of the League of Communists – worker-citizens were, institutionally speaking, not encouraged to formulate, develop, or shape their views at this level. Instead, they were stimulated by the institutional context to think within the scope over which they did exercise meaningful control: investment decisions at the enterprise level. Understandably then, their outlook became a type of 'parochialism': pursuing their narrow-minded, quasi-commercial interests to maximise current income without much regard for broader considerations.

The contradictory forces on which Yugoslav society rested would habitually see conflicting interests give rise to the inconsistent requirements of relaxing and strengthening administrative controls. The system was continually pulled in opposite directions. The primary contradiction of Yugoslav society laid in the labour-managed firm, which encouraged a sort of narrow consciousness and corresponding attitudes, and the society-wide outlook which the Communists hoped to instil through administrative measures. The forces of market relations had an atomising effect on producers in other words, their activity being reduced to their narrow, particular interests. To check against the degenerative consequences of market forces, the League of Communists used a handful of policy instruments. For example:

> The main counterweight to the splintering tendencies of 'socialist commodity production' was the policy of centralized national accumulation, made possible by the Federal Investment Fund, which obligated individual companies to maintain the value of social capital through prescribed rates of depreciation and a minimum rate of savings.[43]

Local government committees exercised indirect control, and kept enterprise activity within the confines of the law and social objectives. In this way, the public interest should have been be safeguarded but this mechanism was proved ineffective:

---

42   Liotta 2001, p. 8.
43   Musić 2011, p. 181.

The communes never quite exercised the dominant role intended for them. Soon very strong anti-communal tendencies made themselves felt. There were objections to interference by the communes in the distribution of enterprises' revenue and to their direction of investment funds which, it was claimed, should have been in the hands of enterprises instead of falling into the hands of commune bureaucracies. The resolution of the First Congress of Workers' Councils in 1957 also demanded that the rights of communes should be clearly defined so that they would no longer put pressure on enterprises and interfere with their proper functions.[44]

Despite intentions, the interventions of the local communities in fact reinforced parochial attitudes, since they blocked 'enterprise plans to invest in other communes (or republics); and they try to ensure that, so far as possible, local enterprises buy their supplies from other local enterprises'.[45]

Another instrument was the appointment of directors to help enlarge the influence of the party over self-managed enterprises, and thereby limit the influence of sectoral, short-term interests of producers over investment decisions. Of course, appointments had to be ratified by the workers' council, but since being in good standing with the party helped the ease of conducting business this was usually a formality.[46] Since the Yugoslav economy was not subject to direct political control over economic developments, due the lack of institutional mechanisms to effect centralised planning, the League of Communists instead absorbed the managerial and directorial layers of firms into the party apparatus to affirm their influence over economic matters. As such, the composition of party membership over time began to skew in favour of administrative staff.

In sum, there existed a contradiction at the heart of the Yugoslav experiment, between the need to assert central control to preserve the general interest, but which absolved local responsibility and distorted incentives, and the need for decentralisation to empower and invigorate producers, but which strengthened particular interests. This structural opposition also manifested in extreme oscillations between policies of centralisation and decentralisation.[47] These capricious shifts in policy resulted in successive periods of chaotic reor-

---

44   Sirc 1979, p. 41.
45   Lydall 1984, p. 77.
46   Sirc 1979, p. 43.
47   Sirc 1979, p. 42.

ganisations of firms and local governments to adjust themselves to the changing structural requirements imposed by the federal government.

Inner tensions, caused by the structural opposition woven into the fabric of Yugoslav society, resulted in increasing pressure to liberalise the economy, to free producers from excessive administrative controls. The Communists had previously feared that workers would increase their consumption at the expense of accumulation if the scope for local self-determination would be increased and had therefore resisted lowering the tax rate that generated funds for investment.[48] However, the dominant 'liberal' faction of the League of Communists eventually caved to these social pressures and implemented several reforms in 1965 which loosened the control of central authorities over economic affairs, and therefore made way for market forces to dominate social production. Decision-making regarding tax policy was delegated to republics or other administrative subdivisions, which were carved out along ethnic-national lines. Each individual republic would decide on its own tax policies, regulations, and investment policies.[49] The reforms also abolished the proviso that at least one-third of the workers' councils were to be composed of shop-floor workers. The federal investment fund had already been abolished two years prior, and in addition, the tax rate on firms would also be lowered. Thus, fragmentation, both along 'republican' (national) lines and economically began to manifest. Ultimately, the inability to reverse this escalating fracture set Yugoslavia on a path toward economic decline and ethnic disintegration.

Where initially the high tax rate had assured that high rates of accumulation could be maintained, there was persistent pressure to lower it, in order to improve the consumption and productivity of workers.[50] In 1965, the discretionary authority of the enterprise over their own affairs was increased in scope. This included the lowering of the tax rate from sixty to thirty percent of enterprise profit.[51] Workers were now considerably freer to decide between the level of accumulation and consumption, which, in practice, resulted in much lower levels of reinvestment. The League of Communists, as self-appointed steward of the general interest, may have recognised the need for higher rates of investment to sustain economic growth, but workers were ill-inclined to pursue the greater interest at the expense of short-term personal gain. Producers, after all, did not own the means of production, and upon exit from the enterprise, would have to vacate the investments which they had made into the collective

---

48 Sirc 1979, p. 43.
49 Ellman 2014, p. 55.
50 Musić 2011, p. 181.
51 Musić 2011, p. 182.

pool of their labour-managed firm. If workers, instead of ploughing profits back into production, choose to distribute residual income among themselves for personal consumption, then workers could 'invest' in durable household items which they personally owned and would not have to vacate upon resigning from their firm.[52] Considered from the narrow perspective of short-term material interests, the workers were right to prefer high consumption over investment. However, in doing so, they ultimately violated their long-term interest as consumers by restricting the flow of funds into accumulation, the source of future consumption. With a lower tax burden imposed on enterprise income, workers tended to disregard accumulation or abuse credit for investment, while soft budget constraints gave unproductive enterprises an undue lease of life. Thus, not only was it in the short-term interest of workers to privilege consumption over investment, firms would also not find themselves penalised in the longer term over their decision to lower their rate of reinvestment or their misuse of credit, since they would be kept afloat by public assistance.

Producers further did not think of themselves as 'entrepreneurs', but as workers, and therefore saw large income disparities as unjust, rather than as rewards for commercial success or risk. An upward revision of income for one group of workers stimulated other workers to follow suit, without regard for the financial well-being of their firm.[53] Workers regarded their personal efforts and expenditure of energy in itself as worthy contribution, regardless of the market value of their output. Hence, whenever losses were incurred because of unsold stocks, workers tended to look to public authorities to cover the losses.[54]

Investment horizons were further shortened by high labour turnover. Workers that expected to have a short employment relationship with a given enterprise would seek to maximise consumption for the duration of their employment there, rather than reinvest profits into the enterprise to potentially obtain higher returns in the future since they might not be around to reap the rewards of these efforts. Labour turnover was exceedingly high in the 1960s, although it improved during the 1970s.[55]

To add to these issues, unemployment became a tremendous social problem and source of concern for the political authorities, with rates surging after the introduction of the market mechanism. The self-managed firms did not attempt to maximise the total amount of profit but rather income per worker. While the overall profits of the firm may be expanded by attracting additional

---

52   Prychitko 2002, pp. 39–40, 48.
53   Sirc 1979, pp. 129–30.
54   Sirc 1979, pp. 175–6.
55   Sirc 1979, p. 73.

workers, this could have a negative effect on the level of 'profit' divided among individual members. Instead, firms over-invested in capital-intensive production methods that would maximise income per worker and restricted employment (in purely relative terms, since in absolute terms, self-financed investments remained low).[56] An overall increase in profit was not treated as a signal to take on additional labour to expand operations, since this would spread the total profit thin among workers. Labour-managed firms therefore exhibited a tendency toward overcapitalisation. The tendency to restrict the inflow of new workers was, in addition, not offset by the entry of new firms into the market, which further contributed to high levels of unemployment:

> The reason was that, since all new enterprises of any size had to be socially owned, no one had an incentive to create new firms except the political authorities, who concentrated their efforts on existing organizations. (...) Workers cannot bid entry into high paying self-managed firms, since their admission would lower the pay of existing employees.[57]

Consequently, unemployment surged and labour productivity suffered, but perhaps more devastating, it also triggered high rates of inflation. The inclination of workers to increase their own wages (and by extension, consumption), regardless of the financial health of their enterprise, and to prefer consumption over sound investment, created a certain inflationary pressure in its own right. At the same time, low levels of investment were compensated by state subsidies and credit in an effort to expand productive capacity.[58] Credit was supplied by banks (which were often under the control of enterprises themselves) without much regard for the ability of enterprises to repay them. Since they were owned by existing firms, they also had little interest in supplying credit to new, competing firms.[59] Enforcement of repayments was often absent and since the real interest rate was zero, if not negative, there were no costs incurred by lending and attempts to impose tight monetary restrictions were bypassed through inter-enterprise credit.[60] In practice credit was therefore abused as a form of subsidy to keep unprofitable or unproductive businesses afloat. Investment criteria for public funds were similarly 'uneconomical' and irrational, which allowed political actors to stimulate economic development

---

56   Sirc 1979, p. 203; Kornai 2007, p. 469; Kukić 2018.
57   Estrin 1991, p. 192.
58   Prychitko 2002, p. 48.
59   Kukić 2018 18.
60   Uvalić 2010, p. 21.

by means of the haphazard pumping of finance into various investment projects.[61] In turn, of course, the ill-advised projects were scarcely allowed to go under. The huge sums of state subsidies made available to firms were partially financed by public banks over-lending to producers, which was contributing to runaway inflation:[62]

> Investment funds were widely financed by borrowing straight from the central bank, which meant that the money supply could be expanding even though the government budget in the narrow sense of the word was balanced or even in surplus. In consequence, currency supply rose.[63]

The workers had become less inclined to participate in management during this period. They rated matters of income, pleasant work colleagues, and career advancement above participation in decision-making; being less concerned with the making of more complicated decisions related to investments or marketing.[64] Technical and administrative staff began gradually to exercise undue influence in decision-making since shop-floor workers judged themselves to be insufficiently competent and informed to make qualified judgements about investments.[65] Thus, the rate of participation in decision-making was disproportionally skewed in favour of the level of skill and expertise of the workforce.[66] This is not entirely a problem of lack of training and education, to be resolved by simply bringing up the level of competence, but also reflected general apathy, i.e. disinterest in taking responsibility for decision-making. Workers tended to abdicate initiative in most matters, delegating it to management, which possessed the capability to make sounder evaluations.[67] Workers often rubber stamped their approval of investment decisions, but also made their approval conditional by employing it as bargaining chip to negotiate modest improvements in secondary work benefits.[68] This tendency was partially the result of the way the system was set up in the 1950s. The workers' collective was supposed to run their affairs themselves, with only minor limitations placed on them by the state. In practice, the lack of time, interest, and

---

61   Sirc 1979, pp. 88–89.
62   Sirc 1979, p. 138; Prychitko 2002, p. 41.
63   Sirc 1979, p. 30.
64   Sirc 1979, pp. 174–6.
65   Musić 2011, p. 178.
66   Devine 2011, p. 95.
67   Prychitko 2002, p. 39.
68   Musić 2011, p. 178.

skill gradually decreased the willingness to participate. Workers were interested in supervising managerial activities, but not in making all significant decisions. The functions and powers of managers were, however, ill-defined, since the communist government had presumed the elimination of all power differentials. There had been no need to define and limit the powers of management, since this separation of productive and executive functions would wither away of its own accord as workers would begin to assume collective responsibility over production and investment decision-making. To the extent that workers did not assume collective responsibility for the whole of the operations of their firm, some of this responsibility necessarily fell on the shoulders of management, which thus began to share more in decision-making authority as direct consequence. Since the communists had not clarified the extent and the limitations of managerial authority by law, the poorly defined discretionary authority that managers wielded resulted in an increasing concentration of power in the hands of management (a cautionary tale for anarchism, undoubtedly).[69]

All in all, market socialism proved to be a recipe for high rates of unemployment, dysfunctional markets, inflationary pressure, and rising debt levels. The imbalanced structure of markets grew out of poor labour incentives, themselves rooted in the system of labour-managed firms, which therefore bore the main responsibility for economic decline. The principal effect of this arrangement was the restriction of demand for labour, the undersupply of investment funded out of reserves and revenue, and over-reliance on borrowing and subsidies – and a willingness by the banking system to extend loans regardless of credit-worthiness, which contributed to high rates of inflation. The maximisation of net income per worker by restricting employment resulted in high levels of unemployment – only partially offset by emigration – and inefficient labour outlays.[70] Workers preferred to abuse credit or subsidies to expand productive capacity, while using residual income to supplement wages. The government, aware of these structural ailments, set out on a frantic search for a definitive resolution to the contradictions. Constant modifications to the system, through various legal acts, were enacted: 'one day enterprises are merged, then they are split into 'economic units', then again into 'basic organisation of associated labour', in short one reorganisation follows another and makes the managers despair'.[71] This had two main effects. First, it increased regula-

---

69   Sirc 1979, p. 179.
70   Kukić 2018.
71   Sirc 1979, p. 185.

tory uncertainty, and thus lowered the effectiveness of medium and long-term business policies – which could be abandoned or nullified as a result of new legislation. Second, the navigation of a constantly changing business environment demanded flexibility on part of the managerial staff, and therefore diminished accountability and transparency toward the workers' councils. This thus allowed for the concentration of additional power within administrative staff.[72] By the 1970s, party theorists believed to have at last found the definitive remedy to the faults of Yugoslavia's self-governing socialism.

3   Bottom-Up Planning and Collapse

From the perspective of Marxism, the qualification of Yugoslavia as socialist raises some conceptual issues. The relationship between enterprises was fundamentally governed by the competition among them. Each enterprise participated in exchange relations to obtain inputs, augment them by the hands and minds of their labour, and return them to market at improved value to secure returns on their investments. Clearly then, the relations among firms were reciprocally independent, and the co-ordination of social production proceeded by the indirect means of the market. The disciplinary mechanism of the competition of capitals, which is the force that drives down the average costs of production, was however, only partially operational due to various administrative controls. By cross-subsidisation, the average earnings of firms shared little relationship with the income of workers. Loss-making firms would be shored up by generous subsidies. The rate of net income, or profit, of firms did not necessarily reflect their level of efficiency, but political dealings. As a consequence, the market could not exert as much disciplinary force as it is free to do under liberal capitalism. Still, the logic of the circuit of capital expressed via the competition among individual capitals emerged more or less automatically and independently from political will, from within the heart of the production and circulation of commodities, and had to be constrained by extraneous instruments after the fact. There was an underlying, endogenous pressure for the accumulation of capital which, according to the social priorities and political characteristics of the ruling communists, had to be curbed to effect socialist transformation. The character of government, and the overall experiment, were clearly disposed toward a socialist direction, then. In Kardelj's own words, 'Self-management is already being practised, it is a social

---

72   Sirc 1979, p. 181.

reality which is, admittedly, still weighed down by and interwoven with various elements of former systems'.[73]

The material reproduction of Yugoslav society depended on a constellation of contradictory social forces and institutional features. The socialist characteristics of workers' councils and social ownership of capital assets were constrained and structured by the competition of capitals, itself kept in check (or distorted) by administrative methods. In some sense, this parallels Marx's own analysis of negative and positive negations of capital. The concentration of capital – and thus the concomitant socialisation of production – he considered the negative negation; whilst production co-operatives were the positive negation:

> The capitalist stock companies, as much as the co-operative factories, should be considered as transitional forms from the capitalist mode of production to the associated one, with the only distinction that the antagonism is resolved negatively in the one and positively in the other.[74]

In theory, their combining would produce the socialist mode of production: co-operative labour on the basis of large-scale directly socialised production. Here in this historical analysis, in parallel to Marx's comments, the Soviet system assumes the role of the negative negation, whereas the Yugoslav system assumes the role of the positive negation. Supposedly, some sort harmonisation of both elements would resolve the internal contradictions of either system – but this is much easier said than done, naturally. To the credit of Yugoslavia's leading socialist theorists, they more or less understood that the contradictions pulling society apart had to be resolved by phasing out competitive market relations.

In the 1970s, renewed ambitions of the party leadership found traction in yet another round of expansive institutional innovations formulated by party theorists. Economic decline would be counteracted by structural reforms that should have restored initiative and economic responsibility and that simultaneously embodied a leap forward in the expansion of socialist relations. The economy would move away from market relations as the primary co-ordinating mechanism of labour-managed firms. Instead, self-managed associations would have to enter into agreements to co-ordinate their activities. This effectively implicated that decisions about the supply of input and the production of output would not be made 'atomistically' on the basis of market signals,

---

73   Kardelj 1976, p. 103.
74   MECW 37: 438.

instead being the outcome of negotiation among the firms involved. This represented a form of economic planning from the bottom upward. The reforms were implemented in 1974 and 1976 and aimed at the strengthening, deepening, and integrating of self-management in all facets of public life. In this way, it was hoped, the bureaucracy, alongside the state, would finally begin to wither away.[75]

The main instruments to realise this policy ambition were the 'Law on Associated Labour' and the 'Basic Organisation of Associated Labour' (BOAL) it legislated into being. Since self-management had been subject to wear and tear – meaning that power had become more concentrated in the hands of managers, even if they were formally elected – the communist leadership decided that enterprises should be split up into these BOALs. It was believed that the decentralisation of decision-making power would reaffirm self-management by cutting through the institutional crevasses in which power had crept, devolving authority downwards, removing it from the hands of managers to re-enfranchise workers at the lowest levels of economic activity directly. This would have to re-energise worker initiative from below.

These basic associations had frequently been part of the same firm prior to the reforms and after having been broken off into several basic organisations had to come together to reach agreements on how to use funds and what investments to pursue. The various levels of organisations, across departments, firms, and branches of industry, would have to enter into these legally binding 'self-management agreements'. Another form of agreement involved political authorities and other stakeholders weighing in on the decisions. These 'multi-stakeholder' agreements were called 'social contracts'. Market competition, in this way, would be replaced by co-operation.[76] To quote Uvalić at length:

> At the macroeconomic level, the 1970s economic reforms introduced new mechanisms of policy co-ordination – social contracts and self-management agreements – as a response to weakened macroeconomic management that accompanied the 1965 reform. Social contracts were to regulate rights and obligations affecting broader economic policies, including the priorities of social plans, the principles and criteria of policies regarding prices, employment and foreign trade, the distribution of income between personal incomes and capital accumulation, to be concluded between enterprises, political representatives, trade unions,

---

75 Prychitko 2002, p. 49; Kirn 2019, p. 197.
76 Estrin 1991, p. 190.

chambers of commerce and self-managed communities of interest; once concluded, they had the force of law. Self-management agreements were also binding agreements, introduced to regulate relations between enterprises and other types of organisations, including banks, in areas of mutual interest such as the creation of firms, investment projects, deliveries, transfer prices, joint transactions and the like. Self-managed communities of interest were also created in order to unite the interests of suppliers and final users of various services, initially in the areas of health, education and social insurance, later extended to other areas such as foreign trade (...). These various types of agreements introduced by the 1970s reforms were intended as specific devices of macroeconomic policy, regulating economic activities in a self-managed socialist economy.[77]

On the surface, these reforms appear attractive from a socialist point of view. Producers would enjoy democratic control over their immediate work environment, but the scope of democracy also extends into the relations among multiple workplaces, civil associations, and local communities, drawing on their particular insights to reach agreements embodying the best course of action. This very much resembles some historical and more contemporary 'multi-stakeholder' models of socialism, such as guild socialism.[78] It would seem then, that this approach to expanding socialist relations provided a solid foundation from which to phase out market relations – containing the seeds for a transition to a socialist, democratically planned economy within Yugoslavia.

However, rather than reinvigorate labour morale, excessive decentralisation of this type bred frustration, creating needless divisions within enterprises over questions of the distribution of responsibilities, funds, and revenue. Decentralisation entrenched and deepened particular interests and sectoral views. Rather than stimulate co-operation, they brought to a fore conflicting interests within enterprises and exacerbated institutional fragmentation.[79] For example, inter-organisational capital mobility was inhibited by the BOALS, since the benefits of investment could be accrued by others subdivisions.[80] Furthermore, whilst intended to reduce the concentration of responsibility, knowledge, and decision-making in the hands of administrative and technical staff, the institutional disorder that emerged from the reforms allowed, perhaps even necessitated, for the League of Communists to use their authority to

---

77   Uvalić 2018, p. 23.
78   For example, Cole 1920, 1921; Gindin 2019.
79   Prychitko 2002, p. 51; Kirn 2019, p. 197.
80   Brus and Łaski 1989, p. 99.

intervene in the activities of producers to grease the wheels of the economy.[81] The effects of excessive decentralisation are well illustrated by the railway system:

> The Yugoslav railways are divided into eight 'completely separate organizations'. Until recently these were further divided into 365 basic organizations, each of which, according to the Law on Associated Labour, had the right to select its own managers, irrespective of the views of the managers of the larger organisations. Moreover, each basic organization had the right to make its own disciplinary decisions, without regard to any damage caused by bad work to the railway system as a whole. With great difficulty, the number of basic organizations in the railways has now been reduced to between 40 and 50. But this still leaves many occasions for conflicts of interest.[82]

Clearly, this devolution of decision-making power narrowed horizons, orientation, and interests to self-destructive levels, raising additional institutional obstacles to the formulation and appreciation of broader interests and viewpoints. This was further reflected in the effects of social plans formulated among producers. If multiple firms arrive at an agreement it will realistically be pivoted toward the benefit of the producers involved, not taking wider considerations into account. The firms would exhibit monopolistic behaviour in formulating their plans, colluding to restrict production and raise prices to increase income at the expense of the general public. The interests of the final users, the consumers, would be violated by being compelled to buy overpriced commodities while rents accrue to producers.[83] However, vetting each proposal to ensure they account for consumer interests would require laborious efforts by political committees:

> If political authorities do participate, either directly or as supervisors (agreements actually had to be submitted to them for approval), the agreements in fact become administrative measures. Full administrative control of the price system is, however, illusory, as prices for at least 500,000 items are involved (...).[84]

---

81   Prychitko 2002, p. 53.
82   Lydall 1984, p. 110.
83   Sirc 1979, p. 126.
84   Ibid.

What emerged was a mismatch of interests at virtually all levels of decision-making. The difficulty of reconciling by institutional means the interests of producers and the interests the community as well as the diffusion of responsibilities strained the performance of the economy. The local associations carried out the social plans that had been devised and settled upon at higher administrative levels. However, these levels of decision-making:

> bore no personal or collective responsibility for poor choices. There was no way to penalize workers for incorrect decisions. Authorities guaranteed that incomes would not fall below a statutory minimum. In law, loss-making enterprises should have been reduced to this minimum but this ruling was rarely applied. Layoffs were virtually unknown and bankruptcies – the ultimate penalty in capitalist systems – were almost nonexistent.[85]

In the 1970s, circa 33 percent of the labour force was estimated to have been employed unproductively.[86] Soft budget constraints continued to allow loss-making enterprise to continue operations and thereby prevent workers and assets from being used more productively in some other capacity. Further, the disincentive for investment had not been addressed. Thus, 'the development strategy increasingly relied on foreign loans and external borrowing'.[87] The misuse of credit to leverage unsound investment policies by firms also continued apace.[88] However, the absolute limits of expansive fiscal and monetary policy would soon be reached. In the 1970s, the rate of investment fell to zero 'even if domestic credits are included',[89] instigated by an external shock: the oil crisis of 1979.[90] During this year, 'Yugoslavia registered a record trade and current account deficit (...) and was no longer able to service its external debt'.[91] Consequently, growth rates grounded to an acute halt in 1979 'once it became difficult to borrow':[92]

> Yugoslav GDP growth averaged around 6 % during the period between the start of reforms in 1952 and the late 1970s, higher than in the Soviet Union

85   Estrin 1991, pp. 192–3.
86   Sirc 1979, p. 199.
87   Uvalić 1992, pp. 10–11.
88   Sirc 1979, pp. 221–2.
89   Sirc 1979, p. 219.
90   Kukić 2018.
91   Uvalić 2018, p. 37.
92   Estrin 1991, p. 191.

or in the capitalist market economies of Western Europe (...). Despite the slowdown in the mid-1960s, growth rates still remained close to 6% during the 1966–1979 period. Yugoslavia registered a remarkable increase in Gross Domestic Product (GDP) per capita, from 1947 to 1981 by more than five times, entering a period of stagnation only in the 1980s.[93]

The 1970s reforms were unable to overcome the structural ailments of the self-management system, and in fact exacerbated many problems. The changes were unable to regenerate worker participation while leaving ultimately debilitating disincentives in place. Buckling under the pressures of over-borrowing, perverse labour incentives, and the dependency on foreign loans, the IMF imposed structural adjustment and austerity on Yugoslavia. In 1989, the system of socialist self-management was abolished. Ultimately, Yugoslavia itself fell apart amid an economic crisis and escalating ethnic polarisation:

> Within Yugoslavia the crucial factor that pushed towards the country's breakup, which was at that time certainly more important than the deficiencies of the economic system, was the renewal and explosion of nationalist sentiment fed by the short-sightedness of political leaders such as Milošević or Tudjman that believed that the key national objectives could be successfully resolved by the disintegration of the federation.[94]

The lessons of this experiment are invaluable for a project of socialist renewal. It calls attention to how a well-intended, but ultimately poorly designed system of socialist self-government condemned workers to become the gravediggers of socialism. The distorted labour incentives, the threat of informal hierarchies and the need to co-opt such corrosive tendencies pre-emptively by institutional means, the problems of excessive decentralisation, the difficulty of phasing out market relations through bottom-up planning, and the limitations to a multi-stakeholder approach to decision-making. Many of these features of Yugoslav-style socialism are reproduced, unwittingly, in contemporary theoretical proposals.

---

93   Uvalić 2018, p. 34.
94   Uvalić 2018, p. 33.

Socialism in Theory, Again

1 Back to the Drawing Board

The disappearance of actually existing socialisms from the world scene has provoked a number of different responses from various socialist factions. Those in the camp of Marxism-Leninism deny the existence of any innate flaws in Soviet-style socialism and instead draw attention to contingent factors in explaining the decline of the Soviet Union and similar regimes. They believe – and as we have established, without good cause – that as long as political command (possibly alloyed with workers' control of some grade) would be secured as the motive force behind production, socialism should work well and outperform capitalism. Others – typically those belonging to the leftmost wing of the communist movement, united in their dismissal of the Soviet experience as 'capitalist' – offer a derivative restatement of communism as response to the crisis of socialism, advancing the conception of the community of freely associated producers. Still others propose that socialism is viable only when it combines two elements that have been proved to work empirically, at least separately: worker-managed co-operatives and the market mechanism. All the particularities of these accounts aside, it is clear that some response is warranted that incorporates the cumulative experience of the twentieth century to bring socialism into the twenty-first, rather than dish up musings straight out of the nineteenth century.

When the necrosis of Soviet-style socialism became all too apparent in the 1980s, a number of theorists returned to the socialist calculation debate, and pondered what role economic planning has yet to play under socialism, if any at all. In spite of the critical importance of this avenue of research – a question of life and death for socialism, in fact – the debate rather remains a niche within a niche.[1] Only a handful of theorists have actively participated in the debate's renewal. In addition to the theoretical difficulties that emerge in such an undertaking, few people outside academia pay attention to these debates. In fact, few people inside academia do so as well; crucially, even socialist theorists fail to take notice. For instance, Magdoff and Williams propose that socialism, by employing democratic planning, could create the conditions for an ecolo-

---

1 See for example: Campbell 2002, 2012.

gically sustainable and equitable society.[2] The positive social and ecological effects that they claim would follow from 'planning' as 'democratic control over the economy' can hardly be subjected to scrutiny however, since their conclusions are tied only to highly amorphous outlines of a socialist economy. We are told that planning ought to be both democratic and bottom-up, but we are not clued in as to how this might actually work, nor are we given reasons that should lead us to believe that it might be workable. They fail to connect their arguments with the theoretical body of literature on socialist economic planning, despite basing central claims on the presumption of its feasibility. They, like most in the socialist camp, treat the whole body of knowledge on socialist planning as more or less non-existent. We are apparently expected to take it on good faith that democratic planning is both feasible and capable of conferring a host of social and ecological benefits that they claim it can.

This is representative of an attitude that is regrettably common. Namely, of the notion that problems of incentives and planning can resolve themselves simply, almost automatically, once people are freed from the shackles of private property and are given collective control over their lives. Historical experience has indeed exposed the graveness of such errors by example of the Bolsheviks, who in their revolutionary zeal severely underestimated the complexity of economic planning and expected enormous gains in productivity and morale that never materialised, to detrimental effect. Today this article of faith survives as a self-complacent attitude in the most radical, left-wing elements of the socialist movement – the 'Old Believers'. The experiences of the Soviet Union and Yugoslavia reveal that the construction of socialism is an exceedingly difficult task, and enormous difficulties lie in wait for those that will attempt to construct socialism in the future. Betting on a spontaneous explosion of collective creativity after setting the revolution in motion; anticipating a sudden epiphany revealing how to run things smoothly under socialism is a spectacularly poor plan and an unconscionable risk. Following this formula – or lack thereof – secures one certain outcome, which is to reinvent the wheel and go through all motions that condemned actually existing socialism to failure previously.

Some socialists justify this nonchalance by rejecting the idea that socialism is an economy, as Buick and Crump maintain for example:

> socialism is more than just not an exchange economy; it is not an 'economy' at all, not even a 'planned economy'. Economics, or political eco-

---

2   Magdoff and Williams 2017.

> nomy as it was originally called, grew up as the study of the forces which came into operation when capitalism, as a system of generalised commodity production, began to become the predominant mode of producing and distributing wealth. (...) Socialism is not an economy, because, in re-establishing conscious human control over production, it would restore to the social process of wealth production its original character of simply being a direct interaction between human beings and nature.[3]

The term 'economics' refers to a social experience which did not exist prior to capitalism and which will again become alien to society after capitalism. The unconscious, blind forces of the market required 'external' and abstract analysis to grasp the invisible laws that guided the hands of producers and consumers. Once market exchange is replaced by the collective, conscious control of producers over production and distribution, the system can be understood without scientific examination of the law-like externalised imperatives that impose themselves over producers and structure their choices accordingly. This notion is tied to the 'direct socialisation' conception, which suggests that we might treat social production as a single, great workshop to be directed rationally and consciously from above – by a democratically mandated workers' council perhaps. All that would remain to be done is accounting and bookkeeping, keeping records of the stocks and flows of materials and re-directing them as needs and wants arise and dissipate. In the words of Lenin, the practices of 'accountancy and control' under capitalism have been 'so utterly simplified' to the extent 'that they have become the extraordinarily simple operations of checking, recording and issuing receipts, which anyone who can read and write and who knows the first four rules of arithmetic can perform'.[4] Producers can simply circulate data and decide amongst themselves on the best course of action given all the information they have pooled.

Democracy does not offer a magical fix for planning problems, unfortunately. The fashionable demand for 'democratic planning' that circulates widely among socialists today usually contains little of substance. Presumably borne out of an attempt to disassociate from the negative legacy of Soviet-style socialism, the appeal of this sort of sloganeering is understandable. After all, if the problem with central, directive planning was that it was excessively centralised, unaccountable to the general public, and barely responsive to consumer wants, then all these faults are resolved when the population itself performs the

---

3   Buick and Crump 1986, pp. 130–1.
4   Cited in Brinton 1970.

economic planning by democratic means – simple enough. On this account, it has been suggested from within libertarian socialism that in communist society a network of mass assemblies and producer and consumer councils could deliberate on how, where, what, and for whom to produce:

> All people in an area would get together on a regular basis to consider, based on an analysis of the amount of materials and labor available, what to produce and how to allocate the products based on the needs (rather than wages) of individuals and families. Producing then in a communist society would rely on two functions: measuring the desire of people for things, and producing both in a collective and accountable manner.[5]

The planning process would incorporate directly the tastes, preferences, and priorities of the consumers and producers in society. It would use a procedure of democratic selection and elimination to arrive at a set of feasible preferences in relation to the available means. Democratic planning avoids the problem of central planners being too divorced from daily realities about both production possibilities and consumer preferences by integrating the producers and consumers (who naturally have intimate knowledge of both) directly into economic planning. Any major problems and issues that might emerge will be smoothed over by drawing on the collective knowledge mobilised in the process of a fully democratic, participatory planning procedure. This is the economic calculation debate solved.

Nevertheless, I want to raise some terminal issues. It would be wholly inadequate for all people in a local community to decide what to produce on the basis of the current level of productive capacity, since this is affected by the level of demand and productive capacity in all other communities. Self-managed workplaces can never be truly independent insofar as their production plans will have to be restructured at some administrative layer beyond the local scope to account for the production plans of workplaces spread across various territories, possibly covering the width and length of the entire globe. Units of production depend on, for example, materials or energy supplied by production sites located in some entirely different region in order for them to produce their output. Moreover, a given amount of output can be produced by various combinations of labour, raw material, semi-manufactures, and equipment; any of which can be requested by any number of production units. To determine where best to allocate these different productive resources to gener-

---

5 Nappalos 2012, p. 301.

ate the best results, these sorts of decisions will necessarily have to be referred to higher levels of administration, and ultimately the central level. As Soviet reform economist Maiminas argued:

> This (...) requires centralized decision-making, since at lower levels it is impossible to grasp the interdependencies. On the other hand, this can move decision-making far above the level of the actual production units and the producers, and this, and also the vast scale of the system, argues for decentralization. An optimum system of information flows, control and regulation must be devised.[6]

We are not to worry much about such co-ordination issues, since each local community of producers or citizens will be able to send deputies, under strict instructions, to higher decision-making bodies, to co-ordinate activities between them by negotiating which inputs they may be able to receive and in return, which output they will be able to supply. As Van der Walt summarises:

> Federalism linking neighbourhoods and workplaces, producers with other producers as well as consumers, would allow large-scale but participatory and democratic economic planning. There would not be a state co-ordinating production from above through a central plan or a market co-ordinating production through the price system but a vast economic federation of self-managing enterprises and communities, with a supreme assembly at its head that would balance supply and demand, and direct and distribute world production on the basis of demands from below.[7]

It is the task of this 'supreme assembly' to ensure that inputs match up with democratically selected output targets for the economy as a whole – in a modern economy with hundreds of millions of unique products this is no small task, especially if the supreme planners only have the physical measurements of these goods to go on in the absence of commensurable units of account. It will have to assemble the data on both these variables and combine them to shape each local plan into a series of interlinked production programmes. These functions that the supreme assembly is expected to carry out are incidentally more or less identical to the main planning agency under war communism, the VSNKh.

---

6   Nove 2011, p. 124.
7   Van der Walt and Schmidt 2009, pp. 68–9.

We should expect that this 'supreme assembly', the anarchist Central Planning Board, will therefore grapple with more or less identical problems related to the (a) lack of rational criteria for determining input requirements and the setting output targets from the vantage point of the vast economy as a whole, and (b) the intractable volume of information that will need to be gathered and digested. The anarchist central planners would have to mix and match many millions of inputs to a set of millions of types of output, whose exact proportions will also have to be specified. They will further have determine the interdependent, integrated activities of productive facilities, i.e. which workplaces will receive what supplies of materials and equipment as well as setting temporal specifications while ensuring their complete consistency. All this by simply casting votes in a mass assembly – conscious, human control of production and distribution.

Producers would transmit information about their input requirements and potential output levels upward by means of their elected, mandated deputies. Once this information has been collected, the supreme assembly would have to confront highly aggregated quantities of millions of goods, which have to be converted – democratically and consciously – into detailed instructions and refer these to production units taking into account spatial and time dimensions. This is, democratic window dressing aside, highly centralised planning. Under Soviet planning, for example, 'consumer enterprises submit their estimated requirements (indents) to the appropriate administration (their administrative superior). The administration checks them, possibly adjusts them, adds them up and sends them to the chief administration of supply of the ministry'.[8]

If the supreme assembly should fail their intractable task of aggregating and processing all this information – and they would fail, being flooded by a deluge of statistical noise – to formulate a series of fully compatible, detailed plans, the supply chain will grind to a halt since production units will not receive the necessary instructions (or non-binding suggestions) to act. They cannot grasp the systemic connectivity from their vantage point since they form only a small part by themselves, and therefore rely on the administrators at higher levels of planning to inform them of these interconnected linkages and structural interdependencies.

Suppose, however, that the supreme assembly should manage to formulate a feasible central plan (i.e. a plan that covers all interdependent activities of the economy as a whole and has smoothed over any discrepancies between supply and demand) each economic unit will subsequently have to be compelled

---

8   Ellman 1973, p. 20.

to actually carry out their part, since the plan would falter if 'one link in this multilevel chain' breaks down. If a production unit would refuse to implement their production programme and act contrary to the information contained in the democratically approved central plan, the entire supply chain will – again – grind to a halt, since the required supplies to carry it through would not arrive. Hence, autonomy is out of the question:

> At each level it must be someone's job to ensure that these things are done. They do not happen 'spontaneously', and they are not and cannot be decided by vote, any more than a train crew or station staff can or should decide whether the 12.30 to Manchester should or should not run.[9]

For bottom-up planning to be effective it are eventually becomes necessary to refer it to the central level, where the decisions taken will need to be binding. We thus arrive at a system of economic planning that is both excessively *centralised* and *directive*, involving the supply of information about productive capacity and preferences to the centre, and the flow of instructions on the basis of that information from the centre to the base-level units – all expressed in physical quantities presumably, since money is abolished. Taken to its logical consequence, libertarian socialism is condemned to fall back on a system of centralised, imperative planning on the basis of material balances, albeit blended with democracy. Not only does such a system fail to satisfy libertarian criteria, the abundant experience of centralised planning relying on material balances shows it to be an infeasible approach in relation to the allocation of resources due to considerable information and co-ordination constraints.

When we disregard the libertarian criterium as inconsequential and consider central planning desirable in some form or another, we are still left to invent a rational set of criteria to aid the 'supreme economic assembly' in executing their tasks. In other words, such proposals, insofar as they lack any mention of decision criteria, bring us no further than what the experiment of war communism has exposed about the nature of economic planning more than a hundred years ago. Furthermore, without even considering many more fundamental issues, such as producers being potentially deceitful in supplying information about material requirements or production possibilities in order to secure more or better resources.

An additional issue resides in determining the proportions of different types of output, which according to Engels would be achieved under communism

---

9 Nove 1991a, p. 36.

thus: '[t]e useful effects of the various articles of consumption, compared with one another and with the quantities of labour required for their production, will in the end determine the plan'.[10] The previous suggestions seem to imply that under 'libertarian communism' citizens, or their delegates, negotiate their preferences and settle upon a final product mix by casting a vote. This presents an obvious problem of scale. The number of goods that are produced and consumed in a modern economy rank in the order of tens of millions. The number of potential output mixes for society as a whole are infinite. Since some needs or wants will have to go unmet (unless resource constraints are conjured out of existence), the members of society would need to express their *relative* preferences for different goods. However, as Nove pointed out: 'In no society can an elected assembly decide by 115 votes to 73 where to allocate ten tonnes of leather, or whether to produce another 100 tonnes of sulphuric acid' – and then repeat the same procedure a couple of million times.[11] Not only would democracy not make centralised planning using material balances workable, it complicates the matter by drawing in an innumerable amount of additional people to make an innumerable amount of qualitative decisions. Such procedures lack the decision criteria that would allow producers to conduct themselves efficiently, rationally, and responsibly. Laibman, then, asks quite correctly, 'is participation something to be maximized, or optimized?'.[12] Furthermore, Castoriadis pointed out that the distribution of consumption goods:

> cannot be based on direct democracy (...) it would be tantamount to a pointless tyranny of the majority over the minority. If 40 percent of the population wish to consume a certain article, there is no reason why they should be deprived of it under pretext that the other 60 percent prefer something else.[13]

Allocation, in effect, would be guided by oral pleadings in mass assemblies, with persuasion and lobbying determining distribution priorities. Since productive resources available to society are necessarily limited, mutually exclusive expressions of demand will necessarily be come to a fore in such meetings. A resultant cacophony would render rational allocation impossible; as also observed under central planning. The implication is strikingly similar to the *de facto* planning processes of administrative command economies, in

---

10   MECW 25: 295.
11   Nove 1991a, p. 76.
12   Laibman 2002, pp. 88–91.
13   Castoriadis 1988, p. 123.

which 'political entrepreneurship' was an important factor. For example, in North Korea, '[b]ecause resources were limited and the transportation system suffered bottlenecks, resources were diverted to politically well-connected enterprises or those whose managers complained the loudest. An enterprise or industry that performed better than others often did so at the expense of others'.[14] Thus, in addition to inadequately and arbitrarily 'resolving' the question of how and where to allocate limited resources, it could also potentially stimulate competition between workplaces and political corruption. Thus:

> Planners heed the signals of shortage and surplus. They try to expand the supply to areas from which more and louder complaints are being received of worse provisions than usual, longer waiting times, and more frequent forced substitutions. To make these transfers, of course, products and resources have to be withdrawn from somewhere. There is rarely a chance to do so from areas with a surplus in the literal sense. So, obviously, they have to rob areas where there are shortage phenomena, but they are less acute than usual.[15]

This also harks back to the experience of war communism, as discussed previously. It was impossible, it turned out, to prioritise allocation in a way that corresponded supply to competing levels of demands in any coherent fashion – arguably, the lack of democracy simplified this process since the volume of preferences that was being expressed was kept in check. Needless to say, when confronting excess demand in relation to different sets of goods, cutting supply in equal proportions across all sectors or consumers is wholly inadequate, since this does not take into account the respective costs and results that are associated with different proportions of output.[16]

Ticktin has suggested that the coefficients, 'as shown in an input-output analysis', would be measured and used as the basis to align production with demand as measured in 'surveys'.[17] Thus, '[t]he planners would obtain the nature of consumer demand by asking people directly', which Mandel had also suggested as solution.[18] The Group of International Communists also believed that it would be a matter of the 'appropriate demand' for a given product

---

14   Savada 1994, p. 113.
15   Kornai 2007, p. 287.
16   Kantorovich 1965, p. xxvii.
17   Ollman 1998, p. 160.
18   Mandel 1986, pp. 5–37.

being 'communicated by distributive organisations'.[19] This does not solve the issue because we are not interested in consumer preferences for products in an absolute sense. We are interested in knowing which *proportions* of goods we should produce since the volume of production has to observe the hard limits imposed on it by resource constraints (time, energy, labour, materials, equipment), and therefore planners will need to know the *relative* preferences of consumers – consequently, simply resupplying facilities and warehouses as inventories deplete does not solve the issue.

Strumilin had described how 'if volume of output (of any good) rises in geometric progression, satisfaction rises in arithmetic progression'.[20] As Nove summarises his proposal of using labour-time accounting; 'every additional unit of labour [*tred*] used in production gives diminishing marginal social utility. At some point the labour effort will produce insufficient social utility to be worth making, and this will represent the limit of production'.[21] What is required, in other words, is to have a mechanism in place which allows for the comparing of efforts and results in order to then allocate resources to their uses where they generate the best overall result. If we produce too much of one type of good we forego producing some other item that might have been more useful. Therefore, according to Albert, the production of output should be increased up to a point 'so that, by not producing that item we can use our productive capability to produce something else that benefits us more'.[22]

In order to make such decisions, society needs to know the trade-off between producing different articles. For surveys of consumer preferences to be an effective tool, therefore, consumers would have to give detailed rankings of different products, to inform planners of the preferred relative proportions of the goods and services that they believe should be made available. These rankings would need to assign 'weights' to different goods according to relative preferences, scoring them on a scale of 1–10, say, and the overall scores should be capped by the amount of consumption permitted by society's productive capacity, since society cannot consume more output than it produces (and it is not a given that we know these constraints, since production units may manipulate data to their own benefit). These rankings will also have to account for the fact that some goods and services require more resources to produce compared to others, making them more costly to society. Hence, the catalogue of products will need to project the costs of each product to consumers according

---

19   GIC 1930.
20   Cited in Nove 2011, p. 56.
21   Nove 2011, pp. 56–7.
22   Albert 2003, p. 124.

to which they can weigh them compared to how intensely they prefer them to some other good. Consumers would thus rate the various goods based on the amount of points they cost and the amount of points they possess.

Note that the actual consumption by households will have to be bound to their consumption list, otherwise the surveys lose their value in the planning of production. If consumers submit certain scores for goods, but end up consuming an entirely different bundle of goods it would throw the planning process off balance. Moreover, since the entire chain of production spans long periods from the point of extracting raw material to the end product becoming available, these consumption requests will have to be submitted months in advance, if not much earlier. In sum, in roundabout way we started by issuing simple questionnaires to consumers to avoid the use of money and prices in communist society, and in the end find ourselves reinventing prices and budgets in a the much more convoluted forms of surveys, rankings, and catalogues as part of preplanning consumption.

It has also been variously suggested that linear programming could be used to make sense of the cacophony of consumer demands and help plan a moneyless economy,[23] which frankly rests on a misunderstanding. Linear optimisation programmes can help calculate the optimal way to use resources given a set of constraints in order to maximise a given objective function. The problem resides in formulating an objective function; in addition to mapping the constraints. If we have a comprehensive list of resource constraints and a detailed list of final output, and we take the latter as the objective function, we can in theory calculate the optimal way to achieve our ends based on the initial conditions and final output targets. There are a great number of variables involved, a large number of productive facilities facing short-run production constraints; time and spatial dimensions that need to be matched (a certain factory fixed in location requiring certain inputs at a specific time); different possible compositions of inputs, and so on. This, in addition to requiring immense computing power, presupposes intimidate knowledge of the initial conditions and the final list of required output. However, neither are 'given' nor readily available to planners for them to run them through optimisation programmes. Producers will have to volunteer reliable data and consumers will have to announce their relative preferences for different output bundles. While broad priorities can be laid down by political procedures, the level of detail needed to formulate a comprehensive plan for a national economy is so voluminous that it cannot be handled by the centre. Without a comprehensive list of relative needs and

---

23   SPGB 2014.

wants, there is no objective function to be maximised and, as we have established, this list cannot be derived from a census. Indeed, Kantorovich pointed out that his method can be used *'not for deciding what to produce but how to produce it'*.[24]

One might instead use mathematical optimisation where the objective function is defined as maximum expenditure given the initial amount of resources, so that the level of production is maximised – to grow the stock of goods and materials by the maximally achievable increment on the basis of primary input availability (i.e. maximise output, as a very poor substitute for 'wealth'). There would be no mechanism, however, that ensures that these outlays link up to consumer preferences, thus rendering this application of technique useless for the purpose of rational economic planning. As a matter of fact, we find much the same mechanism existed in the Soviet Union, as Soviet economist Danilov-Danilyan described:

> our economy can be characterised as cost-inducing (*zatratnoi*), because the economic mechanism for many years orientated enterprises to increase costs rather than economise on them, since it is precisely through expenditure (*zatraty*) that the command-bureaucratic system measures the results of economic activity: there is no other way in the absence of a market, the only known objective instrument by which to compare costs and results.[25]

In short, very little serious thought has been put forth on how allocation and distribution could work under socialism. Rejection of the Soviet experience as 'state-capitalism' tends to produce an intellectual complacency that is conducive to making such errors. Nappalos tells us that Marxist-Leninist regimes 'resembled capitalism more closely than' a moneyless, marketless communist economy.[26] Since the Soviet Union was a failure of (a particular variant of) capitalism, socialists stand to learn little from it, presumably. Yet, libertarian communism (by the account of Nappalos and Van der Walt, at any rate) reproduces fundamental economic problems that socialist economists grappled with in practice, but now spread out diffusely among the level of the neighbourhood, workplace, and federal assembly. This solves nothing, since all that is changed is that now everyone is expected to be a Gosplan planner and deal with the same millions of 'equations' expressed qualitatively, in the absence of commensur-

---

24   Kantorovich 1965, p. 138.
25   Nove 1991b, p. 579.
26   Nappalos 2012, p. 291.

able units of measurement. Thus, far from solving the economic calculation problem through decentralisation of decision-making authority, it increases the information overload problem in actual fact. Indeed, as Laibman expresses agreeably: 'I know this is a bitter pill for many "western" Marxists to swallow, but the Soviet experience, for all of its serious and ultimately fatal flaws, is a vast laboratory of socialist construction'.[27] Refusal to learn from this experience leads socialists to wanting to reinvent the wheel. Disassociating from the Soviet experience, by denouncing it as state-capitalist, will not ensure that a future socialism will trail a different, better path. In fact, each of these previous examples show how it could have the opposite effect, by unwittingly replicating many of the same features that handicapped socialist economies – even committed libertarian communists, it turns out, accidentally find themselves reinventing directive, centralised planning. This, then, is an important additional, instrumental argument why we ought to treat Soviet-style socialism as part of the overall inheritance of socialism.

Nove commented that it 'is extraordinary how' socialists had 'failed to think seriously about how the "associated producers" (...) could in fact control the vast complexities of a modern industrial economy with its millions of different products and multimillion interconnections and interdependencies'.[28] He noted that the level of economic debate in the socialist movement on this subject, compared to debate under war communism, had in fact regressed.[29] Unfortunately, matters have scarcely improved (with a small number of notable exceptions discussed below). For instance, the proposal by Ticktin is virtually identical to Chayanov's proposal (with the useless addition of consumer surveys); many 'models' lack the same economic links for resource allocation as Strumilin's model, such as Fotopoulos' anarchistic 'inclusive democracy';[30] Van der Walt accidentally finds himself reinventing centralised, imperative planning resembling war communism; and some visions, including but not limited to Bookchin's, simply lacks an economic mechanism altogether under the mistaken assumption that 'abundance' would somehow dissolve constraints on production into thin air.[31] Moving forward, we will focus on the positive exceptions.

---

27   Laibman 2002a, p. 117.
28   Nove 2011, p. 59.
29   Nove 2004.
30   Fotopoulos 1997.
31   See e.g. Buick and Crump in *State Capitalism* (1986, p. 132), who conflate the 'folk' definition of 'scarcity' with the technical meaning in economics, and therefore mistakenly assume that mainstream economics postulates that being able to produce 'enough' to satisfy material needs – clothes, food, and so on – would render prices obsolete. Instead,

There is thus a clear need for a *socialist economics* – defying protestations out of the left periphery of the socialist movement. A field of study concerned with finding the incentive compatible, technical means and institutional features by which a society organised around collective ownership can compare the use of resources to the results of their application in order to select a progressively more efficient pattern of utilisation over time. This scientific requirement emerges not from trying to grasp the blind forces and invisible laws of the market, but rather from the blindness of producers to structural interdependencies and the blindness of the centre to the realities and possibilities on the ground – while presupposing the mutual dependence of the centre and local economic units. This necessitates approaching the question of production and distribution under socialism methodically and scientifically, formulating institutional structures and incentive schemes by which producers at the local level and planners at the centre become locked into a symbiotic institutional arrangement.

The Marxist blind spot in this respect is tied to the 'direct socialisation' model of communism, which suggests that society based around social ownership might be treated as a single association and unitarily directed by scientific planning, of which the Soviet model was a particular outgrowth and application. It was forced to grapple with and was handicapped by information constraints that disable any such centralised approach to co-ordination – the instruments of Marxism were not equipped to deal with these unanticipated difficulties. The practical defects experienced by Soviet practice and the attempts to grapple with them become part of an 'economics', which was not due to the 'capitalistic' nature of Soviet-style socialism, but originated in the impossibility of unifying the vast and complex networks of production and distribution at the hands of a single directing centre. Even 'libertarian' communism, which does not necessarily share the 'directly associated socialisation' approach of Marxism, would be reduced to central, directive planning. In either case, 'socialist economics' is not a logical contradiction since socialism is in need of foundations in economic science to deal with the complex interacting variables associated with information and motivation problems that inherently arise from the complications of large-scale production and distribution, rather than exclusively from the social experience of generalised market relations.

'scarcity' exists wherever factors of production – labour and equipment – are required in production. Virtually by definition, the supply of labour and technology is limited, finite, and therefore 'economic' considerations will have to play their part in production and distribution.

The rational allocation of resources requires that both costs and results can be compared, which presupposes that they can be expressed in commensurable ways. This in turn would enable planners to evaluate the trade-off of using different types of equipment in different capacities producing different types of output, since society is necessarily faced with such choices due to inherent constraints on the overall volume of production – the fundamental problem of economics. This problem branches off into a multitude of secondary problems. Secondary problems arise from the manner in which the primary economic problem is dealt with; and so forth. In approaching these problems, taking into account the critical commentary, made decades earlier by Nove, will prove fruitful; to quote him at length:

> It is my contention that Marx had little to say about the economics of socialism, and that the little he did say was either irrelevant or directly misleading. The word 'feasible' is in the title of this book as a kind of flank guard against utopian definitions. One can, if one chooses (and, as I shall show, many have so chosen), *define* socialism in such a way that economic problems as we know them would not, indeed *could* not, exist. If one assumes 'abundance', this excludes opportunity-cost, since there would be no mutually exclusive choices to make. If one assumes that the 'new man', unacquisitive, 'brilliant, highly rational, socialised, humane', will require no incentives, problems of discipline and motivation vanish. If it is assumed that all will identify with the clearly visible general good, then the conflict between general and partial interest, and the complex issues of centralisation/decentralisation, can be assumed out of existence. If human beings in society can see *ex ante* what needs to be produced and the correct way of producing and utilising all products, then there is no need for *ex post* verification; the indirect and imperfect link between use-value and exchange-value, via exchange relations and the market, can be replaced by direct conscious human decisions on production for use. Division of labour will have been overcome, by 'brilliant' multipurpose human beings. 'While not everyone may be able to paint as well as Raphael, everyone will be able to paint exceedingly well'. Everyone will govern, there will not be any governed. Since all competing interests will have disappeared, there will be no need to claim rights of any sort, no need for restrictive rules, laws, judges, or a legislature. Of course, there will be no state, no nation-states (and so no foreign trade, or any trade). The wages system will have gone, as well as money.[32]

---

32   Nove 1991a, p. 11.

This also intersects with a secondary objective of socialist economics. Which is to situate socialism into a process of social development – in a word, *socialisation*. This entails that the formal aspect, the abolition of private property and the conversion of means of production into the collective property of the political community, but also the progressive development of social attitudes consistent with the management of publicly owned property in the greater interests of the community. Thus, 'a long road separates the nationalization of the means of production from their complete socialization, the creation of what we often call a socialist attitude to work and social ownership'.[33] In this regard we should first of all interest ourselves in the initial stages of socialist development, since strong foundations are necessary to consolidate and enable progressive development. A model of feasible socialism will have to be built on reasonable assumptions. We should not abstract away from the realities of society any conditions or circumstances deemed inconvenient. These assumptions should err on the conservative side since pessimism would afford some slack under real circumstances. Although it does not follow from this that we should swing the other way and adopt caricatures of human nature. Neither the 'Homo Economicus' of neoclassical economics nor the 'realist' conception of human nature used in the field of international relations, for example, provide very useful or realistic premises for modelling human behaviour.[34]

To Nove, a feasible socialism meant that 'it should be conceivable within the lifespan of one generation', 'without making extreme, utopian, or far-fetched assumptions'.[35] For our purpose, we will assume that the skeletal model of socialism outlined in this book represents a society as it has just emerged out of a process of social transformation. The citizens of this society are the first generation living under socialism and a mature 'socialist consciousness' in this society has not yet nestled in the minds of its citizens. This means that they share roughly the same mixed motivations and social attitudes that influence the behaviour of workers under liberal capitalism and actually existing socialism (which were very alike). For example, workers have complex motivational orderings, and will generally strive for a comfortable life for themselves and their kin before they do society at large, although they are open to broader considerations about community as well. We will further assume that the scope of knowledge of individuals is restricted by their social standpoint and exhibit practical rationality, whereby they use and filter information heuristically, efficiently, and strategically given their ignorance of the full scope

---

33   Brus 1972, p. 82.
34   See for example Freyberg-Inan 2004.
35   Nove 1991a, p. 12.

of detailed knowledge, to arrive at some deliberate conclusion about means and ends. Lastly, we will assume that 'human nature' is somewhat malleable. On average, people share a propensity toward a range between 'weak egoism' and 'weak altruism' and develop these dispositions to varying degrees in response to the external conditions of their socialisation and material circumstances.

Based on these assumptions we set about designing the social institutions of a feasible socialism. We will need to specify a list of interlocking institutions, assign tasks, divide responsibilities between different levels of administration, design a system of incentives, and formulate rational criteria to help the various institutions in executing their tasks in an informationally efficient manner. This will not only have to take into account that citizens are limited by the extent to which socialist consciousness and civic virtue have developed, but also by the need for the institutional framework to allow for the deepening of social attitudes consistent with socialism. In doing so, political economy for socialism will help to illustrate how and why a particular arrangement public institutions will be effective in dealing with economic problems; as Chandrasekhar argued:

> even if we postulate a socialist economy as a planned economy, until we have specified the precise categories of decisions that are centrally planned, the institutions that would make decentralised decisions, and the fall-out of central decisions for the operational functioning of lower units of command, we have not fully specified the system. We are also left with the problem that the extent and organisational form of decentralisation needs to be defined so as to avoid importing in full the instability and waste of capitalism.[36]

As specified in the introduction, socialism will have to be ambitious, attractive, coherent, and feasible. Expressed differently, according to economic metrics, socialism should be capable of reaching high levels of allocative efficiency, productive efficiency, dynamic efficiency, and macroeconomic stability – in relation to any trade-offs between these variables, socialism should be capable of balancing them in such a way that the greatest improvements in the material welfare can be secured. In terms of our political metrics, socialism should preserve independence from arbitrary power, while encouraging civic duty, collective responsibility, and self-mastery. These are broadly the republican objectives of our project of socialist renewal, discussed subsequently.

---

36   Chandrasekhar 1998, pp. 45–6.

2   The Community of Citizens and Comrades

Lest we forget this is a book of political theory, we will now turn to our account of the tradition of republicanism to provide some indication of the utility republicanism presents for the project of socialist renewal. This appropriation of civic republicanism by socialism is motivated principally by the rejection of inferences woven into the notion of the direct association of modern social production, discussed previously. The 'one vast people's workshop' fallacy lends itself to the implication that social production and administration in communist society will be conducted without social conflict: 'a society in which there are no classes (...) can only be a society of comrades'. By extension, '[s]ince there is no class war, the State has become superfluous'.[37] In early Soviet practice, individual interests were categorically denied and suffocated, instead of channelled into socially desirable directions.[38] If we admit that individual and social interests can diverge to one extent or another in relation to both means and ends under a system of social ownership, and that social conflict can thus manifest over the distribution of material and immaterial goods even where opposing classes are absent, we are suddenly prodded to think of ways to structure the political community of comrades to adjudicate the conflicts that might arise between them. In my estimation, republican institutional features will be able to effectively arbitrate conflicting interests in a socialist regime.

What follows is an exposition of the core conceptual framework of civic republicanism. The intention is not to interrogate the premises of the republican tradition, but rather to provide an overview of its basic conceptual language and values. More specifically, we will draw on 'neo-republicanism' to help formulate an institutional framework of a feasible socialism. The 'classical republicanism' of the Graeco-Roman world was revived in the renaissance, and again rediscovered and renewed in the late twentieth century in academia and re-conceptualised as 'neo-republicanism'.[39] It is this latest reincarnation, which has recovered the progressive elements of the classical republican tradition, that we will appropriate to develop a unique political vision of republican socialism. While, to a certain extent, republicanism and socialism may seem unlikely bedfellows, since neo-republicanism was conceived of as 'post-socialist' challenge to liberalism,[40] the usefulness of republicanism for a socialist programme will become progressively clearer as we move

---

37   Bukharin and Preobrazhensky 1920.
38   Sutela and Mau 1998, p. 59.
39   Honohan 2002; Laborde and Maynor 2008, pp. 2–3.
40   Gaus 2003.

forward. Republicanism is after all, as Pettit puts it, 'congenial' to socialism.[41] Neo-republicanism and socialism share key values ranging from active citizenship and a concern for the concentration of wealth, to an opposition to social relations and structures of domination, critiques of liberal individualism,[42] and a tendency toward universalism and internationalism.

At its most basic core, civic republicanism is a political tradition stemming from the ancient Graeco-Roman world. Classical scholars belonging to this tradition denied that 'government' was the private affair of royalty, instead proposing that the conduct of government was a 'public affair' (*Res Publica*, in Latin). An important political characteristic of the Roman Republic was the separation of powers corresponding to different social bases. Political power was dispersed among diverse public bodies composed of representatives acting on behalf of different classes, such as the patricians and plebeians. Political procedures were constitutionally defined and limited in order to curtail the uncontrolled exercise of power.[43] Republican thinkers of the classical Graeco-Roman world saw it thus:

> Monarchy, aristocracy, and democracy, according to these writers, are prone to degenerate into tyranny, oligarchy, and mob rule, respectively; but a government that disperses power among the three elements could prevent either the one, the few, or the many from pursuing its own interest at the expense of the common good. With each element holding enough power to check the others, the result should be a free, stable, and long-lasting government.[44]

The constitution of the Roman Republic was mixed, balanced between various legislative assemblies and among elected magistrates in a multitude of offices with varying types of powers and functions associated with each. This republican conception of the 'mixed constitution' derives from its concern for the common good, which sets this tradition apart from liberal individualism, which prioritises individual interests above the broader concerns of community. In liberal thought, the political community should create the preconditions that allow individuals to pursue their own conceptions of good life and permit bargaining between rival private interests in the political arena.[45] Citizens, in

---

41   Pettit 2002, p. 142.

42   Brest 1988, pp. 1623–7; Laborde and Maynor 2008, pp. 18–19.

43   Mouritsen 2017, pp. 3–8.

44   Dagger 2004, p. 169.

45   Dagger 2006, p. 155.

the republican conception, should surrender, at least partially, their particular interests to the common good out of a sense of civic duty. It is necessary, then, that citizens experience a sense of solidarity to one another as well as loyalty to core political values of the republic. This should bind all citizens to their common liberty. Social bonds and a shared basis in public life, or civil society, should facilitate the public-spiritedness of citizens. By contrast, liberal individualism, which venerates particular interests, would more likely result in 'corruption', by eroding the public interest. Civic virtue, then, safeguards the republic:

> If the balanced constitution is the characteristic form of the republic, civic virtue is its lifeblood. Without citizens who are willing to defend the republic against foreign threats and to take an active part in government, even the mixed constitution will fail. Republics must thus engage in what Michael Sandel calls 'a formative politics (...) that cultivates in citizens the qualities of character that self-government requires' (...). Constitutional safeguards may be necessary to resist avarice, ambition, luxury, idleness, and other forms of corruption, but they will not be enough to sustain freedom under the rule of law. Replenishing the supply of civic virtue through education and other means will thus be one of the principal concerns of a prudent republic.[46]

To Schnapper, the republic can best be qualified as a 'community of citizens';[47] or, as Lovett and Pettit put it, 'a community of equal citizens governed by law'.[48] This political community rests upon active political participation by the citizenry. Again, this hinges on the willingness to forfeit private interests to some extent. However, '[t]his is not to say that republicans believe that citizens would easily or quickly come to agreement about what the common good requires if only government could be freed from the stranglehold of interest groups'.[49] Political dialogue is necessary for citizens to develop a conception of the common good, but it is not required that a consensus be formed.[50] Deliberation is therefore integral to republican conceptions of governance.[51] The capacity for political dialogue must be nurtured. First, the personal temperaments and

---

46   Dagger 2004, p. 170.
47   Schnapper 1998.
48   Lovett and Pettit 2009, p. 22.
49   Dagger 2004, p. 175.
50   Honohan 2002, pp. 222–3.
51   Peterson 2011, pp. 3–4.

individual qualities of citizens have to be attuned to dialogical exchange in order for a culture of political deliberation to emerge; second, the institutional infrastructure of public life has to be capable of acting as an arena for dialogue or deliberation. This is the basis for self-government in the republican sense.[52] In the 'neo-Roman' conception, self-government is instrumental in ensuring that republican liberty is sustained through political participation; but the 'neo-Athenian' republicans also emphasise the importance of political participation in its own right, for the development of virtue in citizens, under the assumption that the communal nature of humans can be expressed through political participation.[53] Freedom, in this tradition, is understood as self-mastery.[54]

While republicanism is a very broad church, bound only by a fairly loose commitment to a set of concerns and values, neo-Roman thinkers Pettit and Lovett maintain that the republican conception of freedom is the paramount value that underpins the whole edifice of republican thought.[55] All other republican values, such as the mixed constitution, civic virtue, and self-government, flow from the republican conception of freedom: they are necessary instruments to secure liberty by acting as checks on arbitrary power. Republican freedom, or sometimes neo-Roman freedom, is defined as 'freedom from domination' and forms, per this view, the core value upon which republican thought rests. According to the neo-republican view, an individual is considered free when they are not subject to domination, i.e. when they are not tied to the arbitrary will of another. There are some variant definitions of the same core concept, but in all cases republican freedom emphasises independence from arbitrary power, both historically and theoretically.[56] This means that citizens should have a clearly defined range of free choices that cannot be violated on the basis of the capricious whims of a principal actor. This is to say, power in social relations and social structures alike should be 'constitutionally' limited so that citizens can elect to pursue a course of action within a clearly defined range of permissible choices.[57] The boundaries imposed on this range of free choices should be subject to the stipulation that they track the interests of citizens.[58] The political community may, for example, legitimately intervene in

---

52   Dagger 2006, p. 155.
53   Brest 1988, p. 1623; Laborde and Maynor 2008, pp. 2–3; Laborde 2012, p. 6.
54   Laborde and Maynor 2008, p. 3.
55   Lovett and Pettit 2009, p. ???
56   Dagger 2006, p. 155.
57   Lovett and Pettit 2009, p. 17.
58   Pettit 2002, p. 56.

interpersonal affairs – even when they are formally voluntary – to alleviate the dependency of one person upon another.[59]

While republicanism is 'congenial' to socialism in some respects, the political tradition is also marked by an ambivalent relationship to property. Property is a source of power according to republicanism, and its concentration in the hands of a small segment of the community may allow this stratum to leverage their ownership for political influence on the basis of their factional interests at the expense of the common good ('oligarchic harm', as per Arlen).[60] Furthermore, commerce, according to republican thought, promotes particular interests by materially reinforcing the pursuit of private gain in the marketplace. Thus, the 'materialistic 'virtues' of commerce' arguably displaced notions of active citizenship and civic pride. Republicanism, in this sense, 'constitutes a movement back to a status society of a strikingly pre-modern form'.[61] At the same time, republicans saw in property a means to ascertain independence.[62] This notion was mostly advanced within the historical context of small proprietorship and pre-capitalist manufacturing, when all citizens having potential access to some means of production was at least theoretically plausible. The Jeffersonian Republicans, for example, are representative of this strain of thought. With the advent of large-scale industrial production and the increased concentration of capital, radical republicans repurposed the republican conception of liberty. Instead of seeking a redistribution of property into individual hands and households (which became a progressively untenable objective due to the expansion of industrial manufacturing), the labour republicans re-imagined self-control over the means of production in an industrial context.[63] These radical republicans emphasised that large segments of the population did not own means of production nor did they have a realistic chance of ever acquiring them; and were therefore dependent upon the owners of means of production. The capitalists were thus able to subject the workers to their private and arbitrary will – a violation of republican liberty. In order to rectify this, co-operative production was required – or, to borrow a phrase by G.D.H. Cole from another context, 'self-government in industry'.[64] Marx similarly employed the republican vocabulary of dependency, subjection, and domination in his critique

---

59   Lovett and Pettit 2009, p. 21.
60   Gourevitch 2015; Arlen 2019.
61   Honohan and Jennings 2006; Goodin, cited in Honohan and Jennings 2006, p. 2.
62   Dagger 2006, pp. 159–60.
63   Gourevitch 2015.
64   Cole 1920.

of wage-labour.[65] He, too, re-imagined individual self-controlled production of pre-capitalist manufacturing on the basis of large-scale social labour in the form of communism.[66]

For there to be a socialist republicanism it will have to be established that economic affairs are a 'public good' and therefore that public control over economic resources can be legitimately exercised. Secondly, it must be demonstrated that socialism is capable of sustaining republican values in its social institutions, which is the primary focus of this inquiry. Toward the first point I will briefly put forward the following basic argument: Society and their members – the general public – are dependent upon productive resources for access to means of life, and therefore the pattern of their distribution should be subject to stipulations by the public through their political institutions. That is, the division of productive assets is a public affair and should be brought under the auspices of public authorities. The means of production should be employed to the greatest, overall benefit of the community, under the provision that this does not increase arbitrary power over citizens. This argument differs from the labour republican argument that workers become dependent upon a capitalist, since there the focus lies with the interpersonal dimension of the wage-labour relationship. Rather, this argument posits that the private wills of economic actors, particularly capitalists, can shape the entire course of a society, including, crucially, that of government, through nothing but their capacity to direct productive resources in accordance with their privately formulated, narrow private wills.[67] The rest of society, which are relatively deprived, possess a substantially lower capacity for agency compared to the dominant layers of society. This, then, offers a complementary and somewhat distinct argument to those that emphasise how the 'structural domination' of property subjugates workers impersonally,[68] since it accentuates also how the sum of private wills, divided by asymmetrical resource endowments, drives the allocation of resources as well as public policy at the expense of the common good and therefore potentially at the expense of the general welfare of society. That is, this argument centres the common good and social welfare and frames the latter as a republican concern.[69] A society regu-

---

65   Leipold 2020.
66   MECW 35: 751; Chattopadhyay 1991, p. 13; Wheat 2012, p. 263; Leipold 2020a, pp. 8–9.
67   See for example: Scott 2006, pp. 87–9.
68   Muldoon 2019, pp. 7–8.
69   Neo-republicans have sought to disassociate from the 'collectivism' that the emphasis on the common good in classical republicanism implies (see Lovett 2018). In my contention, the common good should become a substantive end at which society and individuals aim

lated by the sum of private wills may be more unstable, which mirrors republican concerns that saw the capturing of the state by private interests as a threat to stable government and durable common freedom. If we conceive of the distribution of productive assets as a direct public concern, then the unfettered reign of private wills in the market is illegitimate. This is especially valid when the weight of respective private wills and the ability of agents to carry them forward depends on vastly unequal access to material and immaterial resources.

Thus, the personal domination implicated in relations of wage-labour, the impersonal domination rooted in the division of society into owners and non-owners of productive assets, and the rule of private wills in market society each provide a clue why articulating a republican socialism might be an attractive political vision to challenge capitalist hegemony. So while republicanism here appears amendable to socialist aims (we will not subject this hypothesis to systematic treatment here), a potential snag resides in the question of the balanced constitution. A primary concern that binds much of republican thought, at least in the neo-Roman forms, revolves around its concern for 'moderation'. A system of government could become corrupted when the balance of power is shifted in a way that power becomes excessively concentrated in the hands of members of one particular social group or class, which subsequently adapts the government to its own agenda and interests. In other words, when governments excessively lean toward the sectional interests of a particular faction they cease to live up to republican standards. The exercise of power should instead be moderated by being spread among the various social bases that constitute the community, to ensure no one section is free to pursue their factional interests to the detriment of the common good. Each citizen or block of citizens is therefore to moderate their own particular demands and wills by institutional mediation for the greater good of the community. An excessive unity of the state would be vulnerable to being captured by the factional interests of the powerful few, and therefore republicans proposed that public power should be carefully balanced to prevent the domination of one class over another. By the same token, the tradition of republicanism has expressed similar concern for an excess of democracy: If popular volitions – their volatile moods and short-sightedness – are not checked by the virtues of higher classes – endowed with a higher capacity for reason – the capricious passions of lower classes would come to dominate the affairs of government and sink society into chaos. This

---

to realise their common liberties and individual goods. For the purpose of this monograph, it should be taken as a postulation that warrants elaboration in the successive inquiries.

negative, aristocratic perception of popular self-government clearly conflicts with the egalitarian premises of socialism. Marrying civic republicanism and socialism into a single union thus poses the challenge of formulating a way to curb the excesses of democracy without relying on oligarchic features to do so.

The focus of this inquiry lies in designing a broad outline of the social structures of a republican socialism. It is with the core republican values – of self-government, mixed constitution, the common good, civic virtue, and republican liberty – in mind that we will attempt to craft an institutional framework of socialist society. For there to be a republican socialism we would need to demonstrate that a socialist society can accommodate public bodies whose respective discretionary authority can be codified, limited, and balanced, to check against them becoming a source of domination. Furthermore, such a socialist model would need to encourage public-spiritedness, active participation, and sensitivity to the common good. The curtailment of commercial imperatives – which reward and reinforce narrow private interests – is a sound objective, then. The social structures will instead have to cultivate, develop, and reinforce the 'weak altruism' innate to humanity in order to promote concern for the general interest. Above all, a socialist republic will need to safeguard republican liberty, encouraging both self-mastery and independence from arbitrary power. All this falls and stands by the ability to formulate a technically feasible economic mechanism based on common ownership by public authorities.

3 Contradictions of Market and Plan – The Menu of Options

An 'economic mechanism' roughly entails an ensemble of incentives and procedures that guide the allocation and uses of resources in an economy. For example, the market mechanism relies mostly on profits obtained in market exchange to set production and distribution in motion and to structure the choices of firms and consumers. A centrally planned economy typically uses instructions passed down a chain of command and material balances to similar effect. It is of course possible to construct hybrid systems by combining various elements, albeit within the constraints of system-specific properties. It is not unusual for market economies, for example, to be complemented with some form of indicative planning, or more commonly after the neoliberal turn, fiscal and monetary policy. Conversely, in the communist bloc, the attempt to stimulate intensive growth by unleashing local initiative usually led socialist policymakers to increase the role of profit calculations and to relax administrative price controls, particularly in Czechoslovakia and Hungary – which called these policies the 'New Economic Model' and the 'New Economic Mechanism' respectively.

Nove had pointed out that any viable socialist economy will have to combine central and horizontal links.[70] In other words, according to Nove, a socialist economy will have to combine both market exchange and economic planning, as also proposed by Gindin or Hodgson for example.[71] It would seem that the problem socialist economics will need to resolve can be reduced to striking the right balance between elements of planning and the market.[72] The difference between the two mechanisms has sometimes been described as '*ex ante*' co-ordination via plan and '*ex post*' co-ordination via market. Meaning that in the market 'independently taken, atomistic, decisions can only be co-ordinated *ex post*', when the commodities enter the market to verify the extent to which output at certain prices align with consumer requirements.[73] The market, in this capacity, registers the degree to which investment decisions correspond to a correct use of resources, measured along the metric of profit rates. However, this can only be known in hindsight. The market relies on a continual overshooting and undershooting of supply and investments to meet market demand. In a planned economy, by contrast, decision-making between interdependent units of production are co-ordinated '*ex ante*', where the economic plan, drawn up by a planning authority, predetermines the 'correct' proportions between alternative uses of productive resources and therefore the investments that should be undertaken by economic units. Hence, the interdependent activities of production units are co-ordinated directly, via planning. This distinction has been overstated, however. Firms operating the market routinely rely on demand forecasting, and usually develop medium and long-term business plans on the basis of prognoses about future market developments; conversely, activity in a planned economy involves uncertainty about future developments that will have to be verified after the fact. Any economy will therefore rely on both '*ex post*' and '*ex ante*' cues to shape and reshape the structure of investments.

It should further be noted that while varying compositions are conceivable, and have been implemented and practised – also with varying degrees of success. Elements of one system cannot simply be grafted on the mechanism of some other type of system and expect to import wholesale the desired effects

---

70   Nove 1991a, p. 43.
71   Gindin 2019; Hodgson 1998, pp. 429–30.
72   Chandrasekhar 1998, p. 35.
73   Devine 2011, p. 121.

of the first into the latter, without also bringing in its negative by-products. More concretely, it is not possible, or at any rate very unlikely, to integrate the market mechanism into a Soviet-style system of centralised planning in such a way that the benefits (dynamic initiative) can be reaped without also inadvertently importing the cyclical instability of the market. And conversely, if political authorities are intend on preserving the stability of directive planning, the role of the market will likely become confined to such an extent that the desired effects of horizontal contracting are cancelled out: 'the combination of a decentralised market – geared towards efficiency – and central intervention – to take account of socialist ethics – can operate in such a way as to mutually extinguish their separate beneficial effects'.[74] The attempts by socialist governments to achieve exactly these ends, producing both stability and dynamic growth, by incorporating markets within the framework of central planning failed to secure a substantive positive transformation. When reviewing various features it is tempting to fall into the trap of perfectionism:

> the idea arose that an 'optimum economic system' must be designed, combining the best possible 'rules of game' and the best operating control mechanisms. Those setting this aim envisage something like a visit to a supermarket. On the shelves are to be found the various components of the mechanism, incorporating the advantageous qualities of all systems. On one shelf, there is full employment as it has been realised in Eastern Europe. On another, there is the high degree of workshop organisation and discipline, like in a West German or Swiss factory. On a third shelf is economic growth free of recession, on a fourth, price stability, on a fifth, rapid adjustment of production to demands on the foreign market. The system designer has nothing to do but push along his trolley and collect these 'optimum components', and then compose from them at home the 'optimum system'.[75]

In other words, different economic mechanisms do not furnish a menu of options from which to pick and choose so that all disadvantages can be counteracted and wiped out. When dealing with the various tools and instruments to structure economic behaviour, attention is to be paid to their mutual implications and the overall properties that emerge from their combination into a system.

---

74   Kornai 1980, p. 156.
75   Kornai 1980, p. 156.

In the planning toolbox, we may discern between three planning tools to shape economic activity: (i) macroeconomic planning, (ii) strategic planning, and (iii) detailed planning.[76] The first tool of planning deals with the major proportions of an economy as a whole, such as the amount of accumulation versus consumption. The second deals with the structure of investments (including the co-ordination of investments, whereas Lange considered this a separate function). Detailed planning is concerned with defining the specificities of product and service output (the quality, quantity, and detailed structure of output). In Soviet-style socialism, as we have discussed in some detail, the ultimate targets were set administratively on the basis of investment priorities and, residually, according to consumption norms. Strategic planning involved setting broad priorities for industrial development and figuring out the rate of capital formation and aggregate output targets implied by these objectives, which were then further disaggregated into the ultimate targets as part of detailed planning for firms.

Under central planning, the 'ultimate task is to attain the ends of the 'headquarters' which is in a position to issue direct orders to lower echelons' thus 'obliging them to achieve those ends'. The elegance and attraction of this model of centralised planning is clear. Political authorities, acting on behalf of society, can formulate the strategic goals for economic development, ascertain the production requirements of these priorities, and then send this information to producers for them to carry out. Why then, Brus asked, 'build up a complicated decentralized organization, steered by indirect means' and 'a roundabout way of getting a change in the structure of production by means of price manipulations if the same effect is obtainable by direct order given to an enterprise?'. This is because producers may strategically conceal their true preferences and capabilities in order to obtain more resources than necessary, as one example. The question, in other words, presupposes 'that information in the course of flowing in both directions and of processing does not undergo serious distortions, e.g., under the influence of particular interests governed by definite material and other motives'.[77]

To circumvent this strategic behaviour, some socialists were quick to propose to let the market do some of the heavy lifting. This conception famously emerged as a theoretical exercise, where Lange proposed to simulate markets until an optimal central plan was obtained and implemented. As Chandrasekhar noted: 'The obvious blending of markets and planning in

---

76   For example: Cockshott and Cottrell 1993.
77   Brus 1972, p. 12.

Lange's model of socialism is ensured through the separation of the structure of decision-making (which is decentralised) and the hierarchical structure of objectives on which those decisions are made'.[78] Even preceding Lange's purely theoretical model of central planning, discussion related to the incorporation of market exchange into a framework of economic planning took place during the 1920s Soviet industrialisation debate, based on more practical considerations. Market exchange, Bazarov argued, would verify the costs and results of productive efforts, rendering it possible:

> to provide an automatic check of the correctness of all actions [and acts like] an automatic calculating machine showing the results of the activities of each branch of the economy, and of each separate enterprise. I firmly believe that (...) the existence of market and economic accounting ('khozraschet') is the necessary prerequisite of any possible planning, whether there will be a world revolution or not.[79]

This lesson was obtained by the experience of war communism, and in particular by the inability to distribute goods without some verification in the form of sales receipts, which could thereby measure the degree to which distribution accorded with the various economic requirements. Similar conclusions were reached decades later by a host of foreign and domestic analysts of the socialist economies at later stages, ranging from Brus and Nemchinov to Itoh and Dobb. According to these 'neo-Marxist' reformers, the vertical chain of command of central planning would need to be complemented by embedded market relations that would serve the purpose of economic accounting. As Soviet economist Leontyev explained:

> It has been demonstrated beyond doubt that the market provides the mechanism for the verification of the extent to which social labour is distributed in optimum patterns, i.e. the extent to which labour outlays correspond to social needs (...) whether the structure of production is in accordance with consumers' preferences, whether production is of the required quality and whether costs are exceeded or not. (...) The signals supplied by the market indicate the extent to which production plans must be subjected to continuous corrections.[80]

---

78   Chandrasekhar 1998, p. 35.
79   Cited in Erlich 1967, p. 73.
80   Cited in Wilczynski 1972a, pp. 226–7.

If market exchange is allowed full free rein in a socialist system, thus being afforded the freedom to not only regulate the market for consumption goods but also, as a general rule, allow all factor inputs to be acquired by free choice from a number of suppliers in a competitive market without directive planning, then we would have the sort of socialism envisioned by, for example, Schweickart and Nove.[81] Firms operating under a regime of free competition would be entrusted to do the detailed planning – there is no need for the CPB to determine the specificities of the assortment of any and all bakeries, say. Macroeconomic planning would consist of massaging out some imbalances through indicative and strategic planning, using industrial policy, taxing negative externalities, subsidising positive externalities, public investment, and so on. In this way, more socially desirable outcomes are generated than would otherwise emerge spontaneously from free competition alone. This is the difference between, as Kosygin referred to it, directive (or imperative) planning of the Soviet kind and indicative planning.[82] Strategic planning, under market socialism, would not be concentrated in the hands of the centre, but be the sum-total of credit supplied by public banks, taxation policies, interest rates, public expenditures, and the investment patterns developed by co-operative federations and individual co-operatives. A market socialism of this type would allow for a public sector (managing natural monopolies), a large co-operative sector and a smaller private sector subject to restrictions.[83] A capital asset tax – its rate determined in the national budget – could be levied as a sort of rent for the use of publicly owned means of production in order to generate funds for public investment, disseminated through a network of public banks.[84] Enterprises would respond to and shape their activities in relation to market signals, such as price levels (freely established by producers), the rates of return, and interest rates; i.e. through market forces within the context of a degree of social control over investment. Assuming that (i) the capital asset tax is set sufficiently high by popular vote to fund the necessary investments, (ii) hard budget constraints can be maintained, meaning there should be 'free exit' out of the market, and (iii) 'free entry' into the market is somehow facilitated, this sort of 'market socialism' would certainly be 'feasible', in the sense that it would could reproduce itself and perform reasonably well. It would, it has to be stressed, require actively avoiding the urge by public authorities to intervene arbitrarily in the affairs of production co-operatives.

---

81   Nove 1991a; Schweickart 2002.
82   In Nove 2011, p. 8.
83   Nove 1991a; Gindin 2019.
84   Schweickart 2002, pp. 53–6.

Market socialism would in any case struggle to avoid business cycles, nor would it likely be able to provision full employment.[85] The empirical record of Yugoslavia's socialism shows how such a system is susceptible to high structural unemployment due to a tendency exhibited by workers to expand production by over-capitalisation rather than by increasing employment, since the latter would eat into their income. Moreover, workers could misuse credit to increase current income and vacate the enterprise before loan repayments are due – although, presumably, this tendency could be partially curbed by stricter monetary and fiscal control (and possibly by keeping tabs on the credit scores of individual workers, affecting future employment in case of records of egregious abuse). Effectively, a market socialism that manages to evade the traps and faults of Yugoslavia's design would be governed by the competition of capitals, with firms subject to the ebb and flow of structural forces beyond their individual control, being at the mercy of the vagaries of the market. Within this ocean over which no conscious control can be exercised, self-government would be limited to vessels of workplace democracy navigating the turbulent waves of market fluctuations. Furthermore, socialism should strive to do away with the motive force of production being tied up with particular, commercial interests. This would otherwise reinforce the impersonality of market exchange being the primary social bonds connecting the socialist community. Since we hope to displace private motives by a general concern for the common good, the more or less free exercise of commerce by co-operative enterprises is unconducive to our aim of disseminating socialist consciousness and civic virtue. Socialists, if conceding the need for markets at all, will therefore naturally gravitate toward amending market mechanisms by introducing considerable administrative checks on their free operation. Among them is Gindin.

He imagines a more proactive role for the state in his version of market socialism, arguing that enterprises in Yugoslavia were excessively autonomous (which does not at all do justice to the depth and complexity of the Yugoslav experiment); and judges Soviet planning to have been overly ambitious. On the basis of this (false) assumption, he proposes a form of socialism that combines a central framework to help structure horizontal relations between firms. For example, he proposes that the central planning authorities should set the wage level of a given industry to balance supply and demand. Within a general framework, sectors are free to further adjust wages to allocate labour-power between different firms. Striking the right balance between markets and planning, to him, also means organising sectoral (and regional) councils, composed

---

85   Brus and Łaski 1989, pp. 105–31.

of representatives of workers drawn from the firms associated with different sectors (and regions). Within the scope of decisions made by these councils, the labour-managed firms dispose of their output via the market. However, the 'central planning board would still allocate funds to each sector according to national priorities'. This logically requires that profits are largely taxed away and pooled into a central fund. Reinvestment decisions are thus centralised and then disaggregated, flowing from the centre via the sectoral councils to the enterprises. Investment criteria, Gindin argues, should be based on enhancing the productivity of those enterprises that underperformed, as well as social criteria (such as promoting full employment). As such, investment funds are not automatically allocated to the enterprises that obtain the highest rates of return. What would emerge, in sum, is an economy structured by vertically determined social guidelines and horizontal market allocation.

Gindin admits that his proposal of reallocating funds based on broad criteria beyond the rates of profit of individual firms may breed resentment among the workers of more efficient firms, but argues that this will diminish as higher levels of socialist consciousness develop. In effect, Gindin's vision of socialism promotes soft budget constraints as a deliberate policy objective. Consequently, the labour-managed firms would be deprived of any incentive to work efficiently since any losses incurred by their operations would be covered by public funds on the basis of a social agenda promoting the growth of productivity. Unproductive enterprises would be able to afford more capital goods in an effort to raise their productivity with their level of productivity being inversely related to the funds made available to them. Because Gindin has misidentified Yugoslav socialism with free markets, he overlooks the fact that soft budget constraints were a major cause for economic distortions in Yugoslavia.[86] Overcoming the tendency of market socialism to gravitate toward adopting weak budget constraints is crucial to its feasibility, whereas Gindin's view expressly proposes to soften them on the basis of social concerns, which does not bid well for the sustainability of this model. Furthermore, if profits are taxed away and the proceeds redistributed via some central investment fund, then firms would have cause to inflate their operating costs to retain control over their net revenue – especially when doing so will make their operations less profitable which, under his scheme, also entitle them to a higher share of the central investment fund.

While Gindin proposes that these issues will resolve themselves as new peaks of social consciousness are reached, his belief, to me, seems unfoun-

---

86 Kornai 1979, pp. 18–20.

ded. The institutional outlines of his model do not align with this objective. Acting in ways that are contrary to the long-term durability and well-being of the community would allow producers to obtain material benefits in the form of supplementary payments. Narrow self-interests that violate the general interest would be continually reinforced by financial compensation. According to Gindin, potential social tensions could be relieved 'by including community representatives in the sectoral and workplace planning mechanisms', but the implementation of a similar solution in Yugoslavia paved the road for the definitive abolition of socialism. Self-managed enterprises resisted the involvement of local and national political authorities in their affairs, and legally mandating producers to have their plans vetted by public officials for approval whittled down the accountability and responsibility of producers. All this inspires little confidence that Gindin's model of socialism would prove workable. Such an economy might spur a host of disincentives and ailments akin to those that resulted in Yugoslavia's socialism coming to a screeching and violent close. Gindin's form of socialism would therefore likely suffer a similar fate in practice.

The sort of competitive market socialism advocated by Schweickart and drawn up by Nove is more feasible than Gindin's. Such a market socialism would not suffer from the major information and incentive problems associated with central, directive planning.[87] The greatest challenge for market socialism, in terms of economic feasibility, would lie in promoting macroeconomic stability and facilitating the free entry and exit of firms into and from the market, as well as devising some capital tax policy to minimise the tendency toward excessive capitalisation. However, before we arrive at the conclusion that competitive markets are the best available economic mechanism for socialism, we will turn our attention to a series of recently developed theoretical models of socialism, beginning by the proposal of 'negotiated co-ordination'.

4   Negotiated Co-ordination and Allocation

The economic mechanism of negotiated co-ordination, which was mainly developed by Devine with some additional support from Adaman was an early attempt to renew the socialist calculation debate by advancing a socialist vis-

---

87   Such problems may emerge as diseconomies of scale internal to large-scale firms but are constantly checked by the disciplinary mechanisms of the market.

ion based on a participatory (or democratic) planning procedure. The basic institutions of the model are familiar and include self-governing production units, intermediate negotiation bodies, and a 'National Planning Commission', which is held to account by national political bodies. The planning process begins by defining, through political means, various social priorities, including the macroeconomic proportions (and in particular the ratio of consumption to accumulation), social policies, and so forth.[88] The planning of investment is divided into major investment, minor investment, and replacement investment. The determining of major investment priorities will be the responsibility of the planning commission, and specific major investment projects are subsequently formulated through negotiation bodies, in which members of the planning board are represented. Minor investment is determined directly by negotiation bodies, using whatever criteria they find expedient to realise social and economic objectives; while replacement investment is at the discretion of individual production units themselves.[89] Economic decision-making will take into account the costs of investments as well as various social factors. For instance, given the choice between two alternatives, the investment project which would generate more fulfilling work may take precedence (provided this is considered a social priority) even if the expected rate of return may be comparatively lower.[90]

To guide such decision making, primary input prices are generated on the basis of macroeconomic priorities. Given the prices assigned to the primary inputs – labour-power, production goods, and raw material – the production units decide upon a particular input mix and set the price of their output on the basis of long-run costs.[91] This distinction between primary input prices and the costs of production allows for the measuring of value added, or net output.[92] Negotiation bodies can thus rely on this quantitative knowledge that measures the performance of individual enterprises, as well as the usefulness of investment projects, and estimates of new technical developments in order to make decisions related to reallocation of resources between production units.[93]

Producers finally offer their commodities for sale on the market, and thus exchange their products. Yet, according to Devine, the use of negotiation as the mechanism to co-ordinate activity means that while market exchange exists,

---

88   Devine 2011, p. 193.
89   Devine 2011, pp. 201–2.
90   Devine 2011, pp. 200, 203.
91   Devine 2011, pp. 197, 202.
92   Devine 2011, p. 198.
93   Devine 2011, p. 208; Devine 2002, p. 78.

market forces do not.[94] Any decision that changes the structure of investment is subject to democratic procedures of negotiation bodies. The regulation of social production, then, is shaped by the conscious participation of all production units, to bring their respective activities into harmony and align them with broader social interests. Such bodies – functional and geographic in scope – would be composed of various stakeholders, including representatives of suppliers, consumers, producers, and the community. Those that exercise effective control over an enterprise:

> include the enterprise's workers, other enterprises in the same line of production, major suppliers and users (...), the localities and regions in which the enterprise is based, and single issue groups with an interest in, e.g., the environmental or equal opportunities impact of the enterprise.[95]

Each interest group would be represented in the governing boards that administer the production units and participate in the decision-making and monitoring of productive activities. The negotiation bodies, through open-ended deliberation, would decide between strategic investment options, weighing enterprise performance against the shared interests in medium and long-term outcomes. There is thus a considerable emphasis on qualitative decision-making to overcome the impersonality of market forces. This also means that the full width of tacit knowledge can be incorporated into the decision-making process:

> The advantage of social ownership, compared to worker-owned enterprises operating within a legislative framework designed to safeguard the interests of other groups, is that it enables the tacit knowledge of all the affected groups to be drawn on in the course of negotiating enterprise policy and practice.[96]

Devine's proposal has been much criticised for his idea that the tacit knowledge of all agents can be drawn into the planning process through participation in the negotiation bodies, since, by definition, this knowledge cannot be made explicit for those not themselves involved in the social process that generates such knowledge. (This is partly nullified if we assume that Devine also means *local* knowledge). At best, tacit knowledge can be used as bargaining chip in

---

94   Devine 2002, p. 76.
95   Devine 2002, p. 77.
96   Ibid.

negotiation bodies, making appeals in good faith by asking other participants permission to act on it. Similarly, as local knowledge (which is thus more broad than tacit knowledge) is aggregated, part of it is destroyed. To an extent, this is inevitable and occurs whenever vertical integration is required (as in any large-scale organisation).

Still, there are obvious benefits associated with a co-ordinating mechanism based on negotiating among a multitude of stakeholders. It restricts market forces through co-operative control over the structure of investment. This naturally means that there is considerable emphasis on self-government and the incorporation of wider interests to shape the participants into a community of interest. Of course, the existence of market exchange will exercise some sort of corrective pressure to economise, independent of conscious control – which, should be noted, is not necessarily contrary to republicanism and arguably economically sensible. The relationship of socialism to such corrective pressures that arise 'automatically' out of the exchange relations is far more controversial, in relation to the Marxist theory of the 'law of value'.

We may well wonder if open ended qualitative deliberation, taking into account the wide variety of interests that are to be represented in negotiation bodies could yield effective and optimal outcomes. Furthermore, the centrality of negotiation bodies in the planning procedure would give rise to the same problems associated with the indivisibility of responsibility. The performance of production units would hinge on decisions made by an external agency (the negotiation bodies), and consequently, should production units perform poorly they may redirect blame upwards. To the extent that higher administrative bodies intervene in the activities of production units, the latter cannot be solely responsible for the outcome of their activity. Any misuse of resources, accidental or otherwise, may be referred back to the qualitative interventions of intermediate bodies. Since the exact role of intermediate bodies in shaping the final outcomes of production units would be difficult (if not impossible) to quantify, any squabbles over responsibility would likely result in the growth of additional administrative bodies to monitor, audit, and mediate between different levels of self-governing bodies. These would not be able to deal with the underlying problem of the muddled, interweaving of responsibility between different levels, however. Hence, while Devine relegates questions of motivation under his model to secondary importance, it is in fact a potentially major stumbling block for a model based largely around deliberation among stakeholders to displace market forces.[97]

---

97   Devine 2011, p. 204.

5   Participatory Planning of Production and Consumption

We will continue our discussion with reference to the allocative mechanism proposed in what we may term the Hahnel-Albert model, which is probably better known as 'participatory economics' (sometimes shortened to 'parecon'). The earliest contours of this theory of economic planning were sketched by Hahnel and Albert in 1978, and subsequently developed in a great number of books and articles.[98] The Hahnel-Albert model details how the market can be replaced by a participatory planning procedure involving negotiations regarding input and output among producers and consumers, mediated by 'indicative prices'. Much like 'negotiated co-ordination', the Hahnel-Albert mechanism, which they summarise as a 'social, iterative planning procedure',[99] was developed as an alternative to both market forces and 'authoritarian planning' alike. In this model, the role of the political community, central planning authorities, and market forces are absent. Instead, economic co-ordination is effected through iterative, planning cycles among consumer and producer councils. Each household belongs to the local neighbourhood consumer council; and each worker is a member of the workers' council of their place of work. The various neighbourhood councils in a given region federate; and likewise, so do the workers' councils. This federalism is applied to from the local to the national level. Consumption may affect individuals or groups at different levels, hence Hahnel and Albert correctly posit that this gives rise to the need to plan consumption in a way that corresponds to each different level of outcome (such as regional social consumption); *ditto* for externalities and the more technical issues of scale that are beyond the grasp of individual workplaces.[100]

Economic planning in their model consists of an iterative process whereby consumption and production councils make proposals about consumption levels and the production of outputs. Each year, consumers are expected to draw up a list of goods and services that they intend to consume over the course of a year; while workers' councils propose a production programme (or 'self-activity proposal').[101] On the basis of this informational input, an Iteration Facilitation Board (IFB – in effect, a 'libertarian' CPB) announces a set of indicative prices (or shadow prices) for all goods and services, which are then projected to the consumers and producers councils. They may each make adjustments on the basis of this information. Imbalances can be identified, pro-

---

98   Albert and Hahnel 1978.
99   Albert and Hahnel 1992, p. 46.
100   Albert and Hahnel 1992, pp. 45–6.
101   Hahnel 2021, p. 132.

posals can be revised, and prices can be adjusted. New indicative prices are generated by moving them up and down incrementally according to the projected levels of supply and demand until inputs and outputs are cleared. Each proposal will have to win the approval of the workers' councils and consumption councils involved at every level. After a certain number of iterations, the outcome of the planning procedure will converge toward an equilibrium and the various plans will be implemented.

The workers' councils propose a list of inputs and outputs to their federation. Each input will be stamped with the costs of production projected by the various workers' councils, whilst the federal councils add the external costs and opportunity costs. To win approval of the other councils at the federal level, each workers' council will have to demonstrate that the social costs of their input will not exceed the social benefits of their output. Each council will vet the proposals of other councils, and if the social costs are excessive, and only then, do the councils have the right to veto the plan proposal.[102] In other words, the procedure allows for the comparison of efforts and results by establishing the 'average social benefit to social cost ratios' of production plans.[103] With each iteration, the plan should draw closer to equilibrium. These decisions will also have to be made according to their scale, of course. Decisions that affect those in a particular region will need to be approved by all councils belonging to that region. In short:

> a neighborhood council must win approval for its consumption request from the other neighborhood councils in its ward; ward councils must win approval from the other wards in a city, etc. Moreover, consumers' councils must win approval of their proposals from workers' councils and vice versa.[104]

The social effects of economic choices are weighed and balanced against the interests of all whom are affected. In this way workers are, for example, compelled to weigh the consequences of using less productive techniques or the production of less costly goods against the losses in consumer satisfaction.[105] Moreover, the workers of a particular production unit have more influence over their working lives, roughly in proportion to the degree to which it affects them. For example, 'if the increased well-being of the workers involved outweighs any

---

102 Albert and Hahnel 1992, pp. 48–9, 52.
103 Albert 2003, p. 129.
104 Albert and Hahnel 1992, p. 47.
105 Albert 2003, p. 104.

excess of social cost over social benefits to others that accompany the change, the change will be enacted'.[106]

By participating in the planning procedure, consumers and producers are confronted with the social consequences of their choices. They are required to take into account the interests of others since each production plan will only be approved when the marginal social benefit obtained by the implementation of their plan is greater than the marginal social costs. The workers' councils have an interest in proposing productive activity that is consistent with the greater, social interest. This focus on wider social interests is achieved without involving the political community in the planning procedure. This puts the social interest on the radar of workers' councils and over time may help in reshaping the consciousness of producers accordingly. Here again we find the crucial intersection between self-government and convergence toward a common good, which is a necessary (although strictly speaking not a sufficient) condition that has to be satisfied from the perspective of republicanism.

The Hahnel-Albert model has been attacked on various grounds, such as its inhibiting of spontaneity on account of annual pre-ordering; an overzealous and fevered pursuit of equalisation,[107] requiring too many meetings,[108] and the CPB acting as a 'Walrasian auctioneer' with enterprises having no say in their external affairs, only responding 'atomistically' to technical parameters.[109] Since the benefit-to-cost ratios provide the sole criterium for approving or disapproving plans, Heyer asks why the procedure cannot simply take place algorithmically, dispensing with the voting process altogether. He further criticises the model over its lack of 'a *democratically legitimized central level* where political debates between delegates and the co-ordination of the overall economy could take place'. The annual pre-order list in particular invokes scepticism and has come under sustained criticism, understandably. After all, can one really expect consumers to specify what they wish to eat for breakfast on any given day throughout the year? What about new tastes, what about spontaneity?

Hahnel believes that an annual pre-order is not as complicated as it sounds. One would simply adjust the consumption list of last year here and there – or in fact, not at all – since some adjustment throughout the year is also possible. According to Hahnel, the divergences of individual consumers from their list may converge in the aggregate – i.e. an increase in consumption by an

---

106   Hahnel 2021, p. 155.
107   Schweickart 2006.
108   Albert and Hahnel 1991, p. 88.
109   Heyer 2022; Laibman 2015, p. 335.

individual consumer may be compensated by the decreased consumption of another. Generally, Hahnel speculates, such imbalances may mostly cancel each other out, and modifying supply would only require minimal adjustments. If this were true, then, as Wright asked, why can production units not simply re-use yearly data on consumption rates that are already available to them and adjust them on the basis of indications generated by various demand forecasting techniques?[110] This would presumably be too 'marketish', to borrow Wright's word. By allowing consumers to give direct input in the drawing up of production plans, the planning procedure is truly participatory. If we leave production planning to 'spontaneous' adjustments made by production units on the basis of demand forecasting, the consumers cease to be active subjects in the area of consumption at least. Thus, this reflects the libertarian views of Albert and Hahnel as well as their 'market abolitionism'.

Albert and Hahnel concede that consumers cannot be expected to be exceedingly detailed in drawing up an annual consumption list. This would be too demanding. But it also raises the following issue. If the consumption lists are not exceedingly detailed, then producers would not know what to produce, nor would they necessarily have an incentive to produce it since the plan gives direction to productive activity. The experience of planned economies does not suggest cause to be optimistic in this regard. Socialist economies concentrated 'the production of specific products into relatively few (often huge) enterprises and by issuing production targets in aggregate form, allowing enterprise managers flexibility in disaggregation'.[111] However, in the Soviet economy:

> [S]ince the central plan was the basis of all activity, the absence of some item from the plan might have resulted in it not being provided. So efforts to reduce the number of centrally planned indicators tended to be futile. If, say, frying pans or electric irons were not in the plan, then they tended not to be produced, and productive capacity would be switched to make things in which the centre expressed an interest.[112]

Hahnel believes that there is not much reason for concern.[113] Just as entrepreneurs in market economies have to make educated guesses as to what specific assortment of output will appeal to consumers, so would the workers' councils in a participatory economy. The producers submit a production plan with

---

110   Hahnel and Wright 2016.
111   Schweickart 1998, p. 12.
112   Nove 1992, p. 367.
113   Hahnel 2021, p. 132.

a certain social benefit to social cost ratio for a certain genre of goods (shoes or shirts, say). Within these aggregate parameters, workers are free to disaggregate output according to their estimates of consumer demand for specific articles, proportions, and variations. They might switch production exclusively to large sized shirts since that would minimise waste, for example, to drive down expenditures and thus 'social costs'; but if producers decide to churn out a large volume of unwanted output these undesired goods will accumulate as unused inventories. The actual social benefit attained by this workers' council would consequently fall, likely well below their proposed and approved benefit-to-cost ratio. This would mean that the workers' council would be able stake a lower claim on resources and income in the future:

> So if their approved production plan had an SB/SC ratio of 1.09 but their actual ratio at year's end turns out to be 1.03, the cap on average effort ratings for workers in the council next year is 103 not 109. Therefore, a worker council that failed to reduce yellow toed shoe production and increase red toed shoe production in response to signals that become available during the year about what consumers truly like would in all likelihood end up with a lower actual social benefit-to-cost ratio and consequently a lower average effort rating for the following year. Similarly, consumers and consumer councils and federations are charged for what they actually consume during the year, not what was approved for them in the plan. Any differences are recorded as increases or decreases in the debt or savings of individual consumers, neighborhood councils, and consumer federations.[114]

This does not resolve the problem to the full satisfaction, even if we assume that the turnover of membership connected to workers' councils would not cause significant distortions (after a poor performance, producers may simply vacate the production unit to prevent their income from being lowered). What would happen when consumers have inaccurately estimated their level of demand for a particular genre of product? Workers' councils have formulated their production programme on the basis of the estimates of social usefulness as measured by this level consumer demand. If demand falls short of this predicted level, the performance ratio of a workers' council may drop through no fault of their own. However, there is no way to discern, in such instances, who is at fault. Did the consumers make mistakes by overestimating their demand, or did the workers'

---

114   Hahnel 2021, p. 167.

council fail to produce sufficiently desirable goods within the categories specified by the consumers? Or a combination of both? While it may be possible to
make some probabilistic analysis to identify where the error lies by comparing
the consumption levels of available substitutes within the same genre of good,
it would presumably be very difficult, if not impossible, to assign responsibility
with the degree of certainty required. Under such circumstances the dreaded
issue of soft budget constraints rears its head. If production units cannot be
penalised for performing poorly, the motivation to use resources efficiently
diminishes. The obvious solution seems to be to dispense with consumption
planning altogether.

The Hahnel-Albert model represents a laudable and ingenious inaugural
theoretical advance of the third round of the socialist calculation debate.[115]
The social consequences of different productive activities are projected to all
producers, to enable them to compare their efforts, to grasp the implications
of using different production techniques, and so on, without ever delegating
authority away to some central planning agency. Producers, as the critics have
it, respond as if 'atomistically' to parametric quantities (costs and benefits), but
these signal the *social* consequences of their and other producers' choices and
reshape their behaviour into more socially desirable patterns of resource utilisation. So while this model reinforces the role of producers and consumers as
such, rather than as citizens of a community of producers and consumers, and
can to this extent be criticised, it is still a far cry from the atomistic forces of the
market that revolve around private activity and gains. The foremost problems
in this model are consumption planning, which clutters responsibility, and –
a feature common to all models – the issues associated with turnover of the
workforce which would enable workers to evade responsibility.

6   Big Computer and Labour Time

The excessive commitment to horizontal co-ordination of the Hahnel-Albert
model, crowding out political control, is an outgrowth of the commitment to
libertarianism and bias against central authority (whatever the particular spe-

---

115   The first round of the socialist calculation debate (circa 1920–44) centred primarily
around the arguments of Mises, Neurath, Lange, and Hayek. The second round (circa 1945–
80) involved the application of mathematical techniques, describing multilevel planning
methods. The third round of the calculation debate (circa 1978–present) was animated
more explicitly by the political commitments of the participants, and centre around the
models discussed in this chapter.

cies), as Laibman also observed.[116] Freed from the limitations of libertarian horizontalism we have a wider range of options to enhance economic planning through vertical integration. If we swing the other way of the spectrum then, we find the Cockshott-Cottrell model of economic planning. Like the Lange-Lerner model, the Cockshott-Cottrell model uses an artificial 'pseudo-market' mechanism to allocate goods. Under this model, the social costs of products are computed through the tracking of the quantity of labour-power (measured in labour time) expended on products as they pass through the chain of production until their final use – i.e. it computes the 'labour coefficients' of products. Prices of goods are initially set on the basis of the cost-price (this being equal to their labour coefficient) and offered on the consumption market where consumers can use their labour tokens, representing their personal share in the total social labour, to appropriate these items for themselves. If stocks deplete at rates faster than they are currently resupplied, the price of a given good is increased above its social costs; if stocks deplete too slowly, the price is lowered. In either case, the price is adjusted to market-clearing levels. The ratio of the market-clearing price to the labour coefficient is used to recalculate input requirements for different products. For example, the price for a particular consumption good may be raised:

> so as to (approximately) eliminate the excess demand. Suppose this price happens to be 12 labour tokens. This product then has a ratio of market-clearing price to labour-value of 12/10, or 1.20. The planners record this ratio for each consumer good. We would expect the ratio to vary from product to product, sometimes around 1.0, sometimes above (if the product is in strong demand), and sometimes below (if the product is relatively unpopular). The planners then follow this rule: Increase the target output of goods with a ratio in excess of 1.0, and reduce the target for goods with a ratio less than 1.0.[117]

In short, if the price is raised above the total amount of labour embodied in the product, it indicates more labour should be directed toward the production of that output, and vice versa. The CPB will plug these numerical 'discrepancies' into an optimisation programme: additional resources are thus allocated to wherever shortages emerge; and conversely, resources are reallocated to more productive uses wherever surpluses emerge. In so doing, the central planners

---

116   Laibman 2015, p. 337; Laibman 2014, p. 226.
117   Cockshott and Cottrell 1993, p. 103.

direct resources directly to grope toward equilibria in response to evolving consumption patterns. The Cockshott-Cottrell mechanism effectively amounts to a digitally enhanced form of centralised planning.

This mechanism of using labour time to allocate resources, as was briefly discussed previously, was also the basis of Strumilin's proposal – in recognition of this fact, Cockshott and Cottrell renamed their model 'Lange plus Strumilin'. Units of labour used up in the production of a particular good should be expanded until the marginal social costs measured in labour time are equal to its marginal social benefit. Workers would receive certificates representing the quantity of labour they contributed to social production. Using these coupons, consumers would commandeer from the stock of consumer goods an equivalent amount of goods, also measured in labour units. Consumers, in other words, evaluate whether the labour expended in the production process for a particular good has been worthwhile. This supplies information about the social utility, or the structure of consumer preferences, in relation to the structure of final output. If, given the average social expenditure of labour for a product, excess demand is observed it implies that, at this level of output, the social utility of the product in question is greater than the amount of labour society has expended on its production. This in turn implies that the amount of labour society should dedicate to the production of that product should be scaled up. This enables planning authorities to compare efforts or costs and results or benefits on behalf of society. Thus, in the words of Marx,[118] under communism 'the determination of value continues to prevail in the sense that the regulation of labour time and the distribution of social labour among the various production groups, ultimately the bookkeeping encompassing all this, become more essential than ever'.

In this way, the Cockshott-Cottrell model realises the long-standing communist ambition of labour-time accounting under a socialist mode of production. In the first phase of communism, Marx argued, the producers of society would receive a certificate representing the quantity of labour they contributed to the total product of society, minus deductions necessary for the common fund. Labour certificates, notes, vouchers, tokens, or credits of this nature are not 'labour money', which Marx criticised. A labour-time currency had been separately proposed by various radical currents within the socialist movement, which believed that the proceeds of labour should go to labour. The basis of exploitation, according to this reasoning, was unequal exchange on the market. By making labour the basis for exchange, the accruing of unearned

---

118   MECW 37: 838.

income (i.e. exploitation) is rendered impossible. As such, producers would need to receive labour notes equal to their labour contributions expressed in work-hours, which could be exchanged for an equivalent amount on the market. The distinction between 'labour money' and 'labour certificates' lies in that former was a 'contradiction', namely by using labour time calculations on the basis of *indirect* social labour (market exchange). That is to say, treating commodities (products of indirect social labour, or private labours) as if they were already products of direct social labour; whereas the latter would merely be a means to regulate individual consumption of articles which are the product of direct social labour. Furthermore, exploitation, Marx sought to prove, had its basis in production, not distribution. Conflating the two, Adam and Tsushima among many others, have shown, is categorically mistaken.[119] Marx had repeatedly stressed that labour vouchers are not money since they do not circulate.[120] Upon their use they would not pass to the producers – being cancelled instead – and would therefore not be a medium of exchange. Consequently, they cannot function as a source of accumulation – they are more akin to coupons than currency. Therefore, the use of paper certificates or electronic credits (labour points) merely regulates consumption by stipulating the amount of social labour that can be 'commandeered' by any one individual for personal consumption – i.e. 'rationing' via quantities of labour. Put differently, the labour certificates serves as a measure of each individual's share in the social product.

'Labour notes' – or whatever equivalent term is preferred – can prove useful for three reasons in comparison to direct allocation (either free access to consumer goods or fixed rations): first, they can cap consumption, compelling individuals to economise and decide carefully between available options thus reducing waste, preventing 'repressed inflation';[121] second, the choices

---

119   Tsushima 1956; Adam 2013.

120   For example: MECW 36: 356.

121   According to Horvat, free access to goods and services was inconceivable since 'needs or wants of human beings are limitless' (see Horvat 1964, p. 132).

    This may be an oversimplification. At a certain point the energy necessary for finding, collecting, storing, and consuming goods and services, even at zero monetary costs, will exceed the utility derived from them, as was also pointed out by Lange (see Lange 1936, pp. 141–2). What is a more persuasive argument against free access is that at zero costs goods and services will likely be used inefficiently. For instance, bread draws more resources from society in its production than low-quality animal fodder, but at zero costs for both goods, a farmer may elect to use bread the same as fodder to feeds its livestock. Attempting to police the use of resources in response would be difficult, intrude on the privacy of citizens, would cost additional resources, and require a bureaucracy with some coercive powers, which contradicts the 'statelessness' of 'free communist' models (see

of consumers reveal the structure of relative preferences for different types and grades of goods, which can therefore guide decision-making related to the allocation of resources between different uses; third, it can induce individuals to contribute to production where moral incentives alone do not suffice.

Kautsky famously dissented from the Marxist consensus that money would be abolished – or wither away – under socialism. According to him, the complexity of calculating the labour contributions contained in each product was prohibitively complicated: 'Consider what colossal labour would be involved in calculating for each product the amount of labour it had cost from its initial to its final stage, including transport and other incidental labour'.[122] The labour expended on a particular article of consumption would require comprehensive and accurate statistical data for each of its components. Each raw material – say, metal, nickel, lithium, cobalt, or whatever may be required – is extracted by a number of labourers working for a definite amount of time. These labourers use tools, made previously by other labourers in a given amount of time elsewhere using materials extracted by yet more labourers using yet other tools to do so, which all counts as an indirect expenditure of labour. The raw material are then transported using a variety of vehicles, each of these means transportation being the product of social labour produced with additional equipment and labour. The infrastructure used to transport the raw material count as indirect productive contribution as well. Not only does the initial expenditure matter, but also the rate of depreciation. Further knowledge is required about the manufacturing of equivalent products by other production units elsewhere in order to calculate the *average* social labour time embodied in each good. All this information will need to be supplied, compiled, and processed. Kautsky thus concluded that:

> Money is the simplest means known up to the present time which makes it possible in as complicated a mechanism as that of the modern product-

---

e.g. GIC 1930). In fact, we see something very similar occurred in the Soviet economy, where capital and land were not priced but allocated for free, being non-labour inputs. Consequently, there was no incentive to economise on these productive resources, which spurred wasteful use of these scarce means, and contributed to poor agricultural performance (Wilczynski 1972a, pp. 34, 37). Similarly, 'in spite of critical shortages of grains, bread was often fed to pigs and cattle because it was cheaper than feeding stuffs' (Wilczynski 1972a, p. 84). Whenever poor incentives produced their inevitable effects, the Soviet government had to turn to the penal code to try and compensate (see e.g. Gregory 2004, p. 145). In any case, all this is rather inconsequential since 'free communism' has no mechanism which allows for the rational allocation of resources in the first place.

122   Cited in Lange 1937, p. 140.

ive process, with its tremendous far-reaching division of labour, to secure the circulation of products and their distribution to the individual members of society.[123]

Currency, according to Kautsky, is not an economic category to be abolished, which would amount to turning back the hands of time. The positive kernel of money should be preserved whilst it is simultaneously combined with a higher form of social organisation in the form of socialism – that is to say, money should be sublated. This would allow society to exercise mastery over money and subordinate its use to the purpose of elevating the overall welfare of the community.

Today this position appears to be less controversial in socialist circles. Marxist-Leninists for example agree that 'money-commodity relations' are preserved in socialism posthumously upholding official Soviet doctrine,[124] and many independent Marxists are agnostic on the question of the role of money in socialism, if not openly supportive.[125] Indeed, the function of 'money' in society may be 'neutral' to the extent that it is subordinated to overriding planning mechanisms, in which case it serves purely accounting purposes – 'control [контроль] by rouble' in Soviet terminology. Money in the Soviet economy was principally used to track the fulfilment of gross output targets (as well as disposing of consumption goods). Enterprises were not free to use money in capacities other than those ascribed by the planning authorities.[126] When the use of money is free to facilitate spontaneous horizontal exchanges of goods, markets acquire a dynamic force by allowing agents to obtain private means by which they can further their private ends. This dynamic force, in which the sum of individual decisions becomes an external, alien force that acts back on individuals, shapes their choices and behaviour and escapes conscious control. The alternative to monetary calculations, calculation *in-natura*, using balance sheets in physical units, of course runs into aggregation problems, since such units are not commensurable. In the Soviet economy, moneyless allocation between state enterprises was briefly reintroduced in 1929–1930, but Soviet practice quickly fell back on monetary units to aggregate physical quantities.[127] Money, in spite of its association with commerce, may turn out to be, as Kautsky

---

123   Cited in Lange 1937, p. 139.
124   For example: KKE 2013; Kozlov 1977, pp. 119–52.
125   For example: Magdoff and Williams 2017; Wolff 2012.
126   Kornai 2007, p. 132.
127   Gregory 2004, p. 91; Harrison 2016; Ellman 1990, p. 14.

was adamant, the best mechanism available to socialism to secure the rational distribution of goods.

Kautsky's arguments against labour-time accounting was very much proved correct by Soviet practice. The Soviet Central Statistical Administration at various times from the 1960s onwards applied the Leontief input-output method to calculate the various commitments of labour-power, expressed in 'person-years' – although expressions in labour hours were possible as well. It tracked how the output, corresponding to the expenditure of quantities of labour, of one industry fed into other industries as input. The balances noted the contents of commodities in units of living and embodied labour-power, rather than physical units – i.e. the sum-total of quantities of labour-power required to produce a unit of output, which is the 'labour coefficient'.[128] However, it was used for analytical purposes, rather than for planning purposes since it required a number of years to complete such detailed calculations.[129] That the ability to calculate the total social labour content of specific goods, or labour coefficients, is technically possible is not particularly contentious. What is not clear is whether these labour coefficients can be calculated speedily enough to serve planning purposes – computation of technical coefficients of various kinds in the Soviet Union, including labour coefficients, lagged several years behind the year of data compilation, and in the case of labour coefficient computations specifically, were calculated only for a limited number of goods. It required enormous computational power to solve the hundred thousands of simultaneous equations necessary to calculate the labour time embodied in products; with one of the theoretical obstacles being the dissolving different grades of labour – complex labour and simple labour – into a single unit of labour.[130]

However, what may not have been possible in the early Soviet period and in Kautsky's time, could well be feasible today using the superior computational force of modern electronic computers combined with information technology. The argument that it is technically feasible to calculate labour coefficients quickly for planning purposes has been advanced by Cockshott, Cottrell, and Michaelson.[131] According to them, the processing power modern electronic computers is such that it is possible to calculate in a matter of minutes the labour coefficients of the millions goods that circulate in an advanced, industrial economy. The relevant data can be submitted digitally, via a network of personal computers located within production units, to a central

---

128   Zauberman 1963, pp. 53–4.
129   Ellman 2014, p. 267.
130   Itoh 1995, pp. 47–8, 53–5; Itoh 1996, pp. 107–8.
131   Cockshott and Cottrell 1993; Cottrell, Cockshott, and Michaelson 2007.

database connected to a supercomputer, which is then tasked with crunching the numbers.[132] Once the numbers are prepared, they can be used as the basis for updating the plan and reallocating resources in light of newly computed labour coefficients. Labour coefficients would give technical expression to the human dimension of social production, and serve as a reminder of the relations of production hidden behind the products that people daily consume. Costs would no longer be expressed in 'dollars', 'euros', 'dinars', or 'roubles', but in minutes, hours, years of labour-time. While planning authorities, armed only with human processing abilities could never solve the millions of equations necessary to arrive at (a) all the labour coefficients for millions of goods; (b) a fully integrated and optimal plan, the processing power of supercomputers is up to the task. In this way, the flow of resources can be determined with the assistance of electronic computers connected to the central supercomputer. Production units manufacturing inputs are instructed to allocate resources on the basis of the optimal solution, and as such no horizontal (i.e. market) transactions are required. Furthermore, enterprise managers are not expected to scale production according to the maximum of profit margins, as in the Lange-Lerner model, but do so simply because they are instructed to.[133] This would also reduce the incentive to manipulate data, in contrast to Soviet-style socialism:

> For enterprises producing consumer goods, this should deter the over-statement of input requirements, since overstatement would result in a higher labour value, and hence a lower ratio of market price to value, compared to the correct statement of input requirements.[134]

Computerised central planning at last resolves the problem of millions of equations.[135] What it cannot do, however, is incorporate local or tacit knowledge because prices and allocation of material goods are adjusted exclusively on the basis of quantitative considerations (within certain politically defined constraints). One potential irrational outcome of direct allocation on the basis of excess supply or excess demand is, for example, that seasonal goods will be depleted quickly in a given period. Quantitatively, this indicates that more input should be supplied. Yet, we hardly wish to increase the supply of Christmas articles available for consumption halfway into January. While Cockshott

---

132   Cockshott and Cottrell 1993, pp. 50–1.
133   Cockshott and Cottrell 1993, p. 107.
134   Cockshott and Cottrell 1993, p. 115.
135   Brewster 2004, p. 69.

and Cottrell admit that 'an element of demand forecasting is also called for here' and argue that 'the current ratios provide a useful guide rather than a completely mechanical rule', it is nevertheless unclear how the scope of enterprise latitude can be marked off from the area of decision-making that is the exclusive domain of the central planning authorities.[136] Evidently, recurrent seasonal patterns of demand may be excluded because such fluctuations follow a predictable cycle that is largely foreseeable by the CPB. However, many (less obvious) qualitative considerations for a myriad of goods cannot be made at the central level. These matters extend to the discovery of opportunities for new lines of products, the potential improvements in productivity by using alternative combinations of inputs or altogether new production techniques, and so on. This type of knowledge is not generated at the level of central planning, but at the level of production and are not expressed by the current structure of labour coefficients. The local, qualitative, and tacit knowledge of the immediate producers, in other words, are excluded from the planning process under the 'Lange-Strumilin' model.

Another issue resides in the reliance on labour-time accounting, the 'Strumilin'-aspect of the mechanism if you like. We can explore these practical problems with reference to a *postbellum* Soviet economic debate. During the early period of administrative command practice in the Soviet Union (1929–1965), production goods were allocated to enterprises at zero cost. No charges were levied on the use of capital goods. This resulted in two forms of waste. First, since production goods were rationed, managers requested additional means of production instead of exploiting existing capacity at a higher intensity. Second, in the absence of a capital charge, production goods were not allocated to where they could be put to use to obtain the maximum effect, but to wherever plant managers pleaded for them the loudest. Moreover, the net results obtained by units of production depend, not only on the total factor costs and user costs of their operations, but also on the degree to which the results of these efforts link up with a definite amount of social wants as expressed by users. However, according to Soviet orthodoxy, any inclusion of consumer preferences in price formation reflected bourgeois theories of marginal utility.

These rather vulgar applications of Marx's theory of value to Soviet practice resulted in two distortions: the neglect of production goods and the neglect of social wants in price formation. The rationing policy for production goods resulted in grave distortions in particular. It motivated managers to hoard capital goods even when they could not be used productively, resulting in acute

---

136   Cottrell and Cockshott 1993, p. 25.

shortages and allocative inefficiency.[137] The effect was 'a chronic bias toward the choice of more capital-intensive methods of production than the economy as a whole can really afford'.[138] Similar distortions occurred wherever the labour requirements for new equipment rose in an absolute sense, as one Soviet plant manager complained:

> There is nothing worse for a plant than to create a new machine if it is twice as labour-consuming as the old one, even if it is twice as cheap and three times as economical as the previous one.[139]

Economic resources should be allotted to different uses according to the maxim that they should be utilised in the capacity that allows for the greatest positive results from the perspective of society as a whole. Since there is no infinite supply of 'capital goods' this implies that it is necessary to add a premium above their initial production costs that covers their usage in a particular capacity to ensure that capital outlays are economical.[140] This would be a 'capital charge', so that in addition to the direct costs, the user costs, the costs of alternative uses associated with means of production, are also reflected in their price. Suppose for example that a piece of equipment can be employed in two rival capacities. The net results might be positive in both capacities, but if its use in one capacity is capable of generating relatively higher returns, there would a hidden, implicit cost incurred by society if the equipment is instead employed in the second capacity by failing to employ it in its most productive way among all alternative possibilities. Hence, productive assets are 'scarce' relative to all possible combinations and uses of resources.

In order to use information about the relative scarcity of production goods and the efficacy of using them in different settings, the price of the piece of equipment will have to incorporate the social opportunity cost in the form of a capital charge, which can be thought of as rent for the use of society's productive assets in one capacity thus preventing its use in another. Producers would, in response to this charge, have to weigh the improvements in productivity obtained by using certain equipment against the social opportunity cost associated with withdrawing the equipment from potentially being used in alternative ways. This renders visible, not only the explicit costs of producing

137   Wilczynski 1972a, p. 176.
138   Dobb 1967, p. 193.
139   Cited in Merrett 1964, p. 404.
140   Dobb 1967, p. 176.

assets (materials and effort) but also the hitherto invisible cost of using means of production in one area, thus preventing its use in another.

According to Marxist theory, capital goods are past contributions of social labour to production. Each piece or tool of production embodies past labour that contributes labour to the production of commodities indirectly. In this respect the Cockshott-Cottrell model presents an improvement over Soviet practice, since: (a) production goods are not rationed but priced according to the amount of labour contained in them; and (b) since the rate of consumption of goods compared to the expenditure of direct and indirect, live and embodied labour is allowed to measure the degree to which social production has been socially necessary or socially wasteful. At the same time, the Cockshott-Cottrell price mechanism is based on the average labour costs of production. And although the CPB in their model might compare the structure of production to the pattern of consumption to help guide the allocation of resources between alternative uses, this reliance on using labour coefficients in products to set prices presents a similar problem. The total quantity of labour contained in a piece of equipment is independent of the productive setting in which it is being used, thus the relative scarcity of productive equipment is rendered invisible to the extent that there is no social opportunity cost that producers have to confront in their choice of technique.

The prices in the economy would thus also need to reflect the scarcity of means relative to demand, in addition to their costs of production – i.e. according to 'cost-preference' relations.[141] To the extent that the supply of productive resources is limited it forms a constraint on the potential total output that society might generate and implies that alternative costs should be included in the price formation for means of production to commit them to their most productive uses; i.e. to approximately ensure the highest possible output within the resource and production constraints faced by society. This principle extends beyond the relative scarcity of means of production, and requires some quantitative measure of the productivity of natural resources, implying the use of differential ground rent levied for the usage of land. For instance, if the exact same amount of labour and effort is applied to plots of land of different qualities they will obviously yield different quantities output. In the absence of differential rent, this would reflect unfairly on the efforts of those labourers who have cultivated the inferior tracts of land.

Furthermore, while it may be narrowly justified from a republican perspective that production activities are subordinated to the central plan – if the plan

---

141   Nove 2011, p. 114; Wilczynski 1973, p. 81.

reflects political priorities established through direct legislation – the scope of economic self-government would be limited to within workplaces, weighing options of how to execute the plan to the best of their abilities. The outlook of the producers would be shaped by this level of active participation, i.e. narrowly circumscribed to their workplace. If economic and political self-government are to be mutually reinforcing, a better balance, if at all possible, must be struck.

7   Multilevel Programming

The model of Multilevel Democratic Iterative Co-ordination (MDIC) advanced by Laibman, which we will discuss subsequently, draws on the experience of Soviet planning, and especially what he calls '*late* Soviet *potential*'.[142] This refers to the reform period of the Soviet Union, after 1965, in which the responsibilities of the central planning authorities were partially devolved to base-level units. 'MDIC' also shares a perhaps a more superficial resemblance to planning techniques based on decomposition algorithms, known variously as 'bilevel optimisation', 'two-level planning', or indeed 'multilevel programming' that came out of the second stage of the socialist calculation debate. Such algorithmic techniques propose to disaggregate large optimisation problems into sub-problems that are resolved iteratively between different levels involved in the planning procedure. If we assume that the planning procedure involves a centre (the CPB) and base-level units (firms), both the CPB and firms perform some of the calculations to arrive at an optimal solution. Such procedures are therefore more informationally efficient compared to a system of comprehensive, top-down planning in which the centre is expected to compile and process all information itself. The decomposition of an optimisation problem into smaller ones reduces the computational requirements, but when the problems contains 'a large number of unknowns and balance equations it requires laborious calculations. For this reason, the history of the development of linear programming methods is, in practice, bound up with the possibility of using electronic computers for such purposes'.[143] Even if it is now technically feasible to perform the required volume of calculations using electronic computer power, we still want to absorb local knowledge in the final, optimal plan. The use of a multilevel mechanism of economic planning may

---

142   Laibman 2015, p. 338.
143   Lange 1971, p. 111.

allow production units to do precisely that, by incorporating such knowledge in the 'responses' they communicate to the centre. Multilevel programming techniques are in effect *informationally decentralised* central planning procedures.

The general gist of multilevel programming is as follows. These procedures involve a dialogue between the centre (the CPB) and base (production units) in which the centre elicits information from the production units in a number of successive approximations (iterations) groping toward a solution that is feasible both in terms of resource and production constraints and the consistency of inputs and outputs, and optimal in relation to the objective function. The local units initially only possess local knowledge about the potential productivity of their efforts and production possibilities, and since the volume of this data is exceedingly large it follows that it may be necessary to allow base-level units to carry out certain calculations themselves, in order to minimise the aggregation of information by the centre. Indeed, '[t]his is what informationally decentralized procedures are meant to accomplish'.[144] Multilevel programming methods seek to coax base-level units into revealing to the centre accurate data regarding production possibility sets, marginal productivities, or output levels. They are to perform calculations and relay the results back to the centre, which uses this information to make appropriate adjustments.

The generic multilevel planning technique involves an iterative dialogue between the centre and firms to find an optimal solution that would maximise the value of the objective function. Heal notes that 'it is probably possible to devise infinitely many iterative and informationally-decentralised planning routines', and indeed various have been drawn up.[145] For example, to Kantorovich, the impossibility of the centre to derive a comprehensive central plan meant that optimisation programmes should be run on multiple layers (national, regional, industrial, enterprise), addressing constrained optimisation problems according to the scale and complexity of their level and compare the results of these calculations to actual performance. Multi-level procedures usually require that they satisfy rather narrow technical conditions (concavity, monotonicity, etc.). The multilevel process may involve the centre quoting prices (in a 'price-guided' planning procedure) or assigning quantities of output to production units (in a 'quantity-guided' planning procedure), or a combination of both[146] – the Lange-Lerner mechanism being an example of a price-guided planning mechanism.[147] The production units respond to the set

---

144   Hurwicz 1973, p. 5.
145   Heal 1974, p. 219.
146   Heal 1974.
147   Hurwicz 1973.

of prices announced by the CPB by setting their output equal to a level that max-
imises profit (i.e. increase output until the marginal costs equal price), which
is taken to be the local optimality criterium. In case of a quantity-guided planning procedure, the production units inform the centre of the marginal social
productivities of the output level. Either the centre gives prices and receives
back quantities of output, or the centre announces quantities and receives
back prices (in the form of marginal productivities) – the details here are of
little importance. Either way, the CPB oversees a process of *tâtonnement* (auc-
tioning) whereby informational exchange takes place until an optimum plan
is discovered and resources are subsequently allocated according to the solution to the optimisation problem. The centre readjusts prices or quantities in
response to the information supplied by the production units in order to come
closer to discovering this global optimum. After a number of iterations (the
number of rounds depending on the scale of the problem and the type of multilevel procedure in question) an optimal solution can be found, provided the
procedure satisfies the monotonicity criterium (meaning that each iteration
yields a solution that is at least as good as the previous one, and preferably
better). If there is insufficient time to find the optimal solution then naturally
we wish to have a solution that is at least better than all previous steps taken
since the initial one. The trouble with all such planning procedures is, however,
that they presuppose that producers supply reliable data in their informational
exchange with the central planning authorities.

Returning to Laibman's model of 'MDIC', this economic mechanism integ-
rates some of the elements of the previous models discussed, and can, in effect,
be seen as a synthesis of many such models – even if it did not emerge as deliberate attempt to combine them.[148] In Laibman's model, enterprises formulate
a draft production programme. Producers initially submit a plan incorporating
their local knowledge to formulate a plan that is 'ambitious' yet also realistically achievable. Once submitted to the central planning agency, the plan is
adjusted by incorporating the knowledge of central planners that can survey
the larger trends and aggregate effects which cannot be grasped from the vantage point of the local economic unit. The plans are aggregated and revised by
the central planning commission according to various metrics such as macroeconomic stability and various politically negotiated social priorities. After
some back and forth between the centre and enterprises, the final production
programmes will eventually incorporate both the local knowledge that was
formerly the exclusive domain of producers as well as the knowledge concern-

---

148   Laibman 2015, pp. 337, 339–41.

ing macro-level reality that was formerly the exclusive domain of central planners. According to Laibman:

> Good work at the center (...) creates a stable foundation for genuine micro-level planning, and this is the basis for achieving one of socialism's most cherished goals: drawing ever larger numbers of working people into knowledgeable and intelligent participation in planning – making them, in effect, stakeholders in society at large, effective owners of the social means of production.[149]

The production plans submitted by enterprises are expected to approximate the highest attainable production possibilities of the workforce and their stock of productive assets. Once the plans have been finalised (brought in alignment with macroeconomic priorities, rendered internally consistent, and reflect the highest attainable productivity) and stamped with the approval of the centre, they are implemented. The plans set the parametric quantities within which producers may enter into exchange relations to bring into operation their production programme. These market relations play the subordinate role of being the 'secondary confirmation of the plan'[150] to assess the 'socially useful results acknowledged in the process of exchange'.[151] Meaning, the exchange of commodities among producers and customers confirms the extent to which economic plans have been drawn up and implemented correctly, i.e. the degree to which they reflected the true potential of enterprises.

A central role in this process is played by the reward function. Since producers are not beholden to revealing their true potential level of productivity, Laibman proposes that enterprises should be encouraged to be both ambitious and realistic, and posits that this can be achieved thus. Production units receive a score on the basis a number of success indicators that determine the size of their supplementary bonuses. Production units are entitled to a higher income rating if they plan a high level of output (ambitious planning), but are penalised (in terms of their performance rating) to the extent that they fail to achieve their aims. In this way, production programmes should reflect ambitious yet realistic goals.[152] We can imagine that production units plan an aggregate level of output for a year, and specify the detailed assortment for shorter plan periods (such as monthly or quarterly periods). For each period, the performance

---

149   Laibman 2015, p. 326.
150   Laibman 1992, p. 66.
151   Kurashvili 1990, p. 32.
152   Laibman 2012.

of the enterprise would be scored according to the degree of fulfilment. Both over-fulfilment and under-fulfilment of achievement targets would be penalised, since both have disruptive effects on the supply chain. Over-fulfilment indicates that producers have under-estimated their level of productivity – i.e. they planned poorly – and imposes unplanned output on logistical chains of storage and transportation. Producers would not benefit from overstating or understating their input requirements or output targets, since they will want to submit a productive plan that approaches the true, achievable limits of their productive capacity. The information that is made available to planners in this process would thus be reasonably reliable estimates, which makes effective planning at the central level possible.

In the simplified model that Laibman employs for the purpose of theoretical clarification, he uses only a central and decentral dichotomy: the local plans are aggregated by the centre immediately.[153] In closer proximity to would-be reality, the plans would presumably first be submitted to regional and branch federations, where the various production units would interact to reshape investment decisions. In light of these interactions, the plans can be redrafted and submitted to the centre. Enterprises revise and then send the plan up to the centre. After being drafted (revised, and re-drafted) the plans are subsequently aggregated and brought into harmony with the social and political objectives (qualitative) and macro-economic proportions (quantitative) at the central level.[154] Through the front door of production units, relevant consumer information is generated that economic units can use to shape their plans, while through its back door the unit is connected to an intricate network of production units that manage their cross-supply chain co-operatively, within a macro-level framework articulated at the central level.

Once the plans of each production unit have been drawn up and approved, the plan becomes 'binding' on all production units insofar as the variable portion of their total income depends on it. The variable income allotted to enterprises will vary according to the degree of correspondence between planned activity and actual activity.[155] Enterprises compete for a higher share of the variable income fund but have to do so on the basis of co-operative sharing of information in order to increase the accuracy of respective enterprise plans – co-operation, then, becomes the best bet for achieving good results. However, under Laibman's proposed model the issue of responsibility again emerges. When the production plans are 'corrected' by higher levels of planning, the

153   Laibman 2002a, p. 119.
154   Laibman 2012, pp. 35–6.
155   Ibid.

enterprises cannot shoulder the full responsibility for their performance. The plan may be corrected in such a way that it no longer reflects the abilities and choices of the work collective; yet, the enterprise is rewarded or penalised to the extent that the plan proved correct in practice. Although Laibman's proposal indicates some way forward, the paramount question central to socialist economic planning – how central authorities can induce micro-level activity to align with macroeconomic interests without intervening directly in the affairs of economic units – still remains unanswered.

PART 2

Remedy

∵

Government in the Socialist Republic

Socialism is based on social ownership of the means of production, which means that the conditions of their use are stipulated by society – or more accurately, the political institutions that are placeholders for society as a whole. The role of political institutions in relation to discussions of the feasibility of socialism should therefore not be sidestepped. It is essential that the political institutions in a collectivist society remain the instruments by which citizens may govern their own affairs, so that corruption in the republican sense – the capturing of public bodies by particular interests – does not occur. After all, the 'reason why we spend so much time on constitutional issues is that we get only one shot at the right organization, because the monopoly of state power cannot afford the luxury of trial and error'.[1] This applies especially to socialist governments, which transfer the stock of productive resources into their hands. The question is very pertinent to the cause of socialism, then, especially since under Soviet-style socialism, owing to the lack of political contestation (which can be traced back directly to the monopoly of power exercised by the Communist Party), corruption deeply penetrated the political system. Such regimes were 'composed of official political relations which are meaningless, and unofficial or extra-statutory ones which are of fundamental significance'. These forms of corruption enabled:

> various pressure groups and interests to decide behind the scenes on the distribution of income and allocation of resources. Such relations do not allow the central authority to be guided by true social priorities, nor to have the capacity to carry out its decisions. Instead, such a system creates pressure for overinvestment exceeding the economy's potential and leading to imbalances in many areas of the economy.[2]

Not only should we be concerned with securing political and civil liberties in their own right, to allow citizens to develop and express themselves fully, the absence of fundamental rights would also form a direct threat to the socialist character of government itself – we have additional instrumental reasons, then, to deal seriously with devising limitations on the exercise of political power.

---

1 Epstein 1999, p. 283.
2 Osiatyński 1988, p. 118.

Under a socialist regime, however, individual ownership of property cannot provide a degree of security against government encroachment into the independence of citizens, since all productive resources fall under the authority and responsibility of the political community – and conversely, the capacity to resist the arbitrary wills of others should not hinge on arbitrary access to privately owned assets. According to liberal critics, this means that socialism will inevitably lead society down the path toward totalitarianism, or as Hayek liked to put it, 'the road to serfdom'. Democracy is supposed to be a means to limit state power, while socialism would supposedly require absolute state power in order to subordinate all economic activity to the single political authority acting on behalf of society, making the notion of a 'democratic socialism' logically incoherent.[3] One would have to give way to the other: either democracy or socialism would in the end survive. This line of criticism, incidentally, very much resembles my own assessment of Van der Walt's anarchist model of economic planning. This 'libertarian' model of socialist planning quickly collapses into directive, centralised planning upon closer interrogation.

If political power in a socialist system becomes usurped by a particular segment of the citizenry, they would have immediate access and control over the total stock of society's productive resources. The means of production would in effect become monopolised by a privileged layer within the population. This ascendant elite would be free (within the limits imposed by the requirements to legitimate their rule vis-a-vis the general population) to dispose of these resources in accordance with their particular will, at the expense of other considerations. The purpose of a socialist theory of self-government, then, is to find the institutional devices by which society can prevent political power from concentrating in the hands of a ruling clique which would in turn be able to direct the use of publicly owned resources according to their partial, factional interests. In socialist theory it is typically assumed that the expansion and deepening of democracy itself will be sufficient to ensure that power is preserved in the hands of the citizenry.

The generic model of 'socialist democracy' relies upon legislative assemblies open to participation by the general public to secure self-government. Citizen assemblies would have the power to propose legislation and elect delegates under an imperative mandate. By transferring decision-making power to citizens directly, society is insured against political corruption, according to this view, because it dissolves the separation of ruled and rulers – without much regard for the process by which an excess of democracy can turn into its

---

3   Makovi 2016.

opposite. It is this view that will be challenged by drawing on the theoretical-conceptual equipment of neo-republicanism. We will develop four key arguments that suggest that democratic procedures can be designed in a number of ways and that simply extending majoritarian rule will not provide the best insurance for the survival of self-government:

- First, the disappearance of class antagonisms would not dissolve conflict between blocks of citizens over the allocation of material resources among alternative ends. The existence of mutually exclusive preferences related to the division of the total product implies that there will be political authority under socialism to mediate these conflicts, and therefore that there should be some counter-balance that places statutory limitations on the exercise of this authority. (Naturally, it is also possible for social conflict to revolve around religious, cultural, or ethnic cleavages);
- Second, there are conflicting interests, not just between different cross sections of the population, but also within individuals. An individual citizen might have a range of conflicting preferences about means and ends as they each relate to their respective horizons. Political procedures, even democratic ones, may be designed in multiple ways, where some among these designs might broaden or narrow the horizons of their participants, which calls attention to the limitations of merely increasing the scope of democracy;
- Third, the geographic fragmentation of a model of 'grassroots'-style democracy strengthens the tendency toward localism and partial interests – all the more so when deputies representing local constituencies act under mandates set and fixed at the local level. Deputies should therefore enjoy a greater scope for discretion, introducing an element of representation, which should consequently be carefully defined and limited to check against the misuse and abuse of representative political authority;
- Fourth, unrestrained democracy relies exclusively on high levels of popular participation to sustain self-government. Since political participation requires a substantial commitment involving a high expenditure of energy and time, we might expect citizens to evade taking full, collective responsibility for political decision-making and their outcomes. If political participation does not exceed a certain threshold, the monitoring intensity of elected officials will decline, in turn potentially allowing power to creep upward, outside the scope and field of vision of the general population.

Instead of relying on maximally extending the principle of democracy into every sphere and direction without any sort of inbuilt checks or balances, it is my proposal that socialism should instead guarantee self-governance by means of an egalitarian constitution that balances a variety of democratic procedures, understood more or less analogously to the mixed constitution of classical republicanism that combined and balanced elements of democracy, aristocracy, and monarchy. This should tip the scales of political outcomes in such way that they are more likely to correspond to the long-term general interests of the community without needing to dilute democracy with elements of oligarchy. We will subsequently outline the main features of the political institutions and complementary practices of the constitutional-democratic republic.

1   Socialist Constitutionalism and the Social Contract

Constitutionalism is usually associated with liberalism, and more particularly with the founders of the republic of the United States of America,[4] and certainly not very much with socialism. Similarly, the conception of the 'social contract' is alien to Marxist theory. As per Marxism, such an ahistorical approach to understanding political power conceals the class antagonisms that underpin society by suggesting a harmony of interest across class divides. Constitutionalism and socialism seem ill-matched. To those moderate republicans influenced by liberalism, such as Hamilton, democracy needed to be limited in order to secure certain natural rights by placing them beyond the scope of immediate democratic decision-making. By constitutional design, various limitations were proposed to bind the role of democracy, balancing political power among the legislative assemblies, the executive branch, and the judiciary. Representation by elected officials also played a role in limited the influence of democracy. The republican tradition places emphasis on virtue and character, and Hamilton believed that representatives would 'most likely' be endowed with 'enlightened views and virtuous sentiments' which makes them 'superior to local prejudices'.[5] This is more or less the mechanism found in contemporary liberal democracies, where professional politicians are supposed to translate popular sentiments into balanced policy proposals, weighing popular grievances and demands against financial and constitutional viability. While what passes for 'democracy' today is mostly associated with representation by elected officials, it is more appropriate (certainly from a historical perspective) to consider this an element of 'aristocracy' – selection of 'the best' (ἄριστος, *aristos*) by ballot; rule by professionals – whereas the original connotation of 'democracy' corresponds more closely to 'government by amateurs'.

---

4   Waluchow 2018.
5   Hamilton, Madison, Jay, and Ball 2007, p. 46.

To Hamilton, the constitutional composition of the republic was intended as 'remedy' against 'diseases', i.e. potential popular demands 'for an abolition of debts, for an equal division of property, or for any other improper or wicked project'. Should such demands surface, various built-in checks and balances would limit and isolate their spread, immunising the republic from self-defeating popular demands.[6] This conception of representation, constitutionalism, and republicanism as an aristocratic check on the radical temperaments of the working classes is the root of anti-republican bias in socialism.[7] Indeed, the republican tradition, spanning back to Graeco-Roman antiquity, has long voiced concerns over democratic excesses, in which commoners are free to act on their self-serving baser instincts, thereby corrupting the character of government. By mixing and balancing different 'constitutions' (systems of government) – democracy, aristocracy, monarchy – the government can be prevented from sliding into corruption. Modified versions of this argument persist today and caution against 'mob rule' or 'ochlocracy': Unfiltered public sentiment, including but not limited to popular prejudice, will cause the majority to disregard and vote away the rights of minorities or pursue economically short-sighted and self-destructive ends. Democracy, then, is supposed to act as a limit on state power, and conversely, democracy is supposed to be limited by extra-democratic constitutional constraints. Constitutionalism, in sum, represents a liberal-republican (i.e. aristocratic) attempt to restrict the direct influence of the mass of commoners over policymaking (i.e. democracy). This elitist conception is hardly compatible with the egalitarian aspirations of socialism, then, which raises the question why socialists should care to complement their politics with republicanism.

It should first of all be stressed that the republican tradition emphasises dialogue and deliberation as a means to transcend partial interests and to collectively formulate a shared viewpoint on the common good. This does more than merely provide an additional institutional platform to express intolerance or prejudice. By bringing opposing views into close contact and creating circumstances under which these views can be expressed, confronted, and mediated, it potentially creates a discursive space for nuance and toleration to emerge out of decision-making processes. Popular participation, far from amplifying prejudice, will likely help to break it down and facilitate the finding of common ground and enhance public civility.[8] Although this requires that certain pre-

---

6 Ibid.
7 See for example: Cockshott and Zachariah 2011, pp. 54–7; Chomsky 1999, pp. 47–8; Bookchin 1991a.
8 Walsh 2007, pp. 45, 56–7.
   Weatherford and McDonnell 2007, p. 196.

conditions are met, such as the use of public talk in which conflicting opinions can be reconsidered and reformulated, or the dissemination of information by experts in a non-authoritarian way.[9] With sound republican institutional mechanisms that facilitate deliberation – such as the use of public forums – self-government by active participation of members of the general public may well be feasible.

My main contention, however, is that democratic procedures in the social-ist commonwealth should not be an unmediated expression of popular will for two principal reasons: (i) social conflict growing out of sectional interests tied to fragmentation; (ii) inner conflict growing out of incompatible interests and preferences existing simultaneously within individuals (for example, narrow, short-term interests versus broad, long-term interests). On the subject of polit-ical authority, my views diverge most strongly from those of anarchism, but also from Marxist orthodoxy. These two key suppositions suggest that political authority should continue to operate under socialism to prevent social strife from spiralling outward uncontrollably. We will turn to the role and scope of political institutions in society in general, and in relation to socialism in par-ticular, which will clarify this proposition more clearly. It will show how con-flicting interests in society will need to be arbitrated by some form of political authority, where traditionally most socialist theory has assumed that the dis-appearance of class antagonisms is the necessary and sufficient condition that will do away with the need for political power. Provided there is no lapse in the structure of my argument, the conclusions indicate that it becomes neces-sary to draw up a composition of institutions as part of the political arrange-ments capable of sustaining community of property, while at the same time limiting the scope of state power in such a way as to prevent its capturing by particular interests. This relates also to the need to centre *citizenship* in social structures. This roughly means that is important that individuals do not relate to one another merely as consumers and producers, regarding others as means to their own immediate economic interests, but instead consider themselves part of the shared social experience of community. The political community will therefore have to assume a pivotal role in the dealings of production and distribution, to overcome narrow horizons engendered by local interests linked to the isolated affairs of individual units of production.

To clarify these issues, a brief treatment of the model of Hahnel and Albert is relevant since it lacks a role for political power. Fotopoulos criticises their model for relying exclusively on producers and consumers for decision-making.

---

9   Walsh 2007, pp. 46–7; Weatherford and McDonnell 2007, p. 210.

In it, the principal (in fact, the only) decision-making bodies are producer and consumer councils. However, as Fotopoulos argues, 'people as workers may have conflicting ideas, views and possibly even interests with people as consumers'. Thus, a public body is required to express the general interest, which in the anarchic model of Fotopoulos, is a general community assembly. While 'the particular interests [are expressed] by workplace assemblies, education establishments' assemblies', and so on, the general interest finds expression in the citizen assemblies of the community. This supposedly transcends 'the division between the general versus the particular interest', which implies that social conflict of this nature cannot arise and by extension that this will remove the *raison d'être* for state authority.[10] Fotopoulos' intellectual predecessor, the better-known Bookchin, too believed that final decisions over workplaces should be left to the communal government, rather than the workplace assembly.[11] In a stateless commonwealth, the legislative powers of 'political' institutions would be limited to decision-making regarding collective infrastructure and public goods – the 'administration of things', rather than rule over people, the 'government of persons'. Citizen assemblies and bounded delegates, without institutional powers of physical coercion, would express their preferences in public matters and allocate resources accordingly. This broad conception of 'statelessness' is shared by Marxism and anarchism. According to Bordiga, representative of Marxist thought in this regard, there is no need for a state 'when society as a whole becomes the master of its conditions of existence', i.e. communistic, since it is no longer 'torn by internal antagonism'.[12] Similarly, Marx had remarked that:

> The character of an election does not depend on this name but on the economic foundation, the economic interrelations of the voters, and as soon as the functions have ceased to be political, 1) government functions no longer exist; 2) the distribution of general functions has become a routine matter which entails no domination; 3) elections lose their present political character.[13]

By contrast, regulation of the actions and affairs of citizens by some central authority could only be characterised as state power and political authority. Instead, social activities in a stateless society would be self-regulated, although

---

10   Fotopoulos 1997, p. 439.
11   Lucardie 2016, p. 39; Bookchin 1991b.
12   Crump and Rubel 1987, p. 134.
13   MECW 24: 519.

not 'anarchically', but instead on the basis of mutual social trust, free agreement, reciprocity, and association[14] – more or less what Proudhon regarded as a voluntary 'social contract'.[15] The community of freely associated individuals would deliberate on collective matters at the local level by participating in public assemblies and selecting a representative from among them to communicate their decisions to other localities and regions for the purpose of coordination.

Tito likewise expressed the Marxist-Leninist idea that the essential unity of socialist society was embodied in the Communist Party by arguing that there were no conflicts between the particular interests of enterprises and the general interest in Yugoslavia, which was quite clearly at odds with reality.[16] The anarchist beliefs of Fotopoulos and Bookchin contain a similar fallacy, by postulating that a public body which expresses the general interest will necessarily nullify particular interests as well as conflicting views of what the general interest should entail. Even in socialist society people will express competing perceptions of the common good or put forward mutually exclusive particular interests, which will have to be mediated, but also ultimately enforced when the need arises. Citizens might advance individual and collective projects, whose strategic calculations, techniques and aims make claims to space, time and additional resources that might conflict with rival projects advanced by others. The constant collision of micro-interests involved in a multiplicity of projects needs to be structured within some sort of framework capable of facilitating, sustaining, and favouring certain projects at the expense of others and ordering them according to the metric of the common good.

According to my understanding, then, the political community, in the name of the general interests of society, should at times overrule the particular interests of individuals, or workplaces and localities. It is entirely plausible that not all differences of opinion and perspective can be smoothed over by deliberation among freely associated individuals, and therefore that not all the fractured and disparate social elements within the community will always align to come to some mutual understanding. By extension, it is perfectly conceivable that political authorities at the national level, motivated by a genuine concern for common welfare, have reached agreements on the direction of public policy that place demands on lower units of administration that are considered excessive or unnecessary from the partial, limited vantage point of the local social unit. This is clearly a potential source of social tension and conflict.

---

14   Holterman 1980; Holterman 2012, pp. 10–13.
15   Proudhon 2011, pp. 562–4.
16   In Sirc 1979, p. 135.

The experience of socialist Yugoslavia is a case in point: work collectives frequently frustrated the implementation of policies formulated at the national level that were intended to promote the interests of society. While Yugoslavia was not an arena in which the common good could be established through deliberative dialogue among free citizens, even in a political community which does allow for this, we might still realistically expect that workers in a given production unit could occasionally object to stipulations of the community without a possibility for reconciliation. Without means to enforce a final decision – taken by a legitimate public body which takes into account both particular and general interests, after every attempt at arbitration has been exhausted to no avail – such a political community may quickly become dysfunctional. Everyone would be free to oppose and obstruct indefinitely any policy or legislation to which they are not partial. More inflexible members of the community, who get their way by obstinately refusing any compromise in spite of majority decisions, might provoke resentment and a general, downward tendency in the willingness of citizens to surrender some personal interests for the benefit of the greater good. It would leave public administration impotent in terms of policy implementation.

Bookchin may argue that the communal assembly should have ultimate sway over all decisions of local economic units, since the effects of workplace behaviour escape their bounds, but he offers no mechanism to resolve any potential conflicts that might arise from such an arrangement – how should society go about settling disputes? Innumerable conflicts over different questions of production and consumption could emerge, which would demand an increasing number of citizen meetings to reconcile such differences. To prevent democratic fatigue, the local communities would likely increasingly rely on vertical delegation, by permitting elected representatives to make more choices on their behalf, increasing their influence on decision-making and outcomes.[17] Levels of political participation might well fall due to its excessive requirements in terms of time and energy, because every aspect of life – with all the intricacies and compartmentalisation of social knowledge that it involves – will need to be democratically 'micromanaged', lacking refuge to other mechanisms, whether markets or bureaucracy. All decisions affecting collective life will need to be made by someone – and since this can neither be some central authority nor a local group guided by partial knowledge, partial concerns, and by extension partial interests – therefore also by everyone at all times. This complexity would allow more power to creep upward, into the hands of

---

17   Lucardie 2016, p. 41.

public officials. Without constitutional limits placed on the powers of public office, there are no institutional mechanisms that regulate the interchange of representatives and citizens. The degree of discretionary power possessed by delegates in the dealings of governance, afforded to them by the abdication of some measure of responsibility by citizens, therefore becomes subject to the arbitrary discretion of the delegates itself. At this juncture, the oscillation from an excess of democracy to a collusive unity among delegates becomes a substantial threat. Thus, the mechanism of unchecked democracy cannot be relied upon to secure a robust freedom. In this respect a republic is better equipped to deal with social conflict compared to a stateless community, since the latter will more likely rely on *ad hoc* methods of enforcement or customary law, and is therefore more susceptible to arbitrary uses of power. A republic, by contrast, has its codes of civil conduct established clearly as general rules, uniformly, transparently, and enforced by an accountable public body.

In a stateless community, the social structure takes shape in accordance with prevailing custom, or customary law.[18] When there is relatively low rates of political participation, the monitoring of delegates suffers. This is compounded by the fact that each tier beyond the local area is indirectly elected via a system of bounded delegates, at least as envisioned by libertarian socialism. Citizens at the base will have limited knowledge of the policymaking intricacies of higher tiers of administration – which are 'black boxes' staffed by indirect ballot and perhaps appointments to commissions – which could potentially allow delegates to misuse political power for their own benefit. Since by acting in different ways new customs and conventions develop, law would over time come to reflect this incremental usurpation of power. If this *de jure* corruption does not occur then at least we might fear a *de facto* shadow administration which circumvents and undermines democratic processes by sabotaging the dissemination of information on which participatory and deliberative democratic processes depend, for example. This may not be done with ill intentions *per se*, but could reflect the creeping conviction that the deputies are better equipped to make decisions, since they are more familiar with the procedures or subject matter. Intricate familiarity with the procedures could allow deputies to massage them to produce outcomes that would benefit them personally, or their own constituency. The rotation of delegates – term limits are also an available policy option in a republic – whenever possible, offers some immunisation against this tendency, but enforcement of this rule is depend-

---

18   Holterman 1980; Holterman 2012, pp. 17–20.

ent on the customs observed by this community alone and cannot be codified into a body of law secured by a judiciary branch. At the earliest convenience, when it is considered opportune to re-elect a representative for an
additional term, a new precedent is shaped that throws out this limitation
on the scope of public office. In a constitutional-republican order the powers
of elected officials are clearly defined and codified, by contrast, and cannot
be changed through an alteration of customs alone. That is not to say that
there is no risk of a constitutional-republican regime sliding into corruption,
of course. Legal norms could fall into disuse, be changed for the worse, or the
judiciary could be undermined. Civic engagement is required in any case, but
the constitutional codifications of public functions are an additional institutional safeguard that a stateless society would lack. In sum, since libertarian
socialist practices are more susceptible to erosion since they are not codified
and secured by independent arbitration, the political community should therefore correspond to a 'community of law', 'legal community', or 'community
based on the rule of law' (NL: '*Rechtsgemeenschap*' or DE: '*Rechtsgemeinsch-
aft*').

To emphasise this further, let us turn to another example. In libertarian
socialism local bodies would operate autonomously and their decisions would
be co-ordinated and enforced by voluntary association alone, i.e. the ability
to opt out. Interdependency and reciprocity between so-called 'free associations' of communities and workplaces would be the glue that holds the system together.[19] Decentralisation, however, cements inequality between communities according to their differential resource endowments. If one community possesses access to particular resources, natural or otherwise, which
could potentially benefit an entire society, then they might possibly withhold
these resources from the rest of society to secure better bargains. This occurred
in Yugoslavia, due to excessive decentralisation, but also during the Spanish
Civil War (1936–1939), during which wealthy collectives effectively monopolised the material assets under their control. Another example occurred during
the course of the Russian Revolution:

> Railways which ran on wood-fired steam engines had acquired planta-
> tions of trees to supply fuel. Local peasants seized the plantations as
> part of 'their' village's land; and by doing so stopped the railways. *Some*
> decisions can be and should be taken locally. In relation to others, at-
> tempting to take local decisions is, in fact, for the locals to decide for

---

19   Van der Walt and Schmidt 2009, pp. 67–70.

everyone else that *there shall not be a railway*, or electricity supply, or an internet, or whatever the large-scale infrastructure item involved is.[20]

A degree of centralisation is required to ensure that resources needed by all are controlled by the political community as representative of the common interests of society as whole. If the effects of decisions transcend the boundaries of a local community or region, for instance, they should be referred to the appropriate level of administration. Central control by a public body would be an effective safeguard against particular interests threatening to undermine the coherence of the system. At the same time, it is not necessary that all decision-making should inefficiently pass through the centre, of course. Socialists have tended to advocate the subsidiarity principle instead,[21] suggesting that decisions should be made at the most immediate scale at which they affect matters – i.e. local matters locally, regional matters regionally, central matters centrally. Some central decisions should be binding on all regional and local public bodies in order to achieve the aims of the decision. In such circumstances a republican regime has at its disposal legal tools to enforce a final decision after independent arbitration. Thus, in terms of the scope and role of political institutions, there should be both a public body which exercises stewardship over the general interest, as proposed by Bookchin for example, but also the means to enforce final decisions, and therefore state authority, which anarchism naturally opposes. Once we acknowledge the need for state power, questions automatically arise about the need to carefully define and limit political authority, since there is a realistic risk of central control resulting in the concentration of unrestrained power. The solution is not, however, libertarian in nature, i.e. to simply do away with central control entirely. This would result in institutional incoherence and paralysis. Rather, the powers of the central body will need to be limited by defining a judicial terrain of legitimate conduct. Indeed, wherever this does not occur – at whichever administrative layer – a 'tyranny of structurelessness' lurks,[22] in which informal groups can increase their power. This effectively means that the powers of public institutions will need to derive their authority from constitutional law embodying the interests of the community in conformity to popular sovereignty, which thus provides the foundation for the functioning of political institutions. By rooting policymaking in legal statutes, it provides citizens with the freedom to know the range of choices available to them; whereas under a system of unrestrained

---

20   Macnair 2005.
21   For example: Devine 2002, p. 75.
22   Freeman 1972.

democracy (majoritarianism), individuals are subject to the volatility of a capricious popular will. Furthermore, since the need for central authority invariably arises in large-scale, complex social organisations, there will need to be various checks in place to prevent power from concentrating at this level.

To summarise, the justifications so far offered for a constitutional regime are as follows. Particular interests and competing perceptions of the common good could give rise to social antagonisms. These antagonisms require institutional mediation and enforceable final decisions to secure the implementation of policies that are intended to promote the greatest good for the overall community. Voluntary association does not suffice in these respects. Furthermore, minorities should not be subject to the whim of the majority, while the majority should likewise have their popular sovereignty secured from usurpation by a minority of political officeholders. It follows from this reasoning that general rules will need to formulated by the political community and enforced by an independent public body. The implementation and enforcement of legal statutes in republican thought is legitimate insofar as it tracks the interests of the affected citizenry, as Pettit explained:

> The promotion of freedom as non-domination requires, therefore, that something be done to ensure that public decision-making tracks the interests and the ideas of those citizens whom it affects; after all, non-arbitrariness is guaranteed by nothing more or less than the existence of such a tracking relationship.[23]

This segues into our subsequent discussion of the second main rationale for pursuing a republican approach to socialism. This is related to the following problematic. If law and public policy of a community are a reflection of the preferences of citizens, then libertarians (of both a left and right-wing persuasion) might object that enforcement would be redundant. If law is truly a reflection of the preferences of individuals then they should not have to assume legal force since individuals would voluntarily act in accordance with their own will – or else they would not be their preference. Republicanism could be charged with paternalism and elitism, therefore, by implying that the true preferences of the citizens are known by legislators or magistrates but not by citizens themselves.

However, we have to take into account that human psychology is somewhat more complex. This can be demonstrated by drawing on the concept of

---

23   Pettit 2002, p. 184.

the 'higher-order volition'. Also known as second-order preferences, they entail one's preferences about one's preferences. For example, an addict's first-order preference or lower-order volition may be for continued substance usage; but a higher-order volition or second-order preference may be to not have this preference in the first place.[24] Similarly, predictably irrational behaviour can be widely observed. One example includes a pension scheme with an opt-in and opt-out variant. When employees in a firm were given the option to opt into the pension plan, few did. This may be taken as an indication that they made the measured choice for another option elsewhere that better suited their needs or preferences. However, when the same employees were all signed up to the plan by the default and asked to opt out if they objected, few again did so. This experiment indicates that the employees were scarcely willing to expend the mental energy to follow through on their higher-order preference for a pension plan when left to their own volition.[25] 'Paternalistic' provisions of universal social security would fulfil the second-order preferences of citizens but universal coverage would not simply follow from individual free choice alone. The uncontrolled exercise of lower-order preferences would likely result in losses in general welfare; and, crucially, not as a matter of preference, since the citizens of such a society might well prefer a different outcome (a society with more stability, security, longevity, and so on, through the universal provision of certain social services).

In relation to socialism, we might argue the following. In a model of socialism which retains market competition, the members of a labour-managed firm may pursue the relative maximisation of income by behaving competitively in an aggressive market, since this is the means by which they can assure their livelihood. They prefer, at some level, to take part in competition – and thereby reproduce the system of free competition – over the immediate other alternative also available to them: operating at a loss, and in due time, insolvency. One might superficially conclude that this is a matter of free choice (and, moreover, that it is the economically sensible thing to do), and should hence not be interfered with. Yet, a higher-order preference of the members of society might be that they prefer a system in which their livelihood does not depend on competition but is secured through co-operation instead. In a 'healthy' market (with free entry, exit, and multiple suppliers), workers would be institutionally compelled to behave competitively to guarantee their livelihood, but that is not to say that they prefer these institutional rules that shape their choices in the

---

24   Frankfurt 1971.
25   Thaler and Benartzi 2007.

first place. Even if co-operation is preferred over competition by all, or at least the majority of society, it may not be the outcome of the aggregate of individual decisions, therefore. As Engels similarly remarked: 'For what each individual wants is obstructed by every other individual and the outcome is something that no one wanted'.[26] In other words, the sum of individual choices may not generate the socially desirable or optimal outcome (not per the standards of technocrats, but from the perspective of the members of the community themselves, it should be noted).

In a socialist model based on voluntary co-operation and commodity exchange but not market competition, capitalism may re-emerge in a similar manner. Members of a high-earning co-operative may at one point use their revenue to sub-contract unemployed workers – in a 'voluntary' society there are no legal restrictions to curb this behaviour – and attempt to undercut other co-operatives to expand their wealth further. In this way they could, at least momentarily, benefit from both competition (by undercutting their competitors) and co-operation (to the extent that their competitors are still bound by their earlier commitment to a compromise of co-operation). The fragile equilibrium based around a voluntary pact of co-operation may disintegrate when at least a few additional firms follow the example of the first and restructure economic behaviour around market forces. Even if it is not consciously willed by the majority of workers, they would be compelled to abide by the competitive pressures emerging as a consequence of the choice of a minority breaking away from the pact.

The behaviour of worker co-operatives in Yugoslavia provides an empirical (and theoretically well-grounded) example of the conflict of interests between different time horizons. By privileging current consumption over future consumption, producers elevated their short-term interest as worker over their long-term interests as consumers. Previously we have discussed social conflict borne from opposing interests advanced by different cross segments of the population, and here arises the issue of conflicting interests contained within individuals. Suppose that a stable majority prefers to organise society on the principles of socialist co-operation, this outcome does not flow automatically from their choices freely made according to the narrow horizons of daily decision-making. It would be necessary to enforce co-operation – a higher-order preference – at the central level through a pact that is binding on all subdivisions that constitute the community. The conditions of this pact, which ought to be the basis of the constitutional order, will need to be formulated by the members of society themselves through direct legislation and subject to periodic

---

26   MECW 49: 35.

re-deliberation. The political arena should thus be a forum in which the long-term and higher-order preferences of the citizenry are expressed. This pact is only effective insofar as the citizens themselves formulate the conditions and statutes, to guarantee that it tracks their interests, and to prevent particular interests (such as those of bureaucrats) from capturing public bodies. This is the nature of the 'social contract' under a socialist constitutional-republican order. It does not exist as an aristocratic check on democracy, nor as a means to gain security in exchange for surrendering absolute freedom, but rather as a means to secure the popular will for a co-operative commonwealth. This is necessary since the outcome of the sum of individual choices does not guarantee the durable reproduction of collective ownership.

The aim of 'socialist constitutionalism' is thus to allow citizens to express their more fundamental interests and higher-order preferences in the form of socialist co-operation. The constitution should embody the moral consensus of the political community, established by relations of political participation and reflecting the common good to which society aspires. In this respect, the unity of the community is established relationally at the level of the constitutional framework, instead of being essentially embodied in the Communist Party. It should ensure that government remains the affair of the community of free and equal citizens and, furthermore, that public policy, social relations, and legislation are vetted against the constitutional body of statutes that reflect these higher goods, and by extension that they do not violate the common interest in socialist co-operation. In effect, a 'social pact' is formulated by means of direct legislation. The excess of democracy, the enslavement of the state by the mob (to paraphrase Cicero), can potentially be circumvented in this way without conceding the need for a displacement of sovereignty into 'aristocratic' or 'oligarchic' checks and balances. This is of course very much distinct from 'liberal constitutionalism', which aims to manufacture a reasonable distance separating policymaking from popular participation. It is also a far cry from the political reality of Marxism-Leninism where:

> power undergoes a curious process of self-legitimation. Whether the ruling group expresses the desires and interests of the majority, and whether the majority of the people supports them, are not measured by whether this support is manifested in some tangible form (for instance, a ballot). The possessors of power have appointed themselves as the manifest expression of the people's interests and the repository of a permanent public good. According to the elliptical thinking described, one can almost say they have legitimated their power 'by definition'.[27]

---

27   Kornai 2007, p. 56.

Socialist constitutionalism can hence be regarded as a non-elitist answer to liberal constitutionalism, liberal republicanism, or for that matter the one-party rule of Marxism-Leninism. The basis of this type of constitution is power sharing among free and equal citizens in all public facets, thus extending these political principles to secure the symmetrical distribution of resources. Rather than distance the citizenry from direct political control, socialist constitutionalism should provide citizens with the legislative instruments to formalise their higher-order preferences for socialist co-operation into a 'social pact', a constitutional order of their own making. By these means, they may shape the foundational rules of socialist society to which all subsequent policymaking is referred. Put differently, democratic procedures should be embedded in an institutional context that inhibits the free exercise of lower volitions in policymaking, instead encouraging second-order preferences to guide the formulation of policy and laws. By combining different democratic procedures into a mixed constitution, the citizenry can formulate their own understanding of their common good and allow these considerations to guide their community. In the following section we will sketch the contours of this constitutional order and address how citizens might realistically formulate the laws of the socialist community through institutions and procedures.

2   Political Institutions and Practices of Self-Government

Socialists and republicans have generally shared a commitment to self-government. Marx and Engels saw in the revolutionary French Republic as well as the Paris Commune, and more generally the democratic republic, with its institutions of democratic participation and direct legislation, a prefiguration of the transitional regime – typically referred to as the 'dictatorship of the proletariat', or alternatively as 'social republic' or 'Republic of Labour'.[28] According to Engels, communists were right to celebrate the French Republic under Jacobin rule;[29] to Marx, the proletarian revolutionary regime began with 'the self-government of the communities' and would encompass the entire population of a given nation.[30] They characterised the democratic republic as 'the specific form for the dictatorship of the proletariat'[31] and identified Jacobin-working class collusion during the height of the French Revolution, as well

---

28   Leipold 2020b, p. 175.
29   MECW 6: 3–14.
30   MECW 24: 519.
31   MECW 27: 227.

as the short-lived insurrectionary Paris Commune of 1871 as such revolutionary dictatorships.[32] In their view, the 'social republic' is a tool for proletarian class supremacy, and once the social transformation had been consolidated, the institutions of self-government would lose their coercive functions and become free and voluntary associations that administer things rather than people.[33] Communism, at least insofar as it concerns canonical Marxism, is a stateless society. However, even in the absence of class antagonisms, as I have argued, society will require political authority. This political authority will – in addition to being defined and limited by a constitutional framework – need to reflect the general interest as understood by the citizenry themselves. Thus, it is required that political institutions allow for some mechanism by which citizens can formulate the laws and policies of their society.

Marx and Engels believed that in bourgeois society elected public officials were seized by private commercial interests, which meant that government turned from the servant of society into its master.[34] To remedy this, they adopted the proposals of radical republicans and socialists. All public functions would need to be elected by universal suffrage; all elected public officials would need to receive an average worker's income; elected officials would need to be bound by fixed mandates; and recall procedures would need to be available to constituencies.[35] These are some of the mechanisms proposed by democratic and radical republicans to guard against 'corruption' of public officials and government as well.[36] The Jacobin revolutionaries, for example, at one point advocated citizen assemblies supplemented with bounded delegates for higher levels of administration, and adopted this in their constitution.[37] Thus, we find that socialist theorists, like Marx and Engels before them, tend to take up the radical proposals of direct legislation. Citizen assemblies, such as those in the French Revolution, were usually taken as the standard model.[38] After the Russian Revolution '*soviets*', or workers' councils, came in vogue and were

---

32   MECW 24: 2; MECW 6: 320; MECW 22: 515–51; MECW 27: 185.

33   MECW 25: 247, 268. Indeed, the term 'dictatorship' was borrowed from Roman law, where it referred to a constitutional proviso which allowed for the temporary concentration of power to quell civil unrest – essentially, a state of emergency (see Draper 1987, pp. 11–13). Only when the state exercises temporary emergency powers to suppress rebellion – like Cavaignac during the Second French Republic – is it rendered a 'dictatorship', according to this understanding (MECW 10: 76).

34   MECW 22: 486–7; MECW 27: 170.

35   MECW 27: 331.

36   Leipold 2020b, pp. 177–8; Mouritsen 2006, p. 30.

37   Lucardie 2016, pp. 62–3.

38   For example: Bookchin 1991a, pp. 50–3.

widely regarded as the revolutionary and 'natural' form of working class political authority.[39] Kautsky, again a dissenting voice, believed on the contrary that
parliamentary forms of political decision-making were an outgrowth of the
absence of slave labour and serfdom in society. From the historical sample of
Ancient Greece he inferred that direct participation by citizens was viable only
because a limited number of free citizens had sufficient time to take part in
political life since they were unburdened by requirements of physical toil.[40]
Without slavery affording a smaller section of the population the right to citizenship, active political participation necessarily became the terrain of professional politicians in modern society. The position of Poulantzas holds between
Kautsky's parliamentary democracy and Lenin's *soviet* republic in a sense.[41] In
his view, socialists should strategically advance their politics through parliamentary bodies while workers' councils would function as the instrument by
which rank-and-file workers apply pressure to the political process, thereby
combining the two institutional elements. Poulantzas, in any case, neglected
to specify the institutional mechanism by which these two forms of political
bodies would jointly operate, failing to demarcate their respective domains of
authority.

All things considered, the socialist republic should provide an institutional
setting facilitating a public sphere for popular deliberation. This political deliberation should be encouraged through face-to-face citizen assemblies, acting as public forums and instruments of direct legislation. This is preferable
to referendums or electronic voting, as proposed by Cockshott and Cottrell
for example,[42] in which no deliberation, no real engagement and interaction
among viewpoints is required, and where, in addition, no compromise, no
modifications, or alternatives become possible in light of the closed questions
that have to be put to a vote. This would make it difficult for shared viewpoints
to emerge out of the political process. However, it is obviously impossible to
gather millions of citizens in a single plenary session to deliberate on political
matters. To Gey, this impossibility is an indictment of participatory forms of
democracy. He points out that 'small, cloistered, homogeneous communities
have become largely irrelevant to discussions' about governance of the modern
state, and the inability of civic republicanism to identify these small homogeneous communities in modern society – which, Gey argues, are the only viable
conditions for participatory democracy to exist – would cause it to reproduce

---

39   See for example: Shipway 1988; Ness and Azzellini 2011.
40   Lewis 2019, p. 68.
41   Poulantzas 2013, pp. 255–65.
42   Cockshott and Cottrell 1993, p. 165.

only the worst qualities of this type of decision-making, namely its conformism and intolerance. Whereas, on the other hand, its advantages, 'its homey, personal, face-to-face means of identifying and achieving common goals', could not be realised on a large scale.[43] Scattering the population into small autonomous communities, as has been proposed by Bookchin for instance, would be an unrealistic and costly solution to this problem (for example: 'Small communities cannot afford their own MRI equipment').[44] Simply put, some assets require such a large expenditure of effort and of materials that it would not be viable to replicate this effort on the level of every local community. Indeed, decentralisation in Yugoslavia led to wasteful duplication of efforts in the area of investments, as well as decreased mobility of resources, lack of co-ordination, and supply chain fragmentation[45] – yet, the level of decentralisation implied by the libertarian vision of Bookchin is still far more extreme and would result in proportionally more waste. By pooling resources, a greater number of communities can rely on fewer assets to meet their needs. So, while retreating into autonomous communities is suitable as a matter of personal lifestyle, it is not a political solution which can adequately address the challenges of contemporary society. Vertical integration of local decision-making, to subnational and national levels is required. How might this be achieved?

We could draw lessons from the Brazilian 'Landless Workers' Movement' (MST), which numbers some 1.5 million members and is administered by a governing structure in which base-level participation is crucial. The local assemblies of the movement's rural settlements – composed of ten to fifteen families – elect two deputies (one male, one female) for managing the settlement's day-to-day affairs, as well as delegates to represent them in the regional, state, and national decision-making bodies.[46] This is, of course, hardly an innovative concept in socialism. But it provides a practical, living example of participatory forms of democracy on a relatively large scale. The MST organises a host of services and activities, including agronomical, health, educational (for example, their schools were attended by 160,000 children, and its literacy programme served 30,000 people circa 2010),[47] recreational, and cultural services, and operates over eighty co-operatives.[48] The emphasis on local empowerment and shared symbols and joint rituals create meaningful communities that

---

43   Gey 1993, p. 815.
44   Shalom 2008, p. 28; see also Nove 1991a, p. 44.
45   Uvalić 2018, p. 36.
46   Vergara-Camus 2005, pp. 11–12.
47   Carter 2010, p. 10.
48   Carter 2010, p. 20; Vergara-Camus 2005, p. 12.

stimulate high levels of participation and mobilisation.[49] The need for base-level empowerment grew out of concerns that leaders could be bought off or assassinated, and thus the MST's ambition is to nurture leadership capacity in every individual member. While, of course, a social movement is distinct from a system of government, we might want to incorporate some elements of their practices. Vertical integration in the socialist republic can be accomplished by the use of delegation for higher administrative levels. At the neighbourhood-level, popular assemblies would be open to participation by all citizens of age. It would deliberate on political matters of local, regional, and national significance and propose legislation. It would further elect delegates to tend to neighbourhood matters on a daily basis since this would be too time consuming to involve everyone. Further, the popular assemblies would select by ballot deputies from among them to represent their local community at higher administrative levels. This would allow citizens to express their views beyond the scope of their immediate locality.

To Cole, there was a clear distinction between delegates and politicians: 'instead of substituting [the delegate's] will for [that of their constituency]', the delegate 'aims at carrying out, not their "real will" as interpreted by [the delegate], but their actual will as understood by themselves'.[50] Indeed, this had been the fear of radical republicans spanning back to the French Revolution. Radicals among the Parisian revolutionists – acknowledging that relying purely on popular assemblies, as in Ancient Greece, was impracticable, given the sprawling scale of their city – proposed that delegates elected to higher political bodies should be bound by fixed mandates, the '*mandat impératif*' conferred to them by their local constituency in the sectional assemblies.[51] Conversely, the constitution of the French Republic of 1791 abolished the imperative mandate positing that the 'representatives elected in the departments shall not be representatives of a particular department, but of the entire nation, and no mandate may be given them'; elected deputies thus acting under the '*mandat représentatif*'. The underlying notion is simply that popular sovereignty is indivisible and should thus be concentrated in the representative body of the whole nation, rather than the popular assemblies that represent only partial sections of the republic. The confederal Dutch Republic abolished binding instructions ('*last*') and consultation ('*ruggespraak*') over more pragmatic details, citing long travel distances required for representatives to return to and consult with

---

49   Carter 2010, p. 20; Vergara-Camus 2005, p. 11.

50   Cole 1920b, p. 51.

51   Lucardie 2016, p. 62.

their constituencies across different towns before again travelling back to the highest legislature to reach a final verdict.

The model of bounded delegation remains the most fashionable alternative to the parliamentary model of government within socialist thought. In such an arrangement delegates should be sent by the primary citizen assemblies to higher levels of administration, to the level of the town or borough (district), municipality (commune), province (department), and to the national level (republic). In this way, it had been proposed, deputies are authorised to merely communicate the decisions taken at the general citizen assembly, ensuring that political power rests with the base at all times. Fotopoulos, for instance, maintains that the 'regional and confederal assemblies' composed of delegates are 'simply administrative councils', whereas the popular assemblies at the base are 'policy-making bodies'.[52] However, Shalom correctly argues: 'We don't want to have delegates mandated by their sending councils, for then the higher level councils will not be deliberative bodies'.[53] What is supposed to guarantee the responsiveness of elected representatives to popular will, in his view, is that they are drawn from the popular assembly itself, 'because [the delegate] has been part of a council and participated in a deliberative process with its members, understands their sentiments and concerns, and is authorized to deliberate on their behalf with other delegates'.[54] Thus, there is an organic connection: 'The delegates are part of – and constantly returning to – their sending council'. Evidently, any important non-routine decision has to be ratified by the lower council or assembly. Furthermore, 'delegates will be rotated', and finally, 'delegates will be subject to immediate recall'.[55]

If the sphere for public deliberation is exclusive to the domain of local assemblies, it stands to reason that the active participants depart from their understanding of local context and opinion. As a result, citizens might pass binding instructions to their delegate that reflect the particular interests of their social standpoint as the residents of their local community, rather than as citizens of the socialist republic. If these assemblies elect a delegate to legislate on their behalf at higher administrative layers on the basis of a fixed mandate, dialogical interaction among different views is handicapped. It would become impossible to formulate some sort of common viewpoint beyond the immediate local level. The whole process begins and ends with local deliberation among spatially fragmented units of administration, thus breeding corres-

---

52   Fotopoulos 1997, p. 404.
53   Shalom 2008, p. 29.
54   Ibid.
55   Ibid.

ponding social divisions. The political process would merely aggregate the narrow, localised interests rather than reshape the various sections and districts into a more or less unified whole that can be guided by concerns for the overall welfare of the national community. This localism is structurally inscribed into libertarian socialism due to closing off all political bodies to deliberation beyond local public meetings. To my mind, this certainly calls for structural amendments to such a model of popular self-government to sensitise citizens to the common good by means of institutional design. The influence of 'localist' prejudices of the population should not be addressed by *ad hoc* interventions into the political process from above by a judicially privileged vanguard party, requiring substantive modifications to the structure of political decision-making instead.[56]

To clarify what I mean in somewhat greater detail, McKelvey assesses, correctly in my view, that 'the people should not be idealized. The majority of people tend to think in concrete and particular terms, not understanding problems in their larger historical and social context'.[57] Thus, he says, 'Most tend to be orientated to the protection of particular interests rather than the good of the society as a whole in the long run'. Socialists are therefore forced to identify some institutional device by which self-governing citizens can be reconciled to broader considerations and general interests. McKelvey argues that the solution should be found in the vanguard party (as per Cuba's model of popular democracy) which contains the most politically advanced and conscious segments of the population. In this capacity:

> Their role is to educate the people, and they play this role through discourses in the popular assemblies and informal discussions among the people. Their challenge is to persuade the people of the best courses of action for the good of the revolution and the good of society in the long term.

There is no guarantee that the work among the popular masses will prove successful, however: 'It therefore is necessary for the sustainability of the revolutionary project that the vanguard maintains the confidence and trust of the people'. This strikes me as all too 'voluntaristic', or contingent if you prefer, since it depends primarily on the cultivation of good-will by party cadres. Because the Communist Party enjoys a legal monopoly as the leading force in polit-

---

56   For an account and defence of this 'Cuban model' of democracy, see McKelvey 2018.
57   McKelvey 2013.

ical affairs it is especially susceptible to careerism which is, at a minimum, no less particularistic than the narrow, short-term interests of ordinary citizens. The collapse of socialist governments in Europe and its causes surely indicate that party officials were vulnerable to considerable particularism and the leading role of the Communist Party did not decelerate the general decline. The solution should instead be sought in the structure of the model of government itself, which ought to be designed in such a way that particular interests are inhibited from producing socially short-sighted outcomes.

Shalom's proposal for elected and flexible representatives is more sensitive to republican concerns for the common good since it would ensure that citizens in communities actively engage with the viewpoints of other communities in order to develop a broader perspective. It facilitates direct participation, by allowing citizens to partake in the public and political affairs by means of citizen assemblies, retaining base-level meetings that have the capacity to send delegates upwards to represent them. However, these delegates operate on the basis of a flexible mandate and are therefore afforded a greater degree of discretion. This permits legislative assemblies at the regional and national levels to become spaces open to deliberative processes by which local perspectives can be reconstituted into a common outlook. At the same time, it enhances the latitude of 'representation' and is therefore more vulnerable to discretions violating the will and interests of citizens. As counterweight to this risk, the functions and authority of public office should be carefully defined and limited by constitutional means to ensure there is no breach of accountability in the exercise of political power.

Since the people's representatives are drawn from the constituency and have to return to their assemblies, they will give account of their own voting behaviour and that of other delegates, as well as the various viewpoints that were circulated. The citizens in local assemblies are thereby exposed to the arguments and views of citizens elsewhere, compelling them to take these into account by considering how some compromise at the regional or national level can be reached that is more reflective of their mutual interests. The delegates therefore act as representative of the local interest at the regional and national bodies, and conversely, come to represent regional and national interests in the local assemblies. By means of this process, the broader interests articulated by delegates in higher level political bodies come to penetrate all local bodies. The local communities are thereby transformed, at least in part, into representative, small-scale placeholders of the national community, being able to identify with its broader concerns and interests. The 'small, local communities', which Gey noted were absent in modern society, can be reformed in this way. Naturally, this would further require a repository of cultural symbols, norms, and rituals that reinforce the sense of social belonging that cuts across localities, so that each local community represents roughly a cross section of the entire republic and comes to identify with the community as a whole – a process of political socialisation to ensure that citizens are permeated by a common attachment to the constitutional principles that secure the status of citizens as free and equal subjects of the republic and a civic duty to take active part in political life and public deliberation to secure this status.

The citizen assemblies conduct their affairs at the level of the neighbourhood. These local assemblies will elect two or so delegates to manage the day-to-day affairs of their immediate locality, and simultaneously represent them in the lower legislative assembly of the commune. The popular assemblies also field candidates for the legislative assembly of their department and the national assembly of the republic. A selection of these candidates is picked by lot or ballot and go on to serve as lawmaker. The frequency at which the popular assemblies will convene should be relatively spread out to prevent political fatigue. They might convene on a monthly basis. During the plenary session of the citizen assembly, representatives of different levels of administration will attend them to account for their choices. It should be noted that all representatives can be recalled by the popular assemblies, even those selected by lot. There might also be another type of public meeting, of a consultative nature convened at the level of districts (towns and boroughs) which lack decision-making power, but which can be used as platform in which people might come forward with concerns that could be included for the agenda of the subsequent popular assembly; where preliminary ideas might be explored; or where delegates might solicit public opinion.

A disadvantage of this 'pyramid'-like structure, where decision-making power rests at the bottom and flows upward to the centre, is that it places multiple tiers between the base and the top. When there is widespread popular participation, involving both deliberation and monitoring, this may not be much of a problem. When this is not the case, however, as Glaser has pointed out, this can lead to an 'undue concentration of power in particular groups of individuals or in higher tiers of political and bureaucratic authority'.[58] We have an empirical basis to suspect that such extensive participation may be absent even when it is facilitated, since attendance to citizen assemblies in Porto Alegre or Swiss *Landsgemeinde* hovered around two and twenty percent, respectively.[59] For widespread popular participation to be sustained, abund-

---

58   Cited in Machover 2009, p. 16.
59   Lucardie 2016, pp. 50–3.

ant quantities of civic virtue are required. Meaningful political engagement 'requires equal access to the resources needed for effective participation'.[60] As Cockshott and Cottrell note:

> those goods and services which are basic prerequisites for full participation in the productive and communal life of the society should be provided as of right, and financed out of general taxation. Prime examples here would be education, health care and child care (...) In order to function as an active, productive member of society one must be well-educated, healthy and free of the need to stay at home with dependent children all day. These goods are necessary to give individuals the 'positive freedom' to control their own lives.[61]

There are some ways to enhance civic virtue, such as through civic education. Comprehensive mandatory public education might include quasi-democratic forums for schoolchildren in which they could deliberate on school-related matters and arbitrate disputes. In this way they can be socialised into norms of civility, dialogue, conflict-resolution, and public-spiritedness – instead of merely socialised into becoming order-takers. They will need to become active subjects, which should help with acquiring a sense of shared responsibility and temperance. Even if civic virtue is nurtured, we have some cause to believe that political participation will be limited. For example, attendance to weekly community meetings in kibbutzim – Israeli agricultural collectives – hovered between twenty to thirty percent, although in varying composition[62] – despite extensive socialisation into collectivist and egalitarian norms. While, from a republican perspective, it may not be strictly necessary that virtually all citizens participate actively in the political process – as long as the composition of attendees is sufficiently balanced to be approximately representative of the citizenry as a whole – a more substantive problem would reside in terms of oversight of delegates. An institutional framework that presupposes sustained and widespread popular participation as primary means to monitor delegates would likely operate under tensions in reality.

---

60   Devine 2002, p. 73.
61   Cockshott and Cottrell 1993, p. 69.
62   Which meant that approximately 71 percent of kibbutz members attended the meetings regularly or occasionally. This seems very reasonable, given the costs of participation in collective decision-making but may not be enough to sustain democratic practices in vast communities bound by an impersonal institutional framework, without also codifying the norms of government. See Blasi 2017.

A society bound by voluntary association alone would have difficulty in reproducing government by free arrangement, since while most people would likely have an interest in broadly influencing the direction of administrative output, it is unlikely that they are willing to devote the demanding amounts of energy necessary to formulate in all the required detail the policies and laws of their society while also monitoring their subsequent implementation. The complexity of modern society will require a correspondingly complex framework of protocols and procedures to structure public administration effectively. If widespread popular participation proves too costly, crevasses will appear in the capacity to monitor the full width of public administration. These would form blind spots that enable deputies to conceal at least some of their political activity from public scrutiny due to a fall in monitoring intensity. Thus, political power would creep into hands of public officials that do have ample access to time and resources to administer the levers of public administration. This is true regardless of the intentions of delegates, since if citizens themselves abdicate their collective responsibility, this vacuum must automatically be filled by the active functionaries elected to act on their behalf. Any model of socialist democracy that presupposes such sustained high-level civic engagement is likely setting itself up for failure. More pessimistic assumptions about the willingness for direct participation need to be integrated into our institutional design to ensure that the political structures accommodating freedom and equality are preserved even when popular participation in political processes falls below a certain threshold. In other words, the sustainability of the socialist constitution should not hinge on direct participation alone.

Machover identifies as an additional drawback of the 'pyramid'-structure the fact that a voter's power is diluted with each additional tier.[63] He shows mathematically that 'the vote of an individual citizen counts for less, has a smaller chance of affecting the final outcome, than in a referendum'. Or in the words of Black, this problem 'will be compounded at every higher level. The majority; the majority of the majority; the majority of the majority of the majority – the higher up you go, the greater the inequality. The more often you multiply by a fraction, the smaller the number you arrive at'.[64] Of course, the chance of a single vote affecting the outcome in any popular vote of millions is astronomically small, essentially nil. This is hardly the point of democratic participation (energy spent on the act of voting outweighs the personal benefits obtained from it by a large margin).[65] Republicanism evades this issue, since it

---

63   Machover 2009, p. 18.
64   Black 2011.
65   See the so-called 'paradox of voting' as formulated by Downs.

does not privilege individual preferences and therefore does not seek to orchestrate a political mechanism that affords the fairest possible opportunity for the largest sum of individual political preferences to influence the direction of the polity – democracy purely for the sake of itself. Instead, democratic participation is first of all an effective check on central political power; secondly, it facilitates sensitivity to the common good;[66] thirdly, it converts the common good as understood by the public into law or policy (rather than the sum of individual self-interested preferences). Put differently, democratic procedures may be an effective way to organise popular sovereignty, with which republicanism is principally concerned, and an ineffective way to organise individual sovereignty, with which liberalism is primarily concerned. An added benefit is that mass democratic rituals create a shared social experience that reinforces a sense of common identity which in turn helps in maintaining public-spiritedness. Thus, political institutions for popular participation should transform subjects into active citizens concerned for the general welfare of their community, and conversely, political institutions should become instruments that advance the common good; rather than act as a mechanism for tallying up individual preferences – democracy, not for the purpose of crude majoritarianism, but with the aim of securing freedom and the general interest. Nevertheless, there is an important point to be made, more sensitive to a republican framework. Machover writes that:

> A free human being, citizen of a free commonwealth, is not merely a member of such a group [a local community] but also, and at the same time, a member of the entire society at large. (...) For some such decisions, local or sectorial interests and viewpoints are relevant, and so it is reasonable for citizens to be represented through a structure that reflects their local or functional affiliation. But there are surely some national-level decisions for which these affiliations are either irrelevant, or should be ignored, even overruled, in order to prevent undue special pleading.[67]

Local self-government arguably binds citizens to the logic of partial interests – even if this is mitigated by flexible mandates at higher levels of administra-

---

66   Similar to: altruistic voter theory (see Jankowski 2007, pp. 5–34) which shows that voting is in part motivated by weak altruistic concerns rather than by a rational analysis of the personal costs and personal benefits that might be obtained by potential electoral outcomes.

67   Machover 2009, p. 17.

tion. The process of political decision-making is tied down by the local community which provides the primary institutional context and political instruments through which citizens express their interests and preferences. Since all decision-making would pass through geographically segmented political bodies, it may discourage the formation of a society-wide general interest. At the same time, we should wish that citizens are afforded access to instruments for direct legislation and political deliberation and thus that this should not be the exclusive terrain of professional politicians. Legislative assemblies that are open to public participation should be maintained as the socialist aspiration, but they should be amended by Machover's proposal for a bicameral legislature. He writes that this should encompass 'a directly elected assembly of representatives [which] functions as the 'lower' chamber, whereas the council of delegates at the corresponding tier of the pyramid serves as the 'upper' chamber'.[68] The lower house of representatives, possessing a greater degree of legislative power, should be elected by direct ballot and proportional representation, in his view. As a result, the legislative assembly should be motivated by the concerns of the entire nation which elected it directly. The upper house, with fewer powers of legislation, would be composed of delegates selected by a passing a series of indirect elections from the base-level upward, permitting a more circumscribed role still for legislative citizen assemblies.

In my view, however, this hierarchy should be inverted. The lower house should be elected by the local popular assemblies, indirectly. In my proposal, the neighbourhood representatives drawn from citizen assemblies act as the legislative council of their district or commune. Popular assemblies may further select candidates from among themselves to act as their representatives at the regional or national level. Since not every neighbourhood can be represented at this centralised level of administration, each candidate elected by their popular assembly will have to pass another election or be selected by lot. Thus, either the delegates at the level of the commune elect the representatives from a short-list of candidates (each put forth by their popular assembly) or they are selected at random. These nominees will compose the lower house of the national legislature of the republic. By according more significance to the citizen assemblies, establishing them as the foundation for the political decision-making, citizens can directly propose legislation at the lowest level sending their proposals upward to earn final approval by the highest legislature, which is composed of the upper and lower chambers. In this way, citizens are given a direct stake in the making of their laws. The importance and respons-

---

68   Machover 2009, p. 23.

ibility afforded to citizen assemblies should reinforce the idea of civic duty and 'politicise' the members of the community into active public service.

The upper house of the national legislature should be a body whose legislative functions are more limited by comparison. The members of the senate should be drawn from the whole territory it represents, as opposed to representing separate electoral precincts and districts. This would make it less disposed to local affiliations and partial interests, and more likely to act on behalf of the interests of the whole community. Volunteers with a sufficient number of signatories backing their candidacy, and who have not previously served as representative in either house for at least some duration, are included in a pool of nominees and a sample is selected by lot to serve as representative. Since this lacks a pre-selection procedure, as would be the case when political parties field their pick of candidates, there should be mandatory work requirements, such as the attending to meetings discussing public affairs and so on. While the various assemblies at different levels of administration have the right to initiate legislation, the upper chambers should vet the policies and laws formulated by these bodies according to the main criterium of the general interest. The members of the upper chamber become representative of the entire nation by virtue of the mandatory meetings among deputies to discuss general affairs from their general perspective. They may vote to approve and disapprove all decisions passed by the lower chamber on the basis of this metric of the general interest. This forces the lower chambers, already under a flexible mandate permitting them to re-organise their interests at the intermediate and national level, and by extension around the common good, to consider the broad implications of their laws and policies as an extra insurance against localism.

Since delegates are not bound by imperative mandates supplied at the local level and since all legislation will have to earn the approval of the upper house of the national legislature, which is representative of the entire community, the overall political procedure is more likely to generate outcomes that approximate the long-run, common interests.

Bicameralism of this type serves an additional purpose. Since policymaking and lawmaking are technical processes, the effective supervision of delegates requires immersion in various policy areas. The large personal costs incurred by citizens in volunteering to oversee public officials and to hold them responsible for their choices form an obstacle in securing transparency. This is especially true where we introduce an element of representation, by providing delegates the discretion to make some choices on behalf of their community without necessarily consulting with them first, which makes accountability all the more important.

In practice therefore, this time-intensive scrutiny of public officials is mostly performed by professionals (ranging from journalists to magistrates or elected officials) who relay their findings back to the public. Citizens can delegate this task of overseeing public administration to a selection from among them who are reimbursed for their time, chosen by lot. Since if both chambers are elected by popular vote, it stands to reason that the political affiliation of their respective compositions would more or less correspond, meaning both chambers would be more likely beholden to the same factional allegiance. This would increase the odds of collusion and deal-making, since political partisanship may inhibit the willingness of members of the upper chamber to critically scrutinise their political allies in the lower chamber, or perhaps conspire against the public by concealing part of their political agenda and motives. The upper house – being chosen by lot from a pool of people have not served in office during the previous terms – would be far less invested in usurping power since there is no chance for their members to reap the fruits of such fraudulent efforts in later terms of office. By having dual-track as well as staggered elections, one chamber elected by popular vote and another by lot, the output of the political process should be approximately consistent with popular will and the general interest by securing a degree of independence from popular caprice without introducing elements of oligarchic decay. This will hopefully generate a proper balancing of direct popular participation in public affairs and political outcomes that are reflective of the long-term, broad interests of the community.

Finally, there are two additional sorts of assemblies that require mentioning. The constitutional assembly, discussed presently, and the annual general planning assembly, discussed more closely in the next section. To affirm and institutionalise the egalitarian or non-elitist character of 'socialist constitutionalism', the socialist republic will have to hold a constitutional convention once, say, 25 or so years – a relatively lengthy interval to prevent chaotic overhauls of the system of government in short succession. During the constitutional assembly (which requires multiple sessions spread out over multiple administrative layers and sequentially), the foundational body of law of the republic may be amended with only a simple majority (as opposed to a qualified majority ordinarily). Each sovereign generation will in this way be afforded the opportunity to give themselves their own constitution, untethered by the decisions of previous generations. This should promote the constitution as a living body of law subject to period re-deliberation according to popular interpretation. The citizens of the republic may amend, overturn, or introduce any aspect of the constitution, with one exception. The sole proviso of constitutional law should be that all constitutional statutes will have universal application, being administered evenly, and cannot therefore have bearing on particular characteristics so that all citizens are equally accountable and protected in the face of the laws of their community.

Constitutional law encompasses the statutes stipulating the procedures and institutions that together compose system of government as well as some sort of bill declaring the obligations and rights of citizens – basic civil liberties and political rights that are necessary for the flourishing of the community should be included, extending to the right to free assembly without interference, the right to free speech and expression, the right to vote and the right to stand in elections, and so on. Political socialisation of the citizenry should have impressed the importance of these basic rights on the members of the political community, to curb capricious tempering with these rights. Still, constitutional statutes over time may become conservative fetters existing only by virtue of tradition and should therefore be periodically revisited, reviewed critically, and be dispensed with if so desired. Moreover, the constitutional body of law contains the architecture, the blueprint if you will, of the edifice of the socialist republic. Citizens may find it necessary to amend the procedures by which they can determine the direction of their community, to improve upon them or to accommodate changes in the sociocultural, demographic, or technological composition of society.

To prevent, for example, a low voter turnout from inadvertently modifying the constitution in ways that are inconsistent with popular will, the constitutional assembly should take place in different stages. Amendments to specific statutes or proposals for new articles and clauses are submitted in local assemblies or by the supreme assembly of republic where they will have to win the support of the majority. The popular assemblies vote on the proposals of the national legislature and vice versa. Thus, each reform will have to be approved by the upper and lower houses of the general assembly of the republic, as well as the majority of votes cast in the popular assemblies. If a simple majority is reached, the draft proposal has been accepted and will be formalised. At this stage, the draft amendments can be broadcasted widely to arouse controversy and public scrutiny to reach larger segments of the population that were hitherto uninterested in reformulating the details of the constitutional body of law. Subsequently, to ratify the draft proposals, each amendment will be subjected to a popular vote by referendum. The much lower personal costs associated with the casting of a vote in a referendum, combined with the potential controversy and the consequential nature of any amendments to the foundational body of law of the national community, should arouse a high turnout thereby guaranteeing that popular will is embodied in the constitutional reforms.

As a final note, the work of people's representatives will need to be assisted in their activities on a number of ends. First, by training elected deputies in the basics of legislation and macroeconomics, primarily. Second, by staggering elections, so that the turnover of experience is not immediate. Third, by executive commissions concerned with different policy area – healthcare, housing, macroeconomics, etc. – staffed by representatives on a rotating basis. This structures the execution of their legislative functions. Hence there is no separate executive branch, with deputies performing both legislative and executive functions simultaneously. Finally, by the administrative apparatus of functionaries and civil servants attached to these same functional divisions and policy areas. They supply lawmakers with information and counsel and assist legislators in the interpretation of technical information, to enable them to make informed decisions.

These are the basic structures of constitutional government in place in my proposal – safe for the legal and defence infrastructures. The popular assemblies in neighbourhoods and towns provide the space and instruments for citizens to shape their community. Their representatives in the national assembly advance their interests, while the upper chamber moderates popular caprice and acts to filter out the durable, long-term general interests.

In sum, the bicameralism of the republic serves diverse and important functions, namely to act as a brake on caprice and factionalism, vet proposals against the general interest, inhibit parochialism, monitor the activity of delegates, in order to check, somewhat paradoxically, against aristocratic tendencies creeping into democratic procedures and to ensure that popular sovereignty and the general will are centred and preserved. There are a number of arguments that justify republicanism over free association. An unchecked democracy is vulnerable to perversion, if: (a) social conflict exists between subdivisions of citizens; (b) the lower volitions of people take precedent over their preferences of a higher order; (c) direct participation is limited, at least in intensity but not necessarily frequency; (d) political participation for most citizens is limited to local forums due to geographic fragmentation at the local level of administration. While we impose certain institutional checks on direct legislation (we can thus speak of a mixed government, and a semi-direct democracy), by introducing bicameralism, the sortition of deputies, a degree of representation, and a body of constitutional law, we do so in the interest of preserving the democratic character of the political process, to curb the usurpation of power. The point of a balanced constitution is for political procedures to generate outcomes that are consistent with the higher-order preferences of the citizenry, as understood by themselves. This can be explained additionally by outlining the process for dealing with the national budget, which we will turn to subsequently.

3   The Role of Central Planning

A socialist regime allows for political considerations and social priorities to guide economic developments directly, whereas under a system of market competition, uncontrolled private initiative based on particular interests primarily determines economic outcomes. This advantage of socialism over capitalism, provided it can be harnessed to its potential, should allow citizens to shape politically the strategy for the improvement of their common welfare. To this effect, socialism will require a significant degree of what is sometimes called 'central planning', despite its connotations with a system of over-centralisation and comprehensive, imperative planning. Since if not for central direction, it would not be the political choices reflecting the overall interests and preferences of the community that set the parameters of economic and social developments, but the sum of narrow individual choices made according to private considerations and particular interests. Central planning is indispensable for a project of socialist republicanism, since the primary aims of both traditions intersect to meet here: considerations of how society's means of production should be used to the benefit of all should be front and centre in political life.

In order to guide the developmental trajectory of society, it is not necessary for the centre to involve themselves in every detail of economic decision-making. The political community, instead, should acquire command over the necessary levers and controls to effectively structure the course of economic development in accordance with politically defined social priorities. This requires some elaboration on the meaning of centralised planning, as Kalecki noted:

> No one would surely dispense with central planning altogether. However, essentially this is not a very meaningful statement, since the notion of planning can be so diluted as to embrace even counter-cyclical intervention in the capitalist countries. What we have in mind here is central planning in the sense [of] planning that embraces the volume of production, the wage fund, larger investment projects as well as control over prices and the distribution of basic materials.[69]

The effective exercise of political command requires the deployment of instruments to determine the amount of total investment, in order to divide the total

---

69   Kalecki 2010, p. 27.

product of society among immediate consumption and deferred consumption for accumulation according to social and political preferences, and by extension the size of the wage fund and, broadly, the structure of income. It further implies the central distribution of investment funds among branches of industry in accordance with socially defined priorities and direct, centralised control over large investments to co-ordinate politically mandated large-scale industrial redevelopments, and finally, the overall determination of the set of relative prices to secure the appropriate macroeconomic balance in relation to investment and employment requirements, as well as to guide microeconomic decision-making and bring it in alignment with social priorities. By moving these levers up and down according to different priorities, economic conduct at the lower levels can be structured in a way to obtain certain socially desired outcomes as defined by a political agenda, itself subject to democratic deliberation.

Principally, centralised planning would be used to maintain stable macroeconomic proportions, and thus implies political authorities setting the levels of income, investment, and prices.[70] Central price determination should play a key role under socialism since market prices would engender competitive pressures (market compulsions) that would cause investment decisions to spiral out of political control, being taken into directions according to the partial interests and partial knowledge of local economic units, ultimately causing the re-emergence of the negative social maladies of market competition (e.g. unemployment, crises of over-accumulation and investment cycles, large income disparities). If the activities of firms are structured according to profit calculations and market conditions, an initial downward shift in the amount of investment undertaken may culminate in an overall decline of output that is greater than the initial change. By adjusting the markups added to the costs of production, so that, for example, a decrease of investment which decreases the rate of expansion of productive capacity, is compensated by lowering the price of articles of consumption, which therefore ensures a proportionate increase in the level of consumption of finished products, the total output furnished by society remains constant. In this way, the release of resources from the sphere of investment is offset by a recruitment of resources into the sphere of consumption goods industries. This secures that the total output by society is subject to constant rates of expansion rather than tied up with the oscillations of business cycles. Under the centralised price-fixing, producers determine the costs of production while central authorities fix prices of products to their aver-

---

70   Kalecki 2010, pp. 48–53.

age current costs and add a markup based on the requirements of foreign trade, investment, social expenditures, and external costs.

In addition to this fundamental role assumed by the centre, the demands placed on centralised co-ordination increase when the rate of accumulation grows. It implies greater control over investment projects by central authorities to ensure that the structural adjustments associated with large-scale investments can benefit from the long-time horizon and vantage point of political authorities to map the interdependencies associated with an industrial overhaul. Thus, the 'difficulty of affording a firm a reliable basis for 'decentralised' long-term decisions at lower levels may well be a reason for retaining centralised planning of all major investment decisions'.[71] When entire industries will need to be restructured to accommodate the introduction of comprehensive technological improvements, there will be a pronounced need for central co-ordination over these industries. The extensive transformation of one industry – perhaps to facilitate a transition in energy consumption – may presuppose the simultaneous expansion of another branch. To effectively restructure industries, the necessary changes will need to be co-ordinated by the central authorities that are able to oversee these broader implications and chart an appropriate course, whereas otherwise a developmental stalemate may emerge where the expansion of each industry is inhibited by the constraints on expansion experienced by another, co-dependent sector – perhaps due to lengthy recoupment periods involved in large investments exceeding the myopic horizons of producers.

Note then, that in addition to being able to internalise external costs in price formation under socialism, a price-signal approach to influence economic decision-making cannot fully serve as a substitute for deploying instruments of centralised planning as part of a proactive investment-approach to securing socially desired ends.

The exercising of these functions involve rather technical matters that should be executed by the expert staff of the central planning bureau and their subdivisions according to a political mandate. The central planning mechanisms are extremely powerful tools in shaping society, and it is therefore imperative that they are applied in the public interest. How can we ensure that the central planners wielding these instruments do not conceal their real preferences and manipulate general plan proposals accordingly? First, by ensuring that they do not have separate partial interests as such, as much as reasonably possible. The members of the national planning commission may be composed

---

71   Dobb 1967, p. 245.

of rotating specialists, randomly drawn from a short-list of candidates, with some selected from all regions to minimise regional differences in the composition of membership to curb the privileging of certain regions over others. Second, the planners should not be entitled to any special privileges or variable bonus payments. Third, the central planning authorities will receive their mandate from political bodies and act as a purely executive agency. It stands to reason that their authority will be codified to limit their scope to executing this mandate and also that the CPB will be subjected to political, journalistic, and judicial scrutiny of their activities. Furthermore, we could imagine that it may be necessary to install an independent supervisory commission of specialists that vets the work of the CPB.

The process of general planning of national budgets calls for more direct participation. It is by political means that citizens should be able to select from alternative development strategies a course of collective action that corresponds most closely to their own understanding of the best approach to improving their common welfare. This democratically sanctioned development strategy should be converted into a set of qualitative and quantitative indicators that structure the distribution of resources and the behaviour of producers and consumers, thereby ensuring that activities at the microeconomic level correspond to and generate the politically formulated macro-level outcomes.

Any society will face choices in relation to the distribution and employment of resources. At the macroeconomic level, the political community will have to decide how to disaggregate the total stock of resources between main categories of alternative uses, primarily between the production of additional means of production compared to means of consumption. In other words, the socialist community will have to weigh the trade-offs associated between increasing future consumption relative to current consumption. In this respect, we have previously noted how under Yugoslavia's market socialism, as far as it concerned the operation of workers' councils, they tended to violate their long-term interests as consumers in favour of immediate increases of their income. Here is an example of a 'democratic excess', wherein self-governing producers act on their narrow and partial interests to the detriment of the greater interest of the community (and therefore ultimately themselves). The institutional context in which they operated structured the behaviour of producers in this way. Having effective discretionary control over the level of investments of their firm, but being unable to influence or shape the national budget by political means, producers were blinded to general consequences of their local choices. Whether democratic procedures generate outcomes that correspond to the long-term, general interest hinges on their institutional setting, then.

In other words, political procedures should be embedded in an institutional configuration of rules and institutions in such a way that their participants are able to overcome their narrow perspectives and partial interests. If we want the members of the political community to come together to identify their common interests in relation to the course of economic development, citizens need to identify with the long-term and overall concerns of their community. This should be achieved by projecting the general, long-term implications associated with different social priorities to citizens and asking them to express their preferences for alternative outcomes by ballot. Put differently, the political decision-making procedure should project to citizens the various trade-offs in social welfare associated with their votes, which is complicated however insofar as this cannot be reduced to a simple and singular scale:

> If, for instance, we maximize the national income expressed in monetary units, or aggregate production expressed in tons, we are dealing with measurable magnitudes. If, however, the problem consists in maximizing magnitudes called social well-being, then the objective thus defined cannot be measured; there is no criterion that would enable us to state that social well-being has increased for instance 'two-fold' or 'tenfold'.[72]

Various factors and variables go into the measurement of social welfare, which are themselves subject to political choice. The benefits associated with the use of more materials to expand the productive base of society should be weighed against their environmental costs; the use of more land should be weighed against the cost of soil degradation or the loss in biodiversity; the devotion of more resources to social consumption against the decrease in personal consumption; the amount of productive investment to improve future consumption against the decrease in current consumption, and so on and so forth. The central planning commission would have to formulate different scenarios that project the approximate consequences and trade-offs of different approaches. Consequently, citizens are compelled to take into account the social effects of their initial set of preferences and rearrange them to concord more closely to their preferred 'social state' (or scenario). The public assemblies will select a national budget by popular vote, which includes the rate of investment and the target rate of growth compared to the volume of consumption, the share of social consumption compared to household consumption, and further the disaggregation of resources designated for public expenditure among different

---

72   Lange 1971, p. 54.

categories of public use (medical care, national defence, R&D, education, transportation, housing, etc.). Since we are dealing with assumptions about future developments, outcomes will fall within a probabilistic range. Still, it allows for social priorities to broadly shape future directions.

Settling on an annual budget for the national community alone would not provide enough latitude to consciously steer the direction of economic, social, and industrial development, due to short-run constraints. Development of the social infrastructure would be a sequence stringing together an endless series of annuals plans without overriding sense of direction (or coherence, since the level of investment may wildly fluctuate by overshooting after a year of underfunding, and then overcompensating the other direction by tightening investments again). Thus, for a period of say, four to six years, citizens will need to choose a number of broad priorities for the development of the national economy during this period, as part of a moving fifteen year perspective target. For the five-year plans, central planners will have to model different trajectories and based on these projections, citizens will have to choose the amount of materials and energy that may flow into and exit from the circuit of production; how much land they wish to use for productive ends or to restore to nature; the increase of the housing supply given demographic trends; the amount of energy consumption and the rate of change in the use of energy sources over the course of the five-year cycle; the relative reduction of one factor cost compared to others (for instance, the reduction of labour costs relative to the costs of means of production); and the incremental growth of national income within given ecological and generational boundaries. These choices form the five-year guidelines for the annual macroeconomic general plan.

As an example, the political community will have to earmark a particular amount of funds for adjustments in the housing supply for the upcoming five years. This amount influences the types, quality, and quantity of living accommodations that can be maintained and constructed for the duration of this period. Suppose citizens choose to devote relatively fewer resources to the construction of new housing for the five-year central guidelines, under the assumption of constant demographic growth, because for some reason or another they prioritise other social aims given the definite availability of resources, it still leaves some scope in alternatives ways of achieving a relative reduction in the costs of housing construction per annum from year to year – by decreasing the construction of new units, decreasing unit costs while keeping construction rates constant, or increasing the share of refurbished housing compared to new construction, which each influence the growth of supply differently. In this way, the five-year general plans form the broader guidelines that set the parameters for the annual general plans. Within the scope of five year parameters, citizens will have to select one of the available yearly strategies of achieving the planned growth of the housing supply (or some other objective) within the limits of the available funds they have themselves previously established.

Planners would project the rough consequences of their choices back to citizens, indicating, for example, the medium to long-term consequence of potentially neglecting non-productive investments (e.g. a reduction in the housing supply) in order to increase current consumption; or a large expansion of productive investments to grow future consumption by large increments (the increased gestation time of investments, the fall in materials-output ratio, and ecological degradation). Within the range of the five-year plan guidelines, the legislative assemblies will have to choose an annual budget out of the number of options prepared by the planning commission. Each year citizens will be invited to participate in the procedure for selecting a central budget, and every five years also for setting the guidelines covering the five-year plan period. In citizen assemblies, annual and five-year plans will be put to a vote. Attendance could be compensated with an average workday's worth of consumption credits. For the five-year general plans citizens will have to identify broad priorities. Citizens may each year choose from a number of alternative yearly strategies for achieving the social priorities contained in the five-year plan. These would be a handful of alternative plans or budgets. Whichever current budget the citizen assemblies select also limits the number of feasible options for next year until the new five-year period allows them to reformulate their general preferences and social priorities. By selecting some target rate of growth over a five year period, it supplies the community with a framework for dealing with the uncertainty of future developments in relation to social preferences for different developmental scenarios – effectively, in order to reduce uncertainty to levels of manageable risk.

According to Kalecki, central planners in a socialist economy face a 'decisional curve', a relationship between the rate of investment and the rate of growth of output.[73] By means of this theoretical device he responded to the Marxist-Leninist orthodoxy which posited that the rate of investment should grow more quickly than the rate of growth of consumption to secure the accelerated growth of national income. Kalecki's argument was that the rate of growth in the socialist economy is constrained by the growth rate of the labour force and technical progress, so that if the share of investment grows beyond a certain point under the assumption of full employment, the rate of growth of output will decline. By expanding the rate of accumulation beyond what the

73   Nuti 1986, p. 339; Sawyer 1985, pp. 248–9.

growth rates of the labour supply and technical productivity can sustain, bottlenecks and investment tension will manifest with resources being stretched thin. The gestation period of investments would extend resulting in more idle capacity, while a higher capital intensity also corresponds to a higher rate of depreciation, with the overall result being a decline in the incremental capital-output ratio. Based on these considerations, the citizen assemblies will have to plot a point along some decisional curve which earmarks the amount of gross investment they prefer given these trade-offs. The national community will have to devote a certain minimum of resources to productive investments to expand the stock of means of production by an amount consistent with the social priority for the growth of future consumption (or national income) by a certain increment (as politically determined for the five-year period). One portion of the investment goods goes to replace the expired means of production, and any portion in excess of this amount accounts for the net investment and therefore the growth rate of the total product.

In terms of annual plans, it is first of all necessary to determine the total amount of productive resources available to society for the upcoming year. The quantities of labour-power and means of production are in principle given since the supply of labour-power is subject to fixed demographic developments in the short-run and the inducement to supply labour would not much change provided nominal incomes remain more or less stable, and the quantity of available production goods are likewise inherited from the previous period. The amount of natural resources that will be used up in production will need to be subject to more direct political influence (although the upper ceiling of extraction is also given in the short-run). By political fiat, the authorities may limit the rate of extraction and depletion of natural deposits to a socially acceptable rate, given the rate of replenishment or substitution availability for these various material inputs. This would also determine the primary input prices attached to factors of production, for instance by raising the prices of material inputs in response to the quantity of demand for them by productive facilities given the constraints on supply determined administratively.

In addition to choosing the ratio of accumulation to current consumption, citizens will have to divide the resources earmarked for consumption between social and individual consumption. They will subsequently also have to choose a particular composition of social consumption. That is to say that they will have to choose how much to allocate to various forms of public expenditure given the implications associated with these choices. How much should be used for infrastructure, how much for housing, how much for education, how much for medical care, and so on. Using more resources in education will mean there is less available for, say, infrastructure. If citizens feel that, education is being underfunded they may choose to divert resources away from, for example, infrastructure. If they feel collective consumption is underfunded more generally they may choose to either lower current household consumption, or decrease productive investment premised on the understanding that this will lower future consumption by an amount. The CPB will have to project the rough implications of these various choices to citizens to ensure that whichever development strategy they choose conforms more or less to their preferences for a future social state. Citizens, possibly united in political associations, may also advance their own budget proposal by popular initiative (requiring a minimum amount of signatories) that falls outside of the general plan guidelines, but a substantial and sudden change of direction would likely prove costly.

By confronting citizens participating in the citizen assemblies directly with the medium-term (and possibly long-term) implications of alternative choices, it ensures that any decision taken is not made in isolation of other concerns (unlike single-issue referenda). For example, citizens will not be able to raise current consumption on partial knowledge of the consequences for future consumption. They will be compelled to take into account all these trade-offs from the perspective of their role as citizens of the national community. The costs and benefits of alternative strategies are contained in balanced general plans, which makes explicit that, for example, the costs of increasing current consumption to the detriment of accumulation will lower future consumption. In this way, the choice for any particular level of investment will embody a more measured preference for a certain scenario compared to the sum of decisions made by individual producers ignorant of broader implications. Thus, the institutional rules allow for the higher-order preferences to take precedence over the more immediate, narrow, partial interests in setting macroeconomic targets.

The size and division of the budget has a direct and noticeable bearing on the daily lives of citizens, which should therefore stimulate a high attendance in the annual 'budgetary' citizen assemblies (despite the personal expenditure and sacrifice required for participation). Naturally, this can be further complemented by a national holiday on the subsequent day with public festivities in central squares and streets to reinforce a sense of common purpose and to underscore the importance of active citizenship. Ideally, observing the direct influence that citizens exercise in this context via the political process should also stimulate them to actively participate more generally in political life.

Since citizens can select from more than two budget proposals in the political procedure, we may need two or three rounds of voting, with the last round having the two most popular proposals up for ballot. If the votes can be tallied up and transmitted quickly, a single meeting of the general budgetary assembly may accommodate three rounds of voting. This is necessary to not cause voter fatigue by asking citizens to show up on multiple separate occasions in short succession. Because the plan proposals deal with high levels of abstraction and are already balanced to take into account the approximate effects for society as a whole (as opposed to policy proposals that suggest how the budget may be used concretely and separately) it is also not necessary to pass the votes back and forth between administrative levels. Only the local citizen assemblies will need to convene while the voting outcome of the process will be binding on the national legislature.

The need for central planning under socialism is substantial, but not all-encompassing. It allows for the more or less conscious steering of economic development according to the preferences of the community. This is moreover a deeply political process because it deals with mutually exclusive plan altern-atives. As such, the procedure rests on *social conflict*: conflicting understand-ings of what constitutes 'social well-being' and conflicting approaches about how best to improve it. Moreover, the centrally determined institutional rules structure the democratic process in such a way that a higher-order popular will may emerge that more closely conforms to the long-term interests of the com-munity as a whole. This can scarcely be expected under an anarchic system of spontaneous order, because it lacks the central political authority to provide an overriding direction to economic choices, being unable to make binding decisions at the central level to effect a general plan for economic development.

Addendum 1: A Note on Public Safety, Crime, and National Defence

In the standard interpretation of Marxism, the state and all its (coercive) func-tions wither away proportionally to the consolidation of communist relations in society. Thus, '[t]here will be no need for special ministers of State, for police and prisons, for laws and decrees'.[74] The administration of society will be borne by a community of free associations of equal individuals, which will collect-ively decide how to allocate collective goods, without the requiring the use of physical coercion to mediate social conflicts. Indeed, this harks back to a central notion in Marxist historiography, which postulates that the primary function of the state is to reproduce the class divisions in society on behalf of the ruling class. Marxist theory therefore proposes that the pre-agricultural

---

74   Bukharin and Preobrazhensky 1920.

form of social organisation was communistic in nature. Without class divisions cleaving society into exploiting and exploited classes, the bands of hunters, fishers, and foragers could socially reproduce themselves freely, without the interventions by some political authority or state power. The archaeological and anthropological record, while not uniformly supportive of the orthodox Marxist theory of primitive communism, affirms the largely communistic qualities exhibited by band societies. In spite of popular convention, these primitive societies were relatively peaceful and egalitarian. The ideas that 'nomadic foragers are warlike', that 'there was a high rate of war mortality in the Pleistocene', that 'the nomadic forager data support the 'chimpanzee model' of lethal raiding psychology', and that 'contact and state influence inevitably decrease aggression in nomadic forager societies' have been rejected as myths.[75] War, if it affected foraging bands, was usually the result of incursions by groups other than foraging bands (e.g. violent intrusions by pastoralists or agriculturalists).

Likewise, the stubborn legend – which apparently appeals strongly to the popular intuitions ('common sense') of people reared in highly stratified societies – of primitive human societies being marked by a strict social hierarchy with alpha specimens found at their apex, akin to ape society – or lobsters for that matter – lacks scientific support. Contrary to such wisdoms found in folk anthropology and pseudoscientific applications of evolutionary psychology; power structures in actuality evolve along the pattern of material development, and a degree of social stratification only emerges in the advent of the agricultural revolution, alongside the spread of neolithic gardens. The classless bands of foragers are transformed into tribes and chiefdoms marked by higher degrees of social hierarchy only when the social form of organisation shifts to settlements that sustain themselves by the cultivation of land or husbandry.[76]

The egalitarian social structure of hunter-gatherer bands was actively shaped by their members and reinforced by an egalitarian ethos. Aided by the enhanced cognition (*ergo*, strategical thinking) and abilities to communicate of modern humankind, those finding themselves on the lower ends of the social hierarchy, it has been hypothesised, were able to form strategic alliances to 'overthrow' the alpha male and establish stable egalitarian social relations via levelling mechanisms (social sanctions against those that violate the collectivist ethic) favouring the group interest.[77] The communistic nature of forager bands provides a window into the full range of human capabilities and social

---

75   Fry and Söderberg 2013, 2014.
76   Service 1971.
77   Gavrilets, Duenez-Guzman, and Vose 2008.

possibilities, since the condition of class divisions is stripped away. Studies into extant hunter-gatherer societies, for example, reveal that there are relatively high levels of gender equality compared to civilised societies, although not an absolute equality across gender divides.[78] Differentiation in physical ability (hunting skills) among men 'does not result in a dominance hierarchy', while it does influence status and mate selection favourably – which is illogical from a purely 'evolutionary' perspective since sustenance was shared, and therefore survival rates were unaffected by differential skill.[79] Although 'some mobile forager peoples have created nearly homicide-free social worlds',[80] homicidal violence is relatively common amongst some band societies.[81] Jones puts the homicide rate among the Hadzas of Tanzania at 40/100,000 between 1985 and 1995, and 33/100,000 between 1995 and 2000, which amounts to 14 and 15 homicides in periods of 15 years.[82] Fry and Söderberg noted 148 lethal events, with one or multiple victims, among 21 forager bands. In Hadza society five lethal events were observed, compared to the median of four, or 3.5 when the Tiwi group are excluded.[83]

Engels had argued that 'prehistoric savagery', or primitive communism, was marked by war and conflict, and it is tempting to assume, by extension, that this had a definite material cause in the form of aggressive competition related to food insecurity.[84] Thus, industrial communism, being able to manufacture the basic necessities of life in abundant quantities, would be clear of such horrific social consequences. It is this assumption that drives optimistic speculation about the scope to which socialism will be affected by criminal infractions of social norms. It makes sense to shed light on the actual causes that drive violence among foragers. The motives for homicide in 20 extant bands analysed by Fry and Söderberg, excluding the Tiwi, were interpersonal conflicts (63.3%), in which revenge killings accounted for ~10% of the total sum of lethal violence, and feuds over a woman for another 7.6%. There were zero cases of a man killed by his wife, but ~9% of all lethal events were instances of femicide. Inter-familial feuds (7.6%), within-group execution (3.8%), execution of outsiders (3.8%), and intergroup events (15.2%) accounted for another portion of the lethal events.

---

78   Fry and Souillac 2017; Marlowe 2010, p. 45.
79   Marlowe 2010, pp. 45–6; Marlowe 2004, 2003.
80   Fry and Souillac 2017, p. 12.
81   Fry and Söderberg 2013.
82   Jones 2016, p. 142.
83   Fry and Söderberg 2013.
84   MECW 26.

Among some foragers, customs permit recourse to semiformal justice, and the accused may be subjected to some form of ritualistic violence in cases where an extreme transgression of social conventions occurred. Alternatively, the aggrieved party may attempt to exact justice by means of retaliatory violence, with a potentially lethal outcome. Thus, if interpersonal conflict (motivated by jealousy, for example) – even in homogenous, closely-knit, communal, stable, and mostly war-free communities – drives antisocial and violent behaviour then we can scarcely expect that this sort of wrongdoing will disappear in an expansive, industrial, collectivist society. Leaving justice at the discretion of informal conduct – without official legal infrastructure with general rules of procedures for complaints, mediation, and penalties – would inevitably lead to arbitrary acts of violence.

These facts call into question optimistic expectations about the near complete disappearance of interpersonal and gendered conflict alongside the abolition of private property. To my mind, it also reinforces the notion that socialist society should actively nurture an egalitarian ethos to diminish the levels of ethnic and sexual discrimination beyond what a structural levelling of material resources alone could achieve. Furthermore, under a socialist regime, the public, through their political institutions and instruments of direct legislation, will be able to instate public agencies to administer justice on behalf of the general population in the interest of public safety and conflict mediation. This would presumably entail some of the familiar public bodies we know today as being part of the criminal and civil justice system, although they would also exist in closer relation to the citizenry which elected to call the bodies into being. This implies a higher degree of accountability to the public, mediated by the lawmaking of political institutions and instruments for direct legislation. There would be some sort of court system to interpret criminal and civil codes and apply rulings, a type of law enforcement agency to deal with antisocial behaviour in communities, and a national-level security force with special divisions to deal with specific forms of criminal and deviant behaviour (homicides, sexual violence, etc.). It would further encompass a system of correctional facilities, custodial clinics, counselling, and restorative justice practices. The justice system would be primarily focussed on rehabilitation wherever possible and reparation whenever called for. We can rightly speculate that equitable social conditions and collectivist culture in socialist society will significantly reduce the need for physical coercion in the administering of justice, but we should not harbour illusions that humankind will rise above this need entirely, at least insofar as our horizons permit us to see. Hence, the use of legitimate force should be defined by codes of conduct within a constitutional-republican infrastructure.

Finally, a few words on national defence. Traditionally, socialists followed the republican tradition in the belief that an armed populace is the best insurance against tyranny. This general training and arming of the population, the militia model of citizen-soldiers, is contrasted to the model of the professional standing army, which was more closely aligned to the political tradition of liberalism.[85] To republicans, the risk posed by a professional army under the command of executive power was unconscionable. The armed forces could so impose a will other than that expressed by a sovereign people. The military *coup d'état* in Chile in 1973 is an infamous case in point. The existence of a standing army with separate loyalties from the socialist government played out disastrously. The putsch decapitated the civilian government and left the population without means to defend themselves. Contemporary socialists therefore tend to uphold the republican principle of the popular militia; disarming professional state functionaries and arming the population – extending the radical concept of 'rule by amateurs' to military defence.

However, high levels of combat effectiveness can be attained only, especially in modern warfare, by high levels of professionalisation in the areas of military training, equipment, logistics, and strategy. While a citizen militia may serve as an adequate warranty for securing common liberty domestically, the threat of external aggression, encirclement, or occupation by a superior foreign military power makes professional specialisation of the armed forces a necessity for survival of a free community. The republican-style militia, initially upheld by the United States, suffered from lack of combat capabilities, observed as early as the US-British War of 1812:

> Many Americans also distrusted standing military forces, believing that a powerful army and navy might pose a threat to their own liberty; and they also possessed an unreasonable faith in the capabilities of the citizen militia. President Madison was typical of many in his discomfort with a professional military and of his embrace of the militia. Toward the end of the war, however, he realized his mistake first-hand when he witnessed the defeat of a force comprised largely of militia at the hands of British regular soldiers outside of Washington. 'I could never have believed that so great a difference existed between regular troops and a militia force, if I had not witnessed the scenes of this day', he remarked.[86]

---

85   A. Smith 1776, Book V; Chapter I.
86   Benn 2003, p. 14.

The Bolsheviks similarly relied on part-time irregular worker-soldiers in the form of 'Red Guards' on the principle that the entire population should be armed, drawing on the concept of the popular militia.[87] By 1918, it had already become clear that the militia model could not be sustained as the need for regimentation and professionalisation arose when faced with serious military opposition by competently organised counter-revolutionary detachments. In response, the Bolsheviks decreed the formation of a regular military force, the Red Army, and recruited former Czarists into its ranks as specialists and officers greatly bolstering the military effectiveness of the revolutionary forces.

Socialists would do well to abandon their belief in the traditional militia model to instead pursue a hybrid form to ensure civilian control over military defence without sacrificing combat effectiveness. This would perhaps include universal basic training and arming of the population, semi-mandatory military service, the formation of territorial defence units composed mostly of reservists and part-time volunteers, complemented by more combat capable full-time regular forces. Territorial forces would be more or less fixed to their geographical location to assist in territorial defence and logistics and serve as recruitment and reserve pool to increase the ranks of regular forces when this need arises, while the professional regular forces would be more widely deployable along shifting battle lines and active conflict zones. This enables general mobilisation as part of a popular military doctrine of total defence, in which all civilian and military resources can be mobilised to serve in diverse capacities (in various combat roles, in support roles, as manufacturers of materiel, propagandists, activists, smugglers, spotters, saboteurs) to frustrate the advance of foreign troops in the event of a full-scale invasion. Naturally, the supreme planning commission will have to marshal all industrial resources and readjust manufacturing to the requirements of defence efforts. The general staff would also need to be subordinated to civilian control, in the form of a civilian security council designated as such by the national legislature and answering directly to it. Further, some sort of military-civilian code stipulating the ways in which civilian life and popular sovereignty should be protected against military infringements of fundamental rights will need to guide military action during the outbreak of an active, armed conflict. To solidify civilian control, political officers should be attached to combat forces, serving adjacent to field officers. They would have the authority to countermand the orders of field officers if they are judged to violate political-civilian directives and fundamental civilian rights or constitutional law. Combining citizen militias with standing armed

---

87   Lenin 1917b.

forces under political command would hopefully achieve a balance between civilian supremacy over military affairs (to ward off military putsches) and combat effectiveness (to deter imperialist aggression).

Addendum 2: A Note on Organised Political Activity under Socialism

Direct legislation will evidently reduce the importance of political parties, but not dispense with their necessity outright. Delegates are primarily responsible to their immediate constituency, organised in the popular assemblies. According to Castoriadis, the existence of political parties in socialist society would be a leftover custom inherited from parliamentary democracy. As such, he believed they would gradually phase out of existence by virtue of the disappearance of social antagonisms over the existence of conflicting particular interests. If, he argued, the citizen assemblies and workers' councils:

> fulfill their function, they will provide the principal and vital setting not only for political *confrontations* but also for the *formation* of political opinions. Political groups, on the other hand, are exclusive environments for the schooling of their members, as well as being exclusive poles for their loyalty. The parallel existence of both councils and political groups will imply that a part of real political life will be taking place outside the councils. People will then tend to act in the councils according to decisions already made elsewhere. Should this tendency predominate, it would bring about the rapid atrophy and finally the disappearance of the councils. Conversely, real socialist development would be characterized by the progressive atrophy of established political groups.[88]

Black makes a similar argument, pointing to a small selection of historical cases of political caucuses manipulating the proceedings of public meetings by rehearsing them in advance. Agreeing to mobilise in large numbers, deciding who will say what and when to overwhelm the popular assembly with superior numbers.[89] All such manoeuvring takes place outside the formal structures for public deliberation, during the course of *private* meetings, depriving the members of the community who have not participated in these caucuses of

---

88   Castoriadis 1988, p. 146.
89   Black 2011.

the ability to influence them. The formal democratic procedure in the popular assembly could be dispensed with since the outcome is already decided by pre-established voting blocks. Democratic proceedings would be reduced to the plaything of increasingly bitter factional rivalries, since victories are not obtained by the powers of persuasion in open dialogue but by those political caucuses that operate at the highest level of machine politics. It closes off hostile political factions to compromise.

At a higher level of abstraction, radical thought held by the Jacobin republicans for example, expressed the belief that the relationship of the citizen and nation should be unmediated and immediate to preserve the universal aspirations and unified sovereignty of the people.[90] A theme of essential unity centred on the nation, overriding sectional interests of clergy or classes, in other words – a theme, furthermore, echoed in the Bolshevik belief of an essentially unified working class bearing uniform interests that could not be expressed by rival factions. The typical Marxist analysis would propose that the Jacobin idea was a 'bourgeois illusion' masking fundamental class divisions. However, even in socialism endemic social conflict in relation to rival claims to resources for distinct individual and collective pursuits should be taken into account. Insofar as intermediate institutions act as sites for the clarification and elaboration of different conceptions of their common goods, and these differences can be structured hierarchically, subordinated to the common good for society, the role of 'corporate' bodies in the articulation of public opinion should be accepted.

Thus, it is my contention that political organisations, particularly interest and pressure groups, will have important roles to play in socialist society. This argument has been influenced mostly by my own personal experience, having been involved in a factional spat within the Socialist Party, ending in my expulsion along with others in 2021 over the accusation that we formed a 'party within a party'. The party leadership was deeply submerged in the belief that party unity should enjoy primacy as precondition for effective political action. This belief, carried over from its past as Marxist-Leninist organisation, bred, in my view, a rigid monoculture. Animated by their self-perception as enforcers of party unity, feeding an intolerance to any and all possible deviations from the party line, the leadership made routine use of extra-official manoeuvring, avoiding formal decision-making procedures and official channels at their convenience – for example by using unofficial, private preparatory meetings of confidants to secure voting outcomes, to isolate or denounce opponents, sub-

---

90   Higonnet 1998.

jecting them to malicious whispering campaigns or shouting them down or vilifying them publicly during party meetings, to push their own candidates in party elections (by expelling direct opponents if all else failed). The party was formed on 'grassroots' principles, which helped the leadership to consolidate their grip over the organisation because local chapters could not be bypassed to co-ordinate opposition horizontally. At least for some decades, local chapters were not permitted to communicate directly out of fear that this would subvert party centralism and therefore corrode the unity over which the party leadership stewarded. The supreme decision-making body, the party council, was composed of chairpersons acting as delegates of local chapters and the party's national board. To the extent that these chairpersons were loyal to the leadership – and they usually had to be, since the nomination process was set up in this way – rank-and-file members were effectively rendered unable to voice dissenting viewpoints in the highest decision-making organ of the party, since horizontal communication was blocked.

When a minority of left-wing dissidents, divided across different chapters, began to co-ordinate directly to promote an alternative agenda, a mass expulsion followed over trumped up accusations of factionalism and coup plotting for operating outside the official channels, themselves tightly controlled by the inner circle of the party, the dominant faction in effect. This miniature version of the sectarian schisms that have historically affected the socialist movement is hardly worth the trouble lamenting – it certainly pales in comparison to major historical episodes of violent and deadly score settling between competing factions of socialists. But this experience has impressed on me the importance of allowing minority viewpoints, whether in organised form or not, to circulate freely outside the officially sanctioned political structures in order to afford minorities a fair opportunity of winning a majority over to their perspective, on their own terms instead of being at the mercy of the good-will of the leading, majority faction. The 'official' channels of the republic – the legislative assemblies – should not be the only public space open to deliberation, since these can fall into self-satisfied conformism and thus be drained of the vibrancy required for political contestation, or perhaps be seized by zealous fanaticism, or become controlled by extra-official instruments, effectively monopolising the circuits for political decision-making in the hands of a single faction.

Under a socialist constitution, the existence of endemic levels of social conflict should be presupposed. These will have to be channelled in such a way that they are mediated by a legitimate public body, to curb their escalation. It implies, in either case, that people will naturally rally around and organise on the basis of their shared views on polarising subjects. It is therefore unlikely that political activism will wither away completely under socialism, which requires an outlet that public assemblies alone cannot supply. Since the forums for public dialogue in the socialist republic are primarily dispersed among geographically segmented districts, it would be difficult for advocates of minority viewpoints to organise themselves politically within the assemblies in order to advance their beliefs upward within the pyramid structure. Delegates will mainly, if not exclusively, voice the broad consensus or majority viewpoint of their constituency, so a minority may find themselves unable to circulate their views beyond local political bodies. Hence, secondary circuits are required through which they can transmit their viewpoints, co-ordinate their efforts, and petition for a change in policy.

Banning political parties from being involved in public meetings is hardly an option. In Cuba, the local popular committees and political gatherings allow citizen to stand candidate for public office, after being vetted and approved. This is not done on the basis of a political platform or party affiliation, but on the basis of a short biographical note and the personal characteristics they exemplify. Political parties are excluded from participating in these local elections. To my mind, this bears resemblance to the party elections of the Socialist Party of the Netherlands. The excessive preoccupation with maintaining party unity means that factionalism is strictly forbidden, to the extreme extent that local chapters for some decades were not permitted to communicate directly, for fear of them forming into a factional opposition block.[91] Likewise, candidates were pre-selected during a nomination process under the control of a committee staffed with loyalists. Some applicants were approved and included in the recommended list of candidates, and some candidates were disapproved for various reasons (inexperience, inactivity, but also over political reasons). These members could still stand in elections but were barred from campaigning or soliciting support among local chapters since this would amount to the transgression of factional activity and violating the party's democracy and unity (that is, campaigning on the basis of views contrary to majority opinion). The actual elections were virtually 'apolitical' and took place during general meetings, which only permitted the candidates to introduce themselves by providing a brief autobiographical synopsis and answer a few short questions. Without ability to interrogate the candidates or being able to come to understand their views via pamphlets or some other means of communication, it was impossible to judge them on their merits or politics – unless you happened to know them personally. Consequently, for all the window-dressing of fair elec-

---

91   See for example Smale 1998, pp. 30, 47.

tions, the odds were stacked against the candidates that did not bear the official approval of the nomination committee and the voting in of the sanctioned candidates were mechanically rubber-stamped by general meetings.[92]

In effect, 'depoliticising' elections – by barring political parties, caucuses, or factions from participating openly – reinforces whatever the current balance of forces happens to be, thus benefiting, what is in fact, the only 'faction' permitted to operate openly and without interference, the majority or dominant faction. Far from securing a neutral or level playing field, it biases political outcomes in favour of the currently prevailing political views, since it deprives the subordinate group – the minority, usually – of their ability to contest the dominant perspective on equal footing. Furthermore, insofar as the intolerance bound up with excessive centralism and unity of this type is justified by the alleged presence of subversive elements scheming and plotting away, it stifles internal deliberations and pushes debate outside of official channels. This in turn demands that rival factions collude outside the formal institutional context in an attempt to struggle for supremacy, which consequently justifies and reinforces conspiratorial beliefs.

Thus, political life should be decidedly political.

Political parties may also be crucial vehicles for monitoring the political activity of deputies, by alerting the public to important causes, influencing the political agenda, fielding candidates, arousing controversy, and in general politicising and mobilising their supporters. On the one end, this should prevent the socialist republic from declining into a condition of stale conformity; yet, it should not be grounds for polarisation. Two factors should moderate political conflict. Political parties cannot hold political office by means of their members, since representatives are bound by the flexible mandate of their constituency and are expected to act in accordance with preferences of the community, rather than exhibit fealty to the political programme of their faction. This will likely increase the role of single-issue pressure groups, since citizens are free to pick and choose their issues rather than cast a vote for a party programme wholesale. Second, while lower chambers are in principle more open to the influence of political contestation and partisanship, which may inhibit the deliberative qualities of the legislatures, this tendency is checked

---

92 The only exception, in my memory, occurred in the party's youth wing in 2019, where the direct opponent to the officially approved candidate for chairperson was narrowly elected, invoking the ire of the party leadership. The factional row escalated and set the youth wing on a course that saw them suspended and eventually collectively expelled from the party – along with opposing candidates running in party elections under the platform of 'Marxist Forum' and individual dissidents – over forming a party within a party in 2021.

by the upper chambers. In this capacity, the upper house is critical in acting as a brake on partisan squabbles by forcing delegates to reach by deliberative means an agreeable compromise that will likely be approved by the members of the upper chamber. Since these are elected by lot, they are not beholden to political affiliations and are unlikely to form into stable voting blocks. Each individual proposal send by the lower chambers to the higher chamber of the legislature will need to earn their approval and the lower house will therefore have to arrive at some consensus that increases the likelihood of being passed in the upper house – the elected deputies are condemned to continually engage in open deliberation to overcome their narrow, factional loyalties.

Production in the Socialist Republic

1   Public Property and Public Domination

Socialism, in the broadest sense of the word, is based on some form of social ownership of productive resources. Here we proceed briefly with a discussion of the appropriate property relations for a republican socialism. For our present inquiry it is necessary to demonstrate that social ownership can be reconciled with the core values of the republican tradition as we have summarised them previously. If, as the detractors of socialism claim, the concentration of productive assets into state hands necessarily implies over-centralisation and a concomitant loss of liberty, then the marrying of republicanism and socialism would prove a futile endeavour. To show otherwise, it will have to be demonstrated that common ownership is able to accommodate active participation by the working population in collective decision-making while preserving independence from arbitrary power at an individual and collective level, which is to be achieved by balancing power among various public institutions. We will briefly go over property relations, types of property that should and should not be subject to public control, as well as discuss the issue of 'public domination'. In short, when we discuss 'property relations' we mean the conventions – whether established by legislation, precedent, or custom – that govern the actual use of objects, symbols, and information by defining: (i) who has the right to exercise or delegate *effective control* over them; (ii) who has the right to residual income generated by their use; and (iii) who has the right of alienation or disposal of them.[1] Social ownership in particular can assume a variety of forms, ranging from state to communal forms of ownership.

We should first of all distinguish between personal possessions and property in which the public has a more direct stake. To Marx and Engels, communism would not deny anyone 'to appropriate the products of society; all that it does is to deprive [them] of the power to subjugate the labour of others by means of such appropriation'.[2] This means that objects of personal use are treated as individual possessions whose consumption is left to the personal discretion of the end user, while productive resources cannot be seized as private, accumu-

---

1   Kornai 2007, pp. 64–6.
2   MECW 6: 500.

lated and subsequently leveraged to subject others to one's private will. This is indeed also the core argument of the republican case for socialism.[3] This means that in communism, as Marx put it, 'no one can give anything except his labour', and 'nothing can pass to the ownership of individuals except individual means of consumption'.[4] This distinction between objects of personal consumption and productive resources is crucial insofar as individual possessions are counted as private matter (aside from the costs incurred by society in their production) and should therefore in principle not be subject to public control, lest we violate important personal freedoms. Objects that should be nationalised and brought under the political control of the community are those productive resources that society depends on for their reproduction, such as natural resources (land, raw materials), production, and certain intangible assets. Since the reproduction of wealth is a highly interdependent, collective activity, the resources necessary for the reproduction and expansion of social wealth should be collectively owned – as is the basic proviso of socialism.

As we have established in the previous chapter, some decisions should be made by the centre and made binding on all regional and local bodies. (We will circle back to this question in the next chapter as well.) For society to exercise effective control over productive resources it is necessary that they are publicly owned at the level of society, rather than by their employees or local community. Employee ownership, for example, will reproduce the atomistically driven commercial imperatives we associate with the centrifugal forces of capitalism. According to Schweickart, the means of production should therefore be owned by the state and to be 'leased' to co-operative enterprises instead of being owned by their employees.[5] In this way, the narrow self-interests that arise from free competition can be managed to different degrees, depending on the terms of lease. Thus, the political community delegates control to co-operatives, whose members may or may not have some claim on the residual income flowing from their use of assets as part of the terms of usage, but not the right to dispose of the assets entrusted to them. Schweickart further points out that income cannot be maximised by simply expanding the firm, being that income is divided amongst the workers and an expansion of business activity usually involves an expansion of the workforce. For this reason, the expansionary and competitive drive in market socialism is reduced compared to liberal capitalism.[6] Hence, social ownership does not by definition

---

3 Muldoon 2019, p. 3.
4 MECW 24: 86.
5 Schweickart 2002, p. 50.
6 Schweickart 1987, pp. 311–12.

imply complete subordination to central authorities, and may even be compatible with a degree of market relations. Whatever the specific arrangement of social ownership and the exact terms of use (which will be discussed later), it is my contention that all productive resources will need to be owned by the political community.

Social ownership does not mean that all members of society should be consulted on the exact use of productive resources at all times, which is neither possible nor desirable. The community, through its public institutions, would stipulate the conditions for the usage of resources via directives, co-management, lease terms, or others forms of regulation. This should prevent the accumulation of assets into private hands and therefore also the enrichment of private individuals at the expense of general welfare. In this respect, 'social ownership' can thus accommodate a variety of forms, from market socialisms to centrally planned economies to freely associated producers administering commonly owned resources. Incidentally, much has been written on the 'tragedy of the commons', and few words are required here other than to say that there is no strong empirical basis for suggesting that commonly owned resources are at a greater risk of being mismanagement compared to other forms of ownership. This is due to 'commons' often, though by no means always, being managed co-operatively by their stakeholders, who share an interest in careful stewardship.[7] In similar vein, the political community should impose terms on users of collectively owned resources that concord with the general interest to ensure that socially and ecologically destructive outcomes are prevented while furnishing a socially desired composition of output. This should create a system of controls that structures the pattern of utilisation of resources in such a way that social priorities can be pursued.

Social ownership should effectively mean that the principle of self-government is extended to the relations governing the use of productive resources. O'Shea points out that public ownership would transfer equal amounts of decision-making power into the hands of citizens, in contrast to co-determination schemes in which power sharing is patterned asymmetrically, being divided equally among the large majority of workers on the one end and the minority of corporate directors on the other.[8] Socialist ownership, in this respect, are the institutional means by which radical republican ends are served, according to his view. The general population, as stakeholders, would possess the democratic means to shape investment decisions, thus being form-

7   Ostrom 1990; Ostrom 2010.
8   O'Shea 2019, p. 12.

alised according to public criteria.[9] All citizens of the community would be enfranchised to exercise control over the collective pool of resources and the division of the social dividends generated by their use. Public ownership is therefore a potentially effective instrument to secure the common good in the area of economic relations. If the economic sphere takes shape as the mirror image of the constitutional-republican political order, it stands to reason that they will strengthen each other. Hence, decentralised units of production should be communities of producers governing their own affairs while the central authority should be the national governing body guided by the social priorities of the overall community laying down the groundwork on which producers operate.

However, transferring the total stock of assets into public hands also carried with it the innate risk of private domination being replaced by public domination, by leaving individuals vulnerable to the potentially arbitrary will of political authorities (who either represent the will of the majority, or less favourably, a minority of public officials). State ownership does not in itself reduce the dependency of workers. In fact, it could exacerbate it when, under conditions of a state monopoly, the ability of 'exit' is compromised, or in the case of an excessive emphasis on unity, the ability of 'voice' is compromised. Indeed, Engels had argued that state ownership in itself did not alter the fundamental nature of wage-labour, if it only substituted the capitalist for the state.[10] Typically, socialists have advocated democratic control over the means of production by producers instead, as will be discussed at some length in the subsequent section. This should ensure a degree of independence from arbitrary government control, but only under conditions of political freedom. The subordination of workers' councils to unaccountable political authorities in socialist countries like Yugoslavia or Poland, for example, undermined this political function of workers' councils.[11] If the workers tasked with the management of publicly owned resources are subject to externally imposed terms that they have no role in shaping or no ability to contest, then public ownership will obviously not enhance freedom.

While a constitutional-republican regime would limit arbitrary power by allowing citizens to formulate the terms of use for public resources, O'Shea correctly notes that this answer does not sufficiently address the dependency of citizens on the public sector for access to means of life. To O'Shea, therefore, citizens should be provided with a basic minimum, through unconditional basic

9   O'Shea 2019, p. 13.

10   MECW 24: 319.

11   Kornai 2007, pp. 464–5; Osiatyński 1988, p. 33; Sawyer 1985, p. 236.

income or unconditional access to basic services such as housing, education, and healthcare.[12] This would guarantee a level of security for citizens that exists independently of the will of political authorities, he argues. While the sentiment is agreeable, we ought, in my view, to substitute universal basic income for a job guarantee policy. While the former would in some cases enhance independence as some individuals may be helped to apply themselves creatively or socially, it may also exert an adverse effect on participation in public life in others. Thus, if universal basic income stimulates inactivity in those with limited access to formal employment opportunities, it could create a socially alienated, idle underclass that becomes unaccustomed to both collective and individual self-control over their lives. The all-round improvement of human faculties depends on becoming an active subject in a multiplicity of social roles necessary for individual development. By creating social distance between individuals and activity under association by affording individuals the means to withdraw from social life and its trials, their development would be inhibited. Social, collaborative activity, such taking active part in collective labour, harbours the potential to harness virtue and character such as social and personal responsibility. Socialist society should emphasise *social obligation*, the basic condition for the reproduction of community, in addition to individual and social *rights*. A job guarantee policy better suits a republican agenda, therefore.

Due attention should be paid to the ways in which public ownership could become a source of individual dependency, and therefore also to the design of institutions to secure their independence from arbitrary power. This should include foundational laws that stipulate that citizens should be afforded unconditional access to the basic means of their subsistence and public services; the right to independent political or religious affiliation; the right to protest, to assembly, and to associate freely for the purpose of collective action. In other words, the basic conditions for the reproduction of individual life, and the capacity for effective political participation, should not rely solely on the charity or favour of the majority of the political community, that might withdraw or withhold these resources. In addition, citizens should have the decision-making instruments to shape public policy concerning the terms of use of productive assets, as well as a degree of control over these assets in their capacity as members of co-operative associations.

---

12   O'Shea 2019, pp. 16–17.

2   Three Public Sectors

While all productive resources should be publicly owned, it does not follow
that they should be treated as undifferentiated holdings of the state, placed
under the direct auspices of the central government. The size and purpose of
different means of production factor into the arrangement under which they
should be managed. For example, particular assets of local importance may be
left to municipal direction (the local water supply, perhaps), while highly concentrated monopolies would demand a higher level of involvement by central
authorities. Since the type of direction required for different units of production depends chiefly on the size of the assets in their custody, the institutional
rules that structure their governance will need to differ according to this metric
so as to obviate the need for 'ad hoc' intervention by the national government.
To effect this, the socialist regime should divide industrial facilities into one
of three main categories, whose labels bear a loose connection to their main
industrial characteristics: (i) the collective sector; (ii) the administrative sector;
(iii) the co-operative sector. The productive resources in all sectors will be the
collective property of society, which holds, by hand of the political authorities,
final sway over their use, returns on their use (net product), and their disposal.
The terms of their use – in other words, the conditions that determine how
the 'use rights' over productive facilities are allocated – will be qualified on a
different basis in each sector, however. Custodianship over productive establishments will be awarded to associations of producers on the condition that
they will exploit the means of production responsibly and productively in the
public interest. If producers make insufficiently responsible use of resources
from the perspective of society, custodianship may be withdrawn and inputs
redirected elsewhere where their use might prove more productive. Furthermore, the production units do not have the right to alienate the publicly owned
assets entrusted to them by society – they have no right to sell them off, or
appropriate, discard or gift them. Lastly, the returns on the use of resources –
i.e. the additions to wealth generated by their use – are appropriated by society, which then, by political methods, decides how to redistribute the total
product of society between different forms of accumulation (the volume and
flow of investment funds) and consumption (the size of the wage fund and
the distribution of income). Public authorities remain the ultimate arbiter over
resources.

    The 'collective sector' would be composed of production units that manage
natural monopolies and public utilities. It is necessary to bring public utilities
under closer management of political authorities due to the principal-agent
relations that are particular to such industrial facilities, as well as the long

investment horizons associated with the high capital intensity of this type of productive establishment. Should the management of public utilities be exclusively left to the democratic bodies of workers – the workers' councils – involved in their reproduction certain difficulties would arise. The production unit responsible for the management of monopolistic resources would enjoy a position of relative power owed to asymmetrical knowledge. Political authorities, which should represent the interests of the general public as consumers of the various public utilities, will rely on the information supplied by the workers' councils to judge whether efficient use of resources is being made. Workers' councils may however conceal information about the optimal level of input requirements in order to increase their partial well-being, by feather-bedding or over-capitalisation for example – which would increase operational costs by consuming more of society's resources without also contributing more to society's well-being. The additional costs are shouldered unto the public without their informed consent. The workers' councils of public utilities would only be accountable to the workforce that elects them and may therefore come to represent their interests at the expense of the wider, social interest. In other words, these workers' councils would exhibit strategic rent-seeking behaviour.

It would be impossible to compare the productivity of a monopolistic production unit to some average norm in order to make inferences about the use and misuse of public resources by workers' councils. It follows that workers' councils cannot be allowed to act as the sovereign body over resources that are natural monopolies. They have both motive and means to work inefficiently, at the expense of the general public. The primary custodians of public utilities should have the interests of the wider public in mind and should therefore be appointed by and accountable to political authorities. One can imagine that the political authorities will stipulate that two-thirds of the governing boards of production units managing public utilities are to be reserved for public officials or consumer representatives appointed by the political community or consumer societies. Alternatively, socialist society can opt for a two-tier board system, in which the governing board (the workers' council) is monitored by a supervisory board composed of public officials with some sort of right to veto decisions that are judged to violate the general interest. These 'external' representatives would be primarily accountable to the general public and consumers, and therefore have their interests in mind, in contrast to the workers' council which is chiefly accountable to the workforce of the production unit and therefore more pivoted toward their sectional interests.

The collective sector would be composed of various (quasi-)monopolistic public services that are expected to recover the costs of their own operations, but that nevertheless operate under relatively softer budget constraints (compared to the co-operative sector, as will be discussed later). The public interest in maintaining critical infrastructure is such that the costs of loss-making operations may need to be supplemented with public funds, due to positive externalities not reflected in individual costs and returns. This is also due to the large size of the initial investment requirements and their long recoupment period, which discourages investors in a market economy from supplying the necessary funds out of private means. Under socialism, similarly, the investment horizon of workers' councils will scarcely extend beyond a decade, let alone the multiple decades necessary to recover the initial investment outlays of large projects. Thus, within the collective sector, the initial investments in particular are made directly by public means, while levies and charges will be used to recover the production costs as much as reasonably possible, but may be topped off by additional public funds.

In contrast, the administrative sector includes all economic units that do not produce discernible output or whose output is on the lower end of the excludability scale (for example, administrative overhead incurred by policy-making and implementation) or basic social services or public infrastructure that are of direct interest to the public (e.g. medical care, waste management), and are therefore included in 'collective consumption' and funded immediately by public means. This may also include access to community health and fitness centres and recreational facilities such as swimming pools and parks, for example. These services would be free at the point of use, being funded out of general means. Consequently, such facilities are not expected to cover their own costs by levying fares or charges for their services. Each unit may nonetheless be expected to minimise costs relative to their output. To measure output, alternative indices (in lieu of a rate of return) will have to be formulated to measure and evaluate performance (e.g. availability of services, quality of services according to consumer complaints or surveys, the reduction of costs for specific service output over multiple years). These measurements may be inferior to a more straightforward calculation of costs and returns, but the social priority accorded to freely supplying social services of this nature to the members of the community may be sufficiently high to justify this for a limited number of primary services. This statement should be qualified, however. Under certain circumstances, goods and services supplied by the administrative sector will also need be made accessible on the condition of a nominal fee. When insufficient public funds have been made available by the political community relative to the demand for basic services at zero costs the resultant overconsumption could be addressed in one of two ways. These scarce services can either be rationed according to wait lists, or a nominal fee is levied to depress demand for these services until the wait lists disappear or at least have been reduced to acceptable levels. Production units in the administrative sector, while not expected to recoup their operational costs, might still have to charge nominal fees to manage demand levels.

Management in the administrative sector would primarily be the responsibility of public officials and consumer representatives rather than the workers' councils, to guard against uncontrolled growth of administrative overhead or other such costs. The governing board of production units that operate in the administrative sector would perhaps be composed of public officials and consumer representatives, while the supervisory board would be an elected workers' council. In either case, some co-determination scheme between workers and public officials would need to be put in place that balances the public interest with the interests of the workers.

Finally, the co-operative sector. This sector encompasses production units that generate output for personal consumption by households. Since it concerns private forms of consumption that vary according to unique, individual preferences in which the public has no direct stake, the production units operating in this sector should be expected to cover their costs of production. This would mean that the social benefit obtained by household consumption should be equal to, or greater than, the social costs of using certain categories of labour, land, and fixed assets. This is measured by the willingness of individual consumers to reimburse these social costs out of their consumption allowance. Where it concerns the co-operative sector, there should be multiple suppliers and producers offering perfect or close substitutes as part of their assortment of output from which households can make a selection of items to consume. The operation of multiple producers in the same branch of industry should enable planning authorities to compare the relative efficiency of different co-operatives to an industry norm of average productivity. If it turns out that some co-operative associations make unproductive use of resources on the basis of such evaluations, inputs and resources can be reallocated to some other capacity where they might better serve collective welfare.

3   Self-Government in Industry – Workers' Councils

Hobson, an advocate of 'guild socialism', noted that in liberal democracy 'we find that the majority of voters, or citizens, possess political power without any corresponding economic power'.[13] A socialist republicanism would rec-

---

13   Hobson 1914, p. 50.

tify this systemic incongruence by extending the principle of self-government to the economic sphere. Thus, for now we will focus on the internal arrangements of 'production co-operatives' (any individual association of producers, or work collective, that people can join as members for the common purpose of contributing to social production as a public service) rather than the process of social co-ordination and harmonisation of the activities of different units of production. 'Workplace democracy'[14] is accepted by all socialist models we have reviewed so far. Theoretical differences are minimal, and furthermore, the widespread availability of economically viable examples of worker, credit, and housing co-operatives attest empirically to their practicability in a wide range of contexts.[15] Nevertheless, what follows is a basic exposition of the idea of workplace democracy, given that it is an important, although not distinctive, part of different post-capitalist models. It allows us to both highlight republican concerns that arise when we set out designing a socialist society and to tweak the proposals to integrate important republican details. The basic rationale underpinning our republican approach toward this matter is that the workplace should act as the microcosm of the overall community; its concrete expression within the sphere of production, where sensitivity to the common good, self-government, dialogue, and active participation rule. The spirit of self-government should ideally be mutually reinforced between economic and political life. This is important since:

> People who spend their lives performing partial tasks, determined for them by others who plan the activity as a whole, develop partial consciousness. People who spend all their time being told what to do, rather than learning how to decide what to do for themselves, develop subaltern consciousness. People with partial, subaltern consciousness cannot take an overall view and share the responsibility of running things.[16]

Thus, active participation in economic decision-making, starting from the lowest economic units, helps socialise workers into a social consciousness that

---

14   Or other more or less interchangeable terms conveying the same essential arrangement, such as 'industrial democracy', 'associated labour', 'workers' self-management', 'workers' management' or 'workers' control' (although not in the sense of Russian 'контроль', which is more akin to supervision). Similarly, 'workers' co-operative', 'producers' co-operative', 'production co-operative', 'labour-managed firm', 'self-managed enterprise', or 'association of producers' refer to more or less similar arrangements of units of production managed collectively and democratically by the workers.

15   Tchami 2007; Pérotin 2014, pp. 34–47; Dow 2003.

16   Devine 2011, p. 134.

disposes them toward assuming responsibility for the active shaping of their collective life, or self-mastery in a word. This should reinforce social attitudes of active citizenship and encourage participation in the multifaceted dimensions of public life. We will proceed with our discussion of how 'workplace republicanism' could be institutionalised and practised.

In Marxist theory, productive activity in communism is based on what we may call 'freely associated labour', or in the precise words of Marx, 'production by freely associated men'.[17] Instead of selling one's labour-power to an employer, the worker joins an association of producers as a member, equal in duties and rights to all other members. Socialist economic thinkers, ranging from Devine to Cole,[18] from Kalecki to Lange,[19] from Hahnel to Schweickart,[20] and so on and so forth, are all in agreement that democratic control by producers over their own affairs should be a fundamental pillar of socialism. There is little room for doubt that such arrangements are feasible. Worker participation in many contexts improves job security, the flow and quality of information, and centres workers' interests in decision-making contributing to improved productivity, engagement, and performance.[21] Numerous studies have indicated a positive relationship between productivity and participation, particularly when it involves sharing the financial benefits of improved productivity.[22] Worker participation increases net productivity somewhat, but not as much as the combination of worker participation and capital assets controlled by workers individually.[23] Furthermore, profit sharing without worker participation does not yield similar improvements in productivity.[24] Low wage differentials within the wider context of worker participation also contribute to productivity compared to higher income disparities.[25] There is some evidence that worker participation in the public sector improves job satisfaction and efficiency and reduces turnover and absenteeism.[26] Finally, the empirical case of Yugoslavia's experiment of workers' self-management attenuates two highly critical lessons: First, it is necessary to promote the *willingness and capacity*

---

17   MECW 35: 90.
18   Devine 2011, p. 190, Cole 1920a.
19   Kalecki 2010, pp. 25–37; Lange 1958, pp. 5–6.
20   Hahnel 2005, p. 189; Schweickart 1998, p. 17.
21   Pérotin 2012, pp. 201, 208.
22   Weitzman and Kruse 1990; Schweickart 2002, p. 60; Levin 2006, p. 114; Pérotin 2012, pp. 195–221.
23   Pérotin 2012, pp. 206–7.
24   Pérotin 2012, p. 210.
25   Schweickart 2002, p. 60.
26   Levin 2006, p. 118.

to participate. Second, it is necessary to formalise representation in workplace democracy. Taking this into consideration, we will sketch the basic features of 'workplace democracy' before amending them with republican attributes.

In the co-operative commonwealth, able citizens should be under the social obligation to contribute labour to social production and in return share in the fruits of this collective effort. The foundational social relationship of production is mediated by the community of citizens, where labour is to be regarded as a public service supplied to the community. The worker, then, does not sell their labour-power on the labour market, but instead joins an association of equal producers as a candidate member before acquiring the status of 'full member' after some duration. Each association of producers supplies part of the total labour of society and together constitute the community of producers as a whole, with each member receiving a share of the total product of society. The basic decision-making bodies of associated labour are two different forms of workers' councils, what Castoriadis called the 'factory council' and the 'general assembly'. He summarises the basic arrangement as follows: 'the factory council exercises authority and replaces the factory's general assembly only when the latter is not in session'.[27] In larger co-operative associations it is expedient for the general assembly to elect a supervisory board as well.

Workplace democracy does not mean that every action of every worker should be subject to immediate majoritarian control, of course. Indeed, the concern that too many decision-making sessions will be required has been raised repeatedly.[28] The general assembly of workers may be a monthly session and make decisions concerning the general organisation and direction of the workplace, leaving some scope for the execution of predefined tasks and functions in daily operations. The general assembly would also elect a governing committee or board tasked with day-to-day administration. The scope of discretionary authority of the workers' councils will primarily concern their internal affairs. That is, the determining of the conditions of employment, the distribution of supplementary income (bonuses), the formulation of by-laws, the growth of productivity and the types of investments required to achieve it, and the approval of annual reports and accounts.[29] The workers' councils will have to formulate their production plan, by choosing equipment, inputs, and the volume and assortment of output. The general assembly would submit

---

27 Castoriadis 1988, p. 98.
28 Castoriadis 1988, pp. 144–5; Laibman 2002b, p. 86; Schweickart 2002, p. 60; Hodgson 1998, p. 415.
29 See Kalecki 2010, p. 35.

input for the production plan, after which the governing committee – especially where it concerns larger associations – will prepare a draft production plan, which will then have to be approved by the workers' assembly after a round of amendments.

The size of the governing board cannot be specified or uniformly established, since it should be informed by the complexity of the day-to-day management. What can be stressed is that the number of board members should tend toward the higher side of the scale since a larger board size in co-operatives was found to increase engagement and productivity.[30] Alternatively, co-operatives may decide that general meetings of workers must be convened at more regular intervals, but the law of the republic should stipulate the minimum number of general assemblies that must be convened. Sustained participation, and not mere passive employee ownership, is after all associated with additional performance gains.[31] Production units would therefore benefit from organising (and should be encouraged to organise) assemblies outside of the mandated minimum number of general meetings. This is only realistic when the workforce of a given association is capable (and, importantly, judges itself to be capable) of governing their own workplace. The adequate training of workers in economic decision-making, accounting, and the dissemination of simplified essential information is a precondition for effective participation,[32] and policies should be in place to ensure this.

If necessary, work teams or departments can be established within the workplace with their own self-governing bodies, provided their authority is circumscribed and subordinate to the highest workers' councils of the association. The exact arrangement depends entirely on the type of work organisation and scalability. Some operations may be co-ordinated through standardisation of work processes, for instance. The routine of such processes makes frequent workers' assemblies less essential, whereas other types of collective labour may demand more deliberation, or mutual adjustment.[33] Members of such workplaces will have to convene frequently owing to the nature of their work. As Levin deduced from empirical observations of existing co-operatives:

> Depending upon the size of the cooperative, participation may be highly informal with discussions and meetings, as needed, and personal discre-

---

30   Pérotin 2012, p. 206.
31   Pérotin 2012, p. 213.
32   Castoriadis 1988, pp. 97–8; Musić 2011, p. 178.
33   Douma and Schreuder 2017, p. 212.

tion in specific work roles. In larger firms the participation may be more formal in terms of work teams and specific decision forums as well as selection of managers.[34]

Even in organisations where standardisation of work tasks is not the default mode of operation, routine decisions will need to be made. An elected manager can operate on the basis of tacit consent of those that they are elected to represent in relation to routine decisions, in order to not bog down production by innumerable meetings that additionally depress morale and therefore undermine the willingness for participation in democratic procedures. Herein lies a risk, namely that new members of the co-operative association will be initiated into ready-made routines which they internalise without critically reflecting upon them, and therefore not becoming full 'owners' of the processes which they reproduce. The rotation of workers 'between production and office areas' and in managerial positions, as suggested by Castoriadis,[35] can alleviate this risk to a degree, since it would familiarise workers with routines at different levels and allow them to reflect upon existing practices from different standpoints. That is to say, they should be given the responsibilities that allow them to become active agents and not mere passive recipients of ready-made routines. Being able to elect their managers for the running of the day-to-day affairs, or to make decisions more directly by vote during the plenary sessions of their general assembly, affords workers the democratic instruments to assume collective responsibility for their immediate, productive environment and to become effective usufructuaries of the assets under their control.

Once workers are transformed into engaged agents within the sphere of production, they can exercise their rights to transform the quality of work processes, integrating executive tasks in production and administrative tasks in preparation of production, exercising control over the pace, character and organisation of their work, to be involved in relevant decision-making regarding their day-to-day obligations, and being able to adjust the course of their association in light of information about performance and results gathered and timely diffused by the central committee of their workplace.

Having so far briefly assessed the preconditions and features of workplace democracy, let us now turn to a republican perspective. Each worker can, and from the perspective of republican socialism should, actively participate in decision-making as a check against the monopolisation of access to, and the

---

34   Levin 2006, p. 115.
35   Castoriadis 1988, p. 117.

arbitrary use of discretionary power to secure freedom from domination within the sphere of production, as per a neo-Roman framework. A neo-Athenian perspective would additionally highlight that self-government in production foregrounds the creative and social nature of humanity as it permits workers to exercise control over their immediate social environment. Since workers have a vested interest in improving the quality of labour, and since self-government commits workers to co-operative initiative, it would bring out their intrinsic social nature. Consequently, it enhances capabilities for self-mastery. This parallels humanist themes in Marxism.[36] Along similar lines, it has been suggested that economic democracy could serve as 'foundation for active citizenship'.[37] Workers become accustomed to participatory decision-making, deliberation, taking different viewpoints into consideration, and the development of shared interests within the context of a collective endeavour and some common goal. Empowering agency in social life, including the workplace, may also address the sense of powerlessness that contributes to reduced political participation.[38] There is some cautious empirical evidence that workplace participation increases political engagement.[39] As Devine speculates: 'Once people become active subjects, making things happen, in one aspect of their lives, they are less likely to remain passive objects, allowing things to happen to them, in other aspects'.[40] Therefore, the skills and spirit of self-government may carry over to political participation, thus contributing to active citizenship.

At the same time, workplace democracy may interfere with political democracy where it concerns a potentially built-in propensity toward 'voter fatigue' owed to excessive numbers of meetings – the amount of deliberative sessions in workplaces and communities may well stretch thin the willingness to participate. In this sense, there may be a trade-off between workplace and political democracy. This can be mitigated in a number of ways, principally through a reduction of the work week and efficient use of decision-making procedures. Kautsky, as mentioned earlier, pointed out that direct political participation in Greek city-states was accommodated by the fact that a relatively small number of free citizens were alleviated of the duty to toil. In addition to having access to training programmes in political decision-making, citizens should have the time and energy for direct participation in political life. This should be achieved by macroeconomic policies that pursue a balanced growth of labour

---

36   Thompson 2019.
37   Brest 1988, p. 1623.
38   Levin 2006, p. 112.
39   Levin 2006, p. 113.
40   Devine 2011, p. 159.

productivity that enables a concomitant reduction of the average workday. Similarly, the planned mobilisation of all labour, by policies of full employment and work-sharing would potentially decrease the average work time per capita. The abolition of commerce will also do away with certain functions that are of high commercial value but of low social value. Moreover, by allowing for the delegation of some authority in the execution of administrative tasks in both workplaces and communities, the number of public assemblies would be relatively limited. This would simultaneously shrink the overgrown and top-heavy managerial apparatuses, which are functionally attuned toward control over employees.[41] All this in turn frees up some labour-power that can be redirected elsewhere in order to reduce the average workload in favour of leisure or participation in civil life. Lastly, it is certainly conceivable that if workers under capitalism can be motivated to attend work meetings to tend to matters of their commercial, corporate firm, it is possible to instil a similar discipline in relation to public assemblies that deal with matters of the public interest by deploying a similar material stimulus. In these various ways, voter fatigue should be minimised.

Evidently, republicans cannot be satisfied with merely extending democracy to workplaces, since this implies that there is no *raison d'être* for a specifically republican vision of economic democracy. Democracy alone insufficiently guarantees freedom in the republican sense. The arbitrary private will of the employer should not simply be replaced by the arbitrary will of the workers, as per the neo-Roman conception of liberty. Within social organisation it is necessary to have a level of discipline and integration, which necessarily means that individuals belonging to an organisation need to surrender some of their personal autonomy for the sake of organisational reproduction and continuity. Even when social organisation is organised on the basis of consensus, personal autonomy is out of the question insofar as individuals are not able to opt out of the agreed upon terms or plans at any given moment. In the sphere of production, the respective individual labours of workers need to be socially integrated. Enforcement of decisions – by various means, such as social penalties – is required. Moreover, workers depend on their place of work for income. It will not always be possible to vacate their workplace at short notice. Therefore, coherent social organisation necessarily creates a condition of interdependency. Under certain circumstances inter-

---

41 For instance: 'The monitoring of work in LMFs [labour-managed firms] tends to be undertaken with peer group monitoring as a substitute for formal monitoring [Bonin, Jones, and Putterman 1993], a mechanism with cost savings for the firm and without necessarily any loss in monitoring intensity' (Doucouliagos 1995, p. 67).

dependency can potentially develop into dependency if a difference in bargaining power develops due to asymmetrical access to immaterial resources (e.g. expertise, charisma). To reiterate, under Yugoslavia's system of workers' self-management, the informal powers of specialists progressively accumulated over a number of decades, partially because managerial authority was not limited by formal statutes. Consequently, there is an inherent risk of workers being subjected to the arbitrary will of other workers – whether a minority (of specialists, say) or the majority that has formed into a durable social alliance against the interests of an essentially disenfranchised permanent minority. Individual workers should enjoy adequate protection against the arbitrary will of other workers, which they may scarcely enjoy if they are at the mercy of an unchecked direct democracy, as in, for example, most anarchist visions of society.

For example, Chomsky characterises anarchism as 'democracy all the way through', unrestrained by state power. To him anarchism 'means democratic control of communities, of workplaces, of federal structures, built on systems of voluntary association, spreading internationally'.[42] Likewise, the acclaimed 'Anarchist FAQ' asserts that '[f]or most anarchists, direct democratic voting on policy decisions within free associations is the political counterpart of free agreement'.[43] Similarly, Van der Walt summarises Bakunin's worldview: 'Anarchism would be nothing less than the most complete realisation of democracy – democracy in the fields, factories, and neighbourhoods, coordinated through federal structures and councils from below upward, and based on economic and social equality'.[44] However, there is a minority of anarchists that reject 'democracy' as 'anti-anarchist', among them Black who does so emphatically.[45] Semantic drift aside for a moment: 'anarchy' and 'democracy' are incompatible terms at a purely etymological level, because 'ἄναρχος' (anarchy) means without ruler, whereas 'δημοκρατία' (democracy) means 'people-rule' – hence making them etymologically incompatible terms, and why 'ἰσονομία' (isonomy) is said to lack either the suffix '-archy' or '-cracy' (authority or rule). As Arendt explained:

> This notion of no-rule was expressed by the word isonomy, whose outstanding characteristic among the forms of government, as the ancients had enumerated them, was that the notion of rule (the 'archy' from ἄρχειν

---

42   Chomsky 2002.
43   The Anarchist FAQ Editorial Collective 2009.
44   Van der Walt and Schmidt 2009, p. 70.
45   Black 2011.

in monarchy and oligarchy, or the 'cracy' from κρατεῖν in democracy) was entirely absent from it. The *polis* was supposed to be an isonomy, not a democracy. The word 'democracy', expressing even then majority rule, the rule of the many, was originally coined by those who were opposed to isonomy and who meant to say: What you say is 'no-rule' is in fact only another kind of rulership; it is the worst form of government, rule by the *demos*.[46]

There are, in my view, various means by which freedom in workplaces can be insured. First of all, according to Dagger, in 'the republican view, freedom is not so much a matter of being left alone as it is of living under the rule of laws that one has a voice in making'.[47] All workers should have an equal say in the matters that affect them, by democratic means. Operational decisions will need a simple majority while changes to by-laws will need a qualified majority. While one cannot discriminate between the degree to which one is affected (and thus assign differential weights to votes) nor the intensity of preferences (two people may be equally affected by a decision but one may be more invested in the outcome than the other), the republican alternative to 'majoritarianism' is to nurture a sense of solidarity and dialogue within workplaces – as outside – to ensure that those who may be widely recognised as being more affected by a decision or more invested in a particular outcome should have their arguments be given their due consideration, even when they represent a minority. Further, (it should go without saying that) to help ensure that the elected standing committee (or governing board) does not become a source of domination over the rest of the workers, the elected managers will need to be accountable to and recallable by the general assembly. In this way, formal equality can be provisioned.

Secondly, the neo-republican solution to the threat of arbitrary power (including majoritarian whim) is to organise the polity as 'a community of equal citizens *governed by law*' [italics added].[48] Where the voluntary associations of anarchism and communism exist by virtue of customary convention, in a socialist republic the sphere of production would be placed under the jurisdiction of a civil code that protects the legal status of production co-operatives as non-commercial associations with a public function. The production unit should be a community of equal producers governed by law, then. The decision-making procedures of the production unit should be subject to by-laws passed

---

46   Arendt 1990, p. 30.
47   Dagger 2006, p. 155.
48   Lovett and Pettit 2009, p. 22.

by the general assembly that form the charter, the articles of association – their fundamental body of rules and regulations of general scope and application. This governing document will specify the rights and duties of workers, thereby providing a framework in which operational decisions can be made at different levels of the organisation. The range of choice and activity of the association of workers is governed by these articles that apply in equal force to all members, rather than being subject to majoritarian or managerial whim.

The civil code of the political community will further provide the broader legal framework in which the by-laws should be embedded to prevent mis-use. The equal distribution of decision-making power, manifested in the general assembly of workers and their elected standing committee, should be anchored in law, and subject to judicial oversight when so needed, to prevent certain workers with a bargaining advantage to leverage their relative strength in order to bend (formally or informally) the rules to their partial will. By placing certain decisions beyond the scope of authority of the workers' councils they cannot suspend, for example, the mandated number of general meetings. Otherwise, managers could whittle down accountability by reducing the frequency at which they call to convene general assemblies, which would render the monitoring of their activity less effective. The remaining general meetings that would be convened say, once per year, would be reduced to hollow rituals. Thus, associational law will have to define the scope and limits of the authority of workers' councils, both the general assembly and the governing board. This would formalise representation and thereby function as check against the incremental usurpation of power by elected managers. In short, the members of production co-operatives will have the option to rely on the representation of workers' interests by electing managers to act on their behalf, without permanently surrendering one degree or another of power to the governing committee. In this way, formal equality is safeguarded by the community of law.

Finally, another check against the potential re-emergence of domination in the sphere of production is the rotation and combination of menial and mental tasks. This would limit the development of a differential bargaining power between workers. Albert and Hahnel suggest that the socialist community should balance job functions within workplaces as well as between workplaces – so-called 'balanced job complexes'.[49] In their opinion, 'empowering' tasks should not be concentrated among twenty percent or so of the population, as they believe they currently are. Albert and Hahnel argue that this

---

49   Albert and Hahnel 1991, pp. 13, 19–21.

poses a risk of the monopolisation of influence by the 'empowered' workers – a potential 'co-ordinator class' – so as to usurp power.[50] Castoriadis had similarly remarked that:

> The roots of possible conflict between workers and technicians therefore are not at all of a technical nature. If such a conflict emerged it would be a social and political conflict, arising from a possible tendency of the technicians to assume a dominating role, thereby constituting anew a bureaucratic managerial apparatus.[51]

Indeed, in socialist Yugoslavia technical and administrative staff exercised undue influence in decision-making since shop-floor workers judged themselves to be insufficiently competent and informed to make qualified judgements on, for example, investment decisions.[52] While formal equality was legally provisioned, informal inequality (in addition to other factors; e.g. political interference that complicating the conducting of business and the absence of political freedoms) eroded self-management. In other words, in addition to formal *de jure* equality, there should be a sufficiently symmetrical distribution of social resources and personal capacities among workers and citizens to participate in collective decision-making. Indeed, this issue could otherwise echo the classical republican slavery-liberty paradox,[53] wherein a labouring population is condemned to menial and physical labour so that a privileged few can apply themselves creatively or intellectually – socialism would reproduce a privileged stratum from within.

Schweickart points out, however, that it is mathematically impossible to equalise job task desirability, according to a cardinal scale, within and across workplaces, as suggested by Albert.[54] Furthermore, whatever the veracity of this aspect of the Hahnel-Albert proposal, it seems to me that 'desirability' is

---

50   Albert and Hahnel 1991, p. 69.
51   Castoriadis 1988, p. 111.
52   Musić 2011, p. 178.
53   This paradox pertains to how classical republicanism reconciled liberty with slavery, in the words of Gourevitch (2013): 'The paradox can be stated logically as a contradiction between two propositions. The first proposition is that republican liberty is a socially constituted condition of independence made possible by the servitude of others. The second proposition is that human beings are equal and thus all legitimate political values must be universalizable, or enjoyable by all. The particularism of a commitment to republican liberty – independence for a particular class, dependence for another class – logically conflicts with the universalism of the commitment to human equality. Hence a paradox'.
54   Schweickart 2006.

not necessarily causally linked to 'empowerment'. What is crucial in relation to power distribution is knowledge diffusion, which may be patterned hierarchically. To the degree that the execution of technical and administrative functions is concentrated in particular sections and departments of the workforce, those not directly engaged in performing these tasks are excluded from day-to-day interaction with the information and knowledge required to meaningfully participate in the making of investment decisions. Thus, this essential information may be effectively monopolised by technical or administrative staff – regardless of the utility derived from participating in certain work. Balancing job desirability, so that on average workers receive an approximately equal amount of gratification from their respective labour efforts will then prove an ineffective means to guard against tendencies toward the monopolisation of information.

Nevertheless, as Castoriadis had already argued, workers should move between departments, and the shop and office floors.[55] Training programmes should be made readily available to facilitate this. Whenever technically feasible, horizontal organisation should be preferred to vertical delegation. Still, the question remains how workers could be encouraged to volunteer for administrative positions, since the willingness to actively participate in administration may be both an effect and cause of participation. Only when workers participate in administration do they acquire the information, confidence, and competency required to participate, which in turn should stimulate their willingness to participate; and conversely, when they fail to participate directly in managing administrative or technical tasks, workers will acquire neither the skills nor the knowledge to participate and therefore neither would they develop the disposition to do so.

By making basic instruction in economic accounting mandatory in public education, by using quasi-democratic forums in educational institutions, and by affording all workers the opportunity to participate in additional managerial training, the knowledge necessary for self-management can be circulated widely. In addition, government might mandate a certain rate of turnover of management, a participation quota in effect. Supplemental income can be made available to achieve effective interaction of socialisation and material interests. Production co-operatives would be allocated additional income on condition of meeting this quota, which would provide each work collective with a material incentive to develop leadership qualities in all their individual members and to rotate the administrative functions amongst each other.

---

55   Castoriadis 1988, p. 117.

In brief, the practice of 'workplace democracy' should be embedded in and mediated by institutional checks of the community of citizens. Unalloyed democracy is unsuitable to the socialist ambition of collective responsibility. It is liable to the erosion of collective decision-making procedures and exposes workers to the caprice of majority or managerial decision-making. To correct for these deficits, the socialist republic should graft democracy on a constitutional body of layered institutional checks and balances. The legal status of production co-operatives will depend on meeting certain legal requirements such as the convening of regular general assemblies, the formulation of by-laws to regulate their internal affairs within the framework of a civil code for the governing of associations, the formal institutionalisation of managerial representation, a participation quota, and so on. The necessary mechanisms can be in place to help ensure that self-government in production is sustainable, without sacrificing technical feasibility or the radical ambition of industrial democracy. The exercise of collective control by workers over their own affairs within a context of balanced institutions would guarantee freedom from domination and enhance self-mastery. The associations of producers would function as vocational centres of civic education. Institutionally nurtured social attitudes of self-government and collective responsibility would have important qualities that could carry over to political participation and vice versa, thus contributing to the overall structural coherence of the socialist commonwealth. This ultimately depends also the broader framework in which the institution of 'workplace republicanism' is situated, extending to the political arrangement (outlined previously) and the economic mechanism for the co-ordination of activity between production co-operatives (discussed subsequently).

General Planning and Parametric Control

We have so far discussed how the *arbitrary* will of the capitalist can be replaced by the *non-arbitrary* will of the workers within the scope of individual units of production. Having for the moment sidestepped the issue of the harmonisation of the diffuse activities of these individual plants, factories, offices, or other sites of production, we can now direct our attention toward the question of whether or not social production should be carried out in the interest of the community. This is to say, should producers dispose of their output on the basis of their narrowly defined commercial interests; or instead, should a public body stipulate the conditions under which products and services ought to be distributed in a way that accords with the general interest for increasing social well-being? This is, in other words, a question of whether free competition around market exchange, or some other mechanism should co-ordinate the activities of production units under a socialist regime. Since free competition produces socially corrosive particular interests – making the free exercise of commerce structurally biased against the concerns for the common good – the aim of a project of socialist renewal, especially where it concerns radical republicanism, should lie in restraining commercial imperatives in production, within the parameters of what is technically feasible of course. Furthermore, if economic and political self-government are to be mutually reinforcing, then the economy should be treated in much the same way as the social sphere of politics, i.e. as a body made up of public and quasi-public organs and agencies whose scope and powers are defined and limited constitutionally, controlled by citizens in their common interests, and in which these public institutions are geared to the promotion of social well-being. One obvious advantage of such an approach would be that it ensures the symbiotic interlocking between the economic and political spheres, unlike economic mechanisms such as 'distributism',[1] in which the logic of commercially-propelled capital accumulation and particular interests, arguably, work in opposition to the logic that government, through pre- or redistributive policies, seeks to enforce – this calls into question the potential longevity of such approaches to securing republicanism in the economy. Conversely, as we have seen, it has been argued that democracy and socialism are structurally incongruous. Makovi argues that 'democracy

---

1 Cooney 2001.

and socialism are fundamentally incompatible, and therefore, that democratic socialism is logically incoherent'.[2] This is supposedly so since democracy is a means of limiting power while socialism would require 'unlimited power' in the sense that all economic resources will be legally concentrated in the hands of the state and their use subject to central control, thus subordinating all local initiative to the central plan (even if 'democratically' established):[3] 'The political and economic systems simply do not match up in any coherent fashion', Makovi concludes.[4]

When setting out to design a socialist economic mechanism, it is clear that we should avoid emulating a model of Soviet-style socialism insofar as such economies suffered from chronic, system-specific deficiencies that cause them to fall short of feasibility metrics. In addition, such a model of socialism is irreconcilable with republican values since it represents an excessive unity of the state. Nevertheless, centring the Soviet experience in the pursuit to formulate a feasible socialism serves a critical purpose rooted in an elementary motive. Any theoretical exercise that proceeds with the formulation of a viable model of socialism is forced to contend with a whole range of questions that puzzled scores of socialist economists of considerable brilliance and ingenuity. Any reappraisal of socialist economics will have to be embedded firmly in the practical experience of twentieth century socialism and interact with the theoretical body of knowledge produced by it – provided we do not intend for socialism to stumble over the same obstacles, replicating the same mistakes.

The lessons obtained by socialist economists and policymakers were acquired under remarkably difficult circumstances and substantial peril, involving many personal tragedies. This agonisingly sluggish learning curve and humbling experience should be a source from which we derive a reanimated body of socialist thought, insofar as we do not aim to replicate this excruciating process on grounds of 'actually existing socialism' not having lived up to its ultimate aims. As contemporary proposals reveal, many socialists unwittingly duplicate some of the major flaws experienced by actually existing socialisms in their proposals – those most vocal in their opposition to Marxism-Leninism simultaneously advance ideas that bear the closest resemblance to early adaptations of Soviet-style centralised planning.

What remains then, for our puzzle, is to combine the various pieces thus far unveiled and examined and to fit them together in such a way that they line up to form into a coherent and viable economic mechanism. From a socialist

---

2   Makovi 2016, p. 3.
3   Makovi 2016, p. 24.
4   Makovi 2016, p. 3.

standpoint, we depart from the assumption that the operation of competitive markets conflicts with affording primary importance to the public interest in the allocation of resources. It more or less follows that some central decision-making body, embodying the general interest, should distribute resources in a pattern of utilisation that increases common welfare by the largest increment. Armed with intimate knowledge of the current endowments of productive resources and their structure, the possible combinations of factor inputs and their yields, as well as knowledge of the necessary product and service output corresponding to the maximum level of consumer satisfaction, the central planning authorities could simply instruct producers to behave in a way that enables resources to be used in such a manner that the maximum net positive effect can be obtained. However, since – as discussed – this information on the current level of productive capacity, the possible feasible options combining materials, labour, and means of production, and levels of social demand for different combinations of output are not readily available to the centre, the planning authorities lack the necessary ingredients to cook up a fully integrated, comprehensive plan that would cover in all the requisite detail the least-cost path that leads from the initial conditions to the maximum growth of the national product. This whole procedure encounters significant obstacles, as Nemchinov summed up:

> In a socialist economy quantitative methods of analysis and the solution of similar problems acquire an incomparably greater significance. The preparation of national economic plans embracing a vast number of mutually related and interdependent economic units and of factors of production, and the co-ordination of these plans – not only in space but also in time – in order to achieve the greatest possible economic or technical effect (at any given moment or in the long run) is a task of enormous magnitude. With the level of development of the national economy and the exceptional complexity of internal economic relations, the problem of finding the best possible system for planning would become insurmountable without a fundamental appreciation of the quantitative methods of economic calculations and without the utilization of the latest computing techniques.[5]

Some socialists have simply assumed that rapid advances in modern computing and information technologies have substantially decreased the information

---

5 Preface to Kantorovich 1965, p. vii.

constraints imposed on the planning process, which is in itself offered as proof of the feasibility of comprehensive planning today.[6] Although such technical work is an important enterprise in its own right, the problem is not simply one related to the quantity of data, but also their quality. The complexity resides in designing a system of planning and control that generates accurate and action-able information in the first place. The enormous volume of technical know-ledge is intimately tied up with highly diffused and tacit knowledge generated by local processes, invisible from the vantage point of the centre. Producers, however, arguably lack the innate motivation to volunteer such information to the planning authorities, especially if it means they will receive fewer sup-plies than they might prefer (or higher output targets, lower bonuses, etc.). Producers will need the right motivation to reveal their true estimates of pro-duction possibilities, as well as the motivation to act on this knowledge. Thus, the socialist planning procedure will need to be informationally efficient, to ensure that the processing of data remains tractable (although less so due to advances in computer technology); but also incentive compatible, meaning that planning protocols are able to distribute the necessary rewards and penal-ties to stimulate workers' councils to reveal their capabilities and to carry out a plan reflective of this potential. In Kantorovich's words:

> Obviously the economy of such scale and complexity cannot be quite centralized 'up to the last nail' and a valuable part of decisions should be retained for the lower levels of the control system. The decisions of dif-ferent control levels and from different places must be linked by material balance relations and should follow the main object of the economy. The problem is to construct a system of information, accounting, economic indices and stimuli which permit local decision-making organs to valu-ate the advantage of their decisions from the point of view of the whole economy. In other words to make profitable for them the decisions prof-itable for the system, [which gives] a possibility to check the validity of the work of local organs' activity also from the point of view of the whole economy.[7]

It is necessary that this should be achieved without violating the political con-straints that are synonymous with the core values of the republican tradition. The conduct of production and distribution should proceed efficiently, without

---

6   See for example: CibCom 2022.
7   Kantorovich 1975.

concentrating excessive authority in the centre; or allowing partial interests at the local level to spiral outward. The common good should be allowed to guide the actions of the centre and local units of production, which presupposes that their pace and direction is determined by self-governing citizens. This means that general planning by the centre should be executed on the basis of a democratic mandate formulated by the legislative assemblies, while production co-operatives acquire a degree of latitude to carry out production as a service in the public interest according to their own collective insights, experience, and knowledge. The various associations will further have to co-operate in bringing about the political macro-objectives at the microeconomic level. This balances self-government between the national and local levels and structures the behaviour of producers according to the social priorities of the national community, as part of a control system of centralised planning and horizontal co-ordination – tentatively designated here as a 'normative collective planning mechanism' or 'normative economic planning' or somewhat more technically, a system of 'general planning and parametric control'. Under such a normative economic mechanism (which is based neither on imperative planning nor on indicative planning), there should be a central framework that defines the parameters of what does and does not count as a socially responsible use of society's assets, and to subsequently allow production units to develop horizontal links within the scope permitted by such parameters.

However, if producers possess a degree of autonomy to establish relations with other workplaces to facilitate the circulation of goods then we can arguably speak of a market economy with, as Nove put it, a 'species of commodity production'.[8] To prevent fragmentation at the hands of autonomously acting units of production, it would be necessary to replace the atomism of market exchange and the profit motive by some other set of success indicators and instruments that link the interests of local economic units to general welfare.

1   Cost Accounting – 'khozraschet'

The model of a socialist economy that will be formulated by synthesising features of different models over the course of this chapter will be based on a central, regulatory framework, which embodies the general interest one the one side, and self-governed production units that possess the constrained autonomy to develop their own plans within the parameters of the regulat-

---

8   Nove 1991a, p. 43.

ory structures, on the other. It should be an essential feature of any socialist model that production units enjoy meaningful independence in developing their activities in the spheres of production and distribution. This flows logically from the supposition that the necessary knowledge to execute economic planning is generated in these processes and is therefore highly contextual, which implies that these spheres cannot be subjected to direct control by administrative means. This concept is somewhat akin to an idea borrowed from Soviet experience, *khozraschet*. The roots of this principle trace back to the 'Thermidorian' phase of the Russian Revolution of 1917–1923. This period saw the Soviet government forced to retreat from their attempts to leap forward in the direction communism in the aftermath of the disastrous social collapse spurred by the civil war and the excesses of war communism.

As Brus and Łaski summarised: 'Lenin was emphatic in admitting that to rely solely on enthusiasm in organizing production and distribution on communist principles was a mistake, and that personal material interest and economic accountability (*khozrashet*) must play a paramount role'.[9] As such, during the period of the New Economic Policy (1921–1928), state enterprises were expected to finance their own operations. The tool of 'profit-and-loss accounting' henceforth became a central benchmark in economic accountancy and performance of the Soviet economy.[10] During the period of administrative command planning (starting in 1929), *khozraschet* remained an instrument to measure the costs and returns of enterprises, allowing enterprises – in theory – to reduce costs or expand output within planned targets defined primarily by gross output quotas. The profit *motive* did not become a functional indicator until the Kosygin-Liberman reforms of 1966. Even then, however, the operative role of profit calculations remained subordinated to plan target fulfilment. For example, in the late 1960s, the promotion of efficiency was mainly attempted through an increase of hierarchical discipline, rather than by expanding *khozraschet*,[11] which would amount to discipline by self-finance – i.e. the tightening of budget constraints for state enterprises, which was only enacted in 1987 under Gorbachev.

The concept, in one form or another, also featured in various reform proposals of a range of Soviet economists – Kronrod and Nemchinov among them – as well as those of Western-based analysts – e.g. Ellman and Dobb. Nemchinov, as an example, advocated what he termed a '*khozraschet*-economy'. He observed

9   Brus and Łaski 1989, p. 37.
10   Smirnov, Radaeva, Esin, and Rusakov 1979.
11   Ellman 1973, p. 56.

that central planning was unable to plan all final output and that material balances in practice focussed on a limited number of goods that enjoyed political
priority (in 1951, 'the detailed version of the five year plan' included a mere
127 products).[12] Given this, Nemchinov proposed a dual-track planning system (later modified somewhat and adopted under Gorbachev's *perestroika*,
rather disastrously it should be added; but more successfully under China's
similar endeavour of *shuangguizhi*), with obligatory plan targets for priority
items and horizontal contracting (wholesale trade) for items that could not
be adequately planned. Prices would remain mostly centrally determined.[13]
During the *perestroika*-era, the principle of cost accounting would again feature prominently in economic debate and policymaking. Voices were raised to
transition to 'full cost accounting', meaning full responsibility accorded to firms
to finance themselves by finding suppliers and customers. One participant
of this debate, Kurashvili, articulated the rationale underpinning *khozraschet*
clearly. He specified that for cost accounting to be feasible, it would require
meeting certain criteria, namely 'self-planning, self-recoupment, and self-financing', or in a word, self-management. Since if, 'the enterprise is not given the
right of self-planning, it cannot be charged with the full measure of obligations
with regard to self-recoupment and self-financing'. The parts and components
are logically interwoven. Thus, '*cost accounting is the economic aspect of the self-
management of enterprises under the conditions of labor emulation and socialist
competition*', he maintained, and continued saying:

> Under full cost accounting, the well-being of the work collective and its
> acquisitions and losses depend entirely on the final economic results of
> its socially useful activity. But the collective cannot be placed in such
> strict dependence (without it there is no full cost accounting) unless it
> is given the freedom, as a basic prerequisite to the economic effective-
> ness of its activity, to plan and decide the questions of what to produce,
> under what conditions to produce, and how to market the product. If such
> questions are decided by the state and if the enterprise is given merely
> an advisory role, [the state] thereby assumes the responsibility for the
> economic consequences of its actions. That is the crux of the matter.
> *Full cost accounting is impossible in the case of incomplete, minimum self-
> management!*[14]

---

12   Gregory 2004, p. 117.
13   Sutela 1992, pp. 78–9.
14   Kurashvili 1988, p. 44.

The need for 'khozraschet' is twofold, in other words. First, cost accounting by production units is necessary in order to compare efforts and results as a *measure* of performance. The effects and costs of using different factors of production to produce different output bundles should be grasped by both the central level and local economic units to enable the best use of resources, which is possible only when these consequences can be presented in the form of quantitative cost-summaries. In order to encourage the *socially rational use of resources* by producers, through the diverting away of resources from less useful applications to more productive ones, the different degrees of productivity attained by producers need to be rendered visible. And accordingly, as the second use of 'khozraschet' in economic conduct, it is necessary to hold production units *accountable* for their performance in terms of their productivity to encourage producers to use society's assets more rather than less productively.[15] Doing so, presupposes that they bear *responsibility* for their choices and activities in relation to the use and application of resources. If, for example, the central authorities allocate resources to producers according to their own calculations, then production co-operatives cannot be held to account for the level of productivity they managed to achieve for the simple reason that they might have received a combination of inputs below their optimal requirements, unbeknownst to the central planning commission.

The basic rationale for securing an autonomous sphere of operations at the local level, among producers and consumers, is as follows: 'the future remains uncertain for both individuals and planning groups so that it involves risk, which means that there must be economic responsibility'.[16] This implies that there has to be a clear division of responsibilities – since if everyone is responsible for everything, no one is responsible for anything. The historical record of 'actually existing socialisms' reveals unmistakeably how the collectivisation of responsibility leads to breakdowns in the operation of material incentives. If political authorities, or some intermediate deliberative body, is involved in shaping investment decisions, but do not share in the responsibility for the out-

---

15   It should be noted, as I have frequently noticed misapprehensions related to the use of 'productivity' and 'efficiency', that productivity increases are not identical to intensification of work rates; while both typically depend on the choice for technical procedures and the associated cycle time per technical, executive task by manual workers. It is entirely feasible to increase productivity and decrease work intensity simultaneously, using certain techniques. The drive for productivity gains is not motivated by a desire to increase labour intensity and reduce the quality of work, but rather to reduce the consumption of materials, energy, and labour (human effort) used up in manufacturing.

16   Sirc 1979, p. 99.

come of these decisions, then production co-operatives would understandably resist being held fully accountable. In order for producers to remain invested in the socially useful outcomes of their productive efforts, it is required that the results and their efforts can be measured, evaluated, compared, and appropriately rewarded or sanctioned if so needed. Thus, as a number of Soviet economists concluded in the 1960s:

> [E]nterprises must be freed from too much interference by central authorities in the details of operation, and moreover the system of incentives must be based on a criterion which combines micro- and macroeconomic interest, so that there is no contradiction between the interest of enterprises and that of society.[17]

This roughly implies that any viable model of socialism requires an incentive scheme that links the activity of producers to the general interest. The macroeconomic objectives, as adopted in the annual and five-year plans, can only materialise when producers can be motivated to contribute productively toward these ends. In the words of Brus: the 'effectiveness of pressure brought to bear by the central plan on the lower levels depends', he said, 'to a large extent, on how far it is possible to reconcile the general social interest with the interests of the various separate economic units and with the interests of individuals (workers, households)'.[18] This requires that macroeconomic goals, established through the medium of centralised planning, are disaggregated into microeconomic metrics that survey the degree of success obtained by production co-operatives in the realisation of the objectives of the general plan. The 'motive force' guiding the hands of producers under this economic mechanism does not emerge spontaneously from local initiative, private considerations, and profit margins obtained in exchange, but are derived from the central plan's social objectives. If producers contribute productively to these objectives, they are rewarded materially and proportionately to the net results of their activity. Provided the incentive scheme is effective in influencing the behaviour of producers, it would structure production and distribution in accordance with the parameters of the general plan – thus allowing for more or less conscious political control over the course of economic development.

In this capacity, *khozraschet* should entail the independence of the basic economic unit in their economic operations within an overall regulative frame-

---

17   Wilczynski 1972a, p. 96.
18   Brus 1972, p. 24.

work. The central framework projects information to producers in the form of independent parameters. This framework allows the central planners to compare the efforts of producers expressed in quantitative terms – the process or production parameters – to the target value that corresponds to an optimal outcome – the 'set-point' or control figure. In response to the data projected to producers, they will have to make adjustments to realign their productive activity with the numerical values that reflect a more socially optimal use of resources. To the extent that they manage to do so successfully, their performance can be reinforced by material rewards to incentivise compliance with the target values generated in the planning process.

If economic accountability is to be organised effectively, production units would have to bear full responsibility for the formulation of their production programme and its subsequent implementation. This principle of local self-direction is probably insufficiently stressed by all models which we have surveyed. For example, the success of production units under Laibman's multi-level planning mechanism depends on the corrections and modifications made to their plans by various higher levels of administration. Likewise, Devine's model of negotiated co-ordination centres deliberation taking place among production units at intermediate administrative levels, shaping investment decisions on which production units depend to develop their own productive activity. Somewhat differently, in the Hahnel-Albert model, the activity of workers' councils is constrained by the information generated by consumption planning. The self-activity proposals of workers' councils are based on planned benefit-to-cost ratios, where the social benefit is inferred from the level of consumption projected by consumers via their consumer councils. Yet, in all these models the workers' councils shoulder the full brunt of responsibility for their performance, even if their success is conditioned or even determined by the involvement of other planning agencies. The more production units are reliant in their activity upon the involvement of other planning bodies, the more difficult it becomes to isolate the effects of decisions taken by production units from the effects produced by the interference of other planning bodies:

> what happens if an investment fails? It is simply impossible to find out who is responsible for the wrong decision. Since decision-making was preceded by a multi-stage iterative process – both in the assembly of information and in the preparation of decision-making – every participating organisation and person is responsible. They are responsible – and yet they are not. They can say that they did not really want the investment in this particular form, but that they were forced to compromise

with the other participants. Ultimately, therefore, personal responsibility for investment decision-making is lost (...).[19]

This would result in (i) pressure emanating from lower units to immunise themselves from accountability thereby weakening the system of material incentives, and consequently significantly reducing the motivation for producers to apply their resources productively; or alternatively, (ii) require a hypertrophy of bureaucratic functions to run audits to isolate the efforts of producers from the effects of administrative interference in order to divide responsibility accordingly. Neither alternative is desirable, and hence material incentives should be allowed to produce their intended effects, which hinges on a clear division of responsibilities.

The alternative to a model of vertically or horizontally interwoven responsibilities in relation to production programming is a system of parametric or cybernetic control. Each production unit should thus be an independent accounting unit, with their own reports, accounting balance, individual members, workers' councils (governing board and general meeting), and by-laws; although they may consist of multiple production sites, work units, or even subsidiaries. The size of these independent production co-operatives will naturally depend on the scale of their operations. Barring external shocks and disruptions, production co-operatives are to be uniquely responsible for their own affairs. Given the objectively determined parameters (success and cost indicators) defined by the centre, producers will need, to the best of their abilities, to determine what combination of factors of production (their choice of technique, level of organisation, semi-manufactures, raw materials, and units of labour) will yield a certain level of output and will generate a socially useful effect. They will need to be able to do so independently, free from arbitrary, *ad hoc* interventions by political authorities. It should be noted that this independence is relative insofar as it stands in relation to both the central framework and the choices of other producers to bid for resources, which constitute the *social* consequences of their choices that have to be weighed and which structure and limit the range of available options. Thus, this 'independence' does not imply that producers should be free to make decisions in isolation of broader considerations for their effects on society, and it pertains only to discretion regarding the social effects of their productive choices and activity. The independent parameters announce to producers the social consequences associated with their choices, and in return, this enables

---

19   Kornai 1980, p. 154.

producers make informed choices about using or abstaining from using different categories of productive resources in an otherwise autonomous capacity.

By employing a system of 'automatic incentives' tied to the control system, the activities of producers are evaluated and rewarded according to dispassionate criteria that should be clear and transparent so that the producers can grasp the approximate consequences of a certain course of action in advance. This generates a level playing field and delineates a sphere of socially responsible economic conduct, thereby significantly reducing the requirements for direct *ad hoc* involvement by planning authorities. Simultaneously, this reduces the need for a complex labyrinth of administrative agencies and rules and interventions, and therefore also reduces the opportunity for either public officials or managers to bend the system to their will and for their own benefit.

2   Planning, Prices, Allocation

We have now established basic feasibility criteria for a socialised, planned economy, around which a mechanism should be modelled. At this point we should begin addressing how socialist society might guide the co-ordination required for investment decisions and the circulation of goods. We cannot be satisfied in the belief that the sum of particular interests is equal to the greater interest of all. What remains to be addressed, however, is how we can reconcile independence at the local level, which we deem indispensable in terms incentive efficacy, with the politically formulated general interest at the central level, which is indispensable in relation to both socialist and republican aims. We have supplied the basic principles above. The politically defined social and macroeconomic priorities of the community will need to be integrated into a control framework, which defines the metrics of success by setting a number of indices along which the activity of production units can be evaluated. These controls should supply target values to producers to guide their choices. Within the parametric framework, workers' councils are fully independent in selecting some composition of inputs that, according to their own insights, allows them to obtain the maximum output, or a close approximation of this optimal level of output. This input-output programme should reflect their best estimates and efforts, informed by their collective experience and contextual knowledge and production plans should therefore not become subject to subsequent modification by planning offices, which lack the ability to pass qualitative judgements of this type. Thus, local decision-making should not imply 'giving up the planned management of the economy', but instead permit 'concentration on general problems' by central authorities, 'leaving the detailed decisions to the lower echelons, provided the latter act according to the rules and with the use of the parameters determined by the central level'.[20] The crucial issue on which the viability of socialism hinges is how informationally efficient, incentive compatible, technically feasible 'rules' can be devised that would encourage activity according to some reasonable approximation of the optimum use of resources, as understood by the central body representing the social interest. This desired 'target value' should closely approach the upper limits of efficiency, but since knowledge of the best potential uses of productive assets is contextual, the centre cannot simply set these values by issuing orders from above.

This problem can be approached by drawing on the Laibman reward function. First, the planning procedure should rely on the use of non-monetary units of account, or 'accounting prices', which are fixed by the centre in accordance with the relative costs of production of different goods (as well as investment requirements, the level of public consumption, and the balance of trade). Producers, using the information contained in the accounting prices, submit a production plan that announces the required inputs and the planned quantities of output. They do so according to a set of rules. First, their production plan should yield a high net output; second, the planned level of net output should be achieved; and finally, the stocks of output should be cleared – i.e. output levels should be constrained by actual consumption. To the extent that producers comply with these centrally formulated norms – which implies that the system of material incentives is sufficiently compelling to structure their behaviour accordingly – the effects obtained by decentralised productive efforts translate directly to effects obtained according to macroeconomic criteria.

Let us examine these rough contours in somewhat closer detail. The socialist republic will presumably intend to maximise their material wealth within ecological boundaries as part of their long-term macroeconomic goals. This can be defined fairly straightforwardly as a minimisation of expenditure of available resources relative to the maximisation of the social benefit of output. This simply means that society should attempt to consume as few resources (production goods, labour-power, raw material, land, energy) in the process of producing as many useful goods and services as possible. Obviously, using more human effort or more materials to produce less useful output represents an unnecessary tax on both workers and the natural environment. To harness efficiency for the purpose of socialist construction, it is necessary

---

20   Brus 1972, p. 14.

that we can compare efforts and results which in turn requires that the disparate and heterogeneous expenditures and consequences for society can be dissolved into a single unit of measurement, a common denominator that expresses both the costs and returns of economic activity. By expressing different and otherwise incommensurable forms of costs (the costs of materials of distinct grade and type, the costs of different classes of labour, etc.) in a single unit of account it furnishes both producers and central planners with the required information about the total costs and potential benefits implied by producing different items. This data can used as rational criterium in economic decision-making, by weighing the costs of using different inputs against the benefits obtained from doing so. Put differently, it should render visible the overall social consequences – the social costs of production, the social opportunity costs, and the social rate of return – of using different resources in different capacities toward different ends. On the basis of such calculations, resources can be allocated according to their most productive uses in order to add to society's wealth – they are indispensable instruments for economic calculus.

Under a collectivist economic regime, these prices should assume the form of non-monetary accounting prices, anchored by the central planning authorities to the average costs of production. These should thus represent 'independent parameters' for producers embodying 'the social scale of preferences' on the one end and the 'true ratios of social costs' on the other.[21] More specifically, as per Kalecki, prices in a socialist society will need to be fixed to the current costs and include a markup. The price of final output is set on the basis of the total costs divided by the quantity of output, which yields the cost-price per unit of output, or unit costs. This conveys to producers what is implied (in terms of what level of costs society incurs and what society gains) by them using a particular combination of factor inputs compared to some other variation of choices. In turn, producers determine the volume of production and 'in the event of disequilibrium the adjustment process takes place through planned quantity adjustment rather than through prices'.[22] The markup added to current costs should be set in relation to the requirements of investment and foreign trade, Kalecki maintained.[23] This means that a markup is added to the cost-price of means of consumption to (i) cover the expenditure of resources used up in collective consumption; and (ii) cover the expenditure of resources used up in the replacement and expansion of productive capacity, or gross

21   Brus 1972, pp. 146, 151–2.
22   Nuti 1986, p. 336.
23   See Kalecki 2010; Nuti 1986.

investment; (iii) be inversely proportional to the volume of savings (i.e. the markup is lowered when the volume of personal savings increases and vice versa); and (iv) balance the requirements of foreign trade. In addition, it should take into account the costs of external effects, in line with the social priorities, defined politically at the national level. Each individual means of consumption will be stamped with the total costs necessary to procure them, furnishing producers with a menu of options from which they can combine factor inputs in a socially responsible way.

The baseline prices of means of production should correspond to the current average of the costs of production, and incremental adjustments up and down from this baseline level should be made according to the opportunity costs. The eventual price levels used by the participants in the planning process would consequently incorporate both the social production costs and the social opportunity costs. The overall set of prices in the national economy will need to be updated at regular intervals to reflect the changing circumstances of production. Representing a moving average, rather than snapshots of any given moment, price levels would be reflective of structural trends rather than accidental oscillations. Hayek had argued it a grave omission that the likes of Lange failed to specify the frequency of price adjustments, proposing that spontaneous price setting in the market was far more flexible in accommodating the changing circumstances of production and distribution.[24] The laborious efforts by the centre to check prices and to continually update them would be a burdensome exercise generating inferior results compared to the adaptability exhibited by decentralised, autonomous actions in the market to accommodate daily changes. Contrary to this claim, computational techniques proposed by Cockshott and Cottrell would furnish 'if not up-to-the-minute then up-to-the-hour estimates' of the (labour) costs of production, which 'is much faster than a capitalist market can achieve'.[25] Be that as it may, the degree of price flexibility should be kept at relatively constant levels to prevent unsound and wild fluctuations that would render economic calculation more unpredictable and unreliable and therefore effect needlessly erratic adjustments in production.[26] In any case, the rapid price-setting capacity of free markets should not be exaggerated, as it is not uncommon for firms in Western economies to only adjust their prices on a quarterly or even yearly basis.[27]

24   Hayek 1940, pp. 134–5.
25   Cockshott and Cottrell 1993, p. 52.
26   Zauberman 1967, p. 275.
27   See Amirault, Kwan, and Wilkinson 2005; Morris and De Vincent-Humphreys 2019; Park, Rayner, and D'Arcy 2010.

Of course, 'one must specify the dynamics of the adjustment process, e.g., by how much prices are to be raised per unit of time given the magnitude of excess demand, etc'.[28] This will require some trial and error and technical refinement of the methods for determining the set of prices and the frequency of their revision, but price updates every monthly accounting period according to the moving average of some duration seems perfectly conducive to rational use – too much flexibility is practically indistinguishable from statistical noise and producers need to be able to rely on some level of stability and predictability. Whatever the exact specifics of the adjustments, the price of production goods should be set closer to their long-run costs compared to consumption goods in light of the longer time horizon associated with investment decisions.[29]

The logistical control of stocks should be subjected to universal standardisation, aided by digital information technology, so that all inputs and outputs can be individually tracked using universal product coding.[30] This allows the general planning bureau to compare production plans to their actual implementation by seeing how the output of one unit of production is fed as input to other producers, and eventually households – which can be thought of as comparing the values obtained in the production process to the target value. Therefore, it also allows the central authority to assess the degree to which both price levels and production plans correspond to actual expenditures in the process of production – or whether, for example, some attempt has been made to manipulate cost data by means of fictitious entries. This would make the set of prices reasonably accurate representations of underlying and objective economic realities, which is crucial because substantial and arbitrary distortions of prices due to mistakes on the end of central planners would make it difficult to hold producers accountable for their performance which relies on the given set of prices.[31] Hence, centralised price-fixing is an exceedingly technical but surmountable task when delegated to techniques involving electronic computers and information technology.

The centrally computed prices will need to form the basic foundation on which the whole planning procedure rests, by supplying producers with information about the social consequences of their choices. A change in the structure of accounting units should effect a change in the structure of production and so on, so that a feedback loop is established between the quantitative parameters and the behaviour of producers to generate socially desired

28   Hurwicz 1973, p. 6.
29   Dobb 1967, pp. 174–5, 199–201.
30   Cockshott and Cottrell 1993, p. 113.
31   See also Brus and Łaski 1989.

outcomes. In this capacity, producers effectively determine the costs of production according to their selection of factor inputs, and prices are anchored to these costs – in the case of joint production producers also need to make some division of costs per type of output (main products and by-products); and for service output and toll goods, producers need to divide quantities of input per unit of output (e.g. consumers serviced, and categories of service).

The procedure for economic planning can be defined thus:

> A production plan, whether it deals with one factory or the economy as a whole, is a type of reasoning (made up of a great number of secondary arguments). It can be boiled down to two premises and one conclusion. The two premises are the material means initially at one's disposal (equipment, stocks, labor, etc.) and the target one is aiming at (production of so many specified objects and services, within a given period of time). We will refer to these premises as the 'initial conditions' and the 'ultimate target'. The 'conclusion' is the path to be followed from initial conditions to ultimate target. In practice this means a certain number of intermediate products to be made within a given period. We will call these conclusions the 'intermediate targets'.[32]

A planning procedure would have to perform two types of computation: '(i) [the] co-ordination calculation which results in determining the set of internally consistent (feasible) programmes, and (ii) [the] optimization calculation which leads to the selection of the optimal programme from a set of internally consistent ones'.[33] Recall for a minute our concise treatment of multilevel programming methods. According to such planning procedures, the centre and base units enter into a dialogue to find solutions to a constrained optimisation problems. This represents a 'shadow market' (per Wilczynski) or 'pseudomarket' (per Robinson) which works by means of an exchange of information, as opposed to an exchange of commodities. In price-guided two-level procedures, like the Lange-Lerner model, the centre quotes a set of prices and production units respond by quoting quantities of output in return. The centre then adjusts the shadow prices on the basis of the responses. The central planning authorities effectively auction goods to production units by announcing a set of indicative prices – a process of *tâtonnement*, in a word. After a num-

---

32   Castoriadis 1988, p. 119.

33   Lange 1971, p. 46.

ber of iterations, the centre should have discovered a range of fully integrated (internally consistent) comprehensive plans, and among these feasible plans, ideally also one or perhaps multiple optimal plans that maximise the value of the objective function – or the best possible approximation under prohibitive time constraints. The planning authorities then select one of the optimal solutions, or its closest approximation, and instruct production units to carry it out. At this stage, no actual market exchange is needed at all, insofar as each unit simply carries out the instructions per administrative fiat (provided they are innately motivated to do so, i.e. if we take strategic manipulation on the basis of partial interests out of the equation).

It is, according to my understanding, inexpedient to attempt to work out virtually a fully integrated and general plan for the national economy, covering all details of production and distribution in advance. Instead, a socialist planning procedure should involve the setting of plans in aggregate amounts via vertical links for the annual plan period. More adaptable agreements involving mainly horizontal links then disaggregate the annual plan into operational programmes of detailed quantities within the stipulated margins of the aggregate plan. Heal points out that the disadvantage of, as he calls it, such a non-*tâtonnement* procedure is that errors in the allocation of resources, once discovered, cannot simply be reversed.[34] Under such a scheme, the planning procedure begins by the planning authorities announcing a set of prices, allowing production units to adopt a detailed plan to carry out on the basis of these prices, and only adjusting the prices and quantities of output once imbalances or suboptimal linkages come to a fore in practice.[35] Productive assets would have already been committed in production in a particular way that might, in retrospect, turn out to have been suboptimal. When the objective function is centrally constructed by planning authorities then problems of uncertainty do not arise to the extent that it accurately reflects planner's preferences. However, given that we want social production to be influenced by actual and evolving household preferences as a measure of 'social usefulness', and since knowledge of future consumption schedules is at best probabilistic, the allocation of resources on the basis of a centrally constructed objective function in advance carries the substantial risk of actual consumption patterns gravitating away from the output schedule as incorporated into the objective function. On this account, two-level *tâtonnement* programming is unsuitable for a socialist project and the solution to the planning problem should be sought elsewhere.

---

34   Heal 1974, pp. 235–6.
35   Patnaik 2004, pp. 3–4.

At the beginning of the annual planning cycle, there are definite reserves of land, labour, energy, materials, and means of production available for production as well as an associated environmental cost attached to their use – the short-run resource and production constraints. The availability of resources will also vary according to the political priorities of the community, which influences the pricing of primary inputs. For example, restricting the rate of extraction of natural resources over ecological concerns will lower the supply of material inputs to the economy and a reduction of the average workday may restrict the supply of labour. The total resource availability and constraints are the 'initial conditions', as per Castoriadis. Within these constraints, each individual quantity of the total stock of productive resources will need to be committed in such a way that they generate the greatest benefit to society – the 'ultimate target'. As mentioned, each product is stamped with the total costs associated with the process of their production, so that producers can weigh and balance the use of different categories of labour, energy, production goods, and materials – the factor inputs – against one another when formulating a production plan for their plant, office, or workplace. The total set of prices for the next planning cycle are initially equal to the average across the previous (sub-)planning period, so they represent the closest and most recent approximation of the actual and relative costs involved.

Each year, all production co-operatives will need to submit an annual production plan to the general planning bureau. The plan announces the amount of labour, raw material, energy, and production goods they intend to use up in production in the aggregate, and correspondingly, also the genre and quantities of output they intend to produce. For each monthly or quarterly sub-period, these cost and output projections are to be disaggregated into exact production programmes, specifying their input requirements and detailed composition of output and their respective time profiles in order to render the plans operational and actionable. Each item also has connected to it their environmental cost. The cost matrix is further adjusted to incorporate the demand schedule of producers, since, for example, the price for energy and materials will be primarily determined by the amount of demand raised for them by productive associations and the price of productive assets will, in addition to the initial factor costs, also need to reflect their relative usefulness based on their employment – in other words, the 'capital charge' corresponding to the relative demand for production goods. The set of prices represents the recorded average costs of over a previous number of plan sub-periods and the anticipated costs for the upcoming period. Based on the updated set of accounting units, producers might need to make adjustments to their production plans so some timeframe should be permitted in which mutual adjustments are possible until a final plan is submitted. The planning bureau could supply 'real-time' updates of the moving average as indicative prices while fixing them at regular intervals to different accounting periods so that producers can know in advance approximately what the operational set of prices will be for the upcoming sub-period. Likewise, producers should communicate changes in their input-output schedule horizontally in advance so that suppliers and customers know to scale their operations accordingly, as reflected in their own revised plan proposals. To reiterate, in formulating these production plans the co-operatives have to observe a number of criteria that serve as the success indicators by which their performance can be evaluated along the metric of the social interest.

The success index of each production unit is composed of a number of individual performance indicators. The first two success indicators form a single scale, in effect – the Laibman reward function. They are the norms of the planned level of net product and the actualised level of output (or the degree of tautness) respectively. The first success indicator of net output encourages producers to set ambitious output targets relative to their consumption of inputs. This reveals the level of efficiency that producers propose can be obtained by them using some selection of society's stock of assets and materials. Since individual units of inputs can only be used in one exclusive capacity, they should be directed to those units of production that have submitted the most ambitious plans in terms of productivity. Since the norm of net output guides the choices of production co-operatives they have an interest in formulating and submitting a production plan that reduces costs and/or expands production.

The second component of the Laibman reward function, the 'norm of tautness' if you will, acts as check on strategic manipulation in the formulation of plans. It prevents producers from setting unrealistic cost reductions or output targets since both under-fulfilment and over-fulfilment in these areas would lower the achievement rating of producers. If producers announce their intention to expand production beyond what they could realistically manage, in order to secure the supply of scarce assets, they would be penalised when failing to achieve their own projections. In other words, the level of productivity that producers propose can be achieved by them will also have to be carried out in practice. Failing to do so will lower their score on the performance scale. Likewise, understating cost projections and subsequently overproducing would not accrue benefits to the producers. For instance, if the labour costs of an economic unit fall below the amount of labour they announced they would employ for the current period, or conversely, if units of labour have been used in excess of their own projections, their success rating is decreased proportionally to the degree of deviation and symmetrically in either direction (i.e. both under-fulfilment and over-fulfilment by equal margins). This mechanism provides producers with an interest in sharing their best and most accurate estimates of their potential productivities. Thus, by means of these institutional rules laid down by the central authority, the producers submit their own 'control figures' (to borrow another Soviet term) or target values representing their estimates of the optimal use of resources given the cost parameters supplied by the planning authorities. Thus, a feedback loop is established, in which the information of producers fed to the centre is aggregated, processed, updated and subsequently fed back to producers in the form of parameters for the use in the reformulation of their plans. This should by no means be a fully automated, algorithmically guided, decentralised control system, since while producers might freely use technical tools or optimisation programming, these purely quantitative tools can be overruled by their manual decision-making using qualitative judgements.

As 'secondary confirmation' of the social usefulness of the production plans, the output will have to be 'validated' by their consumption – there is not much utility in stockpiles of unused goods, however efficiently manufactured. To the extent that households acquire goods at given costs expressed in consumption prices, it serves as verification of the degree of social usefulness of productive efforts. Since the price of each unit of output is centrally fixed at their average costs of production, the producers will have to decrease or expand production until the output matches the anticipated level of consumer demand, evading either excess demand or excess supply (accounting for a margin of error). If stocks deplete at such rates that it cause shortages, it indicates that the social utility of output has been underestimated and more effort, energy, production goods, and materials should have been expended in their production. And conversely, excess of inventories indicates too many resources have been consumed in their production, and these could have been used more productively in some other capacity. Thus, the level of actual consumption at given prices for finished products serves as the validation criterion of the social benefit of productive activity.

Under a policy of central price determination, price competition is rendered impossible, nor would it be possible to increase profit margins by restricting production (as in capitalism) or profit per worker by restricting employment (as in market socialism); nor is there a disincentive for cost-inducement (as under Soviet-style socialism). Producers can only increase their success ratings by reducing costs or expanding production (i.e. by increasing their contribution to society's net product). Suppose for example that a production unit purposefully scales back production of means of consumption, to the extent that central planners prefer to raise clearing prices above their unit costs as a temporary measure to deal with shortages (compared to their preference for rationing scarce goods), the difference between baseline prices and clearing prices is not accrued as profit by the work collective. In fact, this would lower the total variable income of this economic unit, since other production units would be able to produce and clear more output relative to expenditures.

Still, all this requires some means of comparison to measure the 'ambitiousness' of respective plans. Since the ambition of a plan must stand in relation to the production possibilities of producers, which cannot be known by planners, only by workers' councils who might conceal this information, the planning authorities will thus have to find some way to discover the true potential of resources. Laibman has suggested that this measure of productivity may be set according to an industry norm or the historical performance of a given production unit.[36] The latter may be difficult since the composition of output may change over time as older products are substituted for newer ones that may vary in costs – in fact, significant efficiency gains may be obtained by producing newer, improved products rather than the same goods more efficiently. A new type of product may cost twice as much per unit of output to produce as its predecessor, but may also be three times as beneficial. Relying on tracking the change in the costs per unit of output over a period of time (say, a few years) would distort measurements. Deriving an industry norm from the average costs of production would be feasible only where it concerns the manufacturing of identical lines of products manufactured across various sites of production. Hence, if multiple manufacturers produce goods of the same type, society is able to compare the consumption of inputs across producers to set a benchmark of productivity as the industry norm. This presupposes that there are no monopolistic suppliers and manufacturers in the co-operative sector.

A further complication arises since producers at different sites of production face different technological constraints in the short run, for which they may only bear limited responsibility. The conditions of production, even where it concerns identical goods, may vary in such a way that workers are unfairly held to account for them. Society needs access to information about the most productive uses of resources in different capacities, but also of the approximate effort of different collectives, which cannot be gauged directly by the results of their activity given unequal circumstances. To remedy this issue, the planning authorities might assess the degree of relative advancement of co-operatives in comparative rankings of their particular branch of industry on a year to year basis. This should illuminate approximately which producers have put

---

36   Laibman 2015, p. 318.

in additional effort to improve their results given their initial conditions, and are encouraged to implement such improvements by having some amount of their bonus income tied to the change of position in the relative rankings. This would not produce the familiar 'ratchet effect' since the assessment is based on differences in relative performance which are not reset according to planning cycles or based on projections about production possibilities volunteered by producers – nor are relative rankings wholly responsible for additional income formation as part of the bonus system.

At this junction another related issue emerges. Hayek had pointed out, quite correctly, that Lange's planning procedure could not account for special orders, dealing with products with unique, custom-made specifications. To an extent this problem exists in market economies as well and it certainly applies when dealing with the normative planning mechanism sketched thus far. Customers, disadvantaged by asymmetrical knowledge, cannot gain reliable insight into whether the billed expenditures amount to actual expenditures. Similarly, when dealing with large infrastructural projects, a potential contractor may understate cost estimations to secure an agreement. Custom projects do not lend themselves to the mechanism discussed previously for the comparison of costs and productivity. This issue may be resolved by a sort of 'public tender'. Applicants may submit an indent for a product with the exact specifications to an industry planning office and producers may quote the amount of costs they expect to incur and the time schedule in which it can be realised. The applicant may select any offer and manufacturers would be rewarded for fulfilling the order. Since cost projections are less reliable when dealing with custom orders, producers cannot be held to the same standard of mass produced items. The margin for error should be more forgiving, while we can also speculate that over-fulfilment and under-fulfilment are to be *asymmetrically* penalised, skewed slightly in favour of over-fulfilment, but only up to a certain point. If both under-fulfilment and over-fulfilment are equally penalised, and the project can be finalised more quickly than initially projected or with a lower than anticipated labour expenditure, the supplier can bill additional, fictional labour costs to earn the fulfilment bonus in addition to earning compensation for fictitious work hours. There is no incentive to cut additional costs. Conversely, when 'over-fulfilment' is slightly favoured in the reward function, producers have an incentive to complete a custom order more quickly or at lower cost, if this proves possible. The incentive to initially overstate cost projects, in order to more easily over-fulfil their targets, is checked by potential customers being more likely to select the least costly bid with an appropriate time schedule. In either case, as a matter of public record, the degree of orders successfully completed within the margins for error – however specifically determined – can be tracked to provide some indication to customers of the reliability of different suppliers which might factor into their choice.

In sum, the task of the planning headquarters is to administratively determine the set of prices by fixing them to unit costs – the amount of production goods spread over a given period, and the amount of secondary inputs per unit of output. Price levels are the information mechanism that links the production plans to the harmonious macro-structure of the general plan, as opposed to the direct issuing of detailed targets to producers by the centre. The accounting prices, which are based on the costs of production and incorporate information about the relative scarcity of means of production, embody the necessary information for producers to know the extent to which, based on their particular knowledge, they can use resources in socially responsible ways. Thus, they operate independently within a parametric framework. Producers do not set prices, they determine costs and set quantities in relation to prices on the basis of the success indicators that link the interests and activity of producers to the general interest. It combines local knowledge and interests with centralised data about the broad social consequences associated with their choices, including the 'external' environmental costs associated with different production techniques and compositions of input. Based on this knowledge, workers' councils draw up a plan incorporating their best estimates of the potential uses of the various productive assets available to them, without outside intervention. Producers will evaluate their options and select from among them a programme they believe should yield a high value of their performance index. The production programme will need to (i) generate a high net output, minimising costs and maximising output; (ii) which is achievable under normal circumstances; (iii) and which can clear output without either excess demand or excess supply. All this should allow planners to assess the relative productivities of production goods used in different capacities and allocate use rights over them accordingly. Thus, in order to secure access to socially owned assets, production units will have to submit a realistic bid to use means of production efficiently. In this sense, productive resources are not rationed to producers directly according to the insights and priorities of the centre, but are guided in their allocation by the respective levels of productivity that different producers suggest can be obtained in accordance with the rules of the centre.

Since we assume that producers are, at least during the earlier stages of socialist development, motivated largely by their personal well-being, the success indices that together constitute the *performance index* double as the components of the 'bonus forming index' (BFI). This determines the amount of the total social dividend earmarked as bonus allowance for the 'material incentive fund' (MIF) of individual production co-operatives. In other words, a certain portion of income allocated to producers varies according to the value of this index. This amount should be low enough to immunise workers from substantial fluctuations in income (and most certainly from exposure to deprivation and economic insecurity), but high enough to act as effective stimulus for producers to supply both reliable data and adequate expenditures of effort in organising production above what moral incentives alone could achieve. Still, we depart from the assumption of a positive stimulus: workers are not threatened with the withholding of their basic means of life, the fear of unemployment and material poverty being absent. By ensuring that the success indicators and accounting prices stand in relation to macroeconomic objectives such as allocative efficiency, the results obtained by economic units at the local level translate directly to positive achievements in general welfare. By reinforcing positive contributions to society by compensating these efforts materially, the personal interests become aligned with the social interest, which also lays the groundwork for the gradual deepening of socialist attitudes and morale in society.

Before we proceed with our treatment of the planning procedures, we will depart on a small detour discussing in somewhat closer detail the meaning of prices (accounting units) and the 'moneyless' character of a co-operatively planned economy. The accounting units or administrative prices are non-monetary expressions weighing in numeric terms the relative importance implied by producing one unit of output compared to another, given the social costs and relative scarcities of the factors of production involved. By dissolving the use of heterogeneous qualities of materials, categories of labour, and means of production into a common, numeric unit of measurement it renders possible the comparisons of both the costs and results of economic activity. These accounting prices can be thought of as coefficients of the cost relations in the economy and therefore aid in the practice of socialist accounting. The set of prices are not derived from spontaneous market relations, and do not function as medium of exchange since no property rights over commodities are transferred. The *use rights* over productive assets allocated to units of production are conditional on the realisation of their socially rational plan of action, and can be withdrawn or redirected if they fail to use them productively. Hence, the numerical inputs in the universal accounting system are summaries of costs; a common, numerical denominator to render tractable comparisons of alternative uses of resources – i.e. 'production points' expressed as accounting units.

Each economic unit will have accounting statements with a certain numerical value. The primary balance, whose value is set in relation to the control figures, constant costs (e.g. the quantity of fixed assets in their care), and overall performance including the rate of return over a longer period; and a second-ary balance, which tracks the variable throughput of sub-periods. The activities of production co-operatives – the transformation of inputs into outputs, or throughput – are tracked by the universal logistics and accounting system, and checked against their control figures. This generates a score depending on the degree of success, and should also register separately as entries the use of inputs as costs and the supply of output as returns, which respectively deducts and adds points to the accounting balances. The amount of points earned by production co-operatives measures the quantity of goods they may order, given their 'liabilities' (the productivity they owe to society in return for being allowed to use fixed assets). While the equality of changes in input and output between units of productions and the changes in their accounting indexes will have to be observed to maintain the consistency of the structure of the economy, there is no direct exchange of currency; no money is being transferred among firms and customers, the accounting indexes of producers are adjusted by planning offices based on the flows and stocks of goods and assets and their social costs.

Similarly, the markups added on top of current costs are not turnover taxes that generate financial revenue which is subsequently funnelled into investment funds. Markups, by raising prices of the means of consumption relative to the size of the wage fund, decrease the volume of household consumption by a certain increment. This incremental amount should be equal to the quantity of productive resources necessary to expand productive capacity according to the politically established investment requirements – in other words, savings in household consumption obtained by the markup on finished products represent a quantity of resources equal to the total investment fund. The markups lower personal consumption and in turn free up a certain quantity of the total stock of productive assets which can now be employed in the service of manufacturing means of production instead of being devoted to procuring means of consumption. A 'fund', thus, is a reserve of resources earmarked for a particular purpose, instead of a sum of money.

The other end of this stick is the bundle of goods appropriated for personal consumption by households. Any society will face constraints – related to time, productive capacity, labour – in terms of the total amount of final products it can prepare for consumption. Since by producing one unit of output using a particular combination of factors, we forego on producing some other good, consumers will face trade-offs in relation to their choices for end products. We are therefore not so much interested in the level of consumer demand for goods in the absolute sense; as we are in the relative social wants for different potential combinations and categories of output. This implies that the limit of the total volume of household consumption is set by the amount of resources and their productivity that have been made available for the procurement of end products – although not its specific mix.

Since the composition of products consumed by each household varies according to their unique needs and preferences, and given the differential production costs of various items, it is necessary that consumers should make choices on the basis of these social costs compared to their hierarchy of wants and express their preferences by means of consumption within the constraints set by their individual household budgets. This allows for the assessing of the intensity of wants for different outputs based on their differential costs. Thus, given the social costs of producing one item and given what society gives up by producing this item instead of some other, consumers will need to validate this expenditure of resources by using some portion of their consumption allowance to acquire their preferred bundle of finished goods. The consumption allowance of individuals would consist of digital credits or budget points, which are used to appropriate a share of the total stock of consumption goods for themselves. The credits are cancelled after use instead of being transferred to the producer – no money changes hands. The data on the rate of consumption of products, however, is recorded as an entry in the universal accounting system, effectively generating process values. This, naturally, has a dual function. The point-based rating of the unit of production facilitates the allocation of resources (i.e. it determines and caps the consumption of factor inputs by production co-operatives); and determines the value of the BFI (according to the degree of correspondence between the target values and process values, which determines the amount of social dividends allocated to the MIF, and therefore determines in part the rate of household consumption).

The price mechanism in the Soviet economy was two-tiered, insulating retail prices from wholesale prices.[37] The prices of consumer goods bore no particular relationship to the relative scarcity of the means of production, which therefore precluded consumers from influencing the structure of final output by changing their consumption schedules. While this type of dual-track price mechanism produced imbalances in the industrial structure, a different sort of two-tier price system may have some value for a socialist economy still. The accounting price units assigned to means of production may be expressed in an altogether different numerical range than the accounting units assigned to means of consumption. As long as the 'transformation is monotonie', meaning 'the order of numbers expressing the degree of realiz-

---

37   Dobb 1967, p. 191; Wilczynski 1972a, p. 76.

ation of the objective is maintained. For instance, the degree of realization of the objective expressed by numbers: 1, 3, 7, 8 may be replaced by numbers 5, 6, 100, 258'.[38] The costs of means of consumption can be communicated to households using 'consumption prices', while costs of means of production may be expressed as 'production prices' to guide the allocation of resources. This underscores that we are not dealing with a monetary system, in which 'consumption credits' are transferred into the accounts of production co-operatives which they then can use to purchase additional inputs. The socialist economy may also introduce yet another set of prices: The planning authorities may attempt to isolate secular trends from contingent, short-run influences on price levels, and project future shadow prices to production units as part of indicative planning efforts – a triple-track price system, in other words.

Since the use of 'consumption points' by individuals acts as a mere measure for the confirmation of the social usefulness of output, and are non-transferable and nullified after use, their use by consumers *does not generate revenue* for the co-operatives. Producers are only scored points in accordance with their performance in relation to the parametric indicators, but no stream of income is generated that can be divided (among wages, profits, reinvestments, etc.) according to the business interests and acumen of the worker-managers. The point-based allocation of resources prevents workers from illicitly syphoning off earnings to supplement their personal incomes, since the numbers in the primary and secondary accounting balances are purely accounting entries, being numerical weights expressing the relative importance of inputs and outputs and factors of production. Nor should it generate a sense of entitlement over the returns of production co-operatives – a potential hangover of capitalist practices – since the focus is redirected away from individual earnings, and toward the success indicators that measure more directly the contribution of producers to the total social product. Thus, the individual achievement rating of an economic unit measures the degree to which they contributed successfully to the collective welfare of their community; and does not reflect their individual earnings in isolation of wider social implications. This should reinforce the perception that their individual performance equals, and therefore also should be regarded as, their individual contribution to a collective process of wealth production.

---

38   Lange 1971, p. 53.

3   Co-ordination, Investment, Uncertainty

We have thus far outlined the basic features of a parametric control mechanism (cybernetics, in a word),[39] which involves the setting of norms and benchmarks to monitor and compare the recorded activity of local units against their control figures. Having gotten the issue of the role of non-monetary pricing, or accounting prices, in socialist production and distribution out of the way we can return to our discussion of the co-ordination of production in a socialised economy. The primary advantage of socialist economic planning over its alternatives, aside from achievements in the area of social justice, lies in managing future uncertainties by means of the planned co-ordination of economic activity. Since we want economic planning to be compatible with the operation of material incentives at the decentralised level, it is necessary to effect the distribution of economic functions across units of production by means of a parametric framework. Socialist models that propose such a form of parametric control have been criticised for neglecting the social or political dimension in the planning procedure.[40] For example, in the Hahnel-Albert procedure, participation in planning is restricted to workers' councils approving those plan proposals with a higher social benefit to social cost ratio. This is effectively a technical process with little room (or need) for conscious control by the political community. To the extent that planning protocols rely on parametric control, deliberation – which is key in the development of socialist consciousness and active citizenship – is removed from the process. This raises the question whether control mechanisms can encourage co-operative planning among producers, since producers would only respond 'atomistically' to externally given parametric signals in the form of centrally determined accounting prices and performance indicators. Producers could simply submit

---

39   The term 'cybernetics' has acquired futuristic-utopian overtones in socialist circles. Much like the term 'democratic planning', it is often deployed to conceal an absence of elaborate theorisation. Perhaps part of this lack of conceptual clarity is owed to the field of Soviet cybernetics itself, which saw a proliferation of cybernetic phraseology – 'cyberspeak' – pervading all areas of science, from biology, information and communication theory, to linguistics, sociology, and economics without a formal or clearly demarcated definition (see Gerovitch 2002). Far from science fiction, it merely means so much as the regulation of complex, interdependent activities by systemic control through the compilation and transmission of data (see Maiminas 1979). It involves the circulation of information to enable the monitoring of actual activity or trends – which can be expressed numerically as the process value – compared to some normative value often referred to as the set-point, while a controller relies on the back-and-forth flows of data (feedback) to steer the process in the direction of the desired value.

40   Heyer 2022.

their plans in reference to the central framework without relying on horizontal deliberation to achieve a convergence of aims and without any reshaping of interests among producers taking place. At the same time, as noted, independence at the decentralised level is critical to allow material incentives to produce their intended effects. Hence, here we expand on the ways in which the parameters and proportions of general planning effect co-ordination and deal with future uncertainty.

Co-operative planning by means of parametric control would involve 'ex ante' co-ordination and 'ex post' verification. The production norms induce producers to formulate and share, in advance, their plans for the upcoming annual period and sub-periods. The plans are subsequently confirmed, or 'validated', by their actual implementation by recording the degree to which production projections have been realised and output has been cleared. The parametric accounting units and indicators form the basic ingredients for the co-ordination of productive activities among economic units without relying on market competition. This should achieve two outcomes. First, it creates the information infrastructure necessary for a type of deliberate co-ordination to chart the complementary activities of producers in advance, owing to the clearance and tautness norms. Production units will have to communicate and share their best estimates amongst each other, helping each independent economic unit to perform better in turn. By communicating their input requirements and output targets, producers will restructure their respective activities into a set of compatible production plans which are subsequently implemented in practice. Since co-operation, by sharing and aggregating data and levelling risk through social insurance, forms the best bet for producers to achieve a satisfactory performance rating for their productive achievements, the system of material incentives should reinforce an ethos of reciprocity. It is both in the self-interest of producers and to their mutual benefit to submit and circulate reliable data.

Second, the norm of net output creates an incentive that encourages producers to use resources economically. Since the benchmark of productivity is established by comparing the level of efficiency attained by units of production, we can speak of a form of 'socialist emulation' (or 'socialist competition').[41] Not only will workers' councils need to formulate plans that are realist-

---

41   A Soviet term derived from Lenin (see e.g. Deutscher 1952 for a brief discussion), who argued in 1918 that:

'Every factory, every village is a producers' and consumers' commune, whose right and duty it is to apply the general Soviet laws in their own way (...). Model communes must and will serve as educators, teachers, helping to raise the backward communes. The press must

ically achievable – which therefore also stimulates horizontal co-operation – they will also have to submit a plan that strives to operate around, and preferably, above the average level of efficiency in their industry – or the emulation norm. Producers will thus be incentivised to communicate openly about upcoming adjustments in their standard output, even in advance of the formal submission deadline, so that the respective choices of producers are structured into consistent and achievable input-output programmes; but also to strive toward an efficient use of resources according to the benchmark which defines the average level of productivity to be emulated, driving down the consumption of resources. In other words, economic units will co-operate directly in terms of formulating a set of consistent production plans and compete in terms of their level of efficiency based on the emulation norm of their industry. Thus, there is no reason to suppose that parametric control inhibits direct co-operation among different units of production, nor that this would result in collusion.

To help illustrate how co-operative planning in reference to the central guidelines and criteria of the framework will deal with uncertainty, we will proceed with a concise overview of the process of current planning. The first step of the annual planning cycle involves production co-operatives synchronously submitting an annual production plan in aggregate terms for the entire year and the detailed input requirements and output mix for the forthcoming sub-period (their monthly production programme). The plans are submitted to the appropriate office of the general planning bureau and are subsequently promulgated for public scrutiny. The plan proposals in aggregate and disaggregated terms become the 'control figures' by which planning authorities monitor performance – in effect, 'self-planning'. Both central planners and production co-operatives in this way gain immediate insight into the broader trends affecting their sector and along the supply chains on account of the aggregated plans, as well as into the immediate requirements for the upcoming period on the basis of the disaggregated detailed plans. For example, central planners might gain insight into the magnitudes of labour that producers plan to use in relation to the aggregate supply of labour; or of the

---

serve as an instrument of socialist construction, give publicity to the successes achieved by the model communes (...) and, on the other hand, must put on the "black list" those communes which persist in the "traditions of capitalism", i.e., anarchy, laziness, disorder and profiteering' (Lenin 1918).

Evidently, this left enormous scope for determining the basis for judging the activity of some to be 'profiteering' or 'successes' by relying on qualitative or arbitrary evaluations that varied freely according to the interpretation and discretion of public officials.

sum-total of investment plans compared to the size of the central investment fund, given the macroeconomic proportions of the general plan.

The aggregate, annual plans entail the projected costs and output levels for each economic unit. Production units announce the overall amount of labour, energy, quantity of production goods, and material inputs they intend to use up over the course of the plan year to obtain a certain quantity of output. These proportions are their overall input-output norms, the aggregate control figures. It gauges their overall level of productivity, based on the ratio of total output (social benefit) to resource consumption (social costs) under the assumption that their output will meet demand levels more or less precisely. The coarse, aggregate categories of input and output are subsequently disaggregated into details production programmes for each sub-period. The sum-total of input and output for all monthly detailed plans cannot exceed their annual control figures. The detailed plans include the specific input requirements and the specific output mix that producers intend to fabricate during this period. These programmes will reflect reasonably accurate projections of the best use of resources, since producers will draw on their qualitative and quantitative knowledge – their experience, their technical knowledge, and knowledge of local circumstances and evolving consumer wants – to propose a plan that is comparatively more rather than less productive compared to the industry-level emulation norm. By submitting and aggregating the various plans, the particular investment and production choices of economic units become available against broader trends and developments, allowing co-operatives to revise their plans in light of the proposals of other units. If producers anticipate an increase in the demand for a certain type of finished product, for example, the manufacturers of final products will need to scale up their production accordingly and announce a corresponding increase in their input requirements to their suppliers. The same adjustments will need to be made along the entire supply chain, naturally. This should achieve a convergence of aims among producers and of their input-output schedules.

Producers in the same branch of industry possess a shared interest in circulating accurate projections of their own standard output levels that they estimate is necessary to satiate the estimated level of demand. The failure of one unit of production in accurately scaling their activity will negatively impact other productive facilities, reinforcing the need for horizontal co-ordination among producers. Rather than compete for the largest market share (which does not raise income for producers), production units will need to co-operate by sharing their best estimates of supply and demand, allowing other units to draw on the knowledge and projections of all others. By pooling data and maintaining open lines of communication to deliberate, negotiate, and co-ordinate how each independent economic unit should contribute their part to adjust the structure of production within their branch of industry in accordance with modifications in the demand schedule, they enable one another to perform to the best of their abilities. This convergence of interests is assured by rewarding production units for clearing their stock of goods rather than for the volume of sales or profit margins per sale; as well as by the incentive function that promotes the dissemination of reasonably reliable estimates of input requirements and levels of output. This planning procedure, then, should generate a set of internally consistent production plans that simultaneously reflect an efficient allocation and use of resources.

This community of interest among producers may be institutionalised as a federation of production co-operatives. This would include producers operating in the same branch of industry, their suppliers, and a planning office that aggregates and circulates production programmes and cost and output projections denoted in accounting prices. This would be a secondary co-operative, facilitating the transmission and pooling of data to help in the mutual coordination of the setting of output targets and joint expansion or contraction of respective operations in which they share an interest. They would deliberate where and how best to scale production up or down to reflect evolving levels of demand in a way that conforms to their overall interests. This would by and large eliminate the duplication of efforts in the gathering and dissemination of information, parallel development of new technologies, and of rival investments. In this capacity, co-operatives may compile the consumption and online behaviour of consumers and feed this information into predictive algorithms that could potentially become more effective than qualitative knowledge.[42] Thus, 'big data, the producer and discoverer of so much new knowledge, could one day facilitate what Hayek thought only markets are capable of'.[43] Machine learning might aid in the management of increased demand volatility, which is itself brought on by technological advances. However, as Grünberg points out, we should not be overly confident in the predictive capabilities of algorithms, as future developments will always contain a factor of uncertainty and the qualitative knowledge of producers may be needed to overrule automated, algorithmic forecasting techniques for at least the foreseeable future.[44]

It should further be stressed that industrial syndicates or federations – secondary co-operatives – of individual producers are not *and absolutely should not be* democratic bodies that may overrule the individual choices of member

42   Morozov 2019.
43   Phillips and Rozworski 2019.
44   Grünberg 2023.

co-operatives by majority vote. The primary co-operatives will need to retain full discretion in their decision-making, but since all producers also share a common interest in co-ordinating their respective plans as a consequence of the system of norms and controls, it is in their own interest to form themselves into distribution co-operatives to set compatible output targets along the entire length of their supply chain.

Here a crucial point of tension emerges. As noted, it is important that production co-operatives can be held to account for their production plans and the subsequent implementation thereof. However, production units are never independent in the absolute meaning of the word. Each co-operative relies on the timely delivery of products that meet the required quality by other co-operatives to implement their production programme in practice. If a supplier fails to deliver the agreed upon material to manufacturers, the latter can no longer continue producing in accordance with the control figures contained in their production plan. While such a one-sided supply failure or unilateral contractual breach may lead to the temporary suspension of performance tracking of the affected parties by planning offices, the effects of this supply breakdown may ripple outward. For example, consumers may turn to other producers that have not suffered supply issues who are then faced with an unexpected upswing in demand causing their supply to deplete much quicker than anticipated. The entire logistical chain linking suppliers, manufacturers, and consumers is interdependent in this sense.

Since the detailed production programmes of production co-operatives will contain randomly distributed miscalculations, these errors might cancel each other out in the aggregate by stochastic convergence so that a deficit of one input for a production unit might be compensated by the surplus of the same input of another production unit. Such minor discrepancies between supply and demand across units of production could be smoothed over by the distribution of inventory surpluses on the basis of an expectation of reciprocity. Nevertheless, production co-operatives also have – occasional errors notwithstanding – a responsibility to vet potential suppliers for reliability and to map industry risks, such as possibilities related to the temporary or definite ceasing of operations by another co-operative. Based on continual feedback and open lines of communication, combined with cumulative experience in these matters, production units should assess the risk of supply chain disruptions. Still, unforeseen circumstances – incidental delays, delivery issues, swings in demand – will inevitably arise and socialism will have to deal with them adequately.

The production programmes should be fully detailed and itemised if they are to form the basis for robust planning and the reliable premise for productive activity. This level of detail introduces some issues as they relate to future uncertainty – particularly due to the changes in demand, since co-ordination failures of investments is much diminished, if not entirely removed, due to the 'ex ante' planning process. The exact production schedule cannot be known in advance for the entire annual plan cycle, so that producers will need to make adjustments from sub-period to sub-period in the use of their input and the manufacturing of their output. The costs of using fixed assets are constant for, say, an annual period, compared to the variable costs of using quantities of materials that vary from period to period. These non-linearities arguably make the formulation of an input-output schedule more liable to mistakes, since every monthly production plan will have to be manually adjusted for every item. The short-run uncertainty manifests in two ways: producers may fail to enter the correct inputs, accidentally omitting some product; or the anticipated level of demand deviates from the actual rate of consumption and away from the standard output level. Entry mistakes, miscalculations, poor planning, delivery issues, accidents, breakage, and the volatility of demand may each play a part in causing output to deviate from actual demand. Producers are not equally liable for all these conditions and therefore some lenience should be permitted. This is the acceptable margin of error.

Since each production unit is exposed to an amount of risk, there also emerges a shared interest in levelling this risk among production units by means of social insurance. The incidental failure of one production co-operative in acquiring the necessary input may be compensated by redirecting some amount of reserves from other production units as compensation, circulating inventory surpluses among producers that face shortages in the knowledge that this is a mutual expectation. This reciprocity, which may need to be formalised by mutual agreements, naturally only works in the event of incidental supply chain disruptions, as structural negligence in achieving plan targets due to mismanagement will lead to a breakdown of solidarity toward the poorly governed production co-operative. The number of times a production unit may invoke the assistance of other producers may therefore have to be capped by some fixed number per annum.

Workers' councils should be aware of and calculate the risks of their branch of industry. Thus, suppliers and manufacturers will have an interest in maintaining a degree of reserve capacity to collectively absorb unexpected upswings in demand. Naturally, the control norms will need to accommodate such flexibility by allowing for adjustments within stipulated margins, so that some deviations from planned output or capacity utilisation are permitted. The production plans will therefore need to allow for some slack to maintain the overall adaptability of the system to unforeseen changes, as overly taut planning would stifle the flexible conduct of producers and in turn inhibit the effects of material incentives. It is likely expedient, then, for producers to maintain some percentage of excess capacity and concurrently, the planning norms should allow deviation of planned proportions by some percentage, although not by very much. This applies more generally. For instance, production units might experience unexpected breakdowns of equipment, and ordering replacement parts might need to be expedited. The malfunction of some piece of machinery may force producers to suspend their operations, and if this interruption of production is drawn-out because they had – logically – not foreseen technical impairment and therefore have not pre-ordered it in their monthly programme, it may put their performance ratings below their annual control figures. They would lose any interest in operating efficiently during the plan year beyond that point.

To accommodate such misfortunes, and also errors (which have to be subjected to identical treatment since the central authorities cannot be overloaded with audits to distinguish mistakes from malice, and malice from misfortune), we can imagine that it is necessary that each producers are permitted to deviate from their monthly programme by some percentage, and, moreover, underperformance in one period can be wiped from their record by a better than average performance in the next period – perhaps within margins of error divided between quarterly periods. This thus permits producers to order and receive some part of machinery or raw material or whatever else they failed to include in their programme, which they can carry over to their next monthly accounting period – they would have to order fewer quantities to compensate for their over-consumption of resources in the previous period. It also implies that production co-operatives should be permitted to maintain some degree of surplus capacity to deal with demand uncertainty, and to enable upward revisions from their standard output by some margin. Suppliers of inputs (semi-finished products, raw materials, or equipment) may know from experience that on average, say, seven percent of orders will be non-planned indents and determine their standard output accordingly – although this level may also vary across periods so they will find it appropriate to maintain slack in the rate of their capacity utilisation. Hence, some unplanned adjustments are possible from month to month within quarterly periods, provided the sum of adjustments measured in quantities of accounting prices, fall within the margins of the annual input-output norms. Similarly, the failure to meet the clearance norm in one accounting period may be stricken from their record provided they perform well throughout a fixed number of subsequent sub-periods. Lastly, it should be possible for producers to revise the *aggregate* proportions of their current plan once annually, to make up for an initial lapse in judgement or to accommodate unexpected, prolonged changes in the structure of the economy. These built-in margins for errors would ensure that producers are supplied an incentive to retain their interest in improving their performance rather than resign in response to some initial failure by punishing them for honest mistakes or incidental mishaps.

The co-ordination of investments may be approached in similar fashion. Investment, if we recall, can be disaggregated into replacement, minor, and major investments. Small-scale investment choices are subject to the sole discretion of individual production units. The workers' councils are free to determine the quantity and grade of inputs to replenish what they have used up previously, and may choose to scale their operations according to their expectations of the future structure of demand – provided that the social costs of doing so do not exceed the social usefulness of their output. The amount by which they may scale the size of their activity upwards should be capped by some combination of their control figures, their previous rate of return, and the overall investment requirements related to the macroeconomic proportions of the central plan.

Producers will have to respond to changes in future demand by adjusting their productive capacity. Due to the evolving patterns of consumption, the demand for some line of product may fall over time and level of output of this good can be whittled down accordingly. This would not present much difficulty. Producers would have to release part of their labour or production goods. The expected increase in demand for certain output may, however, exceed the current level of productive capacity and therefore calls for the expansion of the size or amount of productive facilities, or both. This cannot be referred to some intermediate planning body, which will, by democratic vote or otherwise, dictate which facilities should be expanded and where new plants might be sited, since this would erase the delineations of responsibilities. However, while bearing sole responsibility for their choices in relation to changes in the demand schedule, producers will be wise to the fact that the outcome of their separate, individual efforts depends on the choices made by other units of production. If producers fail to communicate and co-ordinate their plans to expand capacity or output, there is a substantial chance of a cumulative excess of demand along the width of their industry. There is thus a common interest among production co-operatives in devising a way to absorb a growth of demand. They might for example elect to expand the productive capacity of each facility by equal amounts, so that the expansion costs are spread among the production units.

Each draft investment plan is communicated to all production co-operatives by means of the joint workers' council of the distribution co-operative, where they might further deliberate on these matters. In doing so, some production units might find that their planned level of investment is excessive when compared to the investment choices of other producers, since their combined investment for the expansion of capacity and output would over-saturate the level of demand, for example. In response to this information they would have to scale back the ambitiousness of their initial investment proposal. The co-ordination of production and investment decisions of this type is not achieved indirectly, via market relations, but directly, by deliberation among representatives of primary co-operatives, institutionally encouraged to do so according to the 'rules' laid down by the central planning authority. It is in the self-interest of each association of producers to share their plans and to mutually adjust them according to the information pooled at the level of the industrial syndicate, without modifying them by democratic means. Put differently, it is in the individual interest of production co-operatives to collaborate in terms of setting their levels of output and co-ordinate their investments, while the emulation norm and central price-fixing check against their collusion. But suppose that a rogue production co-operative unilaterally decides to expand their operations to absorb most of a sustained increase in effective demand. This in itself does not grow the income of the workers employed there, since a larger market share is not an indicator of success under the central framework. Each production unit would still be rewarded proportionally to the degree that they clear their inventories of output (at the realised level of efficiency and according to projections).[45] There would not be any competitive market pressures to shape the behaviour of producers. Instead, their best bet to perform well at an individual level would be to co-operatively contribute to the collective success of their

---

45   This only holds when we assume constant returns to scale. In reality, non-constant rates of return would cause different sizes of production to influence the respective levels of efficiency, and therefore success. In industries with increasing returns to scale, production units will want to absorb any increase in demand at the expense of other production units since it implies that production can be expanded while input requirements do not grow by the same proportion, yielding a higher net output. Under such circumstances, the industrial federation will need to facilitate the equal expansion of productive capacity between production units, but it cannot mandate any unit to do so. Still, unilaterally choosing to expand productive capacity by large amounts to force an advantage would need to be counter-acted by the rest of the production units choosing among themselves to grow their capacity modestly, to undercut the efforts to 'monopolise' the growth of their industry and force their rival's hand to trim their expansionary plans. Since increasing returns to scale are usually observed in industries with high concentrations of capital goods – power-plants, ports, telecommunication – potential issues related to the competitive expansion of capacity might be addressed by placing these production facilities under the auspices of public officials in the collective sector.

sector. While it is not mandated by political authorities directly, the system of controls encourages producers to come to some mutually beneficial agreement.

Maintaining some measure of slack in capacity utilisation, mentioned previously, related to the short-run disequilibria in planned output, but the same reasoning applies in more force to the long-run; where it concerns dealing with adjustments in productive capacity. Since future demand is uncertain, high amounts of holding costs of surplus capacity might inhibit producers in expanding their operations. This is especially true for capital-intensive branches of production such as heavy industry and for industrial equipment with substantial longevity and long recoupment periods. Consequently, the cost parameters should be balanced in such a way that, generally speaking, shortage costs are larger penalties in the performance index of producers compared to capacity holding costs in order to encourage producers to meet the overall investment requirements of the central plan. However, incidental and small discrepancies of supply and demand in the short-run may come down to misfortune rather than poor planning and it would be unfair to penalise production co-operatives over small deviations of the rate of consumption from planned output. Likewise, in the long-run, the expansion of productive capacity hinges on estimates on the basis of uncertain demand forecasting. Thus, beyond a certain threshold, the shortage costs associated with the clearance index should slope upward more steeply compared to the holding costs of spare industrial capacity, so that the loss of variable income from substantial shortages is larger than maintaining a level of idle capacity. Producers need to be allowed to maintain a certain amount of reserve capacity to absorb unexpected upturns of demand, but should not be permitted to use productive assets wastefully. This hinges on the parameters of the emulation norm. If more variable inputs could have been used in proportion to fixed costs in order to increase the level of production, producers apparently maintain a level of excess capacity. To allow producers to use the strategic device of purposefully reserving some capacity to deal with unanticipated increases in demand, deviations around the average norm of productivity – the emulation benchmark – will have to be permitted. This should deter postponement of investments since the risk associated with future shortages, beyond small discrepancies and within the acceptable margin for error, would grow more rapidly than the risk of some measure of excess capacity in relation to the emulation norm. At the same time, this does not afford producers *carte blanche* to increase their consumption of resources wantonly – and on the other end, the level of aggregate demand determined by the macroeconomic proportions can be used as an instrument to push up capacity utilisation if there is an overall decline in this rate (in addition, a higher level of tolerance for shortages reflected in the performance parameters may affect capacity utilisation, but frequent adjustments in the proportions of the parameters would increase regulatory uncertainty and therefore shorten the investment horizon of producers). This implies a trade-off between the total loss of variable income from large shortages and across successive accounting periods compared to the partial loss of variable income posed by the risk of maintaining a slightly higher than average excess capacity in their industry. The acceptable degree of variation in the rate of capacity utilisation on the basis of the slackness/tautness of norms may also have to vary according to the concentration of means of production in different sectors of industry, since industries with a high capital-intensity are less able to adjust the quantity of fixed assets in their care even in the long-run. Further, the initial costs of large investments should, naturally, not count toward a single accounting period but spread out over the amount of periods estimated to be necessary for the recoupment of the original investment so that sizeable investments do not unfairly disadvantage producers in terms of their recorded consumption of resources and concomitant rate of productivity relative to the emulation norm on a yearly basis.

A further issue presents itself where the expansion of industrial capacity cannot be absorbed by increasing the size of existing facilities. Under such circumstances, the workers' councils of primary co-operatives will have an interest in siting new units of production due to the shortage costs associated with the parameter of excess demand. While existing production co-operatives do possess a vested interest in setting up new production units, so that sectors would always grow and contract by facilitating the entry or exit of co-operatives according to the changing conditions of industry, they would have no particular interest in setting up well-functioning ones. To the extent that new productive establishments contribute to the total output necessary to satiate the level of actual demand, they serve their purpose for the older line of facilities. However, to the extent that new facility produces output at competitive levels of productivity, they potentially harm the achievement ratings of the older units of production. New production units founded at the initiative of the older ones may therefore be set up in such a way that they face needless liabilities or technological constraints that will need to be overcome by the work collective of the new plant. This dilemma was faced by Yugoslavia's market socialism:

> Under capitalism, a mistake in the original investment is reflected in a fall in the value of risk capital so that anybody taking over later will start afresh because he can buy the enterprise at an adjusted price; under self-management workers take over at the book-keeping value, or at some

value which has little to do with the prospect of the enterprise, but is bureaucratically determined. This saddles them with the responsibility for the original decision in which they have not participated and for which they cannot possibly be held responsible.[46]

To remedy this tendency, new production units would need to be founded as joint ventures of the co-operative federation of its branch of industry. (Alternatively, new industrial establishments may be founded by a prospective association submitting a bid for the use of productive resources.) For a definite period lasting perhaps a number of years or so, the members of the federation would share responsibility for their performance by partially tying the achievement ratings of the new unit of production to the ratings of the older associations. If the new association operates inefficiently, it would decrease the size variable portion of the material incentive fund of the earlier generation of producers. They therefore have a direct stake in creating conditions conducive to a good performance for the new association. By making this the shared responsibility of the co-operative federation it also prevents free-riding – this is the only area where responsibility is shared directly, and the authorities will have to insist that responsibility is shared under the given compromise. Certain production units may otherwise wish to abstain from founding new production units, since it is a risk-bearing operation from which they would benefit regardless of their involvement.

Thus, the socialist planned economy can employ a number of instruments to deal with the inherent uncertainty of medium-term developments and their implications – from one (sub-)planning cycle to the next. This need arises from the premise that we want producers to conduct themselves in the interests of general welfare, while not unfairly disadvantaging producers for not instantaneously adjusting their activity to unforeseeable changes. Before addressing how the socialist regime can get producers to care for the long-term developments of their facility, across a time period of a number of years we will first turn to discussing the structure of material incentives for labour.

4   Labour Incentives

It is the stock of labour-power by means of which society maintains their wellbeing. It forms the active ingredient that purposively combines, by physical and

---

46   Sirc 1979, p. 242.

mental force, materials with means of production to reproduce society's material wealth. The units of labour-power available to society will have to be distributed among the various divisions of production in such a way that society can improve its collective welfare. As mentioned previously, macroeconomic policies should be in place that allow for the full utilisation of labour-power in society. This means that the labour input requirements for the satisfaction of aggregate demand should equal the total supply of labour-power, thus ensuring the full employment of labour – to the extent that macroeconomic proportions have been miscalibrated, job guarantee policies should be in place. Society will further need to level the supply of concrete forms of labour to a definite amount of consumer demand arising out of the scale of social preferences; and encourage workers to behave productively. Labour-power is not however an object upon which the forces of production can exert themselves to shape it according to some will. The reallocation of labour-power from one purpose to another and the promotion of productivity requires somewhat more social ingenuity. To structure the individual productive efforts of workers to align with one social purpose or another requires a complex scheme of material incentives.

We have thus far sketched the outlines of an income policy where personal income is derived from supplying labour to the community, intermediated by joining an association of producers. Meeting this condition is rewarded by being allocated a basic level of fixed income in proportion to the amount of hours worked, which should be sufficient to satisfy immediate needs and wants. A smaller portion of income depends on sharing unbiased estimates of productivity as well as contributing relatively more productive effort to the collective wealth of society. This level of variable income is composed of the differential social dividends distributed to workers according to the value of the BFI of primary co-operatives. Some discussion is still further required to deal with the differentiation of income according to personal qualities and effort. Marx, for example, argued that the distribution of income would, in the initial phase of communist development, be determined by the contribution of producers calculated in hours of labour time.[47] Cockshott and Cottrell suggest that this has the benefit of what may be considered an industrial-day 'levelling mechanism':

> If accounting is done in terms of labour time, then the fraud of professional differentials becomes a little too transparent. Why should a secret-

---

47   MECW 26: 86.

ary get paid only 30 minutes for each hour that she works, whilst professionals in the next office get paid 2 hours for each hour they put in?[48]

An egalitarian income policy is certainly a worthy ambition from a socialist standpoint, but it may not be the most effective in motivating workers to improve their efforts, apply themselves productively, and work conscientiously for the benefit of society, especially where it concerns the first stages of socialist development. Albert and Hahnel believe that rewarding people equally for their productivity is unfair, since it gives advantages to those with superior physical or mental faculties.[49] Marx too was well aware of the inequality implied by equal remuneration, since 'one man is superior to another physically or mentally and so supplies more labour in the same time, or can work for a longer time'.[50] Albert and Hahnel argue that workers should be randomly drafted to evaluate various work tasks according to their intensity, desirability, and so on, in order to score individual labour contributions according to 'effort' and 'sacrifice'.[51] This has some historical precedent. In the people's communes of China, work points were usually assigned on the basis of work rate, tasks, dedication, intensity, and other such norms.[52] While it took into account such varied factors, its drawback was the 'difficulty, if not impossibility, of setting rational norms for so many pieces of work and moreover, of assessing the quality of completed work'.[53] Such difficulty also existed in other socialist countries such as Cuba[54] and the Soviet Union, which both saw an enormous proliferation of largely arbitrary, inconsistent labour norms and chronometric supervision, tied to sanctions and piece rate income. In at least one large Soviet factory, the 'rhythms of production' were guided by a whopping 'thirty-five thousand norms'.[55] Indeed, workers drafted to evaluate work tasks, in the Hahnel-Albert model, will similarly have limited knowledge of many tasks they would be expected to assess, and will therefore produce arbitrary valuations. In other words, their proposal does not fix arbitrariness compared to equal hourly remuneration, but it may be less technically feasible, or at least, more burdensome to carry out.

---

48   Cockshott and Cottrell 1993, p. 38.
49   Albert 2003, p. 36; Albert and Hahnel 1991, p. 42.
50   MECW 26: 86.
51   Albert and Hahnel 1991, p. 42; Hahnel 2005, p. 190; Hahnel 2021.
52   Ahn 1975, p. 647.
53   Ibid.
54   See e.g. Mesa-Lago 2019.
55   Beissinger 1998, p. 134.

Cockshott and Cottrell speculate that it may be necessary to introduce three income categories within workplaces to promote productivity,[56] as had also been practised in some people's communes of China. Indeed, the 'main weakness' of this approach 'was the difficulty of classifying each peasant into one of three grades since each member's performance varied with the specific conditions and types of jobs he performed'.[57] Similarly, Hahnel suggests that the workers' councils may themselves determine how to distribute income among their members, capped by the collective effort rating of their workplace determined by the social benefit to social cost ratio achieved in the previous year.[58] Production units, he suggests, could decide to introduce three income categories and categorise workers according to their respective effort and sacrifice, provided that the total income allocated to producers observes the limits of their collective effort rating. The sum-total of wage bills of all units of production should obviously be capped by the total size of the total wage fund, which is set in relation to the investment fund, otherwise the level of aggregate demand would exceed the constraints of production. The individual members of the production co-operatives would be placed somewhere along the minimum and maximum income scales according to some structure of categories that the workers' council judges to provide the most effective stimulus for their members to work responsibly and productively.

Although it is not possible to quantify the exact contribution and effort – taking into account differential qualities – of different workers, it may be necessary to promote productivity in this way, in spite of arbitrary boundaries that will have to be drawn between different categories of income. This is so since slackers can erode the group cohesion requisite for solidarity, which is unconducive both to the sustainability of republicanism in the workplace and individual productivity. Of course, whenever moral incentives suffice to motivate workers to contribute productively to the goals of the production unit, the workers' councils are free to adopt an egalitarian income policy. However, whenever the overall effect of slackers shirking responsibilities proves larger than the benefits gained from the equalisation of income, the workers' councils may choose to divide workers into different income categories according to their level of responsibility or productive effort.

Laibman proposes that the variable income of an association can be further influenced by including solidarity, community, or ecology measures in the reward function. The achievements of the enterprises in these fields would

---

56   Cockshott and Cottrell 1993, p. 32.
57   Ahn 1975, p. 647.
58   Hahnel 2021.

be rated by relevant institutions, which would be no more arbitrary than academic grading.[59] However, since access to bonuses is a zero-sum game, insofar as the overall variable incentive fund will be fixed by a certain amount to prevent macroeconomic imbalances, socialist society would do well to be cautious in encouraging non-productive social activity by complicating the structure of incentive schemes further. 'Maoist' China again furnishes a factual example to shed light on this issue. The Dazhai brigades in the 1960s and 1970s used a third variant of labour norm remuneration, attempting to de-emphasise an acquisitive morale. Political attitude and activism became important measures of work points allotments to individual peasants and workers, to the detriment of labour productivity.[60] If the portion of income derived from participating in socially conscious extra-productive activity grows at the expense of income derived from solid planning and implementation, it might reduce the motivation to use productive assets efficiently.

A potential source of injustice in dividing workers into different pay scales is that they might be moved from one scale to another on a whim by majority vote. This should be mitigated in a number of ways. First, the lowest rate of income should be enough to cover basic amenities, to prevent workers becoming dependent on the arbitrary will of others by being deprived of the basic material means of life. Second, income should be fixed on the basis of stable professional grading, experience, and competency profiles, rather than fluctuate on the basis of bargaining power between individual workers and the workers' council. Hence, income should be anchored to income categories that are fixed, and income differentiation within these categories should be based on robust evaluative protocols and work experience.

Under socialism, the more or less equally distributed 'wages' of producers represent a reimbursement for the effort and time they invested in collective production – these 'wages' are individual shares in the total social product, differentiated according to individual mixes of achievement ratings. The purpose of wages is not to facilitate the apportioning of labour to different productive ends. The structure of income may not align with the structure of demand for labour, therefore. The question thus emerges whether this would result in substantial imbalances in the supply of and demand for labour-power. Cockshott and Cottrell suggest that:

> In a socialist economy, too, there may well emerge shortages of specific skills relative to the demands of society, and there has to be a mechan-

---

59   Laibman 2015, p. 321.
60   Ahn 1975, p. 647.

ism for enlarging supply. Within a socialised system of education and training and labour allocation it should be easier to project and advertise potential shortages, and to induce recruits into the needed specialisms with the promise of greater choice of work project if they pursue the targeted careers. If this did not ensure adequate numbers of people entering the trade or profession then either direction of labour or the payment of 'rents' over and above the regular labour tokens would be required.[61]

Since information is freely and immediately shared between production units via industrial federations, the work collectives will be aware of the shortages and surpluses of labour-power through horizontal linkages. While labour-power, unlike many other resources, cannot be reallocated at will, moral and material incentives can be in place to seduce workers to (temporarily) come to the aid of other production units that face acute understaffing (and not merely massage certain longer term labour supply developments). We might, in fact, imagine that there would be a short-list of flexible workers – a rapid response, reserve labour force, if you will – in the possession of various skills that volunteer their labour to workplaces that face sudden shortages.

In addressing more structural trends, we should not overstate the ability to manipulate the supply of genres of labour by adjusting the maximum income rate up and downward according to the different labour requirements of the various branches of industry. The experience of the Soviet Union, again, discloses the nature of these limitations:

> Although changes in relative earnings may affect the relative attraction of careers as perceived by schoolchildren and their parents, the gestation period is very long and other factors (such as social prestige and gender) also influence perceptions of the relative attractiveness of different occupations. Hence relative earnings can be changed significantly without in the short run much affecting quantitative labour availability. (It may well affect, however, the quality of work performed in the relatively low-paid occupations. In labour-intensive services such as education and medicine this can have serious adverse effects.)[62]

Related to this is the objection commonly raised against material egalitarianism, namely that a highly compressed or level distribution of income would

---

61   Cockshott and Cottrell 1993, p. 31.
62   Ellman 2014, pp. 269–70.

undermine the willingness of workers to acquire additional skill, resulting in a shortage in the development of much-needed specialist knowledge. The acquisition of skill requires a level of individual investment in terms of time and effort on the part of the worker, while no material benefits may be accrued from this personal expenditure in the future since income is more or less equally distributed – the personal costs cannot be recouped at a later stage. A recurring hypothetical to challenge socialism, there is ample empirical falsification available.

Minimal pay disparities in Cuba (approximately between 4:1 and 5:1) did not result in a shortage of professional or skilled workers.[63] On the contrary, combined with free access to higher education, a compressed wage distribution caused Cuba to face a chronic shortage of manual (low and unskilled) labourers and subsequent delays in construction. It is noteworthy that manual labour was considered less dignified and pay disparities favouring skilled work reinforced this attitude to an extent.[64] Creative and mentally stimulating types of labour tend to be more rewarding in itself, which thus attracts people to invest time and energy – which may also be innately rewarding – in pursuing creative, skilled trades and professional career advancement. This hardly requires reinforcement by material incentives. Ironically, under such circumstances it would perhaps be necessary to introduce differential pay scales favouring those industries that are more physically demanding and intellectually unrewarding (provided there are no economically viable technological substitutes available – in fact, higher manual labour costs may stimulate technical progress), which therefore deserve more compensation to offset the disutility incurred by such work.[65] The problem with increasing pay to recruit more workers is that it may have an adverse or opposite effect. The workers currently employed in those branches of industry may instead elect to work fewer hours without loss of income – especially where it pertains to more unrewarding work in the first place and the preference for leisure is therefore relatively stronger. In the end, it may lead to an overall decrease in the supply of labour to this sector. To curb this effect, bonuses could be disbursed out of the material incentive fund only to those workers contributing labour beyond a certain minimum threshold, such

---

63   Mesa-Lago 2019.

64   Linger 1992, pp. 123–4.

65   In Cuba, it was addressed by organising construction brigades. Thus, '[j]oining a mini-brigade offered the almost-certain material incentive of getting an apartment, plus the experience of learning new skills and sharing in a socially valued project with others' (Linger 1992, p. 124). From the perspective of republicanism, national service mobilisation for the purpose of participating in collective projects of high social value may be an attractive policy option, provided the independence of citizens can be safeguarded.

as the full-time duration. This would retain existing workers, perhaps encourage them to put in additional hours to meet the full work schedule, while also recruit new workers from other industries that are attracted by the promise of higher income.

We should conclude our discussion with the following note. The addition of social dividends to the material incentive funds of production co-operatives will not necessarily produce the same distortions of labour incentives as experienced by the arrangement of labour-managed firms operating under competitive market structures. Under market socialism, producers may restrict membership, especially in response to a rise in price levels, instead of increasing the rate of output by using more labour, since doing so increases income per worker. Market socialism would have a propensity toward unemployment and over-consumption of capital as a result of short-run preference for an increase in average earnings.[66] In other words, by allowing workers to produce relatively less total output, the growth rate of national income is constrained by their choice to maximise income per worker. This 'perversion' under market socialism is accommodated by the structure of social ownership, which among other things inhibits free entry by firms into markets attracted by high profit margins, which is owed to the absence of incentives for new initiatives. Attention is to be paid here to the overall structure of variable income, then. Under socialised planning, a raise in prices (which cannot result from the price-setting power of a firm under a policy of centralised price determination) would not result in the restriction of employment since the strategy for securing the highest income per worker would rely on realising the maximum net output for their association, not average output rates per worker. In other words, when net output can be increased by expanding employment, the production co-operatives have an incentive to enlist additional workers. This then, would not give rise to the negative effects on the rate of employment, as observed under Yugoslavia's market socialism.

5   The Potential for Dynamic Growth

According to my estimation, there is little room for doubt that a socialised, planned economy could far exceed the capabilities of capitalism in terms of achieving high rates of static efficiency – allocative and productive efficiency. Without the asymmetries of market power, without rentiership, without invest-

---

66   See for example: Uvalić 1992.

ment cycles and financial fragility, without speculative finance capital, without wasteful duplications of effort, without profit motive, without unearned income skewing production in favour of luxury while needs go unmet, without unconscious market forces blindly steering the course of social development, the level of static economic performance that can be attained by socialism would prove it to be a superior form of social organisation. Hitherto we have focussed primarily on the static qualities of centralised planning and parametric control, dealing mostly with elements of current or short-term planning. The more challenging issue lies in reconciling the stability generated by centralised planning with the sustained growth of the proficiency and productive powers of labour and the methods of production. As summarised by Gordon, the 'two things that people want most from their country's economic system are growth in their income and security in their income'. And where 'pure capitalism' 'offers growth and insecurity', socialism 'offers security and stagnation'.[67] To prove the superiority of socialism over capitalism, it is expedient to illustrate how socialism is capable of offering reliable and constant growth rates. This is at odds, perhaps, with the growth of 'eco-socialist' proposals related to the 'degrowth' agenda which, semantic and conceptual ambiguity aside, propose that the total social product should remain constant:

> ecological considerations make high rates of economic growth in perpetuity an impossibility, and therefore a constrained 'steady-state economy' – an economy that maintains a constant size, without increasing the throughput of natural resources – is a more likely condition at the end of history.[68]

If, however, the aggregate output of a given society – the total national product – can be increased by growing industries that consume relatively fewer resources – say, certain service output that on the whole uses up few materials, or those industries that simply manufacture more efficiently – while decreasing the size of sectors that consume relatively more resources, the total output of society may increase on the whole while using up fewer natural resources. This is subject to the constraints of the Jevons paradox, which requires correction by administrative means (such as capping the quantity of raw materials that may be extracted from natural deposits by a fixed amount). While there may be a tendency to increase the consumption of natural resources and

67   Gordon 2001, pp. 433–4.
68   Vettesse and Pendergrass 2022, p. 95.

to increase the emission of pollutants when expanding the level of production, there is no *necessary* correspondence between the growth of output and an increase in ecological degradation. For example, between 2005 and 2019, thirty-two countries severed the relationship between growth and CO_2 emissions entirely. Among these countries, Ireland, Singapore, and Poland secured a growth of their total product by 89%, 96%, and 66% respectively, while simultaneously reducing territorial emissions by 24%, 17%, and 1% respectively; and cut consumption emissions by 52%, 22%, and 5% during this period.[69] Naturally, growth as such is scarcely an indication of equitable distribution of consumption among households, and questions of ecological sustainability extend beyond the question of greenhouse gas emissions. The broader point, however, is to insist that there is no necessary link between the growth of output and harmful natural effects.

It should further be stressed that economic growth generates additional resources – assets that might be used to tackle a host of ecological or social problems. What is more important than 'growth' as such therefore, is the *direction* that the pattern of economic growth assumes, and whether it generates resources for the public benefit, or instead generates crises by yielding to private interests. In either case, socialism should be capable of dynamically adapting itself to changing circumstances, for example by contracting certain industries and expanding others. Thus, even if the growth of the national product for its own sake is considered socially impermissible over mounting concerns related to ecological sustainability, society still stands to gain from technical innovation and the diffusion of new technologies. Gains in terms of material savings owed to technological advances would enable society to produce the same level of total output while using up fewer resources. Technical progress bestows important ecological advantages by potentially (and only potentially) reducing the throughput of natural resources, regardless of the growth rate of production.

If the total output of society can be increased within planetary boundaries and if this serves the overall quality of life (not just the material standard of living), there is no reason to abstain from increasing the material wealth by this maximum amount. Whether or not we wish to grow the total product of society relative to the consumption of natural resources and by what amount should – all things considered – be subject to political choice, and not be the unplanned outcome of the sum of private choices based on partial knowledge and particular interests. Socialism should in either case never settle into a

---

69   Hausfather 2021.

stable equilibrium, optimising its static efficiency, but instead strive to move forward, adapting itself to new technological circumstances and exploiting the opportunities arising from them in the public interest. A system of socialised planning and ownership should be capable of growing the rate of efficiency of the use of resources over extended periods of time. The basic critique of socialism in this regard is as follows:

> The LMF [labour-managed firm] will also be characterized by inefficient use of capital, due to distortions in project selection: investment projects having a positive present value may be rejected if they reduce average earnings, while negative present value projects may be accepted if they raise average earnings. But even in the absence of such distortions in project selection, a bias against the reinvestment of net income can be expected, since LMF members are entitled to the current benefits of a project only for the duration of their membership, as they do not participate in subsequent benefits or in the residual capital value of the investment at the time of departure.[70]

The investment horizon of producers would limit the rate of adoption of technological innovations and therefore inhibit their effective diffusion. In order to facilitate intensive methods of accumulation under a socialist regime, we need some means to overcome anti-innovation bias by workers' councils. Producers will have no necessary interest in implementing innovative technology or developing better products. They would presumably prefer to produce familiar goods in a familiar way, to maximise current technical efficiency. Indeed, producers may exhibit a 'conservative bias because new techniques and products are associated with increased uncertainty'.[71] The adoption of new technologies requires adaptation of the level of organisation and the accumulation of experience to use them most efficiently. With a familiar technique, workers' councils know the structure of organisation and ratio and quantity of material inputs that allow them to obtain the maximum quantity of output. If these variables and proportions shift in response to dynamic changes in the structure of the economy, this level certainty diminishes thus acting to brake initiative in the adoption of new technologies by producers. By abstaining from fully developing the technical methods of production, producers may maximise current income at the expense of future growth of total output. These

---

70   Uvalić 1992, p. 18.
71   Brus 1972, p. 23.

narrow interests will bias their actions against the long-run interests of society for improved (more, or at least more sustainable) consumption. This long-term horizon extends to decisions related to research and development (R&D), the development of technical skill among the work collective, and both the volume and structure of investments. If producers disregard these matters over their more immediate concerns of efficiently achieving output targets in the short-run, socialism will eventually decay. Producers under collective ownership would experience the effects of chronic under-investment.

Since producers lack the inherent motivation to introduce new technologies, the imperative to innovate will have to come from political institutions, which represent citizens and therefore embody the interests of their social role as consumers. This is not to say that socialism is inherently biased against innovation in all its forms. If workers are given the ability to act on their local and tacit knowledge, they may adjust work routines accordingly. A rigid centralised hierarchy (corporate or otherwise) may stifle initiative and direct workers to act in certain ways without full knowledge of the actual possibilities 'hidden' away in work processes. Workers, when governing their own facilities or workplaces, may wherever possible simply release this potential to improve production processes. In fact, self-government in production may be an effective solution to some diseconomies of scale experienced by large corporate firms, as Carson summarises the problem:

> The great investors are almost entirely clueless as to what their supposed 'employees', the corporation managers are doing. The CEOs are almost entirely clueless as to what the branch and facility managers are doing. And the management of each facility are almost entirely clueless as to what is going on within the black box of the actual production process. In the light of this reality, Mises' 'entrepreneur' – so carefully and closely involved in the minutiae of choosing between technical possibilities of production, a brooding omnipresence guiding the efforts of every employee – is largely a construction of fantasy.[72]

In corporate firms, those with the authority to make strategic or sometimes operational decisions are often distantly removed, by many layers of dense hierarchy, from interactions with customers. A labour-managed co-operative will be better tuned into consumer requirements without sacrificing economies of scale. Modifying the assortment of products or fine-tuning existing prod-

---

72   Carson 2008, p. 205.

ucts on the basis of qualitative and quantitative information generated by consumer behaviour could be done quite simply without disruption to the workflow, and therefore without notable losses in efficiency. On the other end of the spectrum, progress in the area of developing and diffusing disruptive technologies has typically relied on the public sector directly or indirectly in large part due to the higher tolerance for risk by public authorities for long-term, large-scale vital but low return projects.[73] Major industrial projects and large-scale strategic investments can be implemented successfully directly by administrative instruments. For example, the small selection of high-priority projects allowed Soviet authorities to develop major strategic technologies rapidly.[74] The long-term horizon associated with major investments ensures that there is no immediate pay-off, which inhibits commercial initiative in developing these areas. Hence, public authorities, being less concerned with short-term returns on their initial investments, may display higher levels of willingness to invest in long-term projects related to the research and development of initiatives. Thus, we should expect that public research funded out of the central budget would be capable of developing major technologies in a socialist society. What we are concerned with here is therefore neither the major investments that are centrally directed, nor current planning of minor investments which can be adequately assigned to workers' councils. The issue discussed here relates to sustaining a pipeline of continual and incremental technical improvements of the production process or end products, which may be understood as medium investment horizons related to technical progress.

As Cockshott and Cottrell note: 'For R&D to be effective there must be a transmission belt that spans the stages of pure research, applied research, product development, and mass production'.[75] The development of new technology (both process and product innovation) through publicly funded research would pose major challenges. Under capitalism, the development of new technologies by firms is delegated to salaried researchers and engineers (it is rarely the individual genius of entrepreneurs motivated by private profits that drives innovation). Such intellectually stimulating and creative work is underpinned by intrinsic motivation for purpose, self-improvement, prestige, intellectual fulfilment, proficiency, and so on, which can be harnessed as well under socialism. Researchers and engineers, being privileged to do stimulating and challenging work, can therefore simply be absorbed into public research institutes that may be linked to research universities without a loss in creative

---

73   Mazzucato 2015; Offer 2022, pp. 11–42.
74   Ellman 1969, p. 71.
75   Cockshott and Cottrell 1993, p. 64.

or scientific output. (This implies that, during this stage of socialist development, we presuppose the continued existence of social division of labour that divides workers between functions that combine different proportions of cognitive and manual tasks, i.e. there is some degree of integration of mental and manual labour, but not fully). Furthermore, parallel development and duplicate efforts are a negative effect of commercial confidentiality, and the under-supply of research funds due to beneficial spillovers reaped widely from the results of research are sound reasons to concentrate research, development, and invention into public-administrative hands.

Cockshott and Cottrell maintain that the level of innovation attained by a given society depends chiefly on the amount of funds directed toward research and development and has less to do with the economic system.[76] This is not so, however. They overlook the 'system-specific' qualities (as per Kornai) that engender or inhibit the diffusion of innovations.[77] Under Soviet-style socialism, a crucial factor accounting for economic decline, out of many, was the anti-innovation bias of state enterprise managers. This conservatism was reinforced by the institutional framework of the Soviet economy itself. In terms of indicators related to economic efficiency, according to metrics of neoclassical economics – particularly allocative and technical efficiency – the Soviet economy scored surprisingly well during the course of the 1970s and 1980s.[78] However, slow technological progress meant that more time was available to perfect the use of existing technical means – learning by doing – thus inflating technical efficiency according to static measures. On the whole, initial waste incurred by moving along the learning curve involved in mastering new technologies is over time offset manifold by increases in productivity resulting from the application of new, improved technologies. The social cost of high technical efficiency, in this context, was a much slower rate of intensive growth. Managers, due to disincentives, preferred to produce what they were familiar with in a way they were familiar with, since this could maximise output targets in the short-run, and were resistant to innovation therefore.[79] In other words, dynamic efficiency suffered from the lack of incentives to use new technologies.

The case of Yugoslavia's market socialism is similar, related to under-investment more generally, which was owed to different underlying institutional causes. Producers preferred to use revenue to increase immediate personal

---

76   Cockshott and Cottrell 1993, pp. 63–4.
77   Kornai 2012, pp. 14–56.
78   Whitesell 1990; Murrell 1991, pp. 65–71.
79   Ellman 2014, p. 35; Nove 1992, p. 365.

consumption at the expense of ploughing proceeds back into their firm to expand production, favouring to abuse credit for this purpose. In both models of socialism, narrow investment horizons deferred technical progress.

It should be stressed that under the system of general planning and parametric control thus far outlined, there is also no strong bias *against* the implementation of new technologies. Under Soviet-style socialism, there was no inbuilt reserve capacity for local initiative in the introduction of technical innovations since production goods were rationed in fixed quantities and for definite periods, and no financial discretion existed for producers to use their funds for the adoption of new technologies:

> Before the final approval of the plan, company managers are allowed to make suggestions, so among other things they can initiate the adaptation of a new product or a new technology, that is to say, they can join in the process of innovation diffusion. However, they must ask for permission to realize all significant initiatives. (...) Central planning is not dealing miserly with the resources devoted to capital formation. The share of investment carved out from the total output is typically higher than in the capitalist economies. However, this enormous volume is appropriated ahead of time to the last penny.[80]

Under a system of general planning and parametric control, by contrast, producers can freely submit bids to use equipment at a certain level of productivity, while maintaining a degree of slack to account for miscalculations. And unlike Yugoslav practice, the revenue generated by a firm cannot be pocketed by their workers over being reinvested. The problem faced under normative economic planning, then, could be more accurately stated as an indifference by producers toward innovation. In much the same way, lower management of capitalist firms have no particular reason to obstruct the implementation of new technologies, if so instructed by upper management. Upper management, on the contrary, are partial to technological development, insofar as their prestige and bonus payments depend on promoting their firm as operating at the cutting-edge of their industry, to grow their market share. Management, in a typical large capitalist firm, will therefore issue instructions to the R&D department to develop new lines of products and to lower management to adopt or sell some selection of these new products. It should be noted that the investment horizons associated with these decisions are capped by the short-term returns

---

80   Kornai 2012, pp. 27–8.

demanded by shareholders. In other words, we should not needlessly flatter capitalism and embellish its capabilities. In any case, since the political community replaces the capitalist class as owners of the means of production under socialised planning, it seems that the political regime will have to issue instructions toward this end. These public authorities can, however, scarcely know what these detailed instruction should include since the knowledge required to innovate effectively is highly contextual and usually implicit. Because they cannot issue detailed instructions, they will have to issue these orders in parametric form. This in turn raises the question how these parameters can be established independently and objectively in a way that would not distort incentives. For example, if we simply track the introduction of new goods to the assortment of producers as a measure of innovation, we would in theory possess a yardstick to measure the success rate of new products tied to material benefits. The caveat here lies in that, since knowledge regarding innovation is qualitative, an external agency would have no efficient way of distinguishing nominal innovations from genuine improvements. Producers might make mere cosmetic adjustments to a line of products, supply them under a new name and product code, and submit this as evidence of innovation. It would therefore not be very realistic to imagine that planning authorities could simply award innovation bonuses to encourage dynamic efficiency. It would require intense monitoring and in-depth knowledge of the industry by political authorities (or consumers' co-operatives) to quantify, measure, evaluate, and reward innovation.

The issue could also be solved in a much simpler way. By allowing first adopters of new production techniques or end products the exclusive right to use them for the first number of years, it would provide producers with an incentive to promote innovation since they reap the exclusive benefits of doing so. Such exclusive, temporary use rights, however, are difficult to reconcile with the socialist conviction that the stock of scientific and engineering knowledge should be freely accessible and publicly available – i.e. that immaterial assets are also treated as the common possession of humanity.

It would appear that the norm of net output would at least lead production units to scout out technical improvements that they could adopt. Nevertheless, producers might still be inhibited in adopting new technologies, at least in relatively more stagnant industries. Since all information about innovations and their adoption is a matter of public record, any superior technology adopted by one co-operative would be quickly counteracted by other producers following suit, quickly wiping away the initial advantage gained. While one would be tempted to conclude that this could encourage continual and rapid revolutionising of the methods of production, it could somewhat counter-intuitively also lead to technological stagnation. Given the futility of gaining an initial bene-fit from pioneering new technologies, a tacit agreement might emerge rather spontaneously which swings the pendulum the other direction. Producers would collectively bet on forfeiting investment funds to lower current costs and inflating net output in the short-run while foregoing a higher rate of net out-put in the longer run. Provided this behaviour is exhibited across the industry, producers benefit from averting the risk associated with adapting their organ-isation to new technologies while benefiting from lowering costs by forfeiting investment funds. Conversely, where it concerns expanding industries that are compelled to respond to growing demand by increasing their output, produ-cers – when unable to recruit additional workers to this effect – will have to grow the efficiency of their equipment, which then drives technical progress.

Suppose that we apply a Laibman-style approach to medium-term invest-ment planning, so that producers are expected to draw up a plan spanning four or five-years outlining how they plan to grow labour productivity of their collective or reduce their consumption of energy or other resources compared to their level of output, for example. Producers might formulate an ambitious plan, exceeding the improvements in efficiency proposed by other workers' councils, but will only receive compensation if they actually achieve these goals. However, this would bake into the system a propensity toward over-investment. Realistically, some industries will have to contract so that new, more productive or more sustainable industries may take their place. Ideally, we would like the collectives in an obsolete industry to chart a realistic course for phasing out their facilities and releasing their equipment and workforce so workers can be re-employed in some other capacity that is more beneficial to society. However, if the only strategy for increasing income over time depends on proposing and then achieving higher rates of investment over time it could engender some sort of a crisis of over-accumulation. Producers in a shrinking sector would, against better judgement, attempt to renew their stock of means of production or expand their productive capacity, frantically betting on an unexpected new lease of life for their sector. The cumulative losses of these fruitless attempts might depress the rate of growth of national income.

Another challenge of such an approach would reside in measuring the growth of efficiency over an extended period of time. When the assortment of output of a production unit during this period is not modified, measuring the growth of efficiency would be straightforward. We can measure the unit costs at the beginning of the period and track how it evolves over time. The growth of efficiency over the period of one or multiple years can then be readily measured and appropriately rewarded. The problem lies in that the assortment of output of production units might (in fact, should) change over time. Producers would therefore be able to artificially inflate their recorded efficiency by substituting higher quality goods, which use up more resources, for inferior quality goods, that require less effort to produce. This drives down costs per unit of output compared to the start of the measurements, which therefore gives the appearance of increased efficiency when in fact consumers receive inferior quality substitutes in return. When higher quality alternatives are available to consumers this tendency would be checked by consumers adjusting their behaviour accordingly, but it nevertheless builds into the mechanism a propensity toward producing lower quality output over time. The self-correcting mechanism of consumer selection would be unreliable, at best, since more production units might cave to the pressure of decreasing the overall quality of their assortment over time.

The difficulty of medium and long-term incremental technical innovation under socialism is further compounded by turnover rates of production units. Workers that expect to have a relatively short-term relationship with a given association will not seek to innovate for the longer term (since the benefits would be accrued by others) but instead to maximise income for the time of their employment; thus, we might expect that a higher turnover rate will correspond with a higher propensity toward conservatism.

Having now clarified the main obstacles in relation to dynamic growth under a system of collective ownership, we will turn to sketching the outlines of a mechanism that should be capable of promoting intensive accumulation. The main characteristics of this mechanism are as follows:

- The size of the central investment fund – or the rate of investment – is established at the national level by the highest legislative assembly;
- Public research institutes and universities develop new products and technologies on the basis of qualitative social indicators, and make a list of prospective and viable innovations available for pilots and to producers;
- The central investment fund is divided among the branches of industry and in turn among producers;
- Producers are mandated to use a minimum of $x\%$ of their investment funds to adopt from the list of new technologies a number of new products, averaged out over period of a number of years;
- Successive performance ratings over three to five annual periods potentially allow workers to be promoted in income scale, provided the collective rating of their association has met or exceeded the minimum requirements.

The first insurance against under-investment is that the rate of accumulation is set by popular vote at the central level. Since the issue of immediate consumption versus future consumption is approached from the perspective of citizens belonging to the national community, and not as producers of local firms, the ultimate choice will more accurately reflect the long-term and higher-order preferences of society. The choice for the overall level of investment is not made by producers on the basis of partial interests and their local perspective. The national community may, for example, earmark some twenty percent of their total product for gross investment. This amount of resources forms the central investment fund. This fund is then disaggregated to different branches of industry, which would be roughly proportionate to their size (with some adjustments made to account for the social priorities accorded to different industrial sectors). Each industry-level fund distributes the funds to producers according to their current plans. While producers might submit proposals to use more or less investment funds, they cannot decide to disburse unused funds as personal income to their members. This, then, overcomes the first obstacle of structural under-investment.

Since the political community assumes the role of 'entrepreneur', much like corporate officers sending instructions down the chain of command to develop research projects, political authorities will need to rely on two channels of instructions to prevent frivolous innovation. The first set of instructions should be transmitted to researchers and engineers, grouped into research teams, departments, institutes, and universities. These public research institutes should be instructed in broad terms by political authorities to develop socially useful products and technologies. This might entail a focus on improving technologies according to the metrics of durability (ridding them of planned obsolescence, except for example where the energy savings obtained by introducing new technology is greater than the materials savings from extended product cycles), adaptability (standardising 'plug-and-play' to promote renewal of existing products), equipment that both increases productivity and is human-centred (improving the quality of work), increased user friendliness and safety, and in general, improvements to the quality of life.

Researchers will then propose to pursue different lines of inquiry requiring different amounts of funds that meet social and scientific criteria. These research projects will be vetted by their peers determining where to allocate research funds on the basis of *qualitative indices*. Relying on qualitative indicators serves two purposes. First, it functions as warranty against stimulating nominal innovation. If researchers are rewarded according to quantitative metrics of, for example, the rate of adoption of their prototypes by producers and the subsequent levels of consumption by consumers, it will incentivise both producers and researchers to make nominal changes to existing products for which a proven demand exists to give the false impression of successful innovation. Second, qualitative measurements permit for the requisite degree of flexibility to facilitate innovation. To bring out the inventiveness of researchers requires both funding flexibility and creative autonomy to pursue projects that do not necessary hold the promise of immediate pay-out. If projects are evaluated mainly on the basis of their immediate viability and short-term returns, it will stifle research and inhibit positive spillovers. Research which contributes scientifically relevant output may not always have an immediate real-world application but could be developed further in different directions at later stages. Even research that in hindsight is proven fruitless, might indirectly advance their field by structuring the research agenda which in turn does yield new and more productive lines of inquiries in return. If society wishes to harness the full potential of research and development including positive carry-over from the area of research to practical applications in industry and from industry to industry, it should permit such flexibility by allowing 'waste'. Because of the unique nature of R&D, qualitative indicators, in place of quantitative measurements, will improve the quantity and quality of innovative output. The 'waste' of research efforts is part of a discovery process allowing engineers and researchers to advance the horizon of technological knowledge, whereas innovation would be restrained by binding research to the immediate and narrow requirements of real-world application – measured according to the rate of adoption by producers.

The political community will have to earmark a particular percentage of the total product for research and development which are allocated to research projects based on applications submitted by research teams whose merits should be evaluated by senior researchers along specific qualitative metrics, and more generally, their social and scientific relevance. Because research funding is channelled according to qualitative and social indicators, we can expect that research output will reflect a shift in social priorities, based on the preferences of the political community and the research interests of engineers and scientists. This would likely entail a shift away from the development of frivolous products for short-run gratification and immediate profit, to product and process innovation that places greater emphasis on the increase of durable comforts and substantive improvements in the quality of life. Since here all the conditions for fruitful research and development meet – funding and creative flexibility, principally – there should be no shortage of new prototypes and technologies being researched and developed at any given moment. Once new products have passed all stages of development and approval they are to be included on a list of new products made available for producers to adopt. The issue lies mostly in motivating producers to do so.

Production units will therefore be mandated to use a minimum amount of the fixed investment fund reserved for them to devote to new equipment, spread out as an average quantity over a number of annual accounting periods, and to include new lines of products in their assortment; the frequency of this depending on the length of product cycles per industry, for example. This percentage of funds earmarked for new items and equipment will need to be differentiated according to industries, which harbour varying degrees of potential for technical progress. Furthermore, innovations should be divided between incremental improvement (updates), major improvements (e.g. modernisation), and major innovations (original products) according to the discretion of researchers. The sectoral planning offices will have to determine the mandated overall and specific amounts of new technologies that should be adopted within each branch of industry, again raising the issue of asymmetrical and tacit knowledge. Producers, if behaving strategically in their own narrow interests, will try to whittle down the minimum amount by concealing their true estimates in favour of a smaller amount. To counterbalance this tendency, political authorities should consult with the research offices that are more impartial and may provide more realistic estimates. The norm of net output will also ensure that producers will adopt the technologies that will likely prove more rather than less productive, as opposed to a random assortment to inflate their innovation bonus. The eventual minimum level of mandated innovation will ultimately and inevitably reflect some bargaining between rival interests, nevertheless. This is a necessary compromise. Research institutes, public universities, and design offices, although independent, should also maintain close ties with production units as the latter can provide suggestions about the nature and direction of innovation on the basis of consumer behaviour and user friendliness. Producers also have a stake in feeding suggestions to researchers, since they will ultimately have to use and adapt to new technologies. The information can subsequently be used to attempt to make them into viable technologies. A greater emphasis on the development of technologies that improve both productive efficiency and the quality of work for producers would also help to link the interests of research and development to workers and inhibit their conservatism.

Further conditions in the process of adopting new products will have to apply. First, the introduction of new products will need to pass a pilot period. During this period, the new product will need to be made available to producers or households for a nominal fee – or perhaps only to a selection of consumers rewarded for exceptional performance in their area, ranging from productive to cultural contributions – who will pick new products of their liking. The nominal costs for end products are taken out of the consumption allowance of the consumers, so that they will make a deliberate selection among products based on actual preferences, while at the same time the nominal costs are not reflective of the current costs of production since economies of scale have not been realised given the initial low volume of production at the pilot stage. In the market economy, this is achieved by affording the highest earners the privilege of selecting expensive commodities before cheaper methods of production are developed to scale up the volume of production (or before cheaper substitutes penetrate the market), at which point consumption of the new commodity trickles down to lower income groups. This provides manufacturers with reliable information about which items consumers prefer, and thus which products require expansion or further development. The same result is achieved here without asymmetrical distribution of income. When it becomes a matter of public record which products are preferred by consumers among the 'test demographic' and which less so, their production can be scaled up before they become available to households at realistic and more affordable costs.

Second, new products have to be phased in after the initial pilot period, to allow consumers to express their preference for the old product compared to the new substitute given their comparative, real costs. The older variant cannot be replaced by one stroke, so producers have to observe the rule that products cannot be removed from their assortment from one period to the next, only phased out (barring seasonal patterns). Lastly, a new line of product will need to be adopted into the assortment of multiple plants in order to be able to set an emulation norm around the average level of productivity. Producers will thus have to co-ordinate directly with other units of production about which products should be adopted, as well as consult with manufacturers of the necessary semi-fabricates and equipment whether or not they can supply enough factor inputs to make mass production viable and subsequently enter into contractual agreements with them.

These formal protocols aside, there should also be space for spontaneous initiative. Resourceful individuals should be allowed access to public resources, allotted to them by lottery (after a minimal review of the viability of such projects) or according to a more substantive assessment by some sort of panel of experts in the relevant area. A fund would be established at the national level. Some such projects will evidently have to be discontinued in the face of insufficient demand. Inevitably, this will involve waste of public resources, but a necessary cost to allow creative impulses to flourish in society. The difference compared to capitalism is that in socialism the costs of failed ventures are shouldered by the public rather than by private individuals. This will presumably cause innovators to take more risks since failure comes at no personal cost, which makes it more costly but also potentially more innovative – the cumulative costs of failures should ultimately be offset by the returns obtained from successful innovative enterprises. On the balance, it is important that the net contribution of new initiatives will be positive (taking into account the positive externalities of spontaneous initiative, not merely the rate of return on individual projects) so that society on the whole becomes wealthier as a result of this genre of innovative efforts. The fund for innovative projects will have to be adjusted according to this metric (if it is too large it will direct too many resources away from more useful, alternative capacities; if it is too small the social benefits of spontaneous innovation largely dissipate).

Similarly, we could imagine an official crowdfunding platform in which innovators can pitch their ideas for small-scale projects, and potential consumers can pledge their consumption credits, which are then frozen. If the project is realised, the credits are cancelled (struck from household budget accounts) and the project can withdraw from society the amount of resources saved by the cancellation of the consumption credits; if the project fails to take off, the credits are unfrozen and thus made available to the pledger to consume something else. Innovation of this type would be driven by intrinsic factors, such as the possibility to maintain one's subsistence by offering to society the fruits of one's personal passion and efforts.

All these pathways to innovation should create sufficient conditions for the dynamic growth of efficiency of the socialist economy. We are finally left to address a final and crucial issue. We have implicitly assumed that workers are fixed to their production co-operative. As noted earlier, workplace participation yields the highest improvements in productivity when it is combined with profit sharing, particularly through *individual control of capital assets*. In a capitalist economy, the members of co-operatives have a stake in increasing, or at least, maintaining the value of their capital stock. When they vacate the co-operative, they will be able to pass on their share at increased value. Evidently, this cannot be replicated in a socialist community since all property is collectively owned by society, which raises the issue of how to link the interests of producers to a medium-term investment horizon. The problem herein resides in the periodisation that separates the initial decision from its eventual outcome. If the outcome is much delayed, so that their effects are pushed beyond the immediate horizon of producers, the incentive for sound investment decision-making weakens. For example, if postponement of necessary investments leads to shortage costs at a later point when, perhaps, the composition of membership of the production co-operative has changed substantially, there is not much reason for workers now to make sound initial decisions for improved results later since the negative outcomes of their choices would only begin making themselves felt when they have ceased their association to the production co-operative in question.

According to Hahnel, production units in his model of socialism are motivated to work efficiently because their effort rating is capped by the social benefit to social cost ratio achieved in the previous year.[81] However, when producers fail to achieve a high level of efficiency they could vacate their production association and seek employment elsewhere, or start afresh by founding a new workers' council that begins with an average effort rating. The remaining workers (should there be any), including potential new recruits, would be left to deal with the poor choices of their former associates and predecessors. This disincentive, if increasingly exploited, could have formidable ramifications for the longevity of socialism. It could gradually undermine the willingness to work efficiently. How might we go about remedying it?

The first part of the solution is rather obvious. Namely, to link collective performance to individual members, so their individual income is momentarily capped by the performance of their previous production association when they join some other co-operative. In addition to this, there should be some medium-term performance tracking instrument tied to material incentives to ensure that workers are invested in the medium-term outcomes of their choices. This, again, cannot be the value of the stock of assets under their control, since inevitably, units of production in less productive sectors or obsolete industries will need to contract, and producers should not resist inevitable decline. The metric of success for such producers from the general perspective of society is to successfully navigate this contraction, rather than to maintain or grow the amount of capital in their care. What can be done, instead, is to 'stack' the performance ratings over a number of years, and compare this to the mean in their industry. If the individual score (which may be composed of different membership periods of different co-operatives) does not downwardly deviate significantly from the average under normal conditions, the individual worker may advance to a higher income scale. Thus, workers income would be multiplied by a factor of 1 (junior), 1.1 (medior) and 1.3 (senior).

Effectively, over a number of successive periods composed of a number of years – say, periods of three to five years – the collective performance of work collectives is tracked and whether it has performed reasonably well (that is, above the minimum threshold established in relation to the mean performance of their sector). The membership of an individual worker to one or multiple associations is then recorded and linked to their categorisation according to their level of seniority. If for successive periods the work col-

81   Hahnel 2021.

lective or multiple collectives of which the individual worker has been an associate have exceeded the norm for their industry, the worker is promoted to 'medior' and 'senior' income scales. This particular industry-norm for normal performance does not have to be exceedingly strict, since 'current' emulation norms already push up the level of average productivity for any given year, and the medium-term record of performance is connected to this average. Only significant or flagrant underperformance would result in workers' income levels not being upgraded on the basis of seniority. Conversely, junior members of top level performing associations would perhaps be promoted to 'senior' income scale more quickly (and 'senior' members already allotted to the highest pay scale could be rewarded with priority access to special articles of consumption in their pilot stage of development). This would create the incentive to care, not just for short-term performance (which affects variable income) but also for the longer term performance of their production unit (which affects the individual pay scale of workers). This can be thought off as a 'static' wage scale based on 'current performance' and a 'dynamic' wage scale based on successive performances over a number of annual planning cycles.

Furthermore, when members leave their association, the performance over the next year of their previous collective should contribute to their individual achievement rating and supplementary income in some capacity. This would prevent workers from escaping the consequences of poor choices at the most opportune moment. For the following year, during a 'transitional period', part of their variable income will be derived from the success ratings of their former workplace, beginning with the first six months in which the whole of their social dividends allotted to them is derived from the ratings of their previous production co-operative. Over the course of this year, the share of variable income obtained from the achievement rating of their new co-operative should progressively increase. In effect, their 'portfolio' would consist of their previous and current membership of their production co-operatives – the ratio perhaps related to the length of their previous membership. This should motivate workers to ensure that at any moment in the future, when and if they decide to depart, their current production co-operative has the means to perform well in the upcoming annual accounting period. Since they may not know when their departure will be, these uncertain expectations would push the horizon of individual workers beyond the single transitional year. Moreover, when someone has their membership terminated by the workers' council over substandard contributions to the efforts of the work collective, any positive results achieved by the collective should not contribute to their record or portfolio. Insofar as full employment is secured by the socialist economy, the threat of dismissal will scarcely motivate workers, but if cancellation of membership also prevents them from advancing along the pay scale ladder, it might prove more effective motivationally.

This scheme obviously exerts downward pressure on the flexibility of the labour pool and turnover rates. Workers are free to exit their workplace (i.e. they are not administratively allocated, as under the 'Stalinist' model), although they have somewhat more control over their dynamic pay scale if they do not change workplace frequently – provided the co-operative broadly operates around the average level of their industry. Under conditions of full employment especially, the stability of employment might hinder workers' co-operatives from attracting new members. While this might encourage the diffusion of labour-saving technologies, if and when available in sufficient supply, and should push the average length of association membership to an average of at least five and upward of ten years or so to reduce turnover costs, facilitate the transformation of workplaces to communities of producers, and expand the average horizon of workers, there is obviously also a cost associated with the reduced mobility of labour. This could be exploited to turn associations into stable communities composed of committed worker-members. Socialism should effect a cultural and organisational transformation in the structure of work, so that long-term commitments to individual associations are facilitated, transforming places of work into ethic-bearing communities of involved and developing producers that consider themselves as local extensions of the universalist republic. This further implies that the integration of manual and mental tasks within associations becomes generally organised, so that development of workers can be sustained without constant and high rates of worker turnover (in turn, professional development ceases to be an individualistic enterprise taking place without fidelity to social interests borne by communities of producers).

On a final note, there are multiple dimensions to risk of investments under socialism. Risky ventures do not hold the promise of large future gains, as would be the case under a regime of private appropriation. The mechanism for technical progress would therefore probably rely more on large-scale cycles of technological renewal stretched over decades on the initiative and at the direction of public-administrative authorities as the main source of growth, trickling down by mandating economic units in the co-operative sector to use a minimum of their investment fund for the adoption of new types of hardware and products. While there are lower benefits to be gained by successful investment under a normative planning mechanism, the losses of investments are incurred by society and therefore the risk is collectively shared. While poor investments would affect the income rating of producers negatively, this would not be in proportion to the losses incurred, with excess losses being covered by public authorities. This decreases the risk borne by producers, while the potential benefits secured by achieving a higher income rating would keep them committed to sound decision-making in the area of investment. This would achieve an appropriate balance between risk and reward. Further, co-operative planning between economic units within the parametric framework would do a great deal to diminish uncertainty related to investment cycles and co-ordination failures.

There are a number of reasons, then, why socialism is capable of growing national income at constant rates while simultaneously affording workers substantial security of income. First, both large-scale investment in infrastructure, projects, and research and development by means of central co-ordination and the positive spillover effects into the co-operative sector would create a solid basis for dynamic efficiency. This supplies the long-run horizon necessary for major investments that drive the greater part of income growth; while the medium-term horizon of producers combined with open access to technologies should be enough to ensure the fast diffusion of new technologies. Second, central planning of the macroeconomic proportions and the set of prices creates a reliable point of reference for robust decision-making by producers, while horizontal co-ordination reduces the duplication of efforts and the co-ordination failure of investments. Third, the scope for local initiative and decentralised activity allow producers to act on their contextual and tacit knowledge to the best of their ability.

Addendum: On the Possibilities for Progressive Socialisation

Under realistic assumptions about human motivation and ability, and in reference to empirical experience and theoretical arguments, emerges the broad outlines of a feasible socialism without market competition, based instead on the combination of centralised planning and horizontal linkages within a parametric framework. Having drawn from a variety of theoretical deposits – from Kalecki's centralised planning and Brus' additions to his model, from Laibman's multilevel approach, as well as from the Soviet school of cybernetics, to name but a few sources – we were able to assemble the components of a socialist economy into a coherent and viable whole. This economic mechanism combines the central co-ordination of the major proportions of the economy, of large-scale investments, and administratively determined accounting prices that form the framework of parameters; with co-operative planning of minor investments in reference to decision criteria of the central framework; and socialist emulation, which sets the standard of productivity to be emulated to minimise the consumption of resources relative to total output.

While Kalecki proposed to replace the gross output indicator with net output as the measure of success, he still maintained that central planning should rely on fulfilment and over-fulfilment over the planned volume of production. This incentive structure should, as discussed, be modified by drawing on Laibman's reward function, which is set by the degree of actual fulfilment of pre-planned net output – a sort of 'Kalecki-Laibman' synthesis, reformulated on the basis of Soviet-inspired cybernetic principles. In any case, we have seen how there is no one 'silver bullet' to address the crux of feasible socialism. It is not viable to design an economic mechanism that would operate without snags and hitches and the collectivisation of wealth would not result in an immediate and uncompromising end to all restraints and social hierarchies: *'There are no "pure" and perfectly "consistent" societies. Every real system is built upon the practical compromises of mutually contradictory principles and requirements'.*[82] It requires a fairly complex system of grease and gears to put the hands and minds of workers into motion and render their actions in service of the collective welfare of the socialist community, and while it may work, it would function imperfectly.

The greatest challenge resides in reconciling decentralised initiative and decision-making with promoting long-term investment horizons among producers. The 'simple' act of the abolition of private property and the profit motive will not release a spontaneous surge of creative and moral excellence among workers to the extent that they will become innately motivated to contribute to the greater good, guided only by broad horizons and concern for the far-reaching, general consequences of their choices. Even if they would be, they would lack the information to convert these motivations into operational sets of actions. By contrast, a system of general planning and parametric control rises from the premise actually existing people and extending close attention to the empirical experience of socialism. This model of socialism is more conservative compared to the radical-millenarian visions of socialism from the nineteenth century, but more progressive than the socialist realities of the twentieth. What remains here is to discuss the potential direction of a protracted process of socialisation under republican collectivism.

Before we discuss these possibilities, it should be mentioned that Kalecki had, in his counsel to the socialist government of Poland, opposed proposals to move toward a system of 'automatic incentives'. He had stressed that more

---

82   Kornai 1980, p. 156.

technologically advanced plants would reap higher rewards in relation to net output compared to less technologically advanced factories. The difference in income would not be the result of differential effort but would result from circumstances outside the immediate control of workers. This would put some workers at an unfair disadvantage. Kalecki maintained that under such circumstances of uneven regional or industrial development, a more hands-on, directive approach would be needed to allocate resources, not to where their use might prove most productive, but rather in such a way that the lagging firms could be brought up to the standards of superior plants. He further argued that the growth of productivity could be measured as the change in profits over the course of a number of years.[83] Implicitly then, we have assumed that the model of socialism under discussion is not plagued by any major inequalities in industrial developments or has already successfully smoothed over any such substantial differences in the early stages of socialist construction. This is worth bearing in mind. At the same time, Kalecki's proposals – or some modification involving the movement within relative rankings within different industries – seem effective for the purpose of harmonisation of industrial development across regions and plants before the transition to a system of automatic controls could be attempted. It will take practical experimentation and tweaking to accumulate the experience to balance the system correctly, which implies there are substantial transitional costs associated with socialist construction and suggests that overzealous leaps into socialism should be avoided. A drawn-out transitional process of nationalisation, transferring the means of production into the care of the political community, therefore precedes these problems of economic planning. Hence, a socialised economy relying on a parametric framework is not the first stage of socialist development, but a second or third stage or so of socialist construction – depending on the initial conditions. It presupposes, in any case, a certain material groundwork already.

The structure of material incentives tied to parametric control figures is elaborate (although perhaps not much more complex than the typical tax code, insurance system, or finance markets found in a capitalist country.) It underscores, in my mind, why it is inexpedient to expand the BFI with various ratings for non-productive social activity, as per Laibman's proposals. The system of incentives is sufficiently complicated as it stands. By adding ever more factors and variables that need to be weighed and balanced in the minds and strategic calculations of producers, the workers may lose sight of which efforts

---

83   Osiatyński 1988, p. 45; Kalecki 2010, p. 28.

contribute in which ways to income formation, which would weaken the effects
that the structure of material incentives intends to bring about.

As previously elaborated, household consumption is made up of different
components. In addition to social consumption, workers receive a basic rate
of income in return for their hourly contribution to social production, variable
dividends supplementing this basic rate based on current performance and an
income multiplier based on 'seniority'. The lowest income scale, without additions of dividends or supplemental income, should be sufficient to cover the
basic costs of living and amenities, which are thus guaranteed independently
of the will of others. The basic allowance is the main source of income. The
variable benefits based on current and dynamic performance should be a much
smaller portion, to guarantee substantial income security. The bonuses should
be just enough to get workers interested in getting to know and understand the
social value of their productive efforts as communicated to them by parametric
signals and redirecting their activities accordingly, on the basis of the promise
of gaining access to some additional comforts and without threats to deprive
them of basic income or security of income.

I have not attempted to specify by formal methods how the components
of the BFI should be weighed. This will in any case require some practical
tweaking. It might be necessary to make the payment of the dividends for one
component conditional, if not in whole then at least in part, on meeting some
minimum value of another variable to prevent strategic manipulation. We can
take as warning the later stages of the Soviet economy:

> Parfenov concludes that the 'deliveries' indicator will be effective only if
> it is the sole or predominant determinant of bonuses. He points out that
> where the deliveries indicator has been in use for some time, delivery con-
> tracts have continued to be flouted. He cites the case of the Karaganda
> steel works, which met only a third of its orders for thin sheet steel in
> January 1981 because, with given rolling-mill capacity and 'taut' output
> targets expressed in tons, the best way to ensure output-linked bonuses
> was to roll thick, not thin, sheet steel. In fact the bonus regulations for
> 1982 require any enterprise that falls short of its delivery contracts over
> the year by more than 2% (exceptionally, 3%) to forgo all bonuses.[84]

Different variables could inadvertently influence one another in a way that
would allow producers to massage them in such a way that they could be com-

---

84   Hanson 1983, p. 4.

pensated for a socially irresponsible use of assets. For example, I noted how some discrepancies in supply and demand should be permitted since producers cannot be held to account for unpredictable variations in the demand for different products, yet at the same time the shortage costs will need to rise more steeply in response to increasing rates of excess demand, compared to the holding costs of excess resources to expedite investments in capacity expansion as a check against the tendencies toward under-investment. Such considerations will influence the exact composition of the success and bonus forming indices as calculated by the central planners.

In some readers all this may have raised the following question in their minds – especially when they are accustomed to thinking along the lines of nineteenth-century-style socialism, rather than engaging with the previous century's experience with socialist planning. Why, if we are concerned with the liberation of humankind, do we require an elaborate incentive scheme, with differential pay scales, rewards, and penalties, and so on, to act as discipling mechanism structuring the behaviour of workers in a way that apparently does not correspond to their innate wants or interests? There are three reasons why this is the case, in my view. First, knowledge of social processes is accumulated from the vantage point of the social role adopted by the individual worker. This perspective is necessarily circumscribed, furnishing only partial information that forms the basis for perception and interpretation. To limit the effects of this ignorance, society requires a network of communication and information that summarises and projects the broad, social consequences of individual choices. Unless we assume purely altruistic intentions, there also have to be real, material consequences connected to this web of knowledge and the results of using this knowledge so that individual actions are structured to concord with their general implications, and it thus requires an element of discipline. Second, it should be noted that the incentive scheme is not intended as a way to structure the actions of workers in violation of their inner nature, to override their inherent vices (laziness, resentment, envy, complacency, cowardice, cruelty). We have assumed that, generally speaking, workers are willing to take broader considerations and interests into account and balance them with their own interests, provided they know what these are. Individuals certainly exhibit a tendency toward convenience, even to the detriment of their own welfare at times. However, these vices are locked in cognitive conflict with various virtues, a conflict between base instincts and higher-order reasoning and preferences. People, we assume, are naturally predisposed toward wanting to contribute meaningfully to their community, to be productive, creative, self-disciplined, and challenged as part of their pursuit for personal fulfilment and self-development. Depending on the circumstances of their socialisation, different dispositions – vicious and virtuous habits – are nurtured to different extends. The key is to shape the structural circumstances so that the correct inclinations are cultivated in citizens, by reinforcing attitudes associated with good moral character. Thus, the scheme of material incentives is not intended to suppress human nature, but to nudge these conflicting inclinations in the right direction by rewarding citizens materially for harnessing their intrinsic higher volitions.

Lastly, it should be stressed that it only takes a minority of slackers to gradually erode self-discipline of the majority. If workers put in honest effort to produce and plan responsibly but notice that small groups of workers get by through manipulation, it might very well exert downward pressure on overall productivity. Even if we work from the assumption that the diffusion of socialist morale proceeds rapidly after the reconstruction of society on the basis of collective ownership, the existence of a minority of recalcitrant workers that shirk any responsibility could well reverse these gains and depress morale:

> It is a matter of greatest principle that every working collective in a socialist society consider itself responsible to the entire society for its guardianship over a particular set of productive resources, and for the efficiency with which that guardianship is exercised. Differential rewards, both to collectives and to individuals, follow from this, throughout a long period in which consumption is still constrained by labor income. The system of rewards must be 'gotten right', precisely so that it can eventually be transcended. The ideas that material incentives can simply be denied, or that people's consciousness and behavior can be transformed through a simple act of revolutionary political will, are what give socialism a sense of unreality, and drive people toward advocates of 'the market'; concern for the hard reality of motivation and incentives makes it seem as though it is only the anti-socialists who have their feet on the ground. From this point of view, artificially accelerating equalization of incomes among different classes of labor (so long as such classes exist), and among different individuals within each class (so long as levels of consciousness, effort, skill and educational attainment vary), may have the opposite of the intended effect, causing resentment, demoralization, and cynicism and obstructing, rather than promoting, socialist consciousness.[85]

---

85   Laibman 2012, p. 37.

Indeed, the kibbutzim veered away from their 'communistic' principles precisely because the newer generations (that were less ideologically inclined) felt insufficiently motivated by the separation of income and effort. Thus, these agricultural collectives began 'experimenting with various ways to create explicit links between individual efforts and material rewards, in contrast to the traditional kibbutz principle of "from each, according to ability, to each, according to need".'[86] By proceeding hastily in the direction of a fully egalitarian distribution of income, it substantially increases the possibility that some workers feel better served by the inequalities of market competition. Allowing for a small degree of inequality co-opts such sentiments by disciplining unproductive slacking and rewarding productive contributions.

Over time, the success indicators and performance index should remain just that. An instrument that informs producers of the degree to which their efforts are beneficial to society. This information would allow production co-operatives to make continual adjustments to their production schedules, under the assumption that there exists some social obligation to contribute productively to general welfare and, furthermore, that the character of work is innately motivating, so that the challenge of adapting production to changing circumstances has become rewarding in itself. This also presupposes the gradual integration of mental and manual labour so that work becomes a source of fulfilment. Initial steps in this direction might include drafting and rotating workers to participate in design projects for new lines of products or equipment. However, the attainment of this advanced level of morale will likely require a protracted period of the gradual deepening of socialisation in terms of subjective consciousness and the objective division of labour, before producers will use such information and apply themselves in a socially responsible way without variable income being attached to differential outcomes.

The need for material incentives may be partially phased out, at least concerning variable income, after an extended period of socialisation. The objective basis for this shift in the subjective conditions of socialist society is the incentive scheme connecting the individual interest to the social interest directly. This may be freely reinforced by moral incentives at the local and central levels. By announcing and celebrating the achievements of collective projects or socially determined macroeconomic goals, for instance. Similarly, the consultation of co-operatives for drawing up perspective plans without reinforcing this behaviour by material means would habituate producers to supplying credible estimates of their own accord and for their mutual benefit. Over time,

---

86   Russell, Hanneman, and Getz 2013, p. 2.

the social structure and civic education should nurture a socialist conscious-ness via a process of re-socialisation. Moral incentives and social disapproval of wasteful behaviour, the integration of mental and manual labour thus mak-ing the character of work more intrinsically rewarding, and the reduction of the average work day, combined with the diverting away of resources from inefficient ventures, may gradually become sufficient motivation for producers to conduct themselves productively. Producers would join collective projects that they are innately motivated to contribute their efforts to. While com-pensated for the hours worked, they would also become personally invested in the project's continuation and would therefore use their assets carefully to avoid being deprived of future resources. A fully egalitarian income policy, equalisation of remuneration per hour worked, would enter the realm of pos-sibilities. Income would become a matter, exclusively, of personal preferences related to the trade-off between work and leisure. Such a stage of socialist development would represent a higher form, although it still falls short of the ultimate aspirations of communism as they had been formulated some two centuries ago.

In an advanced stage of communist society, according to the prescriptions of Marxist doctrine, producers would contribute productively to society accord-ing to their own understanding of their ability, and in exchange of supply-ing their productive services to the community, they would be able to draw from the stock of consumption goods some share of products they feel rep-resents a fair compensation for their efforts given their needs and wants. The amount of effort contributed to production as well as the amount of means of consumption acquired by households would be self-regulated and self-deter-mined, without intervening mediation of budgets or prices. Thus in:

> a higher phase of communist society, after the enslaving subordination of the individual to the division of labour, and thereby also the anti-thesis between mental and physical labour, has vanished; after labour has become not only a means of life but life's prime want; after the productive forces have also increased with the all-round development of the indi-vidual, and all the springs of common wealth flow more abundantly – only then can the narrow horizon of bourgeois right be crossed in its entirety and society inscribe on its banners: From each according to his abilities, to each according to his needs![87]

---

87   MECW 24: 87.

It should be stressed, however, that there is no simple linear relationship where production simply overtakes consumption at some point in the steady technical progress of the productive forces – this presupposes that human wants are fixed and static. As the forces of production advance, on the contrary, new technical opportunities emerge that spring new wants and needs into existence. Productive forces then try and catch up with this new set of wants but their technical development in turn engenders the social development of yet another range and direction of preferences. The growth of productive resources will not simply surpass the demand for resource consumption, and consequently, *resource constraints* have to be reckoned with for the foreseeable future *and beyond*. This, in turn, implies that the use of productive assets will necessarily have a trade-off associated with them and that consumption should be constrained by household budgets. Since society would not be able to produce an abundance of goods in the *absolute* sense, the *relative* costs of different techniques of production and the *relative* demand for different goods need to be mapped and reconciled into a common unit of account. Put differently, since constraints on production exist, it follows that the total volume of production will have physical limits and that these limits necessitate for society to determine the relative proportions of inputs and outputs that will need to be produced in relation to the relative wants of end users. Under a communistic arrangement that abolishes money, but also prices and budget constraints for households, society would be unable to grasp the relative usefulness of different productive activities and regress in terms of the level of efficiency at which they can put productive resources to use.

Where does this leave us? Should we abandon the crowning communist objective of the abolition of prices and budgets as hopelessly utopian? Or is levelling incomes the highpoint of socialist construction? Not necessarily. If socialist society is successful in overcoming practical hurdles and socialist consciousness has been universally consolidated, further advances can begin to move society to some yet higher form of socialist development. We can imagine that, initially, the average work day is lowered to a few hours. Producers will be afforded a consumption allowance for those couple of hours, and moral incentives are used as disciplinary tool to ensure that personal efforts of workers gravitate around the average intensity. If this proves fruitful, the subsequent step in socialist construction may be to decouple income and production partially and then altogether. The consumption allowances would then be distributed to households regardless of their productive contributions – a policy of universal, full income distribution.

It is inadvisable, however, to abandon all budget constraints, affording consumers free, unmediated access to the stock of consumption goods and producers unlimited access to the stock of production goods and material inputs. Under this model of communism, the only limitation on their consumption of goods and resources would be their moral restraint. However, even if we presuppose universal dissemination of such selfless attitudes among the community of comrades, the lack of household budgets would render invisible the relative intensities of demand for different products. Households would be ignorant of how immoral their level of consumption is (whether they have taken more than their fair share) and producers would be ignorant of the relative demand for different output mixes, increasing the amount of wasteful production. Even under favourable assumptions of altruistic behaviour and high levels of material abundance, the communist mode of free distribution would decrease the efficiency of the use of resources. Yet it is exactly increases in the size and efficiency of the productive forces of society that are said to create the material foundation for free, communal distribution under socialism. Operating productive resources at lower levels of efficiency would, following this logic, cause society to regress in their level of social development. We are locked into a paradoxical contradiction where progressive material development allows socialist society to shed budgetary constraints, but this results in various losses of efficiency causing society to regress back to its previous level that in turn necessitates the reintroduction of budget constraints (however loose or tight). In other words, it is exactly by means of budget constraints faced by both producers and consumers that the kind of *social efficiency* is generated that allows society to advance to higher forms of social organisation in the first place.

We should be more than satisfied should socialism ever rise to the level of material and moral development where it has become sustainable to distribute, without condition or qualification, a fixed and equal amount of income to all consumers regardless of the amount of labour they in turn supply to society. For all intents and purposes, this very much resembles the distributional maxim that the members of society would supply labour according to their unique set of mental and physical abilities, and in return take according to their needs and preferences – with only the minor adage, that their consumption is constrained by some nominal amount for the purpose of economic calculus and accounting. This is getting far ahead of ourselves, however. We have to deal with more urgent matters in the field of theoretical inquiry and in the area of political strategy and action.

PART 3

Conclusions

..

Postscript

1   Closing Remarks

This monograph has been an exercise in political economy and political theory. Its intention, where it concerns the area of political theory, was to serve as an initial probe – by means of institutional and constitutional design – into how civic republicanism could be integrated into the body of socialist thought and which theoretical innovations and improvements could be derived from doing so. In the area of political economy, it served as an exploration – by means of institutional and mechanism design – of the technical viability of a model of socialism that exhibits republican features. This should be regarded as an initial treatment of the problem of socialist economic planning from the vantage point of the current era, clarifying the basic feasibility criteria for socialism and, by broad strokes, indicating the ways we might go about addressing them. In this respect, the collective planning mechanism has been distinctly *institutional* and *political* in its approach to economics, lacking formalisation. This is certainly an avenue of research that warrants elaboration by means of 'successive approximations' if you will, groping toward a formal model in all the required, technical detail to prepare for further interrogation. Even in the area of the institutional schematics, a trail of unresolved issues is left for future development and examination. In addition, the 'maximalism' of this and similar models of socialism in light of the extreme shifts and developments in the balance of forces in contemporary capitalism represents an obvious strategic obstacle. It is an obvious question whether this type of modelling can answer to actual demands emerging from really existing tendencies, or whether, with the passing of Soviet-style socialism into history, economic imaginaries of this sort have slid too far into being 'arbitrary, rationalistic, and willed' (Gramsci).

For now, we will have to reconcile ourselves to more tentative conclusions. The method of our inquiry was the theoretical design of a democratic republic and socialistic mode of production and distribution, which had to be ambitious, attractive, coherent, and feasible. In order to advance the body of thought designated here as 'republican socialism', it was necessary to disclose viable ways by which society could reconcile community of property to the core republican values – civic virtue, active participation, sensitivity to the common good, self-government, a mixed constitution. By offering this vision I hope to have advanced new theoretical equipment that could potentially help to restore political self-confidence and assertive initiative to the socialist movement.

In particular, our discussion of different models of socialism helped to outline an economic mechanism based on centralised planning and local parametric control which is largely rooted in the cumulative experience of socialist construction, borrowing liberally from its armoury of vocabulary, concepts, and ideas – ranging from *khozraschet* to cybernetics. In this capacity, the book recovers some of the socialist economic thought derived from a context that has now passed into history, for the benefit of a contemporary audience. Many of these ideas built upon the collective intellectual enterprise of research teams and scientists, each contributing elements from which we can derive theoretical conclusions as a whole. While these conceptual innovations cannot be *reduced* to single minds, a handful of individuals have made exceptional strides in their areas of expertise. From Kalecki we borrow his mode of thinking about how the instruments of centralised planning can be employed to secure a harmonious macroeconomic structure in a socialised economy, particularly by means of central price-fixing. In addition, the stress he placed on striking a balance between workers' councils and central authorities and his proposal for using net output as the primary success indicator provide useful ingredients for thinking about socialist economic planning. From his successors, and Brus in particular, we can further borrow ways to think about the technical requirements for effective central control based on the division between the area of centralised planning and the sphere for decentralised activity and local initiative. From Kornai, we obtain further insights in relation of the institutional context and feasibility conditions. This ties into two convergent trends, multilevel, mathematical programming and cybernetic control theory. In this capacity, Kantorovich is still remembered as the most eminent exponent. And from Laibman's multilevel planning – his particular theoretical contributions made outside the immediate requirements for socialist construction – we adopt his reward function in particular. These ideas are incorporated into a cybernetic mechanism which I have elected to tentatively designate as a collective co-ordinating mechanism of normative economic planning. I submit that an advantage of this approach is that it is derived in substantial respects from empirical examination, so that it deals realistically with the problems of incentives, dynamic development and time, risk and uncertainty, and the production and use of economic knowledge. In other words, it does not reduce problems of economic planning to a technical issue of assembling given data points, unlike more static approaches, in which Lange's model in particular excels, although it is not alone in this respect.

There are many more bits and snippets which have served as a source of inspiration and have been proposed by a host of other thinkers – Glushkov, Fedorenko, Nemchinov, Łaski, Osiatyński, Strumilin, Lange, Horvat, Nove, Hahnel, Veduta, Kronrod, Devine, Cockshott. This book, naturally, forms my own take on these approaches and ideas (with the benefit of hindsight) and makes some of the nearly forgotten theoretical developments in socialist thought available in modernised format. I regard this book as a contribution to what should be an ongoing and open-ended dialogue in the socialist movement. An instrumental advantage of my elective approach to socialism – reconciling 'neo-Kaleckian' socialism with Soviet cybernetics, to put it very crudely – is that it reviews the socialist experience critically but seriously and on its own terms, never dismissively and from an alien perspective. The semi-finished proposal etched into the preceding chapters bears a theoretical likeness of the sort that might allow a wide variety of socialists to coalesce around a common pole – petty factionalism aside. The more self-critical adherents of Marxism-Leninism might be drawn to it since it delves deeply into Soviet-style central planning to recover positive lessons for socialism and treats the Soviet experience with due esteem; while members of Trotsky's offshoot of Marxism might recognise some resemblance between the critique of over-centralisation and their own theory of bureaucratic degeneration. The potential attractiveness of this model to democratic socialism should also be obvious, and a systematic outline of socialism might help its advocates overcome their political hesitancy that continually seems to draw them back into the fold of state-guided welfare capitalism – only the anarchists are snubbed by this approach to socialism, insofar as it ascribes a critical role to central authority. Inevitably, however, many Marxist doctrinaires will recoil at some of the pragmatic suggestions, and the model of normative economic planning will certainly prove unable to shake off all dogmatic cleavages within the socialist movement, but it should at least be capable of bridging some sectarian divides.

Naturally, this book does not contain a comprehensive model of socialism. As such, this book does not represent a fully finalised version of a workable model of socialist society. I hope my own attempt invites scrutiny so that we may be able to collectively refine our beliefs to our mutual benefit; to help strengthen our core beliefs; to help improve, expand, and deepen our understanding of theory, and therefore to strengthen our movement and develop the roadmap toward socialism. In this respect, I find the following sentiments expressed by Laibman quite agreeable:

> we should now strive to avoid the error of splintering socialist theory into discrete and warring 'models'. The desire for product differentiation ought

not to prevail over the very real task of developing a complex and nuanced vision, which will undoubtedly incorporate many elements from the various positions currently being put forward. No single model is likely to be adequate to this task, and we should recognise that we are at an early point on a long road of discovery. This road leads to an understanding that will progressively incorporate new qualities as it draws upon (what will hopefully be) a growing Left and working-class movement world-wide.[1]

Whether republican socialism can be regarded as a subset of democratic socialism, or as a separate tendency altogether, is open to interpretation. Discussion of its exact relationship to Marxism has also been mostly avoided. This relationship is ambiguous, to say the least. Whilst communist society has been universally imagined, at least by its exponents, as a society which lacks the coercive powers of the state, only preceded by a transitory revolutionary emergency government (the 'revolutionary dictatorship of the proletariat'), this premise should be put in perspective. If we adopt an overly schematic and formalistic understanding of 'communism', it can necessarily only refer to the Marxist prescriptions of a classless society without state. However, if communism is understood more broadly to mean any society based principally on some form of common ownership – perhaps even certain Jesuitic theocratic communities, 'Democratic Kampuchea' which abolished money and private possessions altogether, or 'war communism' – as well as some theoretical proposals (lamented by Marx and Engels as 'barracks communism'), we can admit that communism may assume multiple forms in theory and practice.

These particular communistic regimes operated on the basis of vertical instructions backed by physical coercion to structure the flow of resources, instead of indirectly by financial means and exchange relations. This effectively de-commodified production and distribution, abolishing currency, and rendered labour-power, means of production, and materials into the immediate instruments of the collective economy. Naturally, it is not our aim to replicate such militaristic regimentation, the point here being that the 'statelessness' of communism is contingent on the constellation of social forces which brings such collectivist arrangements into existence.

The ascription of 'statelessness' to communism in the Marxist scheme of history is a theoretical supposition bound up with optimistic expectations (in fact, I would submit: the received prejudices in the nineteenth century of the linear and rationalistic conception of historical progress) about the enlightened

---

1 Laibman 2001, p. 86.

organisation of society based on scientific principles, enabled by the aboli-tion of class antagonisms. The disappearance of the state is premised on the notion that social conflict can be reconciled by the rational administration of resources in society. As such, the 'statelessness' of communism is a secondary corollary of the more fundamental essence of the organisation of social co-operation arranged around common ownership. This relationship, in my view, breaks down under scrutiny, insofar as social conflict is endemic to human social organisation and cannot be rationally organised out of existence by instruments of scientific social engineering. As such, the classless organisation of society does not (semi-)automatically cause state authority to wither away.

Provided that more fundamental characteristics are actually realised in the constitution of society, such as collective ownership by the political com-munity, we can accurately consider this a form of communistic social organ-isation despite whatever specific form of political organisation presides over it. The constitution of the political community becomes of secondary signific-ance, and may assume the form of a republican regime, voluntary association, or something else entirely. In addition, if we can convincingly argue that the constitutional-republican form represents the highest form of political organ-isation corresponding to socialism as the highest form of social development more generally, then we can successfully re-interpret the Marxist theory of socialism on a republican basis.

2   What I Hope to Have Imparted to the Reader

If I have accomplished my task reasonably well, the book should have conferred to the reader some basic ways to think about the means by which socialist society could be organised, related to its political and economic dimensions. As noted, references to 'democratic planning' and collective decision-making often resemble a wish list of social achievements that socialism should bestow, without tangible means or feasible mechanism to make them a reality under a system of socialised ownership – possibly labouring under the assumption that socialism, in the scheme of history, is the final consummation of social development. These ideas are underpinned by wishful thinking rather than by a serious engagement with political and economic thought. Speaking more generally, effort should be made to revive the field of socialist economics as a serious discipline; and to integrate the political and social scope of socialist thought into the area of socialist economics – in other words, to deal seriously with matters of production and distribution from the perspective of socialism and to end the intellectual embargo on economics. To rectify this attitude, we have outlined some of the primary feasibility criteria and fundamental ways of addressing them in reference to empirical and theoretical data on socialist construction. We have summarised and reviewed some of the basic instruments and institutional features that have been advanced as the equipment to deal with the fundamental problems of organising socialist society. This should have impressed on the reader the complexities of socialist construction and the importance of approaching these issues with the rigour that their intricacies warrant.

Many of the features that I have sketched by broad strokes to form into the crude schematics of the socialist republic are undoubtedly open to contestation, and there are probably many alternative tools and devices that we can conceive of that would achieve the same or similar ends. However, any approach to socialist economic planning and collective decision-making will have to satisfy certain basic preconditions. The theory of socialism being a cumulative, open-ended enterprise – in which the reader hopefully becomes an active participant – does not, however, serve as an excuse to disregard basic realism. The dialogue should involve arguments that deal realistically with resource constraints (presupposing their existence, for one) and all the corollaries that flow from them. This book has hopefully introduced the reader to the necessary ingredients and references to think about the ways in which practical hurdles of the construction of socialism can be addressed and overcome.

In the process of navigating these issues, we revisited some of the ideas developed from within the socialist bloc countries to overcome real-world challenges involved in organising a socialised economy, which are now at risk of being forgotten, and recaptured them to refit these ideas into a modern adaptation of a feasible model of socialist society prepared for a contemporary readership. This should hopefully demonstrate to the reader their relevance to current intellectual endeavours related to the social organisation of socialism. Unfortunately, failures in the twentieth century have resulted in many socialists receding into antiquated ideas from the 1800s about the community of associated producers managing themselves only with the aid of simple arithmetic and book-keeping. These 'traditionalists', unbeknownst to themselves, often propose ideas of lower sophistication than, but of striking similarity to, those that were operational under war communism. Replacing millions of spontaneous interactions of market exchange with an economic mechanism of socialised planning is not a matter of 'winging it' and immediately leaping into a fully maturated socialism by means of immediate 'communisation'; rather it requires tremendous and protracted efforts. It is my hope that the reader is by now aware of these difficulties and has some sense of how we could possibly go about handling them.

3   Moving Forward along the Long and Winding Road

The intent behind my inquiry was to appease my own doubts by discovering a gratifying resolution to the puzzle of socialist planning and social organisation and in this process make my findings available to others who grapple with similar questions. This aim has proved to be over-ambitious. In hindsight, we can discern in this monograph the outlines of a research agenda for modelling socialism, indicating feasibility criteria and the directions in which solutions can and should be sought. The issues and possible solutions raised in this manuscript should be subjected to systematic treatment and critical scrutiny. The theoretical and practical challenges we face are formidable. As a new generation of progressives and leftists emerges, we require a new generation of ideas and theories and therefore of thinkers that take up the mantle of supplying the socialist movement with the theoretical underpinnings and equipment necessary to realise our political ambitions. This should stretch from making socialist political and economic theory available in all grades of theoretical sophistication, from complex 'planometric' modelling to simple summaries published for a more general audience and cadres – and anything in between. It is critical that theoretical prescriptions of socialist society are disseminated widely and do not remain locked away in academia, in isolation of the practical requirements of the socialist movement. By clarifying our destination, we can more effectively chart a path forward that leads to the general emancipation of humanity. Toward this end we require the mutual involvement of political parties, trade unions, and research institutes to develop and supply the theoretical preconditions for the lasting realisation of socialism and thus to enable party theorists, strategists, and activist cadres to formulate a political programme to guide their actions and choices at the operational and strategic levels.

In my mind, it was therefore necessary to first of all establish whether it is technically feasible to re-establish society on the basis of a socialist constitution. The priority of our study was therefore to concern ourselves with the foremost general issues that arise when we attempt to rehabilitate socialism with the aid of the conceptual resources of republicanism. The broad sketches simultaneously provide the outline for a future research programme, which should facilitate the leap into a more mature body of socialist theory. Each chapter warrants more expansive elaboration (probably sufficient for a separate monograph each), developing the technical elements and exploring the political principles in closer detail. Especially where it concerns the dynamics of intensive growth, the theoretical repertoire of socialism is gravely underdeveloped and due attention should be accorded to it.

Some other obvious directions of research also present themselves – although they are too numerous to list in their entirety – which relate to the systematic development of republican socialism in all dimensions. To render republican socialism into a coherent and viable body of political thought, it should develop a normative set of arguments and principles. This implies a systematic treatment of some of the ideas introduced here, such as the expansion and deepening of the concept of socialist constitutionalism. In this respect, socialist republicanism offers a promising new avenue of socialist theory, spanning from research into historical antecedents to current theorising of normative theory and political strategy.

Discussion in this book of how the many particularities and divisions among workers can be successfully reconciled to realise the republican aspiration of universalism has been fully absent. This relates to civic education, mentioned only in passing. This further intersects with the ways in which social cohesion, solidarity, a common identity, and so on relate to tensions of acculturation, patriotism, assimilation, and chauvinism within the political community. A republic cannot sustain itself by formal (in a sense, lifeless) equality alone. Solidarity and public-spiritedness are intricately connected and depend on cultural conceptions of how individual citizens relate to the community at large. By developing these notions into a coherent format, republican socialism contains the promise of a distinctive radical, progressive, emancipatory, universalist identity politics that can challenge and engage with existing variants (liberal multiculturalism, post-colonialism, and nativism) and with the rejection of identity politics altogether (class reductionism, economism).

There are many more threads that should be woven together, and I extend my invitation to anyone whose moral convictions and political commitments are animated by social justice to become active participants in the common ambition of socialist renewal.

> As long as we are living, we need to come up fighting, dust ourselves down, learn from our defeat and, sadder but wiser, struggle to a better conceived victory. Victories do come after bitter and bruising defeats. We need to face the worst, but to hope and work for the best. The motto of Gramsci should be ours as well: pessimism of the intellect; optimism of the will.[2]

---

2 Sheehan 1992.

References

Adam, D. 2013, *Marx's Critique of Socialist Labor-Money Schemes and the Myth of Council Communism's Proudhonism*, Marxist Humanist Initiative: https://www.marxisthumanistinitiative.org/alternatives-to-capital/marxs-critique-of-socialist-labor-money-schemes-and-the-myth-of-council-communisms-proudhonism.html accessed 1 March 2020.

Ahn, B.J. 1975, 'The Political Economy of the People's Commune in China: Changes and Continuities', *The Journal of Asian Studies* 34(3), 631–58.

AKEL n.d., *Our Concept of Socialism within the Realities of Cyprus*. https://akel.org.cy/σοσιαλισμός/lang=en accessed 18 February 2023.

Albert, M., and R. Hahnel 1978, *Unorthodox Marxism: An Essay on Capitalism, Socialism, and Revolution*, Cambridge: South End Press.

Albert, M., and R. Hahnel 1991, *Looking Forward: Participatory Economics for the Twenty First Century*, Cambridge: South End Press.

Albert, M., and R. Hahnel 1992, 'Participatory Planning', *Science & Society* 56(1), 39–59.

Albert, M. 2003, *Parecon: Life After Capitalism*, London: Verso.

Allen, R.L. 1958, 'Economic Motives in Soviet Foreign Trade Policy', *Southern Economic Journal* 25(2), 189–201.

Amirault, D., C. Kwan, and G. Wilkinson 2005, 'A Survey of the Price-Setting Behaviour of Canadian Companies', *Bank of Canada Review Winter 2004–2005*.

Arendt, H. 1990, *On Revolution*, London: Penguin Books.

Ball, J. 2010, 'The Need for Planning: The Restoration of Capitalism in the Soviet Union in the 1950s and the Decline of the Soviet Economy', *Culture and Crisis* 17. https://ojs.library.ubc.ca/index.php/clogic/article/view/191530/188642

Bardhan, P., and J.E. Roemer 1994, 'On the Workability of Market Socialism', *Journal of Economic Perspectives* 8(2), 177–81.

Bardhan, P., and J.E. Roemer 1992, 'Market Socialism: A Case for Rejuvenation', *Journal of Economic Perspectives* 6(3), 101–16.

Bazarov, V. 1917, 'What is Needed for Socialism?' *Marxist Internet Archive*, https://www.marxists.org/archive/bazarov/1917/what-needed.htm accessed 12 December 2022.

Beissinger, M. 1998, *Scientific Management, Socialist Discipline, and Soviet Power*, London: I.B. Tauris.

Belykh, A.A. 1989, 'A Note on the Origins of Input-output Analysis and the Contribution of the Early Soviet Economists: Chayanov, Bogdanov and Kritsman', *Soviet Studies* 41(3), 426–9.

Benn, C. 2003, *The War of 1812*, New York: Routledge.

Black, B. 2011, *Debunking Democracy*, The Anarchist Library, https://theanarchistlibrary.org/library/bob-black-debunking-democracy accessed 24 March 2020.

Blasi, J.R. 1986, *The Communal Experience of the Kibbutz* (electronic book, 2017), New York: Routledge.

Bockman, J. 2011, *Markets in the Name of Socialism: The Left-Wing Origins of Neoliberalism*, Stanford: Stanford University Press.

Boettke, J.P., and P.T. Leeson 2005, 'Still Impossible After All These Years: Reply to Caplan', *Critical Review* 17(1–2), 155–70.

Boldyrev, I., and T. Düppe 2020, 'Programming the USSR: Leonid V. Kantorovich in Context', *The British Journal for the History of Science* 53(2), 255–78.

Bonin, J.P., D.C. Jones, and L. Putterman 1993, 'Theoretical and Empirical Studies of Producer Cooperatives: Will Ever the Twain Meet?' *Journal of Economic Literature* 31, 1290–1320.

Bookchin, M. 1986, *Post-Scarcity Anarchism*, Montreal/Buffalo: Black Rose Books.

Bookchin, M. 1991a, *The Next Revolution: Popular Assemblies and the Promise of Democracy*, London: Verso

Bookchin, M. 1991b, *Libertarian Municipalism: An Overview*, A Social Ecology Publication, http://dwardmac.pitzer.edu/anarchist_archives/bookchin/gp/perspectives24.html accessed 17 March 2023.

Bookchin, M. 2015, *The Next Revolution: Popular Assemblies and the Promise of Direct Democracy*, London: Verso.

Bor, M.K. Material Balances 1979, *The Great Soviet Encyclopedia*, 3rd Edition (1970–1979), accessed 17 October 2020 from https://encyclopedia2.thefreedictionary.com/Material+Balances

Bordiga, A. 1920, *Theses of the Abstentionist Communist Faction of the Italian Socialist Party*, Marxist Internet Archive, https://www.marxists.org/archive/bordiga/works/1920/abstentionists.htm accessed 19 February 2020.

Breslauer, G.W. 2002, *Gorbachev and Yeltsin as Leaders*, Cambridge: Cambridge University Press.

Brest, P. 1988, 'Further beyond the Republican Revival: Toward Radical Republicanism', *The Yale Law Journal* 97(8), 1623–31.

Brewster, L. 2004, 'Review of *Towards a New Socialism?* by W. Paul Cockshott and Allin F. Cottrell', *The Quarterly Journal of Austrian Economics* 7(1), 65–77.

Brinton, M. 1970, 'The Bolsheviks and Workers' Control: The State and Counter-Revolution', Marxist Internet Archive, https://www.marxists.org/archive/brinton/1970/workers-control/ accessed 19 February 2022.

Brus, W. 1972, *The Market in a Socialist Economy*, London: Routledge & Kegan Paul.

Brus, W., and K. Łaski 1989, *From Marx to the Market: Socialism in Search of an Economic System*, Oxford: Clarendon Press.

Buick, A., and J. Crump 1986, *State Capitalism: The Wages System Under New Management*, New York: Palgrave Macmillan.

Bukharin, N., and E. Preobrazhensky 1920, *The ABC of Communism*, Marxist Internet

Archive, https://www.marxists.org/archive/bukharin/works/1920/abc/index.htm accessed 20 February 2020.

Busky, D.F. 2000, *Democratic Socialism: A Global Survey*, Westport: Praeger.

Campbell, A. 2002, 'INTRODUCTION: Designing Socialism: Visions, Projections, Models', *Science & Society* 76(2), 140–6.

Campbell, A. 2012, 'Democratic Planned Socialism: Feasible Economic Procedures', *Science & Society* 66(1), 29–42.

Caplan, B. 2004, 'Is Socialism Really "Impossible"?' *Critical Review* 16(1), 33–52.

Carr, E.H. 1952, *The Bolshevik Revolution 1917–1923*, New York: The Macmillan Company.

Carson, K.A. 2008, *Organization Theory: A Libertarian Perspective*. BookSurge.

Carter, M. 2010, 'The Landless Workers Movement and Democracy in Brazil', *Latin American Research Review* 45(Special Issue), 186–217.

Castoriadis, C. 1988, 'On the Content of Socialism, II [1957]', in *Cornelius Castoriadis, Political and Social Writings: 1955–1960, from the Workers' Struggle Against Bureaucracy to Revolution in the Age of Modern Capitalism*, pp. 90–154, Minneapolis: University of Minnesota Press.

Chandrasekhar, C.P. 1998, 'The Planning Principle: An Unresolved Debate', in *Economics as Ideology and Experience: Essays in Honour of Ashok Mitra*, London: Frank Cass Publishers.

Chandrasekhar, C.P. 2018, 'Learning to Plan: Revisiting the Soviet Experiment', *Marxist* 34, 3 (July–September), https://www.cpim.org/content/learning-plan-revisiting-soviet-experiment accessed 16 July 2020.

Chattopadhyay, P. 1991, 'Did the Bolshevik Seizure of Power Inaugurate a Socialist Revolution? A Marxian Inquiry', *Economic Review* 1515.

Chattopadhyay, P. 1994, *The Marxian Concept of Capital and the Soviet Experience: Essay in the Critique of Political Economy*, Westport: Praeger Publishers.

Chattopadhyay, P. 2005, 'Worlds Apart: Socialism in Marx and in Early Bolshevism', *Economic & Political Weekly* 40(53), 5629–34.

Chattopadhyay, P. 2016, *Marx's Associated Mode of Production: A Critique of Marxism*, Basingstoke: Palgrave Macmillan.

Chomsky, N. 1999, *Profit over People: Neoliberalism and the Global Order*, London: Turnaround Publisher Services Ltd.

Chomsky, N. 2002, 'Activism, Anarchism, and Power', *Conversations with History*, https://chomsky.info/20020322/ accessed 18 February 2023.

CibCom 2022, *Mathematics to Plan an Economy: Introduction to Cyber-socialist Calculus*, https://cibcom.org/mathematics-to-plan-an-economy-an-introduction-to-cyber-socialist-calculation/ accessed 28 November 2022.

Cliff, T. 1974, *State Capitalism in Russia*, Marxist Internet Archive, https://www.marxists.org/archive/cliff/works/1955/statecap/index.htm accessed 22 June 2022.

Coase, R.H. 1937, 'The Nature of the Firm', *Economica* 4(16), 386–405.

Cockshott, P. 2008, *Calculation in-Natura, from Neurath to Kantorovich*: https://pdfs
.semanticscholar.org/0e3a/443d6fb314eb8b160576faa9928aa151d6fb.pdf
accessed 19 February 2020.

Cockshott, P., and D. Zachariah 2011, 'Anti-Republicanism', in *Arguments for Socialism*,
http://eprints.gla.ac.uk/58987/1/58987.pdf accessed 1 April 2020.

Cockshott, W.P., and A. Cottrell 1993, *Towards a New Socialism*, Nottingham: Spokesman
Books.

Cockshott, W.P., and A. Cottrell 1999, *Economic Planning, Computers and Labor Values*,
https://users.wfu.edu/cottrell/socialism_book/aer.pdf.

Cockshott, W.P. 1990, 'Application of Artificial Intelligence Techniques to Economic
Planning', *Future Computer Systems* 2(4), 429–43.

Cole, G.D.H. 1920a, *Self-Government in Industry*, London: G. Bells and Sons Ltd.

Cole, G.D.H. 1920b, *Guild Socialism Restated*, London: Leonard Parsons.

Cole, G.D.H. 1921, *Guild Socialism: A Plan for Economic Democracy*, New York: Frederick
A. Stokes Company.

Cole, G.D.H. 1935, *Principles of Economic Planning*, London: Macmillan and Co.

Conquest, R. 2008, *The Great Terror: A Reassessment*, Oxford: Oxford University Press.

Conte, M.A., and J. Svejnar 1990, 'The Performance Effects of Employee Ownership
Plans', in A.S. Blinder (ed.), *Paying for Productivity: A Look at the Evidence* (pp. 143–
72), Washington D.C.: The Brookings Institution.

Cook, L.J. 1992, 'Brezhnev's "Social Contract" and Gorbachev's Reforms', *Soviet Studies*
44(1), 37–56.

Cooney, A. 2001, *Distributism*, London: Third Way Publications.

Cottrell, A., and W.P. Cockshott 1993a, 'Calculation, Complexity and Planning: The
Socialist Calculation Debate Once Again', *Review of Political Economy* 5, 73–112.

Cottrell, A., W.P. Cockshott, and G. Michaelson 2007, *Cantor Diagonalisation and Planning*, http://www.dcs.gla.ac.uk/~wpc/reports/cantor.pdf?fbclid=IwAR2t-lYm2hP2g
7zJNhbfBf2j95h3WWUeAoxUQB_-bwLofiXslymbcntFncs accessed 23 May 2020.

CPSU 1961, *Programme of the Communist Party of the Soviet Union, 1961*, Moscow: Foreign Language Publishing House.

Crump, J., and M. Rubel (eds) 1987, *Non-Market Socialism in the Nineteenth and Twentieth Century*, London: Palgrave Macmillan.

Dagger, R. 2004, 'Communitarianism and Republicanism', in G.F. Gaus and C. Kukathas,
Handbook of Political Theory (pp. 167–79), Thousand Oaks: Sage Publications.

Dagger, R. 2006, 'Neo-republicanism and the Civic Economy', *Politics, Philosophy & Economics* 5(2), 151–73.

Davies, R.W. 1958, *The Development of the Soviet Budgetary System*, Cambridge: Cambridge University Press.

Deutscher, I. 1952, 'Socialist Competition', Marxist Internet Archive, https://www.marxi
sts.org/archive/deutscher/1952/socialist-competition.htm
accessed 27 October 2022.

Devine, P. 2002, 'Participatory Planning through Negotiated Coordination', *Science & Society* 66(1), 72–85.

Devine, P. 2011, *Democracy and Economic Planning*, Cambridge: Polity.

Dobb, M. 1967, *Papers on Capitalism, Development and Planning*, London: Routledge & Kegan Paul.

Dolgoff, S. (ed.) 1974, *The Anarchist Collectives: Workers' Self-management in the Spanish Revolution 1936–1939*, New York: Free Life Editions.

Doucouliagos, C. 1995, 'Worker Participation and Productivity in Labor-Managed and Participatory Capitalist Firms: A Meta-Analysis', *ILR Review* 49(1), 58–77.

Douma, S.W., and H. Schreuder 2017, *Economic Approaches to Organizations*, Harlow: Pearson Educated Limited.

Dow, G.K. 2003, *Governing the Firm: Workers' Control in Theory and Practice*, Cambridge: Cambridge University Press.

Draper, H. 1987, *The 'Dictatorship of the Proletariat' from Marx to Lenin*, New York: Monthly Review Press.

Dyker, D.A. 2013, *The Future of the Soviet Economic Planning System*, New York: Routledge.

Ellman, M. 1969, 'The Consistency of Soviet Plans', *Scottish Journal of Political Economy* 16(3), 50–74.

Ellman, M. 1973, *Planning Problems in the USSR: The Contribution of Mathematical Economics to their Solution 1960–1971*, Cambridge: Cambridge University Press.

Ellman, M. 1975, 'Did the Agricultural Surplus Provide the Resources for the Increase in Investment in the USSR During the First Five Year Plan?' *The Economic Journal* 85(340), 844–63.

Ellman, M. 1977, 'Seven Theses on Kosyginism', *De Economist* 125(1), 22–42.

Ellman, M. 1978, 'The Fundamental Problem of Socialist Planning', *Oxford Economic Papers* 30(2), 249–62.

Ellman, M. 1986, 'The Macro-economic Situation in the USSR. Retrospect and Prospect', *Soviet Studies* 38(4), 530–42.

Ellman, M. 2008, 'The Political Economy of Stalinism in the Light of the Archival Revolution', *Journal of Institutional Economics* 4(1), 99–125.

Ellman, M. 2014, *Socialist Planning*, Cambridge: Cambridge University Press.

Ellman, M., and V. Kontorovich 2013, *The Disintegration of the Soviet Economic System*, London: Routledge.

Epstein, R.A. 1999, 'Hayekian Socialism', *Maryland Law Review* 58(271), 271–99.

Erlich, A. 1967, *The Soviet Industrialization Debate*, Cambridge, MA: Harvard University Press.

Escoe, G.M. 1996, 'The Efficiency of Soviet Industry', *Comparative Economic Studies* 38(2–3), 71–86.

Estrin, S. 1991, 'Yugoslavia: The Case of Self-Managing Market Socialism', *Journal of Economic Perspectives* 5(4), 187–94.

Feddersen, T.J. 2004, 'Rational Choice Theory and the Paradox of Not Voting', *The Journal of Economic Perspectives* 18(1), 99–112.

Fotopoulos, T. 1997, *Towards an Inclusive Democracy: The Crisis of the Growth Economy and the Need for a New Liberatory Project*, London: Cassell.

Fotopoulos, T. 2003, 'Inclusive Democracy and Participatory Economics', *Democracy & Nature* 9(3), 429–71.

Frankfurt, H.G. 1971, 'Freedom of the Will and the Concept of a Person', *Journal of Philosophy* 68(1), 5–20.

Freeman, J. 1972, 'The Tyranny of Structurelessness', *The Second Wave* 2(1).

Freyberg-Inan, A. 2004, *What Moves Man: The Realist Theory of International Relations and its Judgment of Human Nature*, New York: State University of New York Press.

Freyberg-Inan, A., and V. Birchfield 2005, 'Organic Intellectuals and Counter-Hegemonic Politics in the Age of Globalisation: The Case of ATTAC', in *Critical Theories, World Politics and the 'Anti-Globalization Movement'*. London: Routledge.

Fry, D.P., and G. Souillac 2017, 'The Original Partnership Societies: Evolved Propensities for Equality, Prosociality, and Peace', *Interdisciplinary Journal of Partnership Studies* 4(1), 1–27.

Fry, D.P., and P. Söderberg 2013, 'Lethal Aggression in Mobile Forager Bands and Implications for the Origins of War', *Science* 341(270), 270–2.

Fry, D.P., and P. Söderberg 2014, 'Myths About Hunter-gatherers Redux: Nomadic Forager War and Peace', *Journal of Aggression: Conflict and Peace Research* 6(4), 255–66.

Gaus, G.F. 2003, 'Backwards into the Future: Neorepublicanism as a Postsocialist Critique of Market Society', *Social Philosophy and Policy* 20(1), 59–91.

Gavrilets, S., E.A. Duenez-Guzman, and M.D. Vose 2008, 'Dynamics of Alliance Formation and the Egalitarian Revolution', *PLoS ONE* 3(10), e3293.

Gerovitch, S. 2002, *From Newspeak to Cyberspeak: A History of Soviet Cybernetics*, Cambridge, MA: MIT Press.

Gerovitch, S. 2008, 'InterNyet: Why the Soviet Union did not Build a Nationwide Computer Network', *History and Technology* 24(4), 335–50.

Gey, S.G. 1993, 'The Unfortunate Revival of Civic Republicanism', *University of Pennsylvania Law Review* 141(3), 801–98.

GIC 1930, *Fundamental Principles of Communist Production and Distribution*, Marxist Internet Archive, https://www.marxists.org/subject/left-wing/gik/1930/index.htm accessed 23 February 2020.

Giddens, A. 1990, *Central Problems of Social Theory*, London: Macmillan Education Ltd.

Gindin, S. 2019, 'We Need to Say What Socialism Will Look Like', *Jacobin*, https://www.jacobinmag.com/2019/03/sam-gindin-socialist-planning-models accessed 24 May 2020.

Gluckstein, D. 2011, 'Workers' Councils in Europe: A Century of Experience', in I. Ness and D. Azzellini (eds), *Ours to Master and to Own: Workers' Councils from the Commune to the Present* (pp. 32–47), Chicago: Haymarket Books.

Gordon, M.J. 2001, 'Growth and Security Under Welfare-Corporate Capitalism and Market Socialism', *Brazilian Journal of Political Economy* 21(2) (82), 433–48.

Gourevitch, A. 2013, 'Labor Republicanism and the Transformation of Work', *Political Theory* 41(4), 591–617.

Gourevitch, A. 2015, *From Slavery to the Cooperative Commonwealth: Labor and Republican Liberty in the Nineteenth Century*. Electronic book: Brown University.

Gregory, P.R. 2004, *The Political Economy of Stalinism*, Cambridge: University of Cambridge Press.

Grünberg, M. 2023, 'The Planning Daemon: Future Desire and Communal Production', *Historical Materialism* 31(4), 115–59.

Hahnel, R. 2005, *Economic Justice and Democracy: From Competition to Cooperation*, New York: Routledge.

Hahnel, R. 2021, *Democratic Economic Planning*, London: Routledge.

Hahnel, R., and E.O. Wright 2016, *Alternatives to Capitalism: Proposals for a Democratic Economy*, London: Verso.

Hama, A. 2010, 'Predictably Irrational: The Hidden Forces That Shape Our Decisions', *Mankind Quarterly* 50(1), 257–60.

Hamilton, A., J. Madison, J. Jay, and T. Ball 2007, *The Federalist*, Cambridge: Cambridge University Press.

Hanson, P. 1983, 'Success Indicators Revisited: The July 1979 Soviet Decree on Planning and Management', *Soviet Studies* 35(1), 1–13.

Harrison, M. 2016, 'Foundations of the Soviet Command Economy, 1917 to 1941', Centre for Competitive Advantage in the Global Economy, Working Paper Series, University of Warwick, https://warwick.ac.uk/fac/soc/economics/staff/mharrison/public/cambridge_communism_postprint.pdf accessed 2 February 2023.

Hayek, F.A. v. 1940, 'Socialist Calculation: The Competitive "Solution"', *Economica* 7(26), 125–49.

Hayek, F.A. v. 1945, 'The Use of Knowledge in Society', *The American Economic Review* 35(4), 519–30.

Hayek, F.A. v. 2006, *The Road to Serfdom*, New York: Routledge.

Heyer, J. 2022, 'Basic Problems of a Democratically Planned Economy', Unpublished paper delivered at the conference 'Socialist Futures', Florence, May 2022.

Heywood, A. 2004, *Political Theory: An Introduction*, Third Edition, New York: Palgrave Macmillan.

Heywood, A. 2017, *Political Ideologies: An Introduction*, London: Macmillan Education.

Higonnet, P.L.R. 1979, 'Babeuf: Communist or Proto-Communist?' *The Journal of Modern History* 51(4), 773–81.

Higonnet, P.L.R. 1998, *Goodness Beyond Virtue: Jacobins during the French Revolution*, Cambridge, MA: Harvard University Press.

Hobson, S.G. 1914, *National Guilds: An Inquiry Into the Wage System and the Way Out*, London: G. Bells & Sons Ltd.

Hodgson, G.M. 1984, *The Democratic Economy: A New Look at Planning, Markets and Power*, Harmondsworth: Penguin.

Hodgson, G.M. 1998, 'Socialism Against Markets? A Critique of Two Recent Proposals', *Economy and Society* 27(4), 407–33.

Holterman, T. 1980, *Anarchistiese staatsopvatting: (een paradox?)*, Deventer: Kluwer.

Holterman, T. 2012, 'Anarchisme & Recht', *De As* 179(0), 1–60.

Honohan, I. 2002, *Civic Republicanism*, London: Routledge.

Honohan, I., and J. Jennings 2006, *Republicanism in Theory and Practice*, London: Routledge.

Horvat, B. 1964, *Towards a Theory of Planned Economy*, Belgrade: Yugoslav Institute of Economic Research.

Hudis, P. 2005, 'Directly and Indirectly Social Labor: What Kind of Human Relations can Transcend Capitalism?' *Journal of the International Marxist-Humanist Organization*, https://imhojournal.org/articles/directly-and-indirectly-social-labor-what-kind-of-human-relations-can-transcend-capitalism-by-peter-hudis/ accessed 4 March 2020.

Huerta de Soto, J. 2008, *The Austrian School Market Order and Entrepreneurial Creativity*, Cheltenham: Edward Elgar.

Hurwicz, L. 1973, 'The Design of Mechanisms for Resource Allocation', *The American Economic Review* 63(2), 1–30.

ILO 2016, *Key Indicators of the Labour Market*, Ninth Edition, Geneva: International Labour Office

IMF 1991, *A Study of the Soviet Economy: Volume 1*, Paris: International Monetary Fund.

Inter.kke.gr. 2014, *Programme of the KKE*, Communist Party of Greece, https://inter.kke.gr/en/articles/Programme-of-the-KKE/ Accessed 14 January 2020.

Ironside, K. 2021, *A Full-Value Ruble: The Promise of Prosperity in the Postwar Soviet Union*, Cambridge, MA: Harvard University Press.

Irving, S. 2020, 'Hayek's Neo-Roman Liberalism', *European Journal of Political Theory* 19(4), 553–70.

Itoh, M. 1995, *Political Economy for Socialism*, New York: St. Martin's Press.

Itoh, M. 1996, 'Money and Credit in Socialist Economies: A Reconsideration', *Capital & Class* 20(3), 95–118.

Jakopovich, D. 2015, 'Yugoslavia's Self-management', *Workers Control*, http://www.workerscontrol.net/authors/yugoslavia%E2%80%99s-self-management accessed February 19, 2021.

Jankowski, R. 2007, 'Altruism and the Decision to Vote', *Rationality and Society* 19(1), 5–34.

JCP 2020, 'Program of the Japanese Communist Party', *Japanese Communist Party*, https://www.jcp.or.jp/english/jcpcc/blog/2020/01/program-of-the-jcp.html#_05 accessed 5 June 2020.

Jeffries, S. 2012, 'Why Marxism is on the Rise Again', *The Guardian*, 4 July, https://www.theguardian.com/world/2012/jul/04/the-return-of-marxism accessed 5 June 2020.

Jessop, B., and H. Overbeek 2019, *Transnational Capital and Class Fractions: The Amsterdam School Perspective Reconsidered*, London: Routledge.

Jones, N.B. 2016, *Demography and Evolutionary Ecology of Hadza Hunter-Gatherers*, Cambridge: Cambridge University Press.

Jossa, B. 2014, *Producer Cooperatives as a New Mode of Production*, New York: Routledge.

Kalecki, M. 2010, *Selected Essays on Economic Planning*, Cambridge: Cambridge University Press.

Kalyuzhnova, Y. 1998, *The Kazakstani Economy: Independence and Transition*, Basingstoke: Macmillan.

Kantorovich, L.V. 1965, *The Best Use of Economic Resources*, Oxford: Pergamon Press.

Kantorovich, L.V. 1975, 'Mathematics in Economics: Achievements, Difficulties, Perspectives', Leonid Vitaliyevich Kantorovich Prize Lecture, https://www.nobelprize.org/prizes/economic-sciences/1975/kantorovich/lecture/ accessed 3 January 2023.

Kardelj, E. 1976, 'Socialist Self-Management in Yugoslavia', *International Review of Administrative Sciences* 42(2), 103–10.

Keeran, R., and T. Kenny 2010, *Socialism Betrayed: Behind the Collapse of the Soviet Union*, Bloomington: iUniverse

Kenny, C. 2010, 'What Does the Eastern European Growth Experience Tell Us About the Policy and Convergence Debates?' Unpublished paper, https://charleskenny.blogs.com/weblog/files/russ6.pdf accessed 1 March 2020.

Keren, M., and D. Levhari 1992, 'Some Capital Market Failures in the Socialist Labor-managed Economy', *Journal of Comparative Economics* 16(4), 655–69.

Kim, B.Y., S.J. Kim, and K. Lee 2007, 'Assessing the Economic Performance of North Korea, 1954–1989: Estimates and Growth Accounting Analysis', *Journal of Comparative Economics* 35(3), 564–82.

Kirn, G. 2019, *Partisan Ruptures: Self-Management, Market Reform and the Spectre of Socialist Yugoslavia*, London: Pluto Press.

KKE (Eighteenth Congress of the KKE) 2009, '18th Congress, Resolution on Socialism: Assessments and conclusions on socialist construction during the 20th century, focusing on the USSR. KKE's perception on socialism', *KKE.gr*, https://inter.kke.gr/en/articles/18th-Congress-Resolution-on-Socialism/ accessed 16 July 2020.

KKE 2013, 'Programme of the KKE', *Communist Party of Greece*, https://inter.kke.gr/en/articles/Programme-of-the-KKE/ accessed 14 January 2020.

Knaack, R. 1980, 'The Role of Profit in the Soviet Economy', *De Economist* 128, 393–419.

Kontorovich, V. 2013, 'The Preobrazhenskii-Feldman Myth and the Soviet Industrialization', https://scholarship.haverford.edu/cgi/viewcontent.cgi?article=1172&context=economics_facpubs

Kornai, J. 1979, 'Resource-Constrained versus Demand-Constrained Systems', *Econometrica* 47(4), 801–19.

Kornai, J. 1980, 'The Dilemmas of a Socialist Economy: The Hungarian Experience', *Cambridge Journal of Economics* 4(2), 147–57.

Kornai, J. 1986, 'The Soft Budget Constraint', *KYKLOS* 39(1), 3–30.

Kornai, J. 2007, *The Socialist System: The Political Economy of Communism*, New York: Oxford University Press.

Kornai, J. 2012, 'Innovation and Dynamism: Interaction between Systems and Technical Progress', in G. Roland (ed.), *Economies in Transition: The Long-run View* (pp. 14–56), London: Palgrave Macmillan.

Kowalik, T. 1990, 'Lange-Lerner Mechanism', in J. Eatwell, M. Milgate, and P. Newman (eds), *Problems of the Planned Economy* (pp. 147–50), London: The Macmillan Press Limited.

Kozlov, G.A. 1977, *Political Economy: Socialism*, Moscow: Progress Publishers.

Kscm.cz. 2016, 'Deklarace o socialismu', *Komunistická Strana Čech a Moravy*, https://www.kscm.cz/cs/nase-strana/dokumenty/dulezite-dokumenty-k-minulosti/deklarace-o-socialismu Accessed January 14, 2020.

Kukić, L. 2018, 'Socialist Growth Revisited: Insights from Yugoslavia', *European Review of Economic History* 22(4), 403–29.

Kurashvili, B.P. 1988, 'Restructuring and the Enterprise', *Problems in Economics* 31(5), 23–46.

Kurashvili, B.P. 1990, 'Models of Socialism', *Soviet Sociology* 29(4), 32–52.

Laborde, C. 2012, 'Republicanism', in M. Freeden (ed.), *Oxford Handbook of Political Ideologies*, Oxford: Oxford University Press.

Laborde, C., and J. Maynor 2008, *Republicanism and Political Theory*, Malden: Blackwell.

Laibman, D. 1992, 'Market and Plan: The Evolution of Socialist Social Structures in History and Theory', *Science & Society* 56(1), 60–91.

Laibman, D. 2001, 'Contours of the Maturing Socialist Economy', *Historical Materialism* 9(1), 85–110.

Laibman, D. 2002a, 'Democratic Coordination: Towards a Working Socialism for the New Century', *Science & Society* 66(1), 116–29.

Laibman, D. 2002b, 'Comment [on Devine's "Participatory Planning Through Negotiated Coordination"]', *Science & Society* 66(1), 88–91.

Laibman, D. 2012, 'Incentive Design, Iterative Planning and Local Knowledge in a Maturing Socialist Economy', *International Critical Thought* 1(1), 35–56.

Laibman, D. 2013, 'Mature Socialism: Design, Prerequisites, Transitions', *Review of Radical Political Economics* 45(4), 501–7.

Laibman, D. 2014, 'Horizontalism and Idealism in Socialist Imagination: An Appraisal of the Participatory Economy', *Science & Society* 78(2), 207–34.

Laibman, D. 2015a, 'Multilevel Democratic Iterative Coordination: An Entry in the "Envisioning Socialism" Models Competition', *Marxism 21* 12(1), 307–45.

Laibman, D. 2015b, *Passion and Patience: Society, History, and Revolutionary Vision*, New York: International Publishers.

Laibman, D. 2020, 'Incentives, Optimization, and Democratic Planning: A Socialist Primer', *Science & Society* 84(4), 510–35.

Laibman, D. 2022, 'Systemic Socialism: A Model of the Models', *Science & Society* 86(2), 225–47.

Lange, O. 1936, 'On the Economic Theory of Socialism: Part One', *The Review of Economic Studies* 4(1), 53–71.

Lange, O. 1937, 'On the Economic Theory of Socialism: Part Two', *The Review of Economic Studies* 4(2), 123–42.

Lange, O. 1958, 'The Role of Planning in Socialist Economy', *Indian Economic Review* 4(2), 1–15.

Lange, O. 1971, *Optimal Decisions: Principles of Programming*, Oxford: Pergamon Press.

Leipold, B. 2017, *Citizen Marx: The Relationship between Karl Marx and Republicanism*, Doctoral dissertation, University of Oxford.

Leipold, B. 2020a, 'Chains and Invisible Threads: Liberty and Domination in Marx's Account of Wage-Slavery', in A. De Dijn and H. Dawson (eds), *Rethinking Liberty before Liberalism*, Cambridge: Cambridge University Press.

Leipold, B. 2020b, 'Marx's Social Republic: Radical Republicanism and the Political Institutions of Socialism', in B. Leipold, K. Nabulsi, and S. White (eds), *Radical Republicanism: Recovering the Tradition's Popular Heritage*, Oxford: Oxford University Press.

Leipold, B., K. Nabulsi, and S. White (eds) 2020, *Radical Republicanism: Recovering the Tradition's Popular Heritage*, Oxford: Oxford University Press.

Lenin, V.I. 1913, 'The Three Sources and Three Component Parts of Marxism', Marxist Internet Archive, https://www.marxists.org/archive/lenin/works/1913/mar/x01.htm accessed 19 February 2020.

Lenin, V.I. 1917a, *State and Revolution*, Marxist Internet Archive: https://www.marxists.org/archive/lenin/works/1917/staterev/ accessed 29 February 2020.

Lenin, V.I. 1917b, 'The Tasks of the Proletariat in Our Revolution', Marxist Internet Archive, https://www.marxists.org/archive/lenin/works/1917/tasks/index.htm accessed 4 November 2022.

Lenin, V.I. 1918, 'The Immediate Tasks of the Soviet Government', Marxist Internet Archive, https://www.marxists.org/archive/lenin/works/1918/mar/x03.htm accessed 4 November 2022.

Levin, M.H. 2006, 'Worker Democracy and Worker Productivity', *Social Justice Research* 19(1), 109–20.

Lewis, B. (ed.) 2019, *Karl Kautsky on Democracy and Republicanism*, Leiden: Brill.

Linger, E. 1992, 'Combining Moral and Material Incentives in Cuba', *New School for Social Research* 2(2), 119–36.

Liotta, P.H. 2001, 'Paradigm Lost: Yugoslav Self-Management and the Economics of Disaster', *Balkanologie* 5(1–2), 1–18.

Lovett, F. 2018, 'Republicanism', in E.N. Zalta (ed.), *The Stanford Encyclopedia of Philosophy*, https://plato.stanford.edu/entries/republicanism/ accessed 12 March 2020.

Lovett, F., and P. Pettit 2009, 'Neorepublicanism: A Normative and Institutional Research Program', *Annual Review of Political Science* 12(0), 11–29.

Lucardie, P. 2016, *Democratic Extremism in Theory and Practice: All Power to the People*, London: Routledge.

Lydall, H. 1984, *Yugoslav Socialism: Theory and Practice*, Oxford: Clarendon Press.

Machover, M. 2009, *Collective Decision-making and Supervision in a Communist Society*. Mimeograph. https://www.matzpen.org/docs/Machover-Collective%20Decision-Making.pdf

Macnair, M. 2005, 'Socialism from Below: A Delusion', *Weekly Worker*, https://weeklyworker.co.uk/worker/1071/socialism-from-below-a-delusion/?fbclid=IwAR0qS77d6WB-P_J6bEGZBJvWmdUxHeCV2vjaw5KGx8S0Se3FIWmwHZ139-k accessed 26 February 2020.

Magdoff, F., and C. Williams 2017, *Creating an Ecological Society: Towards a Revolutionary Transformation*, New York: Monthly Review Press.

Maiminas, E.Z. 1979, 'Economic Cybernetics', in *The Great Soviet Encyclopedia*, Third Edition, https://encyclopedia2.thefreedictionary.com/Economic+Cybernetics accessed 17 February 2023.

Makovi, M.B. 2016, *The Impossibility of Democratic Socialism: Two Conceptions of Democracy*, https://ideas.repec.org/p/pra/mprapa/70172.html accessed 7 May 2020.

Malle, S. 1985, *The Economic Organization of War Communism, 1918–1921*, Cambridge: Cambridge University Press.

Mandel, D. 2017, *Democracy, Plan, and Market: Yakov Kronrod's Political Economy of Socialism*, Stuttgart: Ibidem.

March, L. 2008, *Contemporary Far Left Parties in Europe: From Marxism to the Mainstream?* International Policy Analysis, https://library.fes.de/pdf-files/id/ipa/05818.pdf accessed 27 March 2020.

March, L. 2011, *Radical Left Parties in Europe*, New York: Routledge.

Marlowe, F.W. 2003, 'The Mating System of Foragers in the Standard Cross-Cultural Sample', *Cross-Cultural Research* 37(3), 282–306.

Marlowe, F.W. 2010, *The Hadza: Hunter-Gatherers of Tanzania*, Berkeley: University of California Press.

Marx, K., and F. Engels 2010, *Collected Works*, Volume 5: Marx and Engels 1845–47, London: Lawrence & Wishart [cited as MECW plus volume number].

Marx, K., and F. Engels *Collected Works*, Volume 6: Marx and Engels 1845–48, London: Lawrence & Wishart.

Marx, K., and F. Engels *Collected Works*, Volume 10: Marx and Engels 1849–51, London: Lawrence & Wishart.

Marx, K., and F. Engels *Collected Works*, Volume 22: Marx and Engels 1870–71, London: Lawrence & Wishart.

Marx, K., and F. Engels *Collected Works*, Volume 24: Marx and Engels 1874–83, London: Lawrence & Wishart.

Marx, K., and F. Engels *Collected Works*, Volume 25: Engels, London: Lawrence & Wishart.

Marx, K., and F. Engels *Collected Works*, Volume 26: Engels 1882–89, London: Lawrence & Wishart.

Marx, K., and F. Engels *Collected Works*, Volume 27: Engels 1890–95, London: Lawrence & Wishart.

Marx, K., and F. Engels *Collected Works*, Volume 35: Karl Marx – *Capital*, Volume I, London: Lawrence & Wishart.

Marx, K., and F. Engels *Collected Works*, Volume 36: Karl Marx – *Capital*, Volume II, London: Lawrence & Wishart.

Marx, K., and F. Engels *Collected Works*, Volume 37: Karl Marx – *Capital*, Volume III, London: Lawrence & Wishart.

Marx, K., and F. Engels *Collected Works*, Volume 49: Letters 1890–92, London: Lawrence & Wishart.

Mazzucato, M. 2015, *The Entrepreneurial State: Debunking Public vs. Private Sector Myths*, New York: PublicAffairs.

McKelvey, C. 2013, *Popular Assemblies. Global Learning*, https://www.globallearning-cuba.com/blog-umlthe-view-from-the-southuml/popular-assemblies accessed 8 December 2023.

McKelvey, C. 2018, *The Evolution and Significance of the Cuban Revolution: The Light in the Darkness*, Basingstoke: Palgrave Macmillan.

Merrett, S. 1964, 'Capital, Profit and Bonus in Soviet Industry', *Economica* 31(124), 401–7.

Mesa-Lago, C. 2019, 'The Cuban Economy in the 1980s: The Return of Ideology', in S.G. Roca (ed.), *Socialist Cuba: Past Interpretations and Future Challenges*, electronic book, New York: Routledge.

Mises, L. 2012, *Economic Calculation in the Socialist Commonwealth*, Auburn: Ludwig von Mises Institute.

Morozov, E. 2019, 'Digital Socialism? The Calculation Debate in the Age of Big Data', *New Left Review* II/116, https://www.newleftreview.org/issues/II116/articles/evgeny-morozov-digital-socialism accessed 23 May 2020.

Morris, M., and R. De Vincent-Humphreys 2019, 'Price-setting Behaviour: Insights from a Survey of Large Firms', *Economic Bulletin Boxes, European Central Bank*, Volume 7.

Moss, B.H. 1976, *The Origins of the French Labor Movement 1830–1914: The Socialism of Skilled Workers*, Berkeley: University of California Press.

Moss, B.H. 1993, 'Republican Socialism and the Making of the Working Class in Britain, France, and the United States: A Critique of Thompsonian Culturalism', *Comparative Studies in Society and History* 35(2), 390–413.

Mouritsen, H. 2017, *Politics in the Roman Republic*, Cambridge: Cambridge University Press.

Mouritsen, P. 2006, 'Four Models of Republican Liberty and Self-government', in I. Honohan and J. Jennings (eds), *Republicanism in Theory and Practice*, London: Routledge.

Muldoon, J. 2019, 'A Socialist Republican Theory of Freedom and Government', *European Journal of Political Theory* 0(0), 1–21.

Murrell, P. 1991, 'Can Neoclassical Economics Underpin the Reform of Centrally Planned Economies?' *Journal of Economic Perspectives* 5(4), 59–76.

Musić, G. 2011, 'Yugoslavia: Workers' Self-Management as State Paradigm', in I. Ness and D. Azzellini (eds), *Ours to Master and to Own: Workers' Councils from the Commune to the Present* (pp. 172–90), Chicago: Haymarket Books.

Nappalos, S. 2012, 'Ditching Class: The Praxis of Anarchist Communist Economics', in D. Shannon, A.J. Nocella II, and J. Asimakopolous (eds), *The Accumulation of Freedom: Writings on Anarchist Economics* (pp. 291–312), Edinburgh: AK Press.

Ness, I., and D. Azzellini (eds) 2011, *Ours to Master and to Own: Workers' Councils from the Commune to the Present*, Chicago: Haymarket Books.

Neurath, O. 2004, *Otto Neurath: Economic Writings: Selections 1904–1945*, New York: Kluwer Academic Publishers.

Nove, A. 1958, 'The Problem of "Success Indicators" in Soviet Industry', *Economica* 25(97), 1–13.

Nove, A. 1991a, *The Economics of Feasible Socialism Revisited*, London: HarperCollins Academic.

Nove, A. 1991b, '"Allocational Efficiency" – Can It be So?' *Soviet Studies* 43(3), 575–9.

Nove, A. 1992, *An Economic History of the USSR, 1917–1991*, London: Penguin.

Nove, A. 2004, 'The Rise of Non-Leninist Thinking on the Economy', in A. Brown (ed.), *The Demise of Marxism-Leninism in Russia*, New York: Palgrave Macmillan.

Nove, A. 2011, *Socialism, Economics and Development*, London: Allen & Unwin (Publishers) Ltd.

Nuti, D.M. 1986, 'Michal Kalecki's Contribution to the Theory and Practice of Socialist Planning', *Cambridge Journal of Economics* 10(4), 333–53.

O'Shea, T. 2019, 'Socialist Republicanism', *Political Theory* 0(0), 1–25.

Ofer, G. 1988, *Soviet Economic Growth: 1928–1985*, RAND/ UCLA: Center for the Study of Soviet International Behavior.

Offer, A. 2022, *Understanding the Private-Public Divide: Markets, Governments, and Time Horizons*, Cambridge: Cambridge University Press.

Ollman, B. 1977, 'Marx's Vision of Communism: A Reconstruction', *Critique: Journal of Socialist Theory* 8(1), 4–41.

Osiatyński, J. 1988, *Michal Kalecki on a Socialist Economy*, London: Macmillan Press.

Ostrom, E. 1990, *Governing the Commons: The Evolution of Institutions for Collective Action*, Cambridge: Cambridge University Press.

Ostrom, E. 2010, 'Beyond Markets and States: Polycentric Governance of Complex Economic Systems', *The American Economic Review* 100(3), 641–72.

Pannekoek, A. (1950 [1946]), *Workers' Councils*, Marxist Internet Archive: https://www.marxists.org/archive/pannekoe/1947/workers-councils.htm accessed 24 February 2020.

Park, A., V. Rayner, and P. D'Arcy 2010, 'Price-setting Behaviour – Insights from Australian Firms', *RBA Bulletin* 7–14.

Pasvolsky, L. 1921, *The Economics of Communism: With Special Reference to Russia's Experiment*, New York: Macmillan.

Patnaik, P. 2004, 'A Theoretical Note on Kerala-style Decentralised Planning', *The Marxist* 20(1), 1–11, https://www.cpim.org/marxist/200401-marxist-kerala-decentralisedplan.pdf access 21 April 2022.

Pérotin, V. 2012, 'The Performance of Workers' Cooperatives', in P. Battilani and H. Schröter (eds), *The Cooperative Business Movement, 1950 to the Present* (pp. 195–221), Cambridge: Cambridge University Press.

Pérotin, V. 2014, 'Worker Cooperatives: Good, Sustainable Jobs in the Community', *Journal of Entrepreneurial and Organizational Diversity* 2(2), 34–47.

Peterson, A. 2011, *Civic Republicanism and Civic Education: The Education of Citizens*, New York: Palgrave Macmillan.

Pettit, P. 2002, *Republicanism: A Theory of Freedom*, Oxford: Oxford University Press.

Phillips, L., and M. Rozworski 2019, *People's Republic of Walmart: How the World's Biggest Corporations are Laying the Foundation for Socialism*, London: Verso.

Poulantzas, N. 2013, *State, Power, Socialism*, London: Verso.

Prochorov, A.M. (ed.) 1979, *The Great Soviet Encyclopedia*, https://encyclopedia2.thefreedictionary.com/Profit-and-Loss+Accounting accessed 18 July 2020.

Proudhon, P-J. 2011, 'The General Idea of the Revolution in the Nineteenth Century', in P-J. Proudhon, *Property is Theft! A Pierre-Joseph Proudhon Anthology*, Edinburgh: AK Press.

Prychitko, D.L. 2002, *Markets, Planning and Democracy: Essays After the Collapse of Communism*, Cheltenham: Edward Elgar.

Read, C. 1996, *From Tsar to Soviets: The Russian People and Their Revolution, 1917–1921*, Oxford: Oxford University Press.

Richman, S.L. 1981, 'War Communism to NEP: The Road from Serfdom', *The Journal of Libertarian Studies* 5(1), 89–97.

Roberts, W.C. 2017, *Marx's Inferno: The Political Theory of Capital*, Princeton: Princeton University Press.

Robinson, J. 1982, *An Essay on Marxian Economics*, London: The Macmillan Press Ltd.

Roemer, J.E. 1994, *A Future for Socialism*, London: Verso.

Rothbard, M.N. 1991, 'The End of Socialism and the Calculation Debate Revisited', *The Review of Austrian Economics* 5(2), 51–76.

Rothbard, M.N. 2000, *Egalitarianism as a Revolt Against Nature and Other Essays*, Auburn: Ludwig von Mises Institute.

Russell, R., Hanneman, R. and Getz, S. 2013, *Renewal of the Kibbutz: From Reform to Transformation*, New Brunswick: Rutgers University Press.

Savada, A.M., and Library of Congress 1994, *North Korea: A Country Study*. Washington, D.C.: Federal Research Division, Library of Congress.

Sawyer, M.C. 1985, 'The Economics of Michał Kalecki', *Eastern European Economics* 23(3–4), v–x; 1–319.

Schnapper, D. 1998, *Community of Citizens: On the Modern Idea of Nationality*, New Jersey: Transaction Publishers.

Scholl, C., and A. Freyberg-Inan 2018, 'Imagining Another Europe: Building a Pan-European Counter-hegemonic Bloc Around an Anti-austerity Master Frame', *Comparative European Politics* 16(1), 103–25.

Scholl, C., and A. Freyberg-Inan 2013, 'Hegemony's Dirty Tricks: Explaining Counter-globalization's Weakness in Times of Neoliberal Crisis', *Globalizations* 10(4), 619–34.

Scholl, C., and A. Freyberg-Inan 2014, 'Hegemony Reloaded: Why the Anti-Globalization Movement Does Not Benefit from the Neoliberal Crisis', *Zeitschrift für Außen- und Sicherheitspolitik* 12(7), 465–87.

Schweickart, D. 1998, 'Market Socialism: A Defence', in D. Schweickart, J. Lawler, H. Ticktin, and B. Ollman, *Market Socialism: The Debate Among Socialists*, New York: Routledge.

Schweickart, D. 2002, *After Capitalism*, Boston: Rowman & Littlefield.

Schweickart, D. 2006, 'Nonsense on Stilts: Michael Albert's Parecon', http://dschwei.sites.luc.edu/parecon.pdf accessed 7 April 2020.

Scott, J. 2006, *Power*, Cambridge: Polity Press.

Sen, A. 1975, 'The Theory of Economic Planning: Review', *Economica* 42(168), 447–8.

Service, E. 1971, *Primitive Social Organization: An Evolutionary Perspective*, New York: Random House.

Shaikh, A. 1978, 'An Introduction to the History of Crisis Theories', https://pdfs.semanticscholar.org/26af/4e82215aee7170a1183abbd9e7450b0a6cce.pdf accessed 9 April 2020.

Shalom, S.R. 2008, 'Parpolity: A Political System for a Good Society', in C. Spannos (ed.), *Real Utopia: Participatory Society for the 21st Century*, Oakland: AK Press.

Sheehan, H. 1989, *Has the Red Flag Fallen?* Dublin: Attic Press.

Sheehan, H. 1992, *European Socialism: A Blind Alley or a Long and Winding Road?* Dublin: MSF.

Sheehan, H. 1993, *Marxism and the Philosophy of Science*, Atlantic Highlands, NJ: Humanities Press.

Sherman, H.J. 1973, 'The Theory of Socialist Planning: Comment', *Journal of Political Economy* 81(2), 450–58.

Shipway, M. 1988, *Anti-Parliamentary Communism: The Movement for Workers' Councils in Britain, 1917–45*, London: The Macmillan Press Ltd.

Sirc, L. 1979, *The Yugoslav Economy under Self-Management*, London: The Macmillan Press Ltd.

Smale, J. 1998, *De SP: Beroepsrevolutionairen in de jaren negentig*, Dissertation, https://communisme.nu/wp-content/uploads/2020/12/De_SP_Beroepsrevolutionairen_in_de_jaren_negentig.pdf accessed 3 November 2022.

Smirnov, A.D., K.M. Radaeva, A.I. Esin, and G.K. Rusakov 1979, 'Profit-and-Loss Accounting', in *The Great Soviet Encyclopedia*, Third Edition, https://encyclopedia2.thefreedictionary.com/Profit-and-Loss+Accounting accessed 18 July 2020.

Smith, A. 1776, *An Inquiry into the Nature and Causes of the Wealth of Nations: Book V*, Marxist Internet Archive, https://www.marxists.org/reference/archive/smith-adam/works/wealth-of-nations/index.htm accessed Augusts 4, 2023

Smith, M. 2017, 'How Left or Right-wing are the UK's Newspapers?' *YouGov*, https://yougov.co.uk/topics/politics/articles-reports/2017/03/07/how-left-or-right-wing-are-uks-newspapers accessed June 5, 2020

SPGB 2014, *Why We Don't Need Money*, https://www.worldsocialism.org/spgb/publications/why-we-dont-need-money/ accessed 7 April 2020.

Stalin, J.V. 1951, *Economic Problems of Socialism in the USSR*, Marxist Internet Archive, https://www.marxists.org/reference/archive/stalin/works/1951/economic-problems/index.htm accessed 20 June 2022.

Sturmthal, A. 1961, 'The Workers' Councils in Poland', *Industrial and Labor Relations Review* 14(3), 379–96.

Sutela, P. 1992, 'Rationalizing the Centrally Managed Economy: The Market', in A. Åslund (ed.), *Market Socialism or the Restoration of Capitalism?* (pp. 92–120), Cambridge: Cambridge University Press.

Sutela, P., and V. Mau 1998, 'Economics Under Socialism: The Russian Case', in H-J. Wagener (ed.), *Economic Thought in Communist and Post-Communist Europe*, London: Routledge.

Tchami, G. 2007, *Handbook on Cooperatives for Use of Workers' Organizations*, Geneva: International Labour Office.

Tetsuzo, F. 2002, 'Lenin and the Market Economy', *Japanese Communist Party*, https://www.jcp.or.jp/english/jps_weekly/2002-0827-fuwa.html Accessed 14 January 2020.

Thaler, R.H., and S. Benartzi 2007, 'The Behavioral Economics of Retirement Savings Behavior', *AARP Public Policy Institute*, https://assets.aarp.org/rgcenter/econ/2007_02_savings.pdf accessed 1 April 2020.

The Anarchist FAQ Editorial Collective 2009, *An Anarchist FAQ. A.2.11 Why are most anarchists in favour of direct democracy?* The Anarchist Library, https://theanarchistl ibrary.org/library/the-anarchist-faq-editorial-collective-an-anarchist-faq-02-17#toc 19 accessed March 24, 2020.

Thomas, A. 2016, *Republic of Equals: Predistribution and Property-Owning Democracy*, Oxford: Oxford University Press.

Thompson, M.J. 2019, 'Karl Kautsky and the Theory of Socialist Republicanism', in G. Kets and J. Muldoon (eds), *The German Revolution and Political Theory*, London: Palgrave Macmillan.

Ticktin, H. 1992, *Origins of the Crisis in the USSR: Essays on the Political Economy of a Disintegrating System*, Armonk, NY: M.E. Sharpe.

Ticktin, H. 1997, 'What will a Socialist Society be Like?' *Journal of Socialist Theory* 25(1), 145–67.

Tsushima, T. 1956, 'Understanding "Labor Certificates" on the Basis of the Theory of Value: The Law of Value and Socialism', *Marxist Internet Archive*, https://www .marxists.org/subject/japan/tsushima/labor-certificates.htm accessed 1 March 2020.

Tubis, R.I. 1973, *Decision-Making in the Soviet Economic Bureaucracy: Administrative Implementation of the 1965 Economic Reform*, Dissertation, University of Illinois Urbana-Champaign.

Uvalić, M. 1992, 'The Investment Theory of the Labour-managed Firm', in *Investment and Property Rights in Yugoslavia: The Long Transition to a Market Economy* (pp. 17– 28), Cambridge: Cambridge University Press.

Uvalić, M. 2018, *The Rise and Fall of Market Socialism in Yugoslavia*, Dialogue of Civiliz-ations Research Institute.

Van der Linden, M. 2007, *Western Marxism and the Soviet Union*, Leiden: Brill.

Van der Walt, L., and M. Schmidt 2009, *Black Flame: The Revolutionary Class Politics of Anarchism and Syndicalism (Counter-power)*, Edinburgh: AK Press.

Varoufakis, Y. 2020, *Another Now: Dispatches from an Alternative Present*, London: Bod-ley Head.

Veduta, E. 2022, 'Some Lessons on Planning for the Twenty-First Century from the World's First Socialist Economy', *Monthly Review*, https://monthlyreview.org/2022/ 10/01/some-lessons-on-planning-for-the-twenty-first-century-from-the-worlds-first -socialist-economy/ accessed February 16, 2023.

Verbij, A. 2005, *Tien Rode Jaren: Links Radicalisme in Nederland (1970–1980)*, Amster-dam: Ambo.

Vergara-Camus, L. 2005, 'The Experience of the Landless Workers Movement and the Lula Government', *INTERthesis* 2(1), 1–29.

Vettesse, T., and D. Pendergrass 2022, *Half-Earth Socialism: A Plan to Save the Future from Extinction, Climate Change, and Pandemics*, London: Verso.

Wagener, H-J. (ed.) 1998, *Economic Thought in Communist and Post-Communist Europe*, London: Routledge.

Walsh, K.C. 2007, 'The Democratic Potential of Civic Dialogue', in S.W. Rosenberg (ed.), *Deliberation, Participation, and Democracy: Can the People Govern?* New York: Palgrave Macmillan.

Waluchow, W. 2018, 'Constitutionalism', in E.N. Zalta (ed.), *The Stanford Encyclopedia of Philosophy*, https://plato.stanford.edu/archives/spr2018/entries/constitutionalism accessed May 12, 2020.

Weatherford, S.M, and L.M. McDonnell 2007, 'Deliberation with a Purpose: Reconnecting Communities and Schools', in S.W. Rosenberg (ed.), *Deliberation, Participation, and Democracy: Can the People Govern?* (pp. 184–218), New York: Palgrave Macmillan.

Weitzman, M.L., and D.L. Kruse 1990, 'Profit Sharing and Productivity', in A.S. Blinder (ed.), *Paying for Productivity: A Look at the Evidence* (pp. 95–140), Washington, D.C.: Brookings Institution.

West, D.K. 2020, 'Cybernetics for the Command Economy: Foregrounding Entropy in Late Soviet Planning', *History of the Human Sciences* 33(1), 36–51.

Wheat, L.F. 2012, *Hegel's Undiscovered Thesis-Antithesis-Synthesis Dialectics: What Only Marx and Tillich Understood*, New York: Prometheus.

Whitefield, S. 1993, *Industrial Power and the Soviet State*, Oxford: Clarendon Press.

Whitesell, R.S. 1990, 'Why Does the Soviet Economy Appear to Be Allocatively Efficient?' *Soviet Studies* 42(2), 259–68.

Wilczynski, J. 1972a, *Socialist Economic Development and Reforms: From Extensive Growth Under Central Planning in the USSR, Eastern Europe and Yugoslavia*, London: Palgrave Macmillan.

Wilczynski, J. 1972b, *Socialistische Economie*, Utrecht: Uitgeverij het Spectrum N.V. [Original: 1970, *The Economics of Socialism*, London: George Allen and Unwin Ltd.]

Wilczynski, J. 1973, *Profit, Risk and Incentives under Socialist Economic Planning*, Basingstoke: Palgrave Macmillan.

Wolff, R.D. 2012, *Democracy at Work: A Cure for Capitalism*, Chicago: Haymarket Books.

Wood, E.M. 1995, *Democracy Against Capitalism: Renewing Historical Materialism*, London: Verso.

Wright, E.O. 2010, *Envisioning Real Utopias*, London: Verso.

Yorumez, B.A. 2021, *Socialism with a Melancholy Heart: The Red-collars and the Making of Reform Socialism in Czechoslovakia (1945–1968)*, Dissertation, University of British Columbia.

Zauberman, A. 1963, 'A Note on the Soviet Inter-industry Labour Input Balance', *Soviet Studies* 15(1), 53–7.

Index of Modern authors

Index of Subjects

www.ingramcontent.com/pod-product-compliance
Ingram Content Group UK Ltd.
Pitfield, Milton Keynes, MK11 3LW, UK
UKHW020655050626
6257IPUK00010B/62